The Psychological Dimension of Foreign Policy

Joseph de Rivera

Department of Psychology
New York University

James N. Rosenau
Consultant

Charles E. Merrill Publishing Company
Columbus, Ohio

A Bell and Howell Company

To my teachers

Library of Congress Catalog Number: 68-16494

1 2 3 4 5 6 7 8 9 10 — 72 71 70 69 68

Printed in the United States of America

PREFACE

In the winter of 1960 Thomas Landauer and I began talking about a new course at Dartmouth College. We felt that psychology, with its interest in the prediction and control of behavior, should have *something* to contribute to foreign policy and the art of controlling the behavior of nations. We were discouraged, however, by the lack of relevant material and ideas. We probably would have stopped if we had not discovered Charles Osgood's work on "Graduated and Reciprocated Initiatives in Tension-reduction," a possible technique for reducing hostility between nations. We saw how Osgood *had* managed to take psychological material and apply it to foreign policy and, thus, encouraged, we began a seminar in the area. In the succeeding two years I made the course into a regular class with lectures and a research paper. The students often did a remarkably good job, and the results of some of their experiments will be found in this book, referenced as a paper from the Dartmouth course.

In the meantime, Osgood and Sheldon Feldman had begun a wide-ranging search for relevant literature. In 1962, they received a grant for this work from Mr. Earl D. Osborn, president of the Institute for International Order, and this, in addition to grants from the National Institute of Mental Health, made it possible for me to spend half of my time gathering and abstracting ideas from political science and other areas which are unfamiliar to most psychologists. In the course of this reading I learned a great deal from the *Journal of Conflict Resolution* and other inter-disciplinary works inspired by the Center for Conflict Resolution at the University of Michigan. I also became acquainted with the behavioral trend in political science and enjoyed talking with several persons who had been involved in the program at Northwestern University.

In the course of my reading, I came across an article by Edwin Hoyt in which he examined the reaction of American officials to the Korean attack in order to see whether the principles of the United Nations Charter influenced their decisions. (*Amer J. Internat. Law,* 55, 1961, 45-76.) I became convinced that psychology could make its greatest contribution by focusing on the behavior of the officials who were making foreign policy; and thanks to the enthusiastic cooperation of Glen Paige, I soon became immersed in the interview material which he had collected in the course of his investigation of the decision to fight in Korea.

In the fall of 1963 I moved to New York University and began writing this book, often stimulated by the ideas of students in a class on the psychological aspects of foreign policy. Within the Department of Psychology's Research Center for Human Relations I found the time, and the typing power of Dale Schaefer Bailey and Brigitte Hees, to write.

While writing I was constantly encouraged by my association with the Committee for International Relations, a group established by Herbert Kelman within the Society for the Psychology Study of Social Issues. A first draft was read by my fellow members on this committee and I benefited from a two-day meeting devoted to a discussion of the manuscript. Melvin Lerner, Glen Paige, Dean Pruitt, Bryant Wedge, and Ralph White participated, and our discussion was aided by the presence of Allan Evans and Raymond Plating from the State Department.

I have been fortunate in finding a number of psychologists and political scientists who were willing to comment on the manuscript. Murray Horwitz, Irwin Katz, John Neulinger, Charles Osgood, and Morton Schwartz read and commented on individual chapters, and Burt Sapin was kind enough to review five chapters. All of the above persons helped me improve the manuscript. Had I been able to take account of all their criticisms, the book would have none of the weaknesses that remain.

I particularly want to thank Allan Evans, Dean Pruitt, and Jim Rosenau for their ideas and editorial assistance. And I want to thank my wife, Margaret, and my children, Alice, Eric, and Freda, for their help, enthusiasm and patience.

TABLE OF CONTENTS

CHAPTER 1

Introduction

This work is written with two aims in mind: First, to show how contemporary psychology can be meaningfully applied to the behavior of men who are engaged in the formation of foreign policy. Hopefully, such an application will aid us in more accurately conceptualizing how wars occur, how aid programs flourish or fail, and how money is spent. Second, to reveal some gaps in our current knowledge of psychology and to suggest how these gaps might be closed. Application in an unaccustomed area is a severe test which eliminates trivialities and forces a concern with essential principles.

Foreign policy is usually approached from an historical or a political viewpoint. An historical approach describes broad trends in a nation's policy and relates them to the social, economic, ideological, and geographic conditions of the time. To cite examples of each of these factors: At one point in European history a number of royal and aristocratic governments conducted foreign affairs in a relatively harmonious atmosphere which was engendered by their common desire to maintain control over democratic movements. Economic interests helped produce the Tariff Union which influenced the various German states to unite into the German Empire. The structure of the United Nations is based on the ideology of nationalism. German foreign policy has always been influenced by the lack of natural defenses (such as rivers or mountains) and the presence of powerful neighbors; and because of its geographical situation, for over a hundred years, the foreign policy of the United

States was directed towards the North American continent with a deliberate avoidance of entanglement in European affairs.

A political approach usually treats foreign policy analytically. The policy may be analyzed as a response to external stimuli or as the outcome of a struggle between different interest groups within a country. Thus, British policy towards an expansion or contraction of its colonial empire may be analyzed in terms of external presses or by relating it to whether conservative or liberal parties gained control of Parliament. American tariff policy has been influenced by world conditions and by the outcome of a clash between free trade and protectionist interests. Whether money flows into arms, foreign aid, or slum clearance is determined by the actions of other nations and by the conflict between the interests of the departments of Defense, State and Interior, the interests of key congressmen, and the lobbying activities of various industrial and commercial interests. A political approach does not conflict with an historical approach; it simply focuses on the analysis of reactions to other nations or the behavior of interest groups within a broader historical background.

Similarly, a psychological approach — with its emphasis on the individual's perceptions, values, and interpersonal relations — does not conflict with either the historical or the political approach, but rather gives us a more detailed picture of the forces that shape policy. While political analysis has always given some weight to the individual, there is a tendency to invoke psychology only when the abnormal occurs — if there is a distorted perception or a suicide. If the statesman "correctly" views political or economic factors, then we turn to the "objective reality" described by political science or economics. In fact, of course, the individual is always present; and a correct perception, or a particularly creative one, is just as psychological and reflects individual values just as much as does a distorted view of reality. Because we are all human we often take psychology for granted; we assume "human nature" as a constant, or we assume some fixed model of a man — as rational, or "satisficing," or driven by power, etc. — and then describe historical and political developments in terms of this fictional creature who actually has an immense amount of freedom to be different things and, hence, to change the course of history and politics. One danger of taking psychology for granted is the danger of failing to see that things could have happened differently if man had behaved differently — something he is quite capable of doing when he achieves an awareness of his determinants.

Any analysis that divorces history, political science, psychology, and the other social sciences is apt to be incomplete and somewhat misleading. For example, a political scientist is likely to interpret America's policy towards China in the 1950's as a compromise between liberal forces primarily interested in Europe and conservative forces having an interest in the Far East. A psychologist is more apt to focus on the interpersonal clash and the lack of communication between President Truman and General MacArthur. Only when we combine both views do we see that the real clash of interests *and* interpersonal difficulties produced a weak compromise rather than a strong integrated policy.

The interface between political science and psychology has always been an active area. When the founders of the Constitution were debating the powers of the Presidential office, those men who were opposed to a strong executive argued that in certain affairs the President should be *required* to consult with his cabinet. Charles Pinckney maintained that the association would have to be a voluntary one. He argued, "Give him an able Council and it will thwart him; a weak one, and he will shelter himself under their sanction."[1] This psychological argument, based on a knowledge of man's behavior, helped form the consensus for our present political structure. Today, as we shall see, there are new ideas for the organization of government in the latest work of psychologists and ideas for the psychologist in the literature of political science.

Many persons are relatively content with American foreign policy. If they are outside of the government, they see the government as correctly perceiving an objective world situation and adequately coping with it in the only possible way. When something obvious goes wrong, they believe that some person made a mistake and that the situation can be remedied by replacing that person or whatever party is in office. If they are within the government, they believe they see the objective world situation, are doing everything they can to better it, and are choosing the best possible course of action. When something unexpectedly goes wrong, they reassure themselves with the thought that the situation is complex and that the unfortunate outcome either could not have been avoided or can be avoided in the future by some organizational change. Whether inside or outside the government, such persons usually are fairly optimistic about the future and, while they are open to suggestions for improvement, believe that the country is doing pretty well.

Other persons, including the writer, feel that American foreign policy is relatively weak, that government officials are failing to perceive

---

[1] Richard F. Fenno, Jr., *The President's Cabinet* (Cambridge, Mass.: Harvard University Press, 1959), p. 12.

certain aspects of the world situation, that the government is failing to act to change the world situation, and that the way policy is formed needs drastic revision. Those of us with such feelings are motivated by a sense of urgency: by a fear that eventually a nuclear war will occur, by an anxiety that the nation may become less democratic, and by a desire to see other people develop their own unique potentials rather than be destroyed.

Persons who are discontent with the results of American foreign policy do not seem to be able to effectively change the policy. While, undoubtedly, there are a number of problems that should be attacked, I should like to suggest that one basic problem lies in our ways of thinking about human affairs.

In order to maintain any control over his destiny man must continually grasp the essence of the situation in which he finds himself. To the extent which his conceptualization of the situation is inadequate his behavior will not be free, i.e. *self*-determined, and outcomes will be completely determined by forces outside his control. It is my belief that the current defect in our thinking stems from the separation of the various social sciences. In particular, the psychology that has developed to meet our contemporary situation is so separated from history and political science that the psychological dimension of foreign policy is almost neglected and a distorted view of reality results.

In recent years, political scientists have begun working to close this gap and many of the articles collected by Rosenau[2] and by Singer[3] and several of the essays in Knorr and Verba[4] reflect this fact. That psychologists have also responded to the challenge is shown by Kelman's recent volume.[5] *The Psychological Dimension of Foreign Policy* is an addition to this effort to attain a broader conceptualization of foreign policy so that we gain perspective and see it in a larger framework.

Criticisms of American foreign policy often contain the germs of good ideas, but these are masked by their expression in one-dimensional, unrealistic ways. If we can achieve a broader viewpoint, we should be able to forge more creative policies.

I believe that a unified social science can best be achieved by focusing on the interaction between the individual and the situational forces

[2]James N. Rosenau, *International Politics and Foreign Policy.* (New York: Free Press, 1961).
[3]David J. Singer, *Human Behavior and International Policy.* (Chicago: Rand McNally, 1965).
[4]Klaus Knorr, and Sidney Verba, *The International System.* (Princeton: Princeton University Press, 1961).
[5]Herbert C. Kelman, *International Behavior.* (New York: Holt, Rinehart & Winston, 1965).

playing upon him. In the end it is always the individual person who must act and who has the chance of increasing his self-awareness. Therefore, I shall not speak of "the determinants" of foreign policy. Man always determines foreign policy—though he is mercilessly affected by objective forces.

In accord with this point of view, we shall not deal with "psychological factors" but with a way of looking at things that should broaden our perspective. While we shall be concentrating on the psychological dimension of the man-situation interaction, and an historian or political scientist would emphasize other features of this whole, we are concerned with any neglect of these features and are committed to eventually having a completely unified conceptualization.

Now, the dimension that psychology adds is an interesting one that may easily escape attention and that may require the reader to think in an unaccustomed way. Basically, it consists of an examination of patterns of behaviors from a deterministic point of view,* with the subsequent discovery of some interesting relationships which would otherwise go unnoticed. For example, in the course of reconstructing one of the decisions which we shall examine, a political scientist noted that an important official was absent from a crucial meeting. It is obvious that his absence may have been intended, and the layman may speculate that he was purposely excluded for some political or personal reason. The psychologist, however, may see the exclusion as part of a determined sequence of behavior in which certain psychological forces caused the excluded person to play, within the group, a specific role that, under certain circumstances, inevitably led to his exclusion. If the psychologist is correct, it is obvious that a person can gain an additional degree of freedom by controlling the pertinent circumstances.

In investigating these determined patterns of behavior, the psychologist may use simple experimental situations to investigate specific relations which he feels may be important. The reader should be prepared to examine whether or not these relations can be generalized so that they shed light on the complicated behavior of everyday life. He must also be tolerant enough to consider whether the dynamics of unconscious motivation which psychotherapy reveals may also explain some of the behavior of a political leader.

In general, psychology attempts to explicate certain phenomena so that persons can be more fully aware of what determines their behavior. In order to really understand the psychological dimension of foreign policy, the reader must realize that all psychological principles that

---

*As we have noted, behavior is "free" to the extent that it is *self*-determined.

are correct must apply (or potentially apply) to *his own behavior.*
Only if he has this self-understanding, will he be able to apply these
principles to foreign policy and realize new possibilities.

Procedure

In order to "apply" psychology, we must have some material to
work with. Fortunately, there are a number of excellent case histories
of governmental decisions. Decisions that result in a program of foreign
aid, an arms budget, or a war, create as well as reflect a nation's foreign
policy. By interviewing key governmental officials, political scientists
have been able to reconstruct how a number of these important decisions were made. Their published records are the raw material which
we shall subject to a psychological analysis.

In working with this material, a number of limitations must be kept
in mind. In trying to reconstruct exactly what occurred, the investigator
faces a number of problems. He may need a fact that either was never
recorded or is being kept in secret archives. For example, the decision
to defend Formosa set in motion forces which led the Chinese to enter
the Korean war; but Tsou states,

> One cannot ascertain from published records whether it was the officials
> of the State Department or the officers representing the Joint Chiefs
> who, in their meeting to prepare a joint recommendation, initiated the
> idea of sending the Seventh Fleet to the Formosa Strait.[6]

Forced to rely on interviews, the investigator comes against various
distortion problems:

1. The respondent may wish to put himself in a good light. Thus,
   in the "McCarthy Era" every official was inclined to portray
   himself as 100 per cent against communism. Hence, he might
   claim to have supported the defense of Formosa even if he had
   actually argued for keeping good relations with China.
2. The passage of time (and often years pass) leads the respondent
   to remember what is logical in the light of his habits and of future
   developments and to forget incidents or whole series of events
   which do not "fit in" with the final decison. Thus, when an inter-
   viewer asked President Truman about a conversation reported by
   the Chairman of the Senate Committee on Foreign Relations, the

[6]Tang Tsou, *America's Failure in China 1941-1950* (Chicago: University of
Chicago Press, 1963), p. 559.

President replied, "I don't recall calling Senator Connelly in spite of what he says; he's not the one I would call, he couldn't do anything about the situation."

3. For similar reasons, a person may forget having seriously considered an alternative which events caused him to abandon for another course of action. For example, in a recent experiment[7] persons played a game in which they could adopt either a cooperative or a competitive strategy. The experimenters, who had asked each person at the beginning of the game what strategy he intended to follow, found a consistent bias in the player's recall. All those persons who had decided to play cooperatively and had no difficulty in implementing this strategy correctly recalled their initial intentions. However, many players who had made the same decision but had not been successful in reaching a cooperative agreement believed that they had initially decided on a competitive strategy.

4. Because the respondent may be responsible for events which cost both lives and money, he may feel and suggest that events *had* to occur the way they did. Glen Paige[8] suggests that often a decision is reported as "the only thing we could have done" in order to avoid the dreadful responsibility of the real choice that was made.

While the investigator has some ways to combat these distortions (he can discover a great deal from the contradictions between interviews and from the feelings of the respondents), the net effect of the above biases is probably to make decisions appear more rational than they really are. Such distortions, and the fact that officials may fail to perceive important factors which are influencing their behavior, force the investigator to *interpret* what is actually occurring. While these interpretations may often be important insights, they may also be an additional source of error. Because the accounts described in this book are interpretations of behavior, the reader must view them with caution. In the effort to apply a specific psychological conceptualization that reveals a known pattern of behavior, it is always possible that I have unknowingly stretched or chopped the data, (thereby obtaining a "fit" that is more apparent than

---

[7]Gerald H. Shure, Robert J. Meeker, and William H. Moore, Jr., *Computer studies of bargaining behavior: The role of threat in bargaining* (Santa Monica, Calif.: Systems Development Corporation).

[8]Personal communication. For a discussion of some other difficulties, see Richard C. Snyder and Glen D. Paige, "The United States decision to resist aggression in Korea: the application of an analytical scheme," *Admin. Sci. Quart.*, 3 (1958), pp. 342-78.

real). Such errors can only be revealed by the addition of data with which I am unacquainted.

In order to reduce interpretive errors, we would ideally like to have a team of psychologists and political scientists observe decision makers as they are formulating foreign policy. Some of the observers should be completely detached from the policy process so that they have no emotional involvement in the policy. Others should be "participant observers" who are fully involved and can register the effect of this involvement as they reflect an "insider's" point of view. Observation of this sort will become possible when the value of such studies is more recognized and the growth of trust in the behavioral sciences overcomes the understandable secrecy of those officials who are in the politically vulnerable position of being responsible for policy and who are concerned lest premature revelations impede the realization of policy. We will have accomplished enough if this present interpretive analysis of "reconstructions" suggests enough so that it succeeds in demonstrating the value which a "live" study would have. Furthermore, when the opportunity for direct observation occurs, we will know more about what to look for and what problems we shall have to cope with.

A problem related to, but somewhat different from, the technical problems discussed above is posed by the fact that any investigator has certain values which influence his work. I would like to distinguish between the *expression* of values and the *infringement* of values. When Richardson[9] began his study of war, he expressed his (Quaker) values by defining wars in terms of the number of dead rather than in terms of territorial shifts, international law, or financial expenditures. He did not, however, let his values infringe on his work: When there were different estimates of the number of dead, he did not select the highest estimate in order to show how horrible wars were; rather, he maintained his perspective and took the average of the estimates. This book expresses both my basic optimism in the ability of man to control his destiny and an idealistic view of truth. I hope, however, that these values have not infringed on the objectivity of the work. It is particularly difficult to avoid infringement in this area of political or "strategic" thinking because our language is not sufficiently differentiated. Consider the current policy of the United States in Asia. Does the United States *control* Formosa? Not in the sense that the Soviet Union at one time controlled Hungary, but certainly in the sense that the United States prevents the island from coming under the authority of mainland China, supports a

---

[9]Lewis Richardson, *Statistics of Deadly Quarrels* (Pittsburgh: Boxwood Press, 1960).

transplanted regime which otherwise might not be able to survive, and undoubtedly influences some of the island's internal decisions. Because of the lack of a precise term, it is all too easy to have one's values impinge on the facts and to either charge the United States with "imperialism" or pretend that it is simply supporting the "free" world. My only defense against subtle biases has been membership in several different reference groups and the constant criticism of students and colleagues from various disciplines and various political commitments ranging from the extreme right to the extreme left. While undoubtedly there are still many points where lack of knowledge and the infringement of values have created distortions, I believe that it is now at least "even-odds" that any distortion is in the eyes of the beholder rather than the product.

The material that we shall examine in the ensuing chapters stems primarily from four actions that have had an important impact on American foreign policy:

1. The development of the Marshall Plan offers us a chance to see foreign policy affect a critical moment in history — the passing of power and responsibility from the British Empire to the United States. The Marshall Plan set up new historical forces which have influenced all the subsequent foreign policies of the United States, Britain, the Soviet Union, and most of Europe. Its inception is an example of how far-sighted foreign policy in a democracy is dependent on a collaboration between leaders in the administration, the governmental bureaucracy, Congress, and the public. As we shall see, this collaboration required both a beneficial creativity and a distortion of reality that has plagued us ever since. We are fortunate in having an excellent account of the development of the plan from the records of an "insider"; Joseph Jones' book, *The Fifteen Weeks*[10], is written from his viewpoint as the State Department's public affairs officer.

2. The determination of the 1950 arms budget is a good example of the constant routine activity that underlies all foreign policy and often affects it in unexpected ways. While "budget formation" sounds boring and budget setting is a continuous, routine process, we shall see that it can be filled with all the excitement of power politics. It involves a great deal of bargaining between persons with different positions in the government, each of whom is attempting to form alliances in order to obtain the financial support he is seeking or to prevent what he perceives as the excessive spending of some other agency. The 1950 budget is a particularly

---

[10]J. M. Jones, *The Fifteen Weeks* (New York: The Viking Press, Inc., 1955).

interesting budget in that it proved to be far too low in the light
of the 1950 invasion of Korea. The crucial conflicts, bargains, and
alliances behind the budget have been carefully reconstructed by
Warner Schilling in "The Politics of National Defense: Fiscal
1950."[11]

3. The formulation of the document known as NSC-68 (the 68th
paper issued by the National Security Council) challenged the
assumptions underlying the 1950 defense budget and called for
much greater defense spending. It may be viewed simply as an
attempt at influence by officials who were dissatisfied with the
current governmental policy. However, the men working on the
paper attempted to rise above the usual bargaining process and
rationally plan out policy; and, in the light of the Korean War,
their planning and arguments proved correct. Paul Hammond[12]
has carefully described how the paper was developed and how the
very features which made it a rational effort hindered its adoption.

4. The entrance of the United States into the Korean War is an
excellent example of crisis decision making. Unlike the above
actions, the development of this event occurred so rapidly that
only a few key officials participated directly in important decisions.
The crucial meetings and decisions that led the United States to
enter the war were made in a period of seven days and have been
carefully described by Glenn Paige.[13] His reconstruction of what
occurred, like Schilling's and Hammond's, is based primarily on
interviews with most of the available participants.

While we shall focus primarily on the above four cases, we will also
have occasion to examine other important decisions during the Korean
War, such as the crossing of the 38th parallel and the recall of General
MacArthur. In order to avoid too narrow a focus on the Truman administration, we shall at times contrast the methods of that administration
with those of the Eisenhower administration, and we shall often point to
similarities between the processes that occurred in 1947-1952 and
processes that occurred in other nations at other times. In this regard
George F. Kennan's book, *Russia and the West*,[14] is of particular value.

[11]"The Politics of National Defense: Fiscal 1950" in *Strategy, Politics and Defense
Budgets,* eds. W. R. Shilling, P. Y. Hammond, and G. H. Snyder (New York:
Columbia University Press, 1962).

[12]"NSC-68: Prologue to Rearmament," in Shilling, Hammond, and Snyder, *op. cit.*

[13]Glenn D. Paige, *The Korean Decision* (Evanston, Ill.: Northwestern University
Press, 1959).

[14]G. F. Kennan, *Russia and the West under Lenin and Stalin* (Boston: Little, Brown
and Company, 1960).

Although every event we shall examine in this book is at least ten years old, we may succeed in uncovering general principles that are as applicable to today's events as to the past. The decision processes at work in the crisis occasioned by the invasion of Korea appear to be highly similar to those that were occasioned by the discovery of missiles in Cuba. Factors distorting information in 1950 may also have been present in the case of the Dominican revolution of 1965. The value choices involved in the 1950 defense budget are also involved in the dilemma over Vietnam. A history of the specific is of no use unless it reveals those principles which govern our behavior and which we must discover if we are ever to control our foreign policy.

As we search for these principles, we will not necessarily follow actions chronologically — that has been done in the case histories; rather, we shall select fragments from here and there that illustrate known psychological principles or pose problems for psychologists to tackle.

I will not be able to systematically present evidence from all four cases, because the different authors have stressed different things. The account of the Marshall Plan, for example, is excellent in detailing the effects of public opinion but does not describe incoming information processes. The Korean decisions lend themselves to a portrayal of these information processes, but since they occurred under conditions which forced unanimity they do not allow the investigation of the interpersonal bargaining which is so evident in the description of budget making. To insure the proper amount of generalization, I shall try to indicate cases where a particular process is not important and to draw on instances outside the four case histories for evidence that interesting facts are not peculiar to just one situation.

Our focus will be on the behavior of the individual who is influencing the course of governmental action. We are interested in his perceptions and attitudes, his interpersonal relations, his thought processes, how he makes decisions, and how his personality affects these decisions. Because this book is organized around these psychological processes, rather than the historical development, before we get lost in psychological detail it will be helpful to consider the main outline of the historical events.

In the following sketch, and wherever possible, I have purposely omitted the names of the officials whose behavior we shall be observing. It is quite uncomfortable to be under cold psychological scrutiny, and I see no reason to embarrass men who have unselfishly served their country. Unfortunately, in this day of nuclear weapons it is an absolute necessity for our government officials to submit themselves to the kind of observation that would be objectionable to a man in private life.

Recognizing that his behavior affects our lives, the responsible official with any degree of humility will permit independent observation of his behavior. We are all human and capable of making both the mistakes and the creative actions which we shall observe. Some readers may sneer at the less fortunate behavior of various officials. A curse on any such reader who cannot imagine himself in the other's place. May he experience that at which he sneers.

A Sketch of Important Events

In 1945, the cooperative relations that had existed between the United States and the Soviet Union began to be severely strained by conflicting interests in Poland. The American position was that the Polish government should be constituted democratically, whereas the Russians desired a communistic government that would "go along" with various proposals in the Russian national interest. At the Yalta conference, the Russians were pressured into agreeing to free Polish elections but made no real commitment. When the American President died, his successor was confronted with this paper agreement. He chose to insist on the terms of the agreement, and an exchange followed which we shall analyze in the chapter on interactions between the representatives of nations. This exchange was not really satisfactory to either party and it, together with many similar problems, led to a complete deterioration of Soviet-American relations.

In February of 1947, the British government informed the United States that it could no longer afford to maintain Western interests throughout the world and would have to pull back its forces from Greece and Turkey. The British withdrawal would create a power vacuum. The President, the Secretary of State, the Secretaries for the Army and Navy, and key men in these departments recognized this situation and wanted to prevent Soviet expansion. Therefore, they decided to try to give substantial aid to Greece and Turkey. The Congress, dominated by the opposing party, wanted substantial tax cuts, but a group of its leaders were won over when the Undersecretary of State painted a picture of a polarized world and the dangers of Soviet expansion. In a sense (as we shall see in the chapter on consensus formation), the price of congressional cooperation was the start of the Cold War. One key senator suggested that aid to Greece and Turkey seemed only part of a broader situation that should be presented to Congress and the public. This was done, opposition to the aid bill was overcome, and a group in the State Department began to study what countries needed aid and how it should be given.

Several factors influenced this group's recommendations. Among them were the recent failure to obtain agreement with the Soviet Union on the rebuilding of Germany, the perception that Soviet power would benefit from a poor European economy, the fact that Europe was on the verge of starvation, the perception that the economic needs of the rest of Europe were bound up with a revitalized German industry, and the belief within the economic offices of the State Department that a united Europe would be more viable than a host of separate economies. In the chapter on projecting the future, we shall note a number of factors that inhibit creativity; at this time, these were at a minimum, and various leaders combined their ideas until they culminated in the address made by Secretary of State Marshall at Harvard in June 1947. Essentially, he stated that if the European nations would collaborate on a program to build up the European economy, they could expect to receive aid for this program. The "Marshall Plan" was enthusiastically received by European leaders, and the way was paved for European recovery, the lessening of Soviet influence, the North Atlantic Treaty Organization, and the beginning of European unity.

In early 1948, a number of critical events occurred: a communist coup overthrew the Czechoslovakian government, the collapse of Chiang Kai-Shek's regime became apparent, and the Berlin blockade was forecast by a temporary halting of Western trains. These events helped gain congressional action on the Marshall Plan. They also led the State Department to consider pressing for 3 billion dollars of military aid to Europe in addition to the 5.3 billion requested for the Marshall Plan. These requests and other events affected the planning of the defense budget.

In January 1948, the President had asked Congress for 10 billion dollars for the fiscal 1949 defense budget (that is, for June 1948 to June 1949). By March, the Joint Chiefs of Staff had requested a 9 billion dollar supplement. The President agreed to request a 3 billion dollar supplement from Congress. Faced with a revolt from the Air Force, the Secretary of the newly unified Defense Department gained control by promising an added half billion dollar supplement to the Air Force. The President, caught by the kind of conflicting demands we shall study in the chapter on decision-making, agreed to this offer if it were approved by the Budget Bureau. However, the Director of the Bureau advised a *cut* of a half billion dollars and, in May, advised that financial considerations made it necessary that in fiscal 1950 and succeeding years the defense budget should not rise above $15 billion. He argued that if this ceiling were violated inflationary pressures would rise, since the administration could not hope to increase taxes or impose more controls on a Congress that was calling for tax cuts and the removal of price controls.

The Secretary of Defense, alarmed by the Soviet expansion, immediately protested this ceiling at a meeting with the President, the Budget Director, the Secretary of State, and three other advisers. Both the Budget Director and the Secretary of Defense had excellent arguments, and the President turned to the Secretary of State for his advice. For reasons we shall consider in detail in the chapter on consensus formation, the Secretary of State did not support the Secretary of Defense; and on May 13 the President announced the $15 billion ceiling. The only war plan on which the Joint Chiefs of Staff could agree would cost $23.6 billion. Sympathetic with their aims and convinced of the necessity for stronger armed forces, the Secretary of Defense (whom we shall consider in the personality chapter) refused to accept the President's decision as final and spent the next seven months trying to change it. By December 1948, his maneuvers were clearly unsuccessful, and he was replaced shortly afterwards by a man who had been a strong supporter of the President in the 1948 campaign. The aftermath of these events was unfortunate: the former Secretary of Defense committed suicide a few months after his removal. The Congress did not examine the budget wisely. The climate of economy prevailed, and a year later the nation found itself uprepared for the Korean War.

The new Secretary of Defense not only accepted the 15 billion dollar ceiling on the defense budget, he identified himself with economy in the department and planned on cuts in the budget. Meeting high resistance within his department, he forbade all contact with State Department officials, who now supported a higher defense budget. The effects of this communication gap will be noted in the chapter on projecting the future.

But other factors were already at work to call for a policy change. These factors culminated in a paper, NSC-68. It is of interest to examine the forces for and against a change of policy. The Secretary of State had become seriously ill and had to be replaced. The new Secretary (the former Undersecretary) was more defense-minded than his predecessor and was searching for some means of contact with the Defense Department. By September 1949, it was clear that continental China had fallen to the communists, and on the 23rd the President announced that the Soviet Union had successfully exploded the atomic bomb (three years ahead of intelligence estimates). Men in the State Department and on the National Security Council believed that the strategy of the United States should be re-examined. The Atomic Energy Commission was not enthusiastically behind a proposal to build a hydrogen bomb, but the development of a Soviet atomic bomb weakened this resistance. The Chairman of the Commission had to agree to go ahead on the hydrogen bomb but was able to force a reappraisal of the strategic implications of nuclear weapons. The President asked the Secretaries of State and Defense to review American policy. Now the State Department had a chance to reopen communications with the Defense Department, and a ten-man committee began to meet in February, 1950. The central figures on this committee were the Chairman of the State Department's Policy Planning Board and the Air Force representative to the Joint Chiefs of Staff's Strategic Planning Commission.

The Committee successfully bypassed the Secretary of Defense and recommended that American military capabilities be greatly increased. This recommendation was not well received by the Budget Bureau, and in April the President referred the paper to the National Security Council and asked for a specific program and cost estimate. The new program, however, began to merge with routine budget making procedures in the Defense Department, and not much had been accomplished by June 24, 1950. On that date, an unanticipated communist invasion of South Korea upset all planning and led to the Korean War. We shall examine the reasons for such intelligence failures in the chapter on the construction of reality.

It was the opinion of most Washington "insiders" and most Allied elites that the United States would not become involved in the Korean action. Earlier, troops had been removed from Korea because of its low strategic significance, and the Secretary of State had indicated that the defense of Korea was up to the United Nations. As we shall see in the chapter on decision making, what most observers overlooked was that key decision makers might give the invasion an interpretation that would automatically lead them to resist. The decision to fight was actually a series of decisions, a day or two apart, each leading to a greater involvement in the war. Each decision was made by the President after a meeting with a small group of key advisers (see the chapter on small group processes). The brief interlude between decisions permitted congressional, public, and Allied opinion to be weighed.

The first decision was to call an emergency meeting of the Security Council. The second major decision involved furnishing more military equipment to South Korea, using American airplanes to cover the evacuation of Americans and to slow down the North Korean advance, and ordering the Seventh Fleet to prevent a Chinese Communist invasion of Formosa. The third decision was to order full naval and air support to South Korean forces south of the 38th parallel, to augment military assistance to the Philippines and Indochina, and to take all action in the name of the United Nations. The fourth decision was to permit air and naval operations in North Korea and to commit United States ground forces to South Korea.

Following this involvement of the United States in the Korean War, there was a series of developments that led to other decisions of interest. The first occurred when the Commanding General of the United Nations Forces was faced with the problem of how to direct a counter attack against the North Koreans, who now occupied all but the tip of Korea. In the chapter on personality we shall study why in spite of opposition from the Joint Chiefs of Staff, he chose an extremely daring amphibious assault. The success of his plan resulted in the question of whether or not to pursue the enemy across the 38th parallel (see the chapter on decision making). Giving little credence to a Chinese warning that they would intervene if United States troops entered North Korea, the President and his advisers decided to cross the parallel. The advancing troops swept far up the Korean Peninsula until they suddenly encountered stiff Chinese resistance that forced them to a halt. The resistance then vanished, and the Commanding General of the United Nations Forces was faced with deciding whether to regroup and try to establish a defensive line, or to launch a final offensive to capture all of Korea. He chose the latter course of action. In the chapter on commands and communication we shall note that the Joint Chiefs of Staff failed to object to this plan or to order a regrouping of the two main bodies of troops, which they judged to be too far apart from each other. The advancing troops were trapped when superior Chinese forces suddenly fell upon them and exploited their division. We shall examine the Chinese decision to enter the war in the chapter on interactions between the representatives of nations.

In the resulting retreat, it was unclear whether the United States could maintain its forces in Korea without launching attacks against mainland China. The Commanding General of the United Nations Forces, thinking it could not, advocated a broadening of the war. The administration, concerned with maintaining the defense of Europe and lacking confidence in Nationalist Chinese forces, refused to become involved in an all-out war with China. It became evident that the United Nations Forces could hold a line around the 38th parallel; but when the Commanding General of the United Nations Forces publicly pressed for a broadening of the war, the President decided to remove him from his command. We shall examine this dispute in some detail in the chapter on commands and communications. The public reaction to this removal forced a disclosure of the administration's war plans, caused a solidification of attitudes against the Chinese, and gave impetus to a political development capitalizing on false charges of treason in the government.

As a result of the Korean War, the Soviet Union gained by creating enmity between the United States and China but lost some of her control over North Korea. The Chinese gained control over North Korea but lost the opportunity of acquiring Formosa. The United States gained an assured ally in Formosa and affirmed its will to oppose the expansion of communism but lost any opportunity of developing friendly relations with the Chinese. It is estimated that over a million lives were lost. Thirty thousand were American.

Organization of Material

While the foreign affairs of the United States are influenced by extra-governmental events, they are largely controlled by central decision makers. Snyder and his associates[15] have shown that all the historical, political and psychological factors that influence foreign policy — public opinion, material resources, organization of the government, alliance structure, etc. — may be viewed as acting through the nation's central decision makers as they attempt to cope with the actions of other nations. Such an analysis points up the fact that the decision makers' perceptions — their "definition of the situation" — rather than the actual objective situation will determine a nation's foreign policy.

Accordingly, the next four chapters of this book will focus on the psychological dimension of situational definition. First, we shall examine perception and how an individual constructs "reality," then we will study thinking and the factors that affect his projection of the future; next, we shall see how decisions are made; and finally we will turn to the role of personality in decision making.

In these four chapters we shall consider perception, thinking, and decision making in the organization as well as in the individual, for there is more than one important central decision maker. This points up the fact that the relations between these decision makers is often extremely important. Consequently, in the three succeeding chapters we shall examine different facets of these interpersonal relations. We shall first look at the dynamics of a small group, then consider the problems involved in commanding and communicating with "out-groups" in the field, and finally examine the bargaining process inherent in getting a consensus within the government.

---

[15]Richard C. Snyder, H. W. Bruck, and Burton Sapin, *Foreign Policy Decision-Making: An Approach to the Study of International Politics,* (New York: Free Press of Glencoe, 1962).

The policy formed by a government will create events which some other nation's decision makers will interpret in their own way and will react to in the context of their own internal affairs. As each government attempts to build the world it desires, its leaders attempt to influence the leaders of other governments. Since the resulting interaction may greatly affect the relationship between the nations and, hence, their foreign policy, we shall examine some aspects of this process in the last chapter, a chapter on interactions between the representatives of nations.

If the next four chapters of this book deal with how individuals and nations construct their own definitions of the situation and thus form their own individual "worlds," the last four chapters deal with how these "worlds" interact to produce new situational definitions and the isolation, or unity, or destruction of the different "worlds."

While the material within each of the above chapters often fits together, I have resisted any form of tight organization. At this point in our knowledge, any such organization would be quite arbitrary. Because I have used an eclectic approach, utilizing whatever psychological model seems to best fit the data, and since distinct processes are emphasized, the chapters themselves are rather unrelated. Thoughts on perception, personality, bargaining, power, etc., are scattered throughout the book and linked by cross references. Although the coverage is very incomplete, a number of suggestions, hypotheses, and problems clearly emerge.

While this book is not unified around an organizational chart or model of foreign policy formation, it does have a central theme: We can gain the freedom to control ourselves — to meet destiny rather than fate — only if we can conceptualize the forces that act upon us. We must realize the situation we are in if we are to master it instead of having it control us. This book is an incomplete study, a groping toward the knowledge that may free us. The very incompleteness is part of the challenge.

CHAPTER 2

The Construction
of Reality

The Determinants of a Perception

In early June of 1950, a cable arrived at the State Department from the United States' Ambassador to South Korea. This cable was routed up to the Assistant Secretary for Far Eastern Affairs; it reported a heavy North Korean arms buildup along the 38th parallel and pointed out in detail that the North Korean forces now had an overwhelming superiority over the South Korean forces. This piece of information could have been perceived with alarm, it might have suggested a forthcoming attack — the surprise attack that actually did come a few weeks later. In fact, however, it was perceived in a completely different way. The Ambassador had been in Washington shortly before to request tanks and other heavy equipment for the South Korean Army. The Assistant Secretary for Far Eastern Affairs and the group of persons around him perceived the cable simply as being a supporting argument for this request. Because of this interpretation, a message that might have served to warn the nation of a surprise attack was dismissed as another argument for something somebody wanted. How can we account for this unfortunate perception?

It is important to note that here we are talking about what governs a perception rather than a decision. Although the event was perceived one way rather than another, there was no decision; the Secretary was not aware that there were two conflicting possible ways of interpreting the event. He simply "saw" it one way. The "transactional" school of perception[1] has emphasized that perception is always a "choice" or "guess" about the real nature of the stimulus. For example, if a person closes one of his eyes and looks down a dark tunnel at a ball of reflected light, he may see either a large ball that is far away or a small ball that is close at hand. Either perception fits the pattern on the person's retina. Likewise, if the ball of light gradually increases in size (and, hence, the pattern on the retina gets larger), the person may see either a growing ball or a ball that is moving towards him. Either perception "fits the data," for in both cases the retinal pattern would become larger. Note, again, that the person does not realize that a choice is being made — *he* is not making a choice, he simply *sees* a small ball close by or a large ball far away, a growing ball or a ball that is moving towards him.

Now, since there are always a number of possible choices, we must ask, "What determines which choice is made?" Given the stimulus, what determines which of these possibilities becomes a person's reality? The answer, or one of the answers, is "the person's beliefs about related topics." For example, in the case of a ball of reflected light, Hastorf[2] has shown that if a person believes the ball of light is reflected from a ping-pong ball, he will see the light as close at hand; whereas if he believes the same light is coming from a billiard ball, he will see the light as farther away. The choice that is actualized is the choice that does not contradict one's other beliefs.

Now let us apply this thinking to the Secretary's perception of the Ambassador's cable. We must consider the information about a heavy troop buildup as a stimulus that could be interpreted in several legitimate ways. One possibility would be to see an impending attack, another would be to see an ambassador building a case for more money. Which possibility was selected to become reality was determined by the Secretary's other beliefs. Let us therefore inquire into what these beliefs were.

The Secretary probably held three ideas that were commonly believed in Washington at that time. These were that North Korea was a puppet governed by the Soviet Union, that the Soviet Union would not have an atomic capability to offset American nuclear weapons until 1954, and that until it had this capability the Soviet Union would not dare launch

---

[1]See, for example, W. H. Ittleson and F. P. Kilpatrick, "Experiments in perception," *Scientific American*, 185 (1958), pp. 50-55.

[2]Albert H. Hastorf, "The influence of suggestion on the relationship between stimulus size and perceived distance," *J. of Psych.*, 29 (1950), pp. 195-217.

an attack.* Clearly, perceiving the Ambassador's cable as an indication of an arms buildup in preparation for an attack would have conflicted with this system of beliefs which indicated that the Soviet Union would not attack. Hence, the other possibility was perceived.

Perceptual errors of the type we have been describing occur in nearly all intelligence failures. To give two other brief examples: In 1941 the United States had broken the Japanese diplomatic code and knew that Japanese intelligence had been instructed to obtain vast quantities of specific information about Pearl Harbor, including exactly what ships were berthed in what areas. Wohlstetter's study[3] shows that officials were so convinced that Pearl Harbor could not be attacked that they attributed these inquiries to "Japanese diligence" rather than to any special interest in Pearl Harbor. In 1965, when civil war erupted in the Dominican Republic, the rapidity with which arms were distributed was seen as an indication of organized communist activity — whereas it now appears that it was due to the sudden consolidation and emergence of student organizations.

It is difficult even to intellectually grasp the fact that *we construct* the reality in which we operate. We take our perception of the world for granted. We know the house is "out there" because we can see it; we know our friend is trying to impress the person he is meeting because we hear what he is saying; we know that a government is hostile because we can all see the actions it took. We know what is real. We live in this reality and act accordingly. We walk around the house so that we don't bump into it; we feel glad — or jealous — of our friend's desire to impress; we arm ourselves as a warning to the hostile government. We do not stop to consider that *in fact* the house may not be there, the friend may have thought the person a bore, the government may be badly divided. If someone else points out that our perceptions may be wrong we may intellectually admit the possibility, but we continue to act as though our perceptions were true. We are familiar with illusions but dismiss them as interesting playthings. Our reality seems so solid, and we feel so in touch with it, that it is impossible for us to act with the realization that in fact our reality is inferred by us and may not match the reality which future events reveal. It is precisely in this feeling of certainty that the danger lies.

---

*Some officials felt that the Soviet Union might make a localized move somewhere along the communist periphery, but these officials were not charged with any responsibility for Korea and, in any case, suspected that Iran would be a better target.

[3]Roberta Wohlstetter, *Pearl Harbor: Warning and Decision* (Stanford, Calif.: Stanford University Press, 1962).

To summarize what has been said so far:

When an event occurs, it is a stimulus that may be legitimately perceived in several different ways. The perception that actually occurs is the one that requires the least reorganization of the person's other ideas. Without any distortion of the stimulus there may be perceptual error. The person who sees an approaching light may actually be looking at a light whose brightness is increasing; the official who sees a request for money may actually be looking at a warning. Perceptual error will occur when the person least expects it, because the veridical perception will probably be unfamiliar and will go against the person's ideas. *Because of this it is absolutely necessary to have some independent way to check perceptions against reality.* We shall return to this thought later in the chapter.

Just as our beliefs serve to determine which of many possibilities will be perceived, repressed motives seem to express themselves by selecting a perception that relates to their concerns. These motives may exert a continual subtle influence on perceptions, or they may suddenly bias what has been a relatively veridical perception. A possible example of this is provided by President Wilson's perception of the Brest-Litovsk Treaty and his subsequent acceptance of excluding German participation at Versailles. In 1917, President Wilson pleaded for a negotiated peace with Germany rather than a punitive one. A punitive settlement, he said, " . . . would leave a sting, a resentment, a bitter memory upon which the terms of peace would rest, not permanently, but only as upon quicksand." Yet a year later the President had changed his mind. According to Kennan[4], the change resulted from Wilson's peculiar perception of the Brest-Litovsk Treaty, which ended the war between Russia and Germany at the beginning of 1918. As a result of internal chaos, Russia's military strength was extremely weak. The provisional government's decision to continue fighting Germany was a major factor in its downfall at the hands of the Bolsheviks, and the latter wanted peace at any cost. The German government took advantage of this situation to demand control over the entire Ukraine region, and the Bolshevik government was forced to accede to this demand. Now, given the heat of war we might expect a statesman to perceive this action as a ruthless extortion; but we would not expect this to distort his judgment about other issues. Yet Kennan states:

> nothing in the German and Austrian peace feelers of the last months of
> the war, infuriated [Wilson] more than the suggestion that the Brest-

---

[4]George F. Kennan, *Russia and the West under Lenin and Stalin* (Boston: Little, Brown and Company, 1960).

Litovsk Treaty should be maintained in force as the price for a German accommodation with the West. It was, in fact, the draconic nature of the Brest-Litovsk settlement, as he saw it, and the fear that it might disturb his favored scheme, that finally swung him from his aversion to a dictated peace to an acceptance of the idea of total victory and unconditional surrender.[5]

If Kennan is correct, we can only infer that the Brest-Litovsk Treaty meant something very personal to the President. Kennan suggests that Wilson had an image of himself as a defender of the helpless and innocent against the injustice of the mighty. Accordingly, he tried to play this role in the Mexican troubles of 1912-15, and his failure made him all the more eager to prove his approach in some other circumstance. After the Russian revolution, he began to picture the Russian people as frustrated idealists who needed his help and would respond to his sympathy. Therefore, he began to identify himself with their needs and to base his post-war plans on giving them support.

Now, the Georges'[6] analytic portrait of Wilson shows a man with a tremendous need for power which he could not admit to himself (and hense hid in his idealistic championing of the helpless). This was a man who had had an overpowering father, who had submitted to his father's will, and who now wanted power for himself and could not bear the thought of yielding to another's power. Imagine, then, his feelings when Germany took advantage of the powerless Russia with whom he had identified. He saw the nation he identified with having to submit to a tyrant. This was the excess meaning which the Brest-Litovsk settlement had — himself submitting again! A possible interpretation of the stimulus was selected by his repressed concerns and given a personal meaning.

The resistance to change of a belief

We have been concentrating on the fact that our perception may be in error because our beliefs lead us to select the wrong possible interpretation. We must now look at a related consideration — since the perceptions of events are selected by our beliefs, it may be very difficult for events to change our beliefs. Let us examine how this operated in the case of one key decision maker, President Eisenhower's Secretary of State.

An individual in the position of Secretary of State may have relatively little or a great deal of influence on foreign policy, depending on his

---

[5] *Ibid.*, p.123.

[6] Alexander and Juliette George, *Woodrow Wilson and Colonel House* (New York: The John Day Company, 1956).

relations with the President and on his own personality. In this particular case, the beliefs of the Secretary had an immense influence; the
President relied on him completely, and the Secretary relied on his own
beliefs rather than on the advice of his subordinates. Holsti[7] notes that
he carefully guarded his own position of influence with the President
and permitted no competition. All four of the President's foreign policy
aides left the government after clashing with the Secretary.

President Eisenhower was committed to exploring all avenues that
might lead to a rapprochement between the United States and the
Soviet Union. In particular, he wished to obtain an agreement on the
control of nuclear arms. At the time of his inauguration in January of
1953, the Iron Curtain was solidly closed and there were no prospects
for serious negotiations. However, the internal changes resulting from
Stalin's death in March of 1953 combined with the advent of thermo-
nuclear weapons and the realization of their destructive capacity created
a thaw that was apparent in 1954. Bechhoefer's[8] history of the disarmament talks shows that the talks began to progress in 1954 and that
progress continued into 1957. At the same time, the Soviet Union lifted
the Iron Curtain to permit cultural exchanges, reduced the strength of
its army, withdrew troops from Austria, and adopted a conciliatory
attitude towards Finland. We wish to examine how these events were
perceived by the man whom the President relied upon to carry out his
announced policy.

The man who served America as Secretary of State from 1953 to
1959 wrote in 1950, "Soviet Communism starts with an atheistic, God-
less premise. Everything else flows from that premise."[9] One of the conclusions which the Secretary drew from that premise was that the Soviet
Union could not be trusted to keep its word. Davis notes,

> He had a deep suspicion of the Communists, abundantly justified by
> events. He believed that a nation operating by principles was at a dis-
> advantage when dealing with an unprincipled nation, and feared that if
> we were drawn into agreements with the Kremlin on particular issues
> the effect on public opinion might be to undermine our ability to keep
> up our guard. He was determined that we should not be taken in.[10]

---

[7]Ole R. Holsti, "Cognitive dynamics and images of the enemy," *International Affairs,* 21 (1967), pp. 16-39.

[8]Bernhard C. Bechhoefer, *Postwar Negotiations for Arms Control* (Washington:
The Brookings Institution, 1961).

[9]Ole R. Holsti, "The belief system and national images: a case study," *J. Conflict
Resolution,* 6 (1962), pp. 244-52.

[10]Saville R. Davis, "Recent policy making in the United States government,"
Daedalus 89 (1960), pp. 951-66.

Consequently, the Secretary of State gave arms control a low priority. He saw as his mission the welding together of an alliance of nations against Communism. Whenever there was a decision between arms control and alliance strength, he chose to support alliance strength. This policy, of course, eventually defeated the arms control talks. For example, Bechhoefer notes that the Soviet Union was most interested in the separation of the antagonists in Europe and in conventional disarmament. It is conceivable that an agreement on these points might have been exchanged for an agreement on the control of nuclear weapons and arctic inspection points that interested the United States. However, an agreement on a neutral zone in Europe or on conventional disarmament would have involved the solidification of the split between East and West Germany. The Secretary of State was not willing to upset America's harmony with West Germany to secure an agreement with a party he did not trust. When the chief American negotiator gave his Soviet counterpart an informal preview of a control plan which had not yet been cleared by Germany, the Secretary of State denigrated the chief negotiator's position by having him reprimanded, making him clear all subsequent moves through NATO, and sending a deputy to "assist" him. According to Davis, the Secretary of State also encouraged a general atmosphere of pessimism about the chances of getting any arms control agreements. He did this by supporting the anti-test ban positions of the Chairman of the Joint Chiefs of Staff and the Chairman of the Atomic Energy Commission and by steering talks away from agreement between scientists to disagreements on a political level.

The Secretary's intransigency was based on his belief that a communistic government was essentially evil. There is no doubt that the Secretary of State was an intelligent person. Given the fact of the great Soviet "thaw" that followed the death of Stalin, did he really fail to change his belief about the Soviet Union? And, if so, how could he have failed to do so? We are fortunate to have a detailed study of the Secretary's perceptions of the Soviet Union. Holsti[11] has considered all of the Secretary's publicly available statements—a total of 434 documents including Congressional testimony, press conferences, and addresses. Correspondence with the Secretary's close associates established that these public statements also matched his private beliefs. In these statements, the Secretary made a total of 3,584 assertions about the Soviet Union. Holsti asked judges to place each of the assertions into one of four categories: assertions as to whether Soviet policy was friendly or hostile, assertions as to whether he perceived Soviet capabilities to be strong

---

[11]Holsti, "The belief system and national images," *J. Conflict Resolution,* 6 (1962).

or weak, assertions as to whether Soviet policy was succeeding or failing, and assertions expressing the belief that the Soviet Union was either "good" or "bad." The judges then rated all the assertions within each category. (For example, assertions in the first category might be rated as indicating that the Secretary saw Soviet policy as very friendly, friendly, slightly friendly, neutral, slightly hostile, hostile, or very hostile.) With these data before us, we can ask how Soviet policy affected the Secretary of State's belief in the worth of the Soviet Union.

We might expect that when the Secretary began to perceive Soviet policy as becoming more friendly (when, for example, the Soviets relinquished Austria), he would also begin to evaluate the Soviet government as "good" rather than "bad." Conversely, if Soviet policy toughened, we might expect the Secretary to perceive the government as more evil. To ascertain if this were true, Holsti examined the Secretary's statements during each of twelve consecutive six-month periods of time and related the Secretary's perceived hostility (or friendliness) of the Soviet Union to the Secretary's evaluation of them as bad (or good). He found that there was no relation at all (the correlation was $+.03$)! That is, whether the Secretary perceived Soviet policy as hostile or relatively friendly did not affect his beliefs — his evaluation of the Soviet Union — one iota.

How did the Secretary account for relative Soviet friendliness? The data show that he assumed that Soviet capabilities had lessened (the correlation is $+.76$). That is, whenever the Soviet Union became relatively friendly, the Secretary perceived it as weaker rather than nicer! For example, he saw the withdrawal from Austria as due to the failure of Soviet policy in Western Europe, and saw the reduction of Soviet armed forces by a million men as forced by industrial and agricultural weaknesses.

Now, of course, it can be argued that the Secretary's reaction was the correct one, but even if that is so the study raises an important question: If there were factions in the Soviet Union who desired friendlier relations with the United States, what could they have done (in the realm of political practicability) to convince the Secretary of State of their sincerity? It would appear that no matter what the Soviet Union could have done, the Secretary would have interpreted the very acts that should have led him to *change* his belief, in such a way as to *preserve* his belief.

The difficulty of changing deep beliefs has been noted in a completely different context by Conant.[12] He has pointed out that time after time the adherents of a scientific theory have refused to abandon their theory

---

[12]James C. Conant, *On Understanding Science* (New Haven, Conn.: Yale University Press, 1947).

in the face of negative evidence from opponents. The theory dies only when it fails to gain new adherents. The resistance of beliefs to evidence is also shown in Cantril's[13] study of reactions during the fear of an invasion from Mars. Panic ensued when Orson Wells' "Wars of the Worlds" was presented over the radio as an extremely realistic series of new broadcasts. On hearing that Martians were approaching and that evacuation was recommended, some persons thought to check the validity of the news but they only confirmed its truth by whatever evidence was at hand. Thus, a person might look out of his window to check the story. If many people were seen, he might confirm the story by seeing that the evacuation had begun; if none were seen, he might confirm the story by seeing that the evacuation had already been completed in that area.

We have been treating a person's perception of reality as though the person were an isolated individual. It is time that we considered some of the effects engendered by his relations with other persons. The most important of these effects is the stability of beliefs induced by membership in a group. A person almost always belongs to at least one group of persons whose opinions he values. He cares what these particular persons think about him, and he tends to see things from their perspective. This perspective affects what is important to him and, therefore, what he attends to. Furthermore, since changing his view of reality means losing emotional contact with the group, his beliefs are anchored in what the group perceives as real. In the chapter on communications we shall see how groups can have quite different realities, how their realities are resistant to change, and how this prevents successful policy integration.

A somewhat different effect is produced by the need to communicate effectively to others and to convince them of one's own beliefs. If one wants to be taken seriously one has to largely accept the reality in which others are operating, and thus one begins to think and perceive in their terms. Furthermore, as Bauer[14] has indicated, when a person attempts to convince others of a point he builds an argument that is directed to their concerns and is a selection of a portion of the truth. This aspect of the truth then becomes rigidified as "the way things are." For example, in order to discourage the wishful thinking of some person who hoped to encourage a revolution in the Soviet Union, many experts discovered and stressed stabilizing factors within the Soviet

---

[13]Hadley Cantril, *The Invasion from Mars; A Study in the Psychology of Panic* (Princeton, N.J.: Princeton University Press, 1960).

[14]Raymond A. Bauer, "Problems of perception and the relations between the United States and the Soviet Union," *J. Conflict Resolution*, 5 (1961), pp. 223-29.

Union. They built models of the Soviet Union that did not permit change to occur. As a result, these experts cannot now objectively assess slower changes occurring in Soviet society. An expert's audience has an effect not only on what the expert says but also on what he sees — because what he says must seem to follow from what he sees.

Bauer points out that when an expert builds a model of events, he tends to overrationalize the actions of the society he is studying. Everything that happens must be accounted for by his model, nothing can be regarded as an isolated accident. This compulsion to fit everything into one's model is a particular problem when the data are sparse — as they are when one is dealing with a country other than one's own. For example, a Soviet diplomat may interpret American Middle Eastern policy as being determined by the large American oil companies. He may not realize that the more politically powerful segment of the American oil industry is domestically based and would be happier without competition from Middle Eastern oil.

Overrationalization is a particular problem when the other society is in competition with the expert's own. Competition almost forces the expert to assume that his opponent is rational so that the expert may play the game in an optimal way. The problem is that this adoption of rationality as an optimal strategic assumption becomes confused with one's perception of the real situation. A statement such as "The Russians will attack us as soon as they believe they have a military advantage" may be a good assumption on which to base policy, because *if* it were true the consequences would be enormous. But a person using this assumption begins to believe that it is a true picture of the world when it *probably* is not true. A good strategic assumption becomes confused with a good description of the other nation's behavior and intentions. For strategy, the *possible* is important, but this may become confused with the *most probable* at the expense of exaggerating our perception of the opponent's rationality, power, and aggressiveness. Bauer[15] suggests:

> This confusion of strategy-setting with perception is preserved on the individual level by the phenomenon which has become known as dissonance reduction. Apparently, most of us find it a source of strain to act on an assumption that we do not believe is the most probable state of affairs. Accordingly, we 'adjust' our perception to bring the probabilities into line with the possibilities.

---

[15]Raymond A. Bauer, "Accuracy of perception in international relations," *Teachers College Record,* 64 (1963), pp. 291-99 (p. 294).

Yet another factor that biases the expert's perception of another country is that his model of (beliefs about) the other country is always slightly out of date, since it is based on recent history rather than current events. Since the model does provide a way of organizing many facts, the expert tries to preserve his model against evidence that would suggest its change. He selects those aspects of the data that conform to his model and considers the rest "nonessential." When the data are ambiguous — as when one is looking at a society that is not his own — Bauer[16] notes,

> . . . one's theoretical model becomes simultaneously more necessary and potentially more dangerous. There is an increased tendency to interpret the very data which would lead one to change one's model in such a way as to preserve that model. Without the model one could not say if change had taken place, but with the model one is less likely to see the evidence for change. To compound this error, . . . the ideologies in both camps are so concerned with the differentation of one system from the other that a discussion of points of similarity is resisted.

Individual differences

We must now turn to a different implication of our analysis of perception. Since different persons have different beliefs, it should follow that they will have different perceptions of the same event. For example, early in 1950 government officials had a number of different beliefs that affected their perception of the Korean invasion. The Chairman of the Joint Chiefs of Staff believed that the Soviet Union might try to move into Iran. A high official in the State Department believed that Soviet foreign policy was quite cautious in its expansionism. The President believed that a nation did not become belligerent unless it thought its opponents too weak to fight. Hence, when news of the Korean attack first reached government officials, it was perceived in slightly different ways. The Chairman of the Joint Chiefs of Staff appears to have seen the event as a diversionary move before a major blow against Iran. The State Department official interpreted the invasion as a tentative probing action. (He was reminded of Lenin's remark that if one's bayonet runs into concrete he withdraws, while if it hits a soft belly he continues to thrust.) The President saw the attack as similar to Hitler's invasion of Czechoslovakia.

The first perceptions of an event are extremely important because they influence the decision of how to respond to the event. If the inva-

---

[16]Bauer, "Problems of perception," *J. Conflict Resolution,* 5, p. 227.

sion was analogous to Hitler's assault on Czechoslovakia, then the Russians must have been gambling on the United States to avoid fighting. One can imagine the President's anger rising at this audacity and can understand his determination to resist the attack, even if the resistance would be unsuccessful. Any other course would be appeasement. Given this perception, one can understand why the President later stated, "Every decision made in connection with the Korean War had this one aim in mind: To prevent a third world war and the terrible destruction it would bring to the civilized world."[17] Given this perception of the situation, one can understand why the President was willing to abandon some of his plans and incur the political costs of the war.

If, on the other hand, the invasion was seen as a diversionary move, one would hesitate to commit troops to a strategically unimportant peninsula. And if the attack were seen as a tentative probing, there would be no reason to become angry — one could simply reinforce the South Koreans so that the bayonet would meet a concrete wall instead of a soft belly. That is, the attack would be seen less as a gamble based on the United States' timidity than as a routine attempt at expansion.

The President's view of the Korean attack as similar to Hitler's invasion of Czechoslovakia was not as accurate as it might have been. In retrospect, it appears that to the extent to which the Soviet Union was involved, it was not gambling on the United States' weakness of will as much as on the United States' disinterest in Korea. And whereas Hitler's Nazi party was based on aggression and needed to fight in order to survive as a political force, the Communist party seems to have viewed the invasion as a tentative expansion in order to offset the United States' gains in Japan and the increased power of the Communist Chinese. The perception of the tentative bayonet thrust was proved more accurate when the Russians failed to support the invasion, after the United States decided to resist it. However, the President's perception had the advantage of mobilizing the nation's will to fight. A challange to one's will and a reference to the historical fact of Munich summoned the nation's emotional strength; whereas the stopping of a tentative bayonet thrust and a recall of the Communist attempt to win Greece (a more accurate analogy) might have left the nation uninvolved. The perception may also have helped the President to decide to fight. We shall return to this idea in the chapter on decision making. On the other hand, the President's interpretation may have had some unfortunate consequences. Its emotional quality may have encouraged the protective blockade of

---

[17]Harry S. Truman, *Memoirs*, Vol. 2: *Years of Trial and Hope, 1946-1952* (Garden City: Doubleday & Company, Inc. 1956), p. 248.

Formosa, exaggerated the evil intent of the Soviet Union to the extent that it became a factor in the rearming of Germany, and discouraged the setting of strict limits on American war goals.

It should be noted that, from a contemporary perspective, all of these perceptions may possibly have been in error in attributing the major responsibility for the invasion to the Soviet Union. On the one hand, it is clear that Soviet advisors were heavily involved in the North Korean government and army, that most of the troops were trained and equipped by the Russians, and that the Soviet Union had direct control over gasoline supplies. On the other hand, one defector from the North Korean government has stated that the North Korean leader decided on the invasion when he was assured by the leader of the large South Korean Communist Party that there would be widespread popular support in South Korea for the invasion. Furthermore, a Polish advisor who was attached to the North Korean army has stated that the Russian advisors made some attempts to prevent the invasion. Thus, the North Koreans may not have been the puppets which they were perceived to have been; and while the Soviet government obviously failed to hold the invasion back, it may not have really been the *instigator* of the invasion.

Note how the perception of a stimulus is just as important as the stimulus itself. We never respond to the actual event or situation but to our view of it. The actual motivations of the Russians and the actual importance of Korea did not determine American action. According to Paige,[18] at the time of the invasion the expert opinion in Washington was that the President would not act to resist the invasion. The experts were incorrect because the President perceived the invasion in a way that made armed resistance the only acceptable alternative.

The Soviet Union may not in fact have been as determined to expand as Hitler's Germany; but if American officials perceived this to be so, then the rearmament of West Germany followed as a conclusion. As Thomas[19] has succinctly noted, "If men define situations as real, they are real in their consequences."

If there are differences in the perception of an event among persons similar enough to be high American officials, one can imagine how differently an event may appear to persons from different cultures. A person from a different culture literally lives in a different world of

---

[18]Glenn D. Paige, *The Korean Decision: June 24-30, 1950* (Glencoe, Ill.: Free Press, 1968).

[19]W. I. Thomas, quoted by M. R. Merton (ed.), *Social Theory and Social Structure* (Glencoe, Ill.: The Free Press, 1949).

reality — so much so that a person who is thrust into a different culture actually experiences a kind of "culture shock" in which he is quite disoriented. This difference in worlds has two serious consequences for international relations. First, as Wedge[20] has documented, a visitor to another country perceives events in a way that fits in with his own beliefs and, hence, often does not get a valid picture of that country. Second, in attempting to anticipate the reactions of other nations, officials often fail to view events from the other nation's perspective. Hence, there is a failure to anticipate the other's reaction, and, as we shall see in the next chapter, this failure often contributes to poor policy planning.

The perception of persons

While we have been speaking of the perceptions of events, the perception of another person's actions is no different in principle. We are, again, faced with a complex stimulus that permits several possible interpretations. And the perception that does, in fact, occur is influenced by factors such as beliefs and other knowledge extraneous to the stimulus itself. A neat experiment that demonstrates this process has been performed by Strickland.[21] He assigned certain students to supervise the work of others. Each of these "supervisors" was responsible for insuring that the output of two students met specified standards. The situation was arranged so that the supervisor could closely watch the production of one worker but could not easily monitor the output of the other. The experiment was planned to insure that, to the supervisor's knowledge, both of his workers produced the same amount of work. After several periods of work, the supervisor was instructed to choose which worker he should watch more closely. In almost all cases, the supervisor's choice indicated that he perceived the student who had been working without close monitoring to be more trustworthy. The reason should be clear — while the outputs were the same (and, hence, the supervisor was confronted with the same stimuli), the supervisor knew from his own experience that the other student might have been working only because he was being watched. However unjustly, his perception of trustworthiness was influenced by this extraneous knowledge.

Now let us consider an example of interpersonal perception in public life. In early 1948, the President was confronted by a Secretary of

---

[20]Bryant M. Wedge, *Visitors to the United States and How They See Us* (Princeton: D. Van Nostrand Co., Inc., 1965).
[21]Lloyd H. Strickland, "Surveillance and trust," *J. Personality*, 26 (1958), pp. 200-215.

Defense who wanted an extra $9 billion for his budget. The President knew that there was tremendous interservice rivalry in the newly unified Defense Department. In the light of this knowledge, he perceived that the request for more money stemmed from the interservice rivalry rather than from an integrated defense plan. Since he wanted an integrated plan with a low budget, the President perceived that the Secretary of Defense had not exerted enough leadership in unifying the services and keeping their budgets under control. Rather than seeing a legitimate plea for more money, he saw a weak leader.

In order to assess the validity of this perception of the Secretary of Defense, we must look at the interservice argument between the different Chiefs of Staff.[22] The minimum war plan to which they could all agree consisted of plans for a strategic air offensive from Britain with combined Naval and Army operations to hold open a line of communication into the Mediterranean. While this plan had something important in it for each service, it was a compromise which involved a reduction in what each really wanted, since the Air Force wanted to develop intercontinental strength, the Navy large carriers, and the Army a standing force in France and Germany. The problem with this minimum war plan was that it required $23.6 billion. To lower this to the $15 billion Presidential ceiling required some service to surrender its mission, and unfortunately there was no common doctrine to guide how this should be done. The resultant disagreements were not simply a matter of service pride and politics; there were genuine differences in belief about the importance and cost of each activity. The Air Force argued that strategic bombing was the most efficient way to win the war, while the Army felt that ground troops ultimately had to win any war. No one was sure whether bombers could really get through to their strategic targets and whether the use of nuclear weapons would be politically feasible. The Army argued the necessity of defending Western Europe, but no one was sure how many divisions were needed to hold the Rhine. The Navy argued the value of carrier operations in furnishing tactical air support, but no one knew whether carriers could really survive in the Mediterranean Sea.

It is clear, then, that there was no "correct" solution to the war plan and budget problem. The Secretary of Defense could have forced a solution by arbitrarily picking one course of action, but the arbitrary nature of this solution would have resulted in the mass resignations which his successor incurred after doing precisely that. The Defense

---

[22]Warner Schilling, "The Politics of National Defense: Fiscal 1950," in *Strategy, Politics and Defense Budgets,* eds. Schilling, P. Y. Hammond, and G. H. Snyder (New York: Columbia University Press, 1962).

Secretary decided to avoid the conflict an arbitrary choice would have forced. He was in sympathy with the needs of all the services because he was convinced that the Soviet Union was expanding rapidly. Consequently, he resolved to battle for the only solution — more defense money.

This analysis shows that the President's perception of the Secretary of Defense was incorrect. Rather than being a man who failed to exercise determined leadership to solve interservice wrangling, he was a man who believed the service's requests were essentially legitimate. Why did the President perceive the Secretary as a weak leader rather than a man whose opinion differed from his own? In addition to his knowledge of what seemed to be needless interservice competition, there may have been two other reasons. First, the Secretary was somewhat of a rival, a man who was a potential leader of the more conservative half of the Democratic party and who often insisted on his views, even when they were opposed to the President's. He sometimes seemed a little contemptuous of the President. Under these circumstances, the President, who respected the Secretary's ability, may have had to dislike him a little in order to keep from feeling inferior. Second, while the President had to decide to put a ceiling on the defense budget in order to prevent inflation, he must have been in conflict about his decision. To perceive the Secretary's budget request as stemming from the Secretary's inadequate control over interservice rivalry must have lessened this conflict, whereas a perception of a clear-cut difference of opinion might have heightened it.

The stimulus in the above case was the Secretary of Defense's request for an extra $9 billion, and, clearly, either the perception which the President entertained or a perception of the Secretary as a dedicated man with strong opinions on defense would have fit this stimulus. But what kept the stimulus so meager? What prevented the President from having contact with other stimuli from the Secretary that would have forced a more veridical perception? Why, in particular, did the Defense Secretary and his friends fail to object to the President's perception of him? The answer probably lies in the fact that perceptions, even when they are incorrect, often lead to behavior that supports the perception. When the President turned down the Secretary of Defense's budget request, he did not say that he felt the Secretary was failing to exert leadership over the feuding armed services, or that he should have done more to control the testimony of the various services before Congress. If the Secretary really had been failing to exert leadership, this would not have helped matters. Instead, the President told the Secretary that a budget increase would hurt the economy and, in the long run, would lead to a public reaction against defense spending that would hurt the services.

Now, we do not know how the Secretary of Defense reacted to this explanation, but I believe we can hazard a guess. When a person presents an explanation that sounds weak — which is obviously only half of the picture — we become suspicious. The Secretary of Defense probably sensed the insincerity in the President's position. It was clear to him that the nation needed to spend more for defense and the economy had to give. He was confronted by a President turning down his request with an argument which he sensed the President really did not believe. The Secretary might have perceived that the President felt that defense needs were being inflated by interservice rivalry that was not being controlled because of the incompetent leadership of his Defense Secretary. However, this perception would have been painful and might have hurt the Secretary's belief in himself. There was an "easier" perception available, a perception which fitted well with the mild contempt the Secretary sometimes had towards the President. The Secretary seems to have perceived that the President was basing his decision on what the public would like instead of what the nation needed. He saw the President making policy with an eye on the forthcoming election and thus devalued the President just as the President had devalued him.

Probably, in this way, one misperception led to another, and no correction ensued. It is not surprising that the Secretary of Defense failed to support the President in his attempt to get reelected and that this, in turn, lost him the President's confidence. The reader should note how no party really *distorted* any information and how no one was really to *blame*. Given the personalities involved, their different responsibilities, and the atmosphere of politics, the whole process was as determined as a Greek tragedy.

Changing views of reality

We have been considering how beliefs determine our reality by dictating the selection of one of a number of possible interpretations of the stimulus. Nevertheless, a stimulus can lead to a perception that influences our reality and, hence, our beliefs, *if* none of the possible interpretations of the stimulus can be easily accounted for. Consider a cable from the Ambassador to Korea, which reached the Assistant Secretary for Far Eastern Affairs a few weeks after the cable we discussed earlier. The first paragraph of the new cable listed four attacks at different points along the 38th parallel. The second, and last, paragraph stated, "It would appear from the nature of the attack and the manner in which it was launched that it constitutes an all-out offensive against the Republic of Korea." In spite of initial beliefs to the contrary, central decision makers perceived an invasion of South Korea. Hence, one of their beliefs had to change.* It is interesting to note that their first reaction was to check their own estimates of Soviet capabilities to see whether, perhaps, the Soviet Union *was* as strong as the United States and might be risking a global attack. Only after this check proved negative did they fully believe in a relatively limited attack. And, as we have mentioned, the belief that North Korea was a complete satellite was never questioned.

While in the above case a new stimulus changed the decision makers' beliefs, there are many examples of changes that occur in spite of the lack of new, otherwise inexplicable stimuli. Consider the many government officials who at one time would have been horrified at the thought of a wall separating East and West Berlin; how did these same officials gradually change their belief and come to regard the wall as tolerable and no obstacle to negotiations? Consider Admiral Radford, who was once a critic of strategic bombing and opposed to what he called the "indiscriminate bombing of cities." How did it happen that three years later he was in the forefront of those advocating strategic bombing and the infeasibility of a nuclear test ban?

In the absence of new and inexplicable stimuli, perceptions only change when the interpretation that was dominant is eliminated for some extraneous reason. There are two possibilities. First, the person may find that actions based on his perceptions are not working. He may then be forced to act in a way that appears strange to him in the light of his perceptions. If this action is successful, the corresponding potential interpretation of the stimulus becomes perceived. Second, the person may look at the stimulus from a different and possibly more complete perspective. Thus, consider our example of looking at a ball of light with one eye. Suppose a person sees the ball as close. *Telling* him that the ball is actually farther away does not change his perception. But if he tries to touch the ball and repeatedly fails, he may be forced to reach out far past where the ball appears to be. On touching the ball, the perception may shift so that the ball is seen as larger and farther away. Or, if the person is permitted to use both eyes, he gains a perspective that eliminates some possible interpretations and, hence, may create a shift in perception of the stimulus.

Let us consider the first of these reasons for change. Psychologists have emphasized two different factors that may be involved when

---

*The Ambassador could have been perceived as exaggerating if he had not had the reputation of being a cautious, responsible person.

actions lead to new perceptions: the rewarding of the action, and the new psychological forces that may be called into play. The role of rewards seems relatively straightforward. For example, according to Jones,[23] a crucial factor in Vandenberg's shift towards internationalism was the response to a policy speech which he made in the Senate. In this speech, he surprised his colleagues (and maybe even himself) by strongly advocating a concern with the future of other nations and the necessity of avoiding an isolationist position. Internationalists were delighted, and congratulatory letters, calls, and telegrams poured in from all over the country. While the Senator's beliefs were probably beginning to shift in response to his viewing new aspects of international affairs, there can be little doubt that the large reward he received for his Senate speech played an important role in speeding the change of his belief.

Some of the new forces that may be called into play when a person acts incompatibly with his current perception have been described by Festinger[24] and by Kelman.[25] Festinger postulates a general force that operates to make a person's ideas consistent with one another.* Hence if a person performs an action that is incompatible with his beliefs, his knowledge that he has done this will have to be made consistent with his beliefs. If this dissonance can be resolved by referring to some external reason for the action, the person's beliefs will not have to change. If, however, there is no obvious external reason for the action, the person will have to change his beliefs so that they will be the reason for his action.

When the Berlin Wall was first erected, there were relatively few obvious reasons for not tearing it down. At least, many government officials seem to have perceived this as a real alternative which they failed to exercise because the situation took them by surprise. Since these officials believed that a split of Berlin was unthinkable, Rosenau[26]

---

*Rather than postulating a general force towards consistency of beliefs and actions, Kelman considers an array of different factors. For example, he points out that the change of beliefs follows if the action creates a commitment that is difficult to revoke and, hence, leads the person to search for new information that will make his new association more profitable, or if the person's self-esteem is threatened and can be defended by a change of belief.

[23]J. M. Jones, *The Fifteen Weeks* (New York: The Viking Press, Inc., 1955).
[24]Leon Festinger, *A Theory of Cognitive Dissonance* (Stanford, Calif.: Stanford University Press, 1962).
[25]Herbert C. Kelman, "The induction of action and attitude change," *Preceedings of the XIV International Congress of Applied Psychology* (Copenhagen: Munksgaard, 1962), pp. 81-110.
[26]James N. Rosenau, *Calculated control as a unifying concept in the study of international politics and foreign policy,* Research Monograph No. 15 (Princeton: Center of International Studies, 1963).

has pointed out that dissonance would have been operative and would have required them to change their belief to one of tolerance for the split. While, no doubt, other factors were involved in the officials' change in belief, it would appear that the reduction of dissonance might have been an important factor.

Dissonance theory may also be useful in understanding why some persons change their beliefs when others do not. Snyder[27] furnishes an interesting example in his discussion of some problems President Eisenhower had with his method of obtaining a satisfactory defense budget.

If the Joint Chiefs of Staff had produced a defense budget based solely on military factors, their request would have been so high that the Administration would have had to deny part of the request, thereby exposing itself to the criticism that it was not furnishing the nation with an adequate defense. To avoid this embarrassment, the President asked the Joint Chiefs of Staff to arrive at a defense budget based on economic as well as military considerations. Admiral Radford sympathized with the President's political position and perceived the President's request as legitimate. Therefore, although he was forced to suppress military considerations for economic ones, he felt that he had a real choice in formulating the most desirable defense budget. The careful reader will note that Admiral Radford was in a situation where he was maneuvered into *voluntarily* advocating a budget that was lower than the one called for by his beliefs. Therefore, we would expect his beliefs to change to support his new position as to what was a desirable defense posture. On the other hand, the Army Chief of Staff felt that the administration was *pressuring* him to put economic considerations ahead of military ones. He perceived the situation as one where he had no real choice. Consequently, while he went along with Admiral Radford's recommendations, he did not change his beliefs and later made statements that embarrassed the administration.

Turning now to the second reason for change, changing in order to follow a new perspective, we note that a person may achieve a new viewpoint by joining a group that has a reality different from the one he is accustomed to or by stepping into a new role that forces him to see things from a different point of view. Thus, Lieberman[28] has demonstrated that workers who become foremen begin to change their beliefs about unions, incentive pay, and seniority. Let us see how this applies to the shift in Admiral Radford's beliefs.

Admiral Radford was a critic of strategic bombing when he was

---

[27]Glenn H. Snyder, "The 'new look' of 1953," in Schilling, Hammond and Snyder, *op. cit.*

[28]Seymour Lieberman, "The effects of changes in roles on the attitudes of role occupants," *Human Relations,* 9 (1956), pp. 385-402.

Vice Chief of Naval Operations. His position required him to champion naval power in the budget struggle with the Army and Air Force. Hence, he argued against relying on strategic bombing by the Air Force on the grounds that tactical air support (which could be supplied by carriers) was more effective militarily and did not involve the mass killing of civilians. When Admiral Radford became Chairman of the Joint Chiefs of Staff, he was faced with problem of insuring an adequate national defense that would not disrupt the national economy. He perceived the politically potent fact that strategic air power was the most inexpensive way of buying some security. This view of the problem he was confronting led him to change his beliefs about strategic bombing. In his new position, the only way the Admiral saw to solve his problem was to advocate strategic bombing and thus modify his beliefs.

While Admiral Radford changed his beliefs because of his insight into solving a problem, he confronted the problem in the first place because he had assumed his new role of Chairman of the Joint Chiefs of Staff. Functioning in a new role often changes beliefs by forcing the person to examine issues from a different perspective. Bauer, Pool and Dexter[29] have argued that this point is an important aspect of how foreign travel changes beliefs. They point out that when an American businessman travels abroad he must take the role of a spokesman for American interests instead of his usual role of spokesman for his business' interests. Their study shows that if a businessman came from a small company and had not traveled abroad, his beliefs about free trade could be predicted simply by knowing whether free trade would benefit or harm his business. But the beliefs of a businessman who had traveled were not as easy to predict. Speaking of such men, the investigators note,

> They became more internationalist in the sense that they took more foreign facts into account in their calculations, but in another sense they became more nationalist. They came to answer questions in the light of what seemed to them the interests of America in the world, not in the interests of one firm in America.[30]

The Determination of the Stimulus

Thus far, we have been treating the stimulus as a concrete thing or event that is placed in front of a person, to be perceived in any of a

---

[29]Raymond A. Bauer, Ithiel de Sola Pool, and Lewis A. Dexter, *American Business and Public Policy* (New York: Atherton Press, 1963).
[30]*Ibid.*, p. 472.

number of different ways. We must now recognize that to some extent the person determines what stimuli confront him in the first place. This occurs in two different ways. First, the person's actions (which were based on his *perception* of the stimulus) may affect the actual nature or presence of the stimulus. Second, the person decides what stimulus or aspect of the stimulus he will *attend to*.

Perception as a determinant of the stimulus

The simplest instance of this occurs whenever a person's perception affects what physically happens to the perceived stimuli. For example, when the Ambassador to Korea's first warning cable was perceived as a "back up" for his request for funds, the cable itself was filed away. Consequently, all of the information in the stimulus was lost, and none of the other potential perceptions had a chance to occur. A few weeks later, when key officials gathered to decide how to meet the invasion, they wondered about the true size of the North Korean forces. In their guessing, they continually underestimated North Korean strength. The Ambassador's cable, filled with accurate details on the North Korean forces, lay in the files completely forgotten.

A more complicated effect occurs when the perception leads to communication problems. Thus, as we saw earlier, the President's perception of the Secretary of Defense led him to not disclose his real reasons for declining the latter's request. This behavior *created* a stimulus for the Secretary, who interpreted this evasion of the President as an indication of his political motivations. The Secretary's perception, in turn, changed the actual nature of his response to the President and, hence, he became a different stimulus for the President.

Perhaps the most well known form of perception affecting reality is the "self-fulfilling prophecy." In this effect, the person's perception of reality leads him to take actions which *produce* what he believed he had seen all along. Thus, to the extent that President Eisenhower's Secretary of State created Soviet hostility by refusing to seriously negotiate on arms control measures, he produced the very hostility he perceived. Similarly, when the United States took action against China in 1950 because it perceived China to be in league with the Soviet Union, it may have forced the Chinese into a closer alliance.

Attention as a determinant of the stimulus

It is obvious that we are most likely to attend to stimuli that have to do with our interests and needs. However, it is also true that our *beliefs* affect not only how we perceive a stimulus but also whether a stimulus is there in front of us. We build or select an environment that provides us with the stimuli we want, and we turn away from unwanted intrusions. Studies such as Hyman and Sheatsley's[31] have repeatedly demonstrated that a person selectively exposes himself to information that is consonant with his beliefs. Our beliefs are quite stable; we resist changing them. Our beliefs bias our attentive processes so that we usually attend to events that are compatible with our beliefs. Then, when potentially incompatible alternatives occur, we perceive the one that preserves our beliefs. Only if a person is unusually aware of this, will he go out of his way to maximize the opportunity to test his beliefs against the real situation so that his beliefs may be adaptively influenced by rewards and insights.

Now, a bureaucracy can attempt to guard against individual biases by requiring that messages be routed to appropriate officials and that these officials initial each message. Thus, the bureaucratic structure could insure that the Assistant Secretary of State for Far Eastern Affairs would attend to the Ambassador to Korea's cable. Such a message may be misperceived, but at least it is assured of being a stimulus. Unfortunately, there is no way to guard against biasing by bureaucratic interests; that is, the design of the whole bureaucratic routing system to insure attention to the stimuli the bureaucracy thinks are important, sometimes creates a bias against important information. One way a democracy attempts to circumvent this problem is to have elected officials at the head of the government. This insures that there will be political as well as bureaucratic channels of information, but it again raises the problem of an important official's personal biases and the biases introduced by his policy. If a stimulus is important enough, it will eventually come to a President's attention — but valuable time may be lost, and the situation may grow to be dangerous. We need to become more conscious of these natural selective processes and to study possible safeguards that might be erected.

Consider the following example of inattention cited by Cantril.[32] In May of 1960, a carefully conducted poll of 1,000 Cubans showed that a strong growth in optimism followed the revolution. Eighty-six per cent of the people were in favor of the Castro regime, and it seemed clear, in the light of these data, that there was no hope of stimulating the Cuban people to take action against Castro. A report of this poll was widely distributed in the American government but seems to have

---

[31]H. Hyman and P. Sheatsley, "Some Reasons Why Information Campaigns Fail," *Pub. Opin. Quart.*, 11 (1947), pp. 413-23.
[32]Hadley Cantril, *The Human Dimension: Experiences in Policy Research.* (New Brunswick, N.J.: Rutgers University Press, 1967).

not been attended to. At least, the government went ahead with its ill fated invasion attempt in 1961. In a somewhat similar manner, data showing that an explosive situation existed in the Dominican Republic were completely ignored before the outbreak of civil war.

We have been speaking about whether or not a stimulus is physically in front of a person. Once a stimulus is before a person, selective processes again operate to determine which aspects of the stimulus are attended to. The Ambassador's cable about an invasion was viewed with an eye to the situation in Korea rather than to the Ambassador's grammar. While this was a very functional selection, it should be apparent how easily a person could attend to irrelevant details and thereby miss important facts. In short, a person cannot only turn his eyes or instruct his secretary to sort his mail so that he views some stimuli rather than others, but can also, having his eyes on the stimulus, search for evidence of poor socio-economic conditions or evidence of communist infiltration. He can learn to use his attention to select those aspects of the stimulus that interest him.

Any stimulus is initially amorphous; it is not a psychological stimulus until the person attends to some aspect of it. In order to act, the observer selects an aspect of the stimulus which he can distinguish and thinks important. He determines the aspect of the stimulus to which he responds.*

In order to control his attention to select a given aspect of a stimulus, the person has to learn appropriate responses. If he has never learned to recognize communist infiltration or neo-colonialism, he cannot look for them. This fact leads to another biasing influence: if a person is not interested in or familiar with a given area, he may not be able to see an aspect of the stimulus to which an expert can easily attend. Conversely, if a person is set to pay attention to certain aspects then the appropriate responses are available and he is much more likely to see these aspects of the stimulus — even if others are more important.

In the first section of this chapter, we saw how a perception was determined by the stimulus and a person's past experiences and beliefs. Now we see that the stimulus itself is determined by a person's attention. The reader should note that both the perceptual and attentive processes are usually completely intertwined, so that both determine how a person constructs his world. A person cannot be said to attend to a stimulus

---

*Thus, Lawrence states, "There is a sensory input; this is acted upon by the coding response, an implicit reaction that is controlled by factors other than the proximal stimulus; the consequence of this interaction is (the stimulus as coded) and it is the latter that is directly associated with the overt behavior." Lawrence, Douglas H. The nature of a stimulus. In Sigmund Koch (ed.), *Psychology: A Study of a Science,* Vol. 5, (New York: McGraw-Hill, 1959), p. 189.

unless he perceives it, and yet every perception involves a selective attention. Still, there are two important differences between attention and perception. First, the aspect of a stimulus to which one attends does not *contradict* any other aspect of the stimulus. One can look at either communist infiltration or socio-economic conditions, first one and then the other; for both aspects may be there. On the other hand, one perception of a stimulus is incompatible with a different perception. One can see only one reality: there either is or is not a given amount of communist infiltration; there either are or are not poor socio-economic conditions. Second, in attention, if the person has a number of responses available, he has some direct control over the stimulus or the aspect of the stimulus which he selects. If he desires more control, he learns further discriminations. In perception, on the other hand, all of the stimulus elements to which the person is attending determine an *involuntary* organization of these elements into one of several possible perceptual responses.* The person cannot voluntarily control his perception, and we have seen that the changing of perceptions is a quite involved process.

Distorted and creative perceptions

In the section on perception, we noted that when a person confronts a stimulus he can form a number of legitimate interpretations or perceptions that fit the stimulus. Even if a perception is in error — that is, if the person revises his perception when he comes in contact with more of the stimulus — we can hardly call it a *distorted* perception. However, we must not conclude that all perceptions are legitimate. The stimulus has an *objective structure* that limits the number of possible legitimate interpretations. Thus, given an image of a ball, we may see it as small and close, or larger and farther away — but we cannot see it as smaller and farther away. Such objective structures limit the perception of any event and are an exciting field of study in their own right. (Within social psychology several interesting structures for interpersonal relations have been explicated by Fritz Heider.[33])

---

*Technically speaking then, the attentive response is an operant, while the perceptual response is more related to classical conditioning and insight learning. Attention is a response set, perception a stimulus organization. Unfortunately, little is known about how each process affects the other. Most experimental work in learning has concentrated on the attention process by studying the learning of arbitrary connections between an aspect of the stimulus and the "correct" response. Thus, a rat may be taught to move toward the brighter of two stimuli or a person taught to group together all Chinese characters with two crossing lines. What is needed is more information about how attention affects perceptual insight.

[33]Fritz Heider, *The Psychology of Interpersonal Relations* (New York: John Wiley & Sons, Inc., 1958).

We may now define a distorted perception as a perception that does not fit the objective structure of the stimulus. Such a perception is possible only when a person does not attend to all of the relevant aspects of the stimulus. Suppose, for example, that the stimulus is the simple one below:

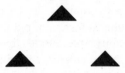

A person could organize or perceive this stimulus in various ways. He could see it as "three triangles," or "one triangle," or "the face of a pyramid," or "the faces of three pyramids," etc. All of these perceptions fit the objective structure of the stimulus. Distorted or poor perceptions, such as "three spots," "two triangles," or "a figure," are not as accurate because the perceiver has not attended to all of the relevant dimensions of the stimulus.

A possible example of such a distorted perception may be found in North's[34] account of the German Chancellor's perception of European forces in 1914. The Chancellor and other officials perceived Russia as bluffing in its expression of support for Serbia against Austria. In part, this perception was based on the belief that England would certainly remain neutral. This perception of affairs was held by failing to attend to a dispatch from the German ambassador in England, who clearly warned against counting on British nonintervention. We shall see some of the dynamics behind such distortions in the next chapter.

To turn now to *creative* perceptions, we may note that some perceptions are *deeper* in that they capture more of the essence of the structure than a cursory inspection reveals. Thus, in the above figure, "four triangles" captures more of the stimulus. The importance of the accuracy of a perception can hardly be overstressed: as stimuli increase in complexity, fewer perceptions seem to capture their essential structure and creative insight becomes important. Indeed, one can view creativity as perception based on attention to the structure of a complex stimulus. This is what Michelangelo was referring to when he said that he did not create a statue but simply freed its form from the rock. A great musician is confronted with the same page of notes as his students, yet his music reflects a different perception of these notes. Thus, Pablo Casals instructs his students to try to see behind the notes into the

---

[34]Robert C. North, "Perception and action in the 1914 crisis," *J. International Affairs,* 21 (1967), pp. 103-122.

structure they reflect. This is not, of course, to say that there is only one correct interpretation of a set of notes — another great cellist would play them differently. But both great interpretations reflect a structure which lesser interpretations miss.

One of the most intriguing facets of this process is that any great interpretation also reflects the person who renders the interpretation. That is, a creative perception is based not only on the essential structure of the stimulus but also on the essential structure of the personality of the creator. Insight into the structure of something "out there" seems to always be linked to the structure of the inner person. While this is most apparent in the arts, it seems to be true in all fields. The biographer of Josiah Gibbs has noted how the theories of this founder of physical chemistry could only have been formulated by a man with his personality. The great jurist Benjamin Cardozo has noted the influence of personality on judicial decisions and agonized, "Why would the pure light of truth be broken up and impregnated and colored with any elements of my being?" And Admiral Nelson was noted for exploiting his unique perceptions of the structure of battle formations. In the chapter on decision making we shall examine some related issues. Though it is beyond the scope of this book to explore this facet of creative perception, we can note that it is probably just as important in a politician as in any one else. Certainly, it is just as important for their perceptions to fit the structure of reality. The perception of the Korean invasion is a case in point. Information about the Korean invasion was a complex stimulus, and the President's perception (which reflected his personality) grasped enough of the structure of the stimulus so that he acted in an unexpected way, and with reasonable success. As we have noted, the inaccurate aspect of his perception may have contributed to the lack of preciseness in the American response.

To summarize what has been said thus far:

The construction of reality depends on two intertwining processes: An attentive process that determines what is selected as the stimulus, and a perceptual process that determines which of several possible alternative views of the stimulus is actually perceived. The attentive process depends on response categories which the person has learned in the past and on the person's goals and beliefs. The perceptual process depends on the nature of the stimulus which the person confronts and on the person's beliefs. The alternative selected to be perceived will be the alternative that requires the least reorganization of the person's beliefs. The two processes, thus, interact to determine what the person attends to and how well his perception fits the real stimuli which he must cope with if he is to achieve his purposes. A perceptual error may be retained and become a distortion if the person's attention is restricted to a limited aspect of the stimulus situation. A creative response occurs when a person's attention is unusually broad and yields a perception that accurately reflects the structure of a complex stimulus and relates it to the person's goals.

"Perception" in the Organization

We have been considering perception in the individual; let us turn to perception in the organization. It does not seem to me that we should speak of an organization as though it were either an individual or a machine. Its behavior is not motivated in the sense that a person feels himself to be motivated, nor is it determined by the constraints that govern the behavior of even the most complicated machine. An organization does not really perceive events or make decisions; that is done by the individuals in the organization. On the other hand, an organization does exist in its own right — it is not simply the sum total of the individuals in it — and it does act. Information may or may not reach central decision makers, and these men may or may not issue orders which thousands of men will probably obey. Our current language and thinking is not precise enough to indicate exactly what an organization is and how it behaves; we are forced to rely on terms such as "perception," "threshold," and "sensor" — terms which really apply to the behavior of individuals or machines. With these limitations in mind, and with a concern for how we should conceptualize organizations, let us examine how an organization "perceives" information. As an example, we may consider how the United States government first perceived the Korean invasion.

The invasion began at 4:00 a.m. on Sunday, June 25, 1950 (Korean time), when about 100,000 North Korean troops attacked South Korean forces at many points along the 38th parallel. The "peripheral sensors" of the government were United States military advisors who were stationed in most South Korean regiments. The advisors in different regiments began reporting to the Korean Miltary Advisory Group (KMAG) headquarters (the first "relay station" of the system) that their regiment was under heavy attack. Reports began to come in to this station about 5:30 a.m. Men at this station, used to reports of numerous border incidents, were not expecting an invasion (the "relay station," therefore, had a high threshold for sensitization). However, by 7:00 a.m. so many widely scattered reports of serious fighting had been received that the chief of KMAG headquarters notified the Deputy Chief of Mission of the United States Embassy. The Deputy Chief soon suspected that a full fledged invasion was underway. He had the hypothesis that this was so, but one does not awaken superiors at 7:00 a.m. Sunday morning with a hypothesis. It was 8:00 a.m. before he *knew* that a large scale attack was underway, and he phoned the United States Ambassador to Korea. While the Deputy Chief can be considered as a relay station in the organization's information system, he was a man who formulated a hypothesis and tested it before he made a decision to send information further in the communication hierarchy.

Nor did the Ambassador passively forward the news of an invasion to the State Department. If he had done so, he would have forwarded the news as a KMAG report. But he knew that men in the State Department would want *his* evaluation of the situation — he automatically took into consideration that more central elements of the chain would want an opinion from someone they could trust, rather than from someone they did not even know. Of course, an ambassador could have accepted the KMAG's belief as his own and reported an invasion, but this ambassador had a reputation for carefulness. Indeed, it was this very reputation that insured that his report would be accepted at face value by men who were not in a position to check the information first hand. The Ambassador, therefore, personally went to KMAG headquarters to evaluate the situation before he took the responsibility of notifying the State Department. By 9:30 a.m., he had evaluated the attack and had sent the cable (which we described earlier) to the State Department.

When the Ambassador was walking to KMAG headquarters, he was spotted by an alert reporter who inquired how he happened to be up so early. The Ambassador told him of the reports of a full scale attack. A second channel of communication began as the reporter hastily filed a report with the United Press. A third channel to Washington also started via the embassy's military attaché, who began relaying messages to the Defense Department.

By 10:00 a.m. (9:00 p.m., June 24 in Washington), the United Press had phoned the State Department to inquire about the report of fighting. The Ambassador's cable had not yet arrived, and a public affairs officer phoned the Assistant Secretary for Far Eastern Affairs, who happened to be at a dinner party with the Secretary of the Army. Both men went to their departments to check on the news. The Secretary of the Army phoned the Secretary of Defense, who had just received word of the attack from the Defense Department. The Secretary of Defense told the Secretary of the Army to take the responsibility of keeping up with the attack.

Figure 1. *A Diagram of the Communication Pattern in the Korean Invasion (Washington times are in parentheses)*

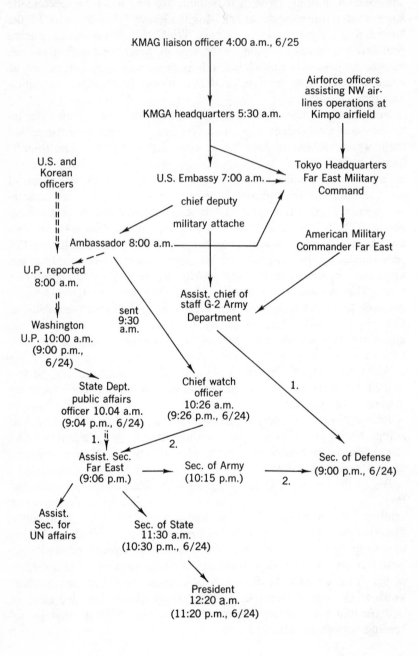

The Assistant Secretary for Far Eastern Affairs cabled the Ambassador for information. Minutes later — 9:30 p.m. in Washington — the Ambassador's cable arrived. It was decoded by 10:15 p.m., and the Defense Department was notified. It is to be noted that this cable formed the basis of all action for the next thirty-six hours. Since the information had come from a reliable man with a reputation for carefulness and caution, the Assistant Secretary immediately phoned the Secretary of State (it was 10:30 p.m.). Although the full extent of the attack was not appreciated, the two agreed that it could not be merely another border skirmish. Therefore, at 11:20 p.m., the Secretary of State decided to phone the President, who was not in Washington at the time, to tell him of the attack. We may now, somewhat arbitrarily, consider the organization to have "perceived" the Korean invasion, and we shall stop our description of communications at this point. A diagram of the communications is shown in Figure 1. Note that there was a delay of eight hours and twenty minutes between the beginning of the attack and the notification of the President. An organization's perceptual response time is, therefore, considerably longer than an individual's. Responsible communication of novel information necessarily means slow communication in an organization.

Figure 1 shows that the chain of communication had more than one channel. In the case of the Korean attack, there were two separate official channels and one unofficial channel of information to Washington. (In fact, a fourth channel began from the President of the Republic of Korea to the American Secretary of State via the Korean Ambassador to the United States.) Multiple channels give the organization a degree of protection against individual biases that might otherwise prevent the receipt of information.

The channels of communication on which the organization's perception depends consist of chains of individuals. These individuals are not passive relays; each has his own perceptions, and each must decide what to report up the chain. A chain of communication consists of a series of decisions by individuals. Since this is true, the organization's "perception" is affected by the perceptions of each of these individuals and by the relations they have with each other. We have already seen how the perception of an individual can affect the response of his organization; how do interpersonal relations affect organizational "perception"? First, interpersonal relations are often important in determining communication channels. It should be observed that the Secretary of Defense did not phone the President; he waited for the action of the Secretary of State. One reason lies in the fact that Korea was a responsibility of the State Department, but perhaps of greater importance was the fact that the Secretary of State had a much closer relationship with the President than did the Secretary of Defense. Second, the relations between people may also determine what information is referred through a given communication channel. In detailing the tremendous amount of information which a President receives, Sorensen[35] has remarked,

> What [the President] actually considers and retains may well be the key to what he decides, and this in turn may depend on his confidence in the source and on the manner in which the facts are presented. He is certain to regard some officials and periodicals with more respect than others. He is certain to find himself able to communicate more easily with some staff members than with others.

Parenthetically, we should note that sometimes the behavior of an official shows a bias for certain kinds of approaches. Thus, Lasswell and Almond[36] have demonstrated that one official may go out of his way to help a person who makes a request in a non-aggressive way, while another official in the same position may ignore such requests but help persons who accompany their requests with demands and threats.

Finally, we have seen that the reputation of the man in the field is of great importance in enabling central personnel to assess the incoming information. When one must act on the basis of another man's judgment, one desires a man he knows and trusts. Had the Ambassador to Korea been a less respected man, the United States response would have been considerably slower. In fact, events developed with such speed that the invasion might have progressed beyond the point where the United States could have intervened.

While it might seem that the above points are almost self-evident, they are often forgotten when another nation's response is evaluated. For example, when the United States dropped an atomic bomb on Hiroshima on August 5, 1945, it was believed that three days would give the Japanese time to surrender before the second bomb was dropped. But Hiroshina was largely destroyed by the first bomb, and the central Japanese decision makers had no one whom they could trust to evaluate the rumored information that a radically different kind of bomb had been used. They had to send a trusted man from Tokyo to interpret the bombing. This kind of delay prevented a quick decision

---

[35]Theodore C. Sorensen, *Decision Making in the White House* (New York: Columbia University Press, 1963), p. 39.
[36]Harold Lasswell and Gabriel Almond, "The participant-observer: Studies of administrative rules in action," in *The Analysis of Political Behavior,* ed. Lasswell (London: Routledge and Kegan Paul, 1949).

to surrender; and meetings were still deadlocked when the second bomb was dropped on Nagasaki.

Once the organization had "perceived" the invasion, it began to "attend" to many pertinent details. This occurred when the President requested men in key positions to answer various pertinent questions. The organization's information networks were used to gather the knowledge needed for an adequate response. The intelligence network was used to ascertain whether a global communist attack was in progress (it was not). The Defense Department net furnished information as to the strength and location of American forces. Experts on the Soviet Union in the State Department were queried for news of Soviet intentions and probable Soviet reactions to different moves which the United States might make. In short, the organization's "perceptual system" consisted of many possible communication nets, which, within two days, were used on many different problems. In this sense, it should be noted that the organization's information processes involved the memories of individual officials as well as their perceptions. What are the laws that govern an organization's "perceptual" process?

Snyder and Paige[37] have attempted to formulate a number of important relations that they feel will always be true. With some changes in formulation, four of these are:

1. The less adequate the inflow of information about external events, the more reliance on information within the unit making the policy decision. This information will be in the form of memory of past experiences. The more the above is true, the fewer will be the number of policy alternatives considered.
2. The more limited the information, the greater the emphasis on the reliability of the source.
3. The greater the confidence in the existing information, the greater the amount of contrary information and source reliability necessary to change the current interpretation.
4. The more routine the times, the more information must have crisis-like qualities if it is to gain top-level attention.

In addition to suggesting the above laws, Snyder and Paige have prepared an interesting table for evaluating the communications during the first weeks of the Korean crisis. They rated the different kinds of information available at different stages of the decision making. For example: information on the progress of fighting, on the relative strength of the armies, and on enemy intentions, was rated as the week pro-

[37] R. C. Snyder and G. D. Paige, *The United States Decision to Resist Aggression in Korea: The Application of an Analytical Scheme* (Evanston, Ill.: Northwestern University Press, 1958).

gressed. The ratings were on four aspects of the information: the amount of information used relative to the amount actually available, the amount used relative to the amount needed, the reliability of the information, and the degree of confidence in the interpretations made on the basis of the information. For an example, let us consider the information on the relative strength of the armies. The ratings show that in the beginning of the week only "medium" amounts of the information actually available were used (a reflection of the forgetting of the Ambassador's first cable). This state of affairs continued until halfway through the decision week, when this particular rating rose to "high." On the other hand, the ratings show that confidence in interpretations based on strength of the armies started at a medium rate and became low at the end of the week.

In general, it may be said that confidence in interpretation of most of the information was higher than either the amount of information or its reliability.

Intelligence Failures

After carefully reconstructing the failure of intelligence to anticipate the Japanese attack on Pearl Harbor, Wohlstetter[38] states,

> The history of Pearl Harbor has an interest exceeding by far any tale of an isolated catastrophe that might have been the result of negligence or stupidity or treachery, however lurid. For we have found the roots of this surprise in circumstances that affected honest, dedicated, and intelligent men. The possibility of such surprise at any time lies in the conditions of human perception and stems from uncertainties so basic that they are not likely to be eliminated, though they might be reduced.

Now that we have considered how individuals construct reality and the nature of the communication channels that underlie the organization's "perception," we are in a position to understand an organizational intelligence failure. Let us look at the intelligence failure in the Korean case. The Korean invasion came as a complete surprise. Virtually none of the military aid that was due Korea according to the 1949 Mutual Defense Assistance Act had reached the country. A third of the South Korean Army was on leave, the Chief of the South Korean Navy and the Deputy Chief of Staff of the Army were in Honolulu, and the acting Commander of the Korean Military Aid Group was in Tokyo;

---

[38]Wohlstetter, *op. cit.,* p. 397.

100,000 North Korean troops, 1,400 pieces of artillery, and 126 tanks had not served as a warning signal. How did this intelligence failure occur?

We may consider the problem of anticipating the Korean invasion as a problem in signal detection. That is, out of the hundreds of messages that bombarded government officials, how could the organization have detected those messages signaling a forthcoming invasion? Studies of a person's ability to recognize a stimulus embedded in other stimuli have shown that at least three factors are important: the signal-to-noise ratio (i.e., the strength of the signal relative to the strength of confusing background stimulation), the expectancies of the observer, and the rewards and costs associated with announcing the signal as present. Let us consider each of these factors as they affect governmental officials in the organization.

Holding the strength of a signal constant, it is obviously easier to detect the signal if there is relatively little background "noise." In the case at hand, there was a considerable amount of such "noise" — numerous border skirmishes in Korea, recent reports of Soviet troop movements in the Balkans, rumors of forthcoming attacks on Iran, and the surveillance of no fewer than ten "danger spots." On the other hand, the reader must not suppose that the signal consisted of just one cable. Intelligence sources made several reports of troops moving up to the 38th parallel. It is hard to evaluate the strength of the signal because, while there were many intelligence reports about the arms buildup in North Korea, there was no red flag. A capacity to invade is not the same as an intention, and no one said, "I believe there is going to be an invasion." Consequently, it is difficult to estimate just what the signal-to-noise ratio actually was, and one can only wish that systematic studies were made of fluctuations in the noise of intelligence reports and the best way to increase the signal-to-noise ratio. After the Korean invasion, it was easy to go over intelligence reports and see evidence of the invasion's preparations; before the invasion, this was more difficult to see.

If a person expects a signal, he is much more likely to be able to detect it. We have already observed how the Assistant Secretary of State for Far Eastern Affairs did not expect an invasion and, hence, failed to detect it even when he was confronted with a rather strong signal. An equivalent mistake would probably have been made by any person in the Secretary's position. We noted at the time how the correct perception of information is particularly difficult when it goes against one's beliefs. Research in simulated intelligence operations has repeatedly shown the biasing effects of the operator's beliefs. Consider the following demonstration by Bavelas.[39] He took a detective story, cut out every couple of sentences, pasted them on cardboard, then mixed up the sentences in a box with sentences from other stories. Persons participating in the experiment were told that a crime had been committed and that they should use the box of information to find out about the crime and who was responsible. Each person was given five assistants. Bavelas reports that almost every person began by having his assistants go through the sentences to find clues. As soon as information of interest was reported, the leader began to form a hypothesis that controlled the next step of the search process. For example, if an assistant came up with the information that a knife had been found, the person might hypothesize that a murder had been committed, probably by a man. He then might request information on possible male suspects. After half an hour of search, the experiment was stopped and an objective test was given to all the participants to determine how much information they knew.

Two important results were obtained. First, it was established that the average assistant knew more facts than the average person directing a search operation. Second, it was discovered that the only way to have the leader correctly determine the crime was to prevent him from forming hypotheses until many pieces of information were in his possession.

What was happening is evident. A person would form an idea of the state of affairs on the basis of a little information. Once he had this idea, it was almost impossible to change it because it governed his perception of future information. The hypothesis of a male murderer prevented the perception of information about a woman smuggler, and the leader would end up knowing less than his subordinates about the real state of affairs. The only way to prevent this was to prevent the leader from thinking until his first hypothesis could be based on enough information to ensure that the hypothesis was a good one. Perceptions of information that were dissonant with the hypothesis did not occur.

It may be objected that a failure in one person does not explain the failure of an organization. However, in many cases, almost all of the high level decision makers have the same set of ideas. In the Korean case, most officials believed that the North Koreans were Soviet puppets, that the Soviet Union was not prepared to engage the United States in war, that if there was going to be a war it would be in the Near East rather than Korea, that if the North Koreans were determined to win South Korea they could probably gain their ends by subversion,

---

[39]Alex Bavelas, Personal communication.

and so on. As one intelligence official later remarked, these common beliefs were a wall against which all intelligence reports were evaluated. Furthermore, every high official knew of the pressures on the American defense budget; they knew that plans would not permit the strengthening of South Korean defenses. Ransom[40] has noted,

> There had been no consideration given . . . to providing for the defense of Korea against limited war or satellite aggression. Intelligence, in a sense, was thus falling on deaf ears.

"Self evident" beliefs are involved in most intelligence failures. For example, only five months after the Korean invasion, military intelligence failed to correctly estimate the strength of the Chinese forces that were quietly entering Korea. Intelligence estimated between 60 and 70 thousand Chinese troops, when in fact there were 300 thousand Chinese troops waiting to fall on the advancing U. N. forces. Again, we find evidence of blinding biases present in the intelligence agency. For example, intelligence felt that since the North Korean forces were virtually defeated, the Chinese would be poorly advised to enter the war at such a time. Three days after the first skirmish with Chinese forces, the Far Eastern Command's intelligence summary stated,[41]

> From a tactical viewpoint, with victorious U. S. Divisions in full deployment, it would appear that the auspicious time for such [Chinese] intervention had long since passed; it is difficult to believe that such a move, if planned, would have been postponed to a time when remnant North Korean forces have been reduced to a low point of effectiveness.

As in Bavelas' demonstration, the Far Eastern Commander's chief intelligence officer interpreted all information in the light of his belief that it was a bad time for the Chinese to intervene. When aerial reconnaissance failed to find masses of Chinese troops, he took this as evidence supporting his hypothesis and did not worry about the possibility that the masses of troops were well hidden in small groups. As in Bavelas' demonstration, men in the field had a much better idea of the actual situation. For example, the Commander of the Marines in the field was so worried at this ignoring of Chinese strength that he wrote the Marine Commandant in Washington, constructed an airfield in case

---

[40]Harry Howe Ransom, *Central Intelligence and National Security* (Cambridge: Harvard University Press, 1958). p. 174.

[41]Robert Leckie, *Conflict: The History of the Korean War, 1950-1953* (New York: G. P. Putnam's Sons, 1962).

emergency evacuation was necessary, and delayed carrying out orders to move forward. He thereby avoided a trap and managed to evacuate the bulk of his troops.

The rewards for correctly detecting a signal and the costs for failing in detection or making a false report have a striking effect on how well a person detects a signal. Swets[42] has demonstrated this effect by having persons listen to a background noise and guess whenever they thought an additional sound had been added to the noise. Keeping the signal-to-noise ratio constant and working with a ratio so small that the observer thought he could not tell the difference between noise and noise-plus-signal, he showed that if the reward for detection is high and the cost of an incorrect guess is fairly low, then the observer "guesses" correctly far more frequently than would occur by chance. If there is a low cost associated with failing to guess, while a high cost is associated with guessing incorrectly, the person will not guess enough. Swets' work shows that it is incorrect to think that a signal will be detected simply because it is strong relative to the background noise. The rewards which a person gets if he detects the stimulus, and the costs he must pay if he fails or gives a false report, are as important as the signal's strength in determining whether the person will perceive the stimulus.

Within the government, the intelligence service places a high cost on failure to report a signal. Since nobody wants to be blamed for an intelligence failure, far too many false leads swamp the information channels at a high level in the State Department and elsewhere. On the other hand, at the Assistant Secretary level, there is a high cost placed on falsely reporting a signal to be present when actually nothing is there. No one wants to bother a Secretary of State or a President with false information. Unfortunately, the result is a *filter* which may be at the wrong place in the system. While central decision makers have a broader view of world events, persons nearer the source of intelligence might be better judges of the accuracy and importance of information mainly relevant to one nation.

Filters are also sometimes placed incorrectly for *outgoing* information. Wohlstetter[43] notes that, a week before Pearl Harbor, Washington officials believed that the Japanese were going to strike somewhere but failed to issue strong enough warnings to the Pacific Fleet. This failure was due partly to fear of the cost of a false warning (it would decrease future credibility and interrupt training) and partly to a lack of realization that

---

[42]J. A. Swets, "Is there a sensory threshold?" Science, 134 (1961), pp. 168-77.
[43]Wohlstetter, *op. cit.*

the men in the fleet, lacking certain background information held by the central officials, misinterpreted what warnings were issued. The importance of adequate feedback can hardly be overstressed. Without it, men in the field cannot be sure that their messages are being perceived correctly by central decision makers and vice versa. Had the Ambassador to Korea been aware of how his messages were being taken, he might have been able to correct the situation.

The fact that the communication of information is affected by rewards and costs helps explain why the entire communication system is biased by the ideas and plans of the top decision makers. A subordinate is rewarded for communicating information that interests his superior. If he insists on communicating information that his superior feels unimportant or biased, it is likely to prove costly. Hence, subordinates soon learn their superior's ideas, plans, and way of thinking. If a person is "in" with his superior, he is likely to share his biases. The man with different ideas is likely to be "out," to have communication problems, or to actually leave the organization. When a subordinate has ideas which his superior may disagree with, he may be tempted to water down his report so that it is more acceptable. As a result, the superior may easily interpret it in a way that does not alert him to facts he should know. In the Korean case, several of the Ambassador's advisors believed an invasion would occur, but others thought it unlikely. Rather than making a judgment, the Ambassador sent the cable which we considered at the start of this chapter. Had he known how his cable would be perceived, he might have acted differently — but, in general, rather than risking the costs of being wrong or arguing with an unsympathetic superior, the easiest thing to do is to pass up scraps of raw intelligence information. These are always welcome, since they can be interpreted in any way.

One might suppose that policy makers would encourage intelligence operations to risk specific guesses about the future. However, Hilsman[44] reports that only about half of the policy makers he interviewed felt that the intelligence service should issue warnings or make any interpretations of the facts it gathered. As a result, there is continual disagreement about the role which the intelligence community should play. Currently, there are various compromises. For example, within the State Department, the Bureau of Intelligence and Research does write some policy oriented memoranda that estimate future developments in the light of proposed policy. These memoranda may also put forward

---

[44]Roger Hilsman, Jr., "Intelligence and Policy Making in Foreign Affairs," in *International Politics and Foreign Policy,* ed. James N. Rosenau (New York: The Free Press, 1961).

suggestions in order to insure the consideration of possible opportunities for action.

Whereas, theoretically an intelligence service gives the facts on which policy is based, often, particularly over the short run, policy is made and *then* supported by intelligence. In general, in spite of what *we* have seen, everyone in the government seems to believe that the truth is perfectly obvious when all the facts are known. Actually, this reasoning is partly a rationale to avoid giving the intelligence service any more power than can be helped. As Ransom[45] has indicated, policy makers have a legitimate fear that information may be interpreted to be used as a weapon for influencing policy. There is also a concern that intelligence operators interested in policy may become the advocates of some pet scheme at the expense of reporting facts. Consequently, the interpretations they present often meet with skepticism. Unfortunately, the major effect of these attitudes may not be to purify intelligence but rather to discourage the reporting of clear estimates of what will happen.

It must not be assumed that an intelligence failure, such as the failure to anticipate the Korean invasion, is a rare event. No government is free from intelligence failures, many of which are due to the ignoring of information that does not conform to the ideas and plans of those at the top of the organization. Let us review a few historical examples. These are taken from Kennan's book, *Russia and the West.*[46]

1. In 1917, both the French and British Ambassadors to Russia tried to warn their governments of the coming collapse of the Tsarist regime. Such a collapse could only have been averted by Russian withdrawal from the War. The foreign ministers of France and Britain would simply not believe that collapse was coming. It would ruin their plans for the war! When unmistakable evidence of disintegration was thrust before their eyes, they believed the deterioration resulted from German influence rather than a fundamental weakness in the Russian government.

2. In 1926, Stalin was repeatedly warned by Chinese Communists that Chiang Kai-shek was becoming unfriendly to the communist forces within the Kuomintang. But Stalin himself had helped the Kuomintang grow and had integrated communist forces within it; furthermore, he had had Chiang trained in Moscow. Some of Stalin's rivals were opposed to Chiang and the idea that Chiang was now unfriendly was upsetting politically and met neither Stalin's plans nor his emotional commitment. Stalin ignored the information; within a year Chiang had slaughtered his communist allies.

---

[45]Ransom, *op. cit.*
[46]Kennan, *op. cit.*

3. In 1941, Russia was warned that the Germans were about to attack them. The United States commercial attache in Berlin relayed detailed plans to Washington that were given to the Russian Ambassador to the United States. But such an attack would have made the Soviet-German non-aggression pact and the cooperation flowing from it completely meaningless — it would have ruined Russia's plans. Consequently, the information was interpreted as propaganda to split Russia from Germany. Three months later, when Hitler struck, the Russians were completely unprepared.

This list could easily be lengthened. For example, the United States government failed to predict not only the Korean War but also the Polish and Hungarian uprisings, the Israel attack on Egypt, the riots accompanying the Vice President's tour through South America in 1958, the communist development of the Cuban revolution, the success of Sputnik, and the revolt in the Dominican Republic. The reader may be assured that some of the processes we have described are involved in all of the above failures. Let us see whether our knowledge of these processes can help us suggest some remedies that might reduce the likelihood of future intelligence failures.

Organizational constraints

In attempting to find a way to increase the accuracy of organizational perception, we must keep three constraints in mind. All of these stem from the fact that any large organization contains competing interests. The first constraint is that important officials work under a time pressure generated by the work needed to integrate different interests within a bureaucracy. I have not read an account of a bureaucratic operation or had a talk with a person in a policy-making position that has not touched on the necessity of swimming or sinking in the continuous stream of things that must be done. There is the press of one problem after another with memoranda to be read, memoranda to be commented on, memoranda to be initiated, and meetings to attend. If an official wants to have his views influence policy, he must keep abreast of a dozen developments and initiate a dozen actions. He may have a half hour to draft a memorandum which he would like a day to think about. One may get a feeling for this constant turmoil by reading Ogburn's[47] brief description of State Department operations. As a result of this

---

[47]Charlton Ogburn, Jr., "The Flow of Policymaking in the Department of State," in *The Formulations and Administration of United States Foreign Policy,* ed. H. Field Haviland, Jr., (Washington: The Brookings Institution, 1960).

time pressure, officials do not have the time to judiciously weigh different points of view.

The second constraint is that the conflict of interests often prevents any action that is not absolutely necessary. If an office makes recommendations on the basis of perceiving a problem that *may* erupt in the future, the recommendations will probably not be accepted because they will interfere with actions that are required by another office to cope with problems that currently exist. The fact that the foreseen problem may not develop is a powerful argument against the recommended action. As a result, the already overworked official is not inclined to worry about things that *may* happen in the future.

The third constraint involves the fact that there are often legitimate differences of opinion as to what a situation is really like. Typically, these differences in perception are bound up in differences of values and personal attachments and provoke severe conflicts within the organization. For example, Feis'[48] account of American policy in China in 1944 shows a complete divergence of opinion between the Ambassador and a group of Foreign Service officers. He states:

> This divergence reflected different estimates of the strength and vitality of the Communist movement among the Chinese people. [The Ambassador] did not think it had great or lasting support. Several of the Foreign Service officers were thoroughly convinced that it had. . . . both favored and urged reform. But [the Ambassador], impressed by the obstacles which made it hard for the Generalissimo to take unusual measures, was not downcast by the signs of lethargy. The others were convinced that only thorough and rapid reform could save the government.

When an official finds himself in such a disagreement, he may fight for the adoption of his policy and consequently become involved in a dispute that prevents him from sympathetically examining opposing ideas.

Just as the individual official tends to perceive what fits in with his beliefs, the organization tends to "perceive" whatever will allow it to act. That is, the organization will "view" as reality whatever will help establish a consensus. The individuals in the organization will then have to respond in terms of this construction.

Now, if one keeps these constraints in mind — if one realizes the fact that officials have little time to explore anything, little inclination to explore what *might* happen, many pressures to argue for the policy they currently believe in rather than to explore an opponent's perceptions, and a need to believe in whatever will establish a consensus —

---

[48]Herbert Feis, *The China Tangle* (Princeton: Princeton University Press, 1953), pp. 260-64.

then it is evident that even the most open minded official usually *will not* cope with the biases inherent in his beliefs and perceptions.

A Suggestion

Once we recognize the above fact, it is apparent that the organization itself must institutionalize a procedure that forces officials to try to disprove their own beliefs. That is, we would suggest that an organization should have a routine procedure for systematically searching out information that goes against its view of reality.

We have been speaking of organizations in general and not simply the United States government, because it appears that all organizations need such a procedure. For example, when a business organization looks for a new market, it often hires consultants or instructs its own men to gather facts that would support an investment in a new area. We would argue that it should also hire men to make a case *against* expanding in the new area. With both sets of facts before it, the management would protect itself against wishful thinking and could make a more rational choice. Ordinarily, superiors in all organizations fail not only to instruct their investigators to look for information that goes against their ideas and plans, but also to *collect* what negative information is passed upwards. In spite of the blocks to the upward communication of negative information and the failure to actively search for dissonant facts, some clear estimates do come to the attention of top officials. But such pieces of information come through singly and lack the strength which a number of independent reports would have. Consequently, each piece of negative information is rejected by different officials who perceive it the wrong way or explain it away by any plausible line of reasoning. Since these officials keep no record of their rejections, the evidence is rejected in pieces before it can build up into a convincing case. Within the individual, information that would prevent an intelligence failure is not perceived or is explained away. Within the organization, the information never builds up to form a strong enough case to overcome the powerful psychological opposition in top decision makers.

While some leaders try to insure that their organization examines many different alternatives, organizations, like individuals, generally suffer from not devoting enough energy to stating their assumptions and trying to disprove their own hypothesis. In fact, there is usually a bias in the direction of securing agreeable information. In 1949, the United States tended to take information from Chinese nationalists rather than Chinese Communists, just as in 1919 the British relied on information from Kolchak rather than the Bolsheviks. In a democracy, the responsibility of making a case against current policy is often left to the party that is out of office. Unfortunately, in the case of foreign policy, the administration often wants a bipartisan agreement. While this helps the accomplishment of necessary legislation, it hinders the making of a good opposition case. The problem is compounded by the fact that the opposition may feel that it is politically unwise to challenge the assumptions promulgated by the party in office.

We would suggest that whenever an office or department or administration considers or has a policy, it should be obligated to assume the responsibility of assigning a group *within* the office, department, or administration to make an opposition case. Such a group should:

1. Be composed of competent men who are identified with the office, department, or administration, and who have the trust and confidence of the leadership and access to it.

2. Be given a fair opportunity to periodically present their case.

3. Be given feedback so that they are assured the leadership understands the case they present.

4. Be given the authority to ask the leadership to state the assumptions on which the policy is based.

5. Be committed to the leadership so that they do not attempt to gather political support outside the office, department, or administration.

It is particularly important for such a group to continue functioning *after* the organization is committed to a policy. Usually, after a decision has been made all persons are expected to pull together to implement the policy. At this point, those who cannot so commit themselves generally leave the organization. Consequently, once it is committed to a policy, the organization becomes even blinder than an individual.

The suggested group would:

1. Continue to actively look for information contrary to the office, department, or administration's ideas and plans.

2. Serve as a repository for such negative information.

3. Insure that filters in the information system were properly placed, that adequate feedback were being given, and that unpopular views were being heard at high levels.

4. Make out the most reasonable case possible for alternative beliefs and plans.

5. Be ready to suggest new policy if and when changing conditions substantiate the opposition's viewpoint.

In order to avoid the sabotaging of the current policy to which the organization is committed, members of the group charged with the responsibility of collecting negative evidence should only present such evidence to the top leadership at periodically scheduled meetings. In the chapter on concensus formation, we shall see *how* these meetings should be arranged in order to maximize the possibility of meaningfully integrating different policies.

We may anticipate the following objections to our suggestion. I will attempt to answer each of them in turn.

1. There are differences of opinion within any organization that force an examination of the issues.

Unfortunately, we cannot rely on disagreements to air issues. Most intelligence failures are examples to the contrary. There was no disagreement on failing to provide for an adequate defense of Korea. And, as in the case of China, when there is disagreement, it may result in harmful conflict rather than a productive review of issues.

2. Government policy necessarily operates within a framework of common beliefs. Policy makers must pay attention to this area of agreement and cannot give real consideration to alternative policies that fall outside of this framework. A decision maker cannot take information that does not fit with his policy, cannot consider knowledge that is not in accord with his actions, cannot tolerate criticism once he is committed to a given policy.

While this is currently true, we know that under appropriate conditions the framework of common beliefs responds to good arguments. The suggested procedure may aid this change process so that beliefs respond more quickly to reality.

3. Dissident groups will take advantage of the procedure to mobilize opinion outside of their office or appeal to higher authorities.

This is currently the case. The suggested procedure will contain dissidence since it provides a clear means of loyal and effective protest.

4. The discrepancy of values within an organization would prevent the suggested procedure from working. It is idealistic to expect men with different values not to use information to gain power in the struggle to have their own values influence policy. Indeed, this is part of our democratic process.

But the suggested procedure does not seek to separate information from values and the desire to influence policy. Rather, we wish to channel this desire into a more effective expression of values. The current competition of values either is stifled or produces compromise policies that yield results satisfying no one. We want a procedure that produces policies that truly integrate different values and yield results that meet these different values.

5. Neither time nor manpower permits the extravagance of using a policy maker's time to argue against current policy.

We believe that the time of a limited number of valuable men can best be conserved by the suggested procedure. At the moment, time is dissipated in warring factions within a department or administration. A procedure that formalizes disputes would produce a unity that would make the organization more effective.

We have spent quite a bit of time on intelligence failures because it is relatively easy to illustrate the various factors involved. I feel, however, that intelligence failures (in the narrower sense of the term) are a relatively minor problem. What bothers me a good deal more is the probability that our view of reality may be so inaccurate that we are failing to see ways to increase the cooperation of different nations in ending poverty and war and advancing human dignity. We cannot afford to be overly confident in what appears to us to be the reality. We need to listen carefully to what seem to be improbable ideas, and we need to try to really understand the feelings of other people. I believe that to do this we will need to instigate institutional changes similar to the one suggested.

CHAPTER 3

The Projection
of the Future

In the last chapter, we saw that each of us is somewhat imprisoned in a world which we perceive to be reality. Operating within this world, we attempt to imagine what the future will be like and what plans we should make in order to attain our goals. Such thinking may be highly creative, or it may be quite unrealistic, failing to consider important factors that will determine what will actually happen. In this chapter we shall examine some of the psychological forces that affect what is and what is not considered by the officials making foreign policy.

Constraints on Action

In evaluating the planning of foreign policy, one must remember that there are always many brute facts that prohibit certain actions and, hence, place severe constraints on any serious planning. For example, the planner must consider:

Limited resources of money, patronage, time, information, and trusted subordinates.

Previous commitments, such as the promise of his predecessor to guarantee some nations military security (a promise that must be kept if the office's honor is to be maintained), the promise of a subordinate to give economic assistance (if the subordinate's reputation is to be maintained), and his own statements (if his own honesty is to be maintained).

65

Precedents which the public, Congress, or newsmen expect to be followed.

Circumstances: For example, the Truman administration, which was committed to Europe, could not direct public attention to problems in Asia when the fall of China made it politically damaging to acknowledge the emergence of a new situation.

The momentum of current policy that resists attempts to direct resources into new channels and secure a different consensus.

Political factors, such as the winning and keeping of key supporters who may have their own ideas on what policy should be, and the avoidance of making new enemies.

Responsibilities, such as concern for other officials who have taken political risks to aid one, and a general concern for the national honor.

While some of the above factors play a positive role in preventing poor policy, when we consider all of the constraining influences operating at a given time, there seems so little room for free and rational action that there is a danger of resigning oneself to the inevitability of policy errors. We believe, however, that this feeling is unwarranted. While often the above constraints actually do determine policy, it is not necessary that they do so. If the administration has rational goals, then the constraints we have listed will simply modify rather than make the policy. There are often alternative ways of dealing with constraints if one knows what one is doing and is conscious of what is occurring. The trouble is that the constraints which we have listed do not always operate consciously but become aspects of subtler processes that begin to distort the thinking of officials. A person has a good chance of coping with a constraint he is aware of; it is when he is unaware of a constraint operating on his thinking that he loses control. There are certain biases in the policy process that often lead to poor planning, not because of any constraints on action but because of a *conceptual failure* — *a failure to grasp the meaning of the situation.* Let us examine an example of this — the failure of the United States in 1948 to budget adequate funds for defense in the light of its policy to contain communism.

Conceptual Failure

After the Second World War, the President of the United States made a basic decision to try to balance the budget and reduce U.S. ground forces. In fact, the President wanted personally to start reducing some of the national debt that had built up during the Second World War.

There were many reasons for this position. Certainly, the majority of Congress favored balancing the budget; there were many pressures for tax cuts; and the country was tired of selective service and did not want to raise troops. In September, 1947, the President asked the State and Defense Departments to recommend places where troops could be withdrawn without endangering U.S. security.

The Joint Chiefs of Staff recommended that U.S. troops in Korea be withdrawn to Japan. They stated that Korea was of little strategic interest. In case of a war, the troops would be of no use if the U.S. took the offensive and might get trapped on the mainland in a defensive action. Korea would be a difficult place to fight in, and the only possible defensive use of troops would be in preventing enemy airbases in Southern Korea, a task which bombing attacks could handle just as easily. While some men in the State Department were concerned about protecting South Korea for its own sake as a nation, their cause was weakened by the difficulty experienced in establishing a satisfactory democratic government in Korea. The government that was finally established excluded most liberal elements. However, since the Department was concerned about maintaining an independent Korean nation in order to prevent the expansion of the Soviet Union, it requested that troops be left in until South Korean forces had been strengthened. This strengthening was performed, and by July of 1949 the last U.S. troops had been withdrawn. Just before the final withdrawal, two congressmen asked if token forces could be left. They were told by the Defense Department that the U.S. might become involved in internal Korean problems if this were done.

It appears that no one really worried about South Korea being attacked in a *limited* war. When congressmen questioned the administration on South Korean strength, they were told that it was adequate. Sometimes "adequate" seems to have meant "adequate to preserve internal order"; at other times, "adequate" meant "to resist a North Korean invasion that did not have strong Soviet support." The Commander Far East advised that South Korean forces were adequate to maintain *internal* order; but, with a semantic slippage that may be frequently observed, when a policy paper was worked up for the Security Council he was quoted as saying that the combat readiness of South Korean forces *justified withdrawal!* The second-class status accorded to Korea was reflected in a speech made by the Secretary of State in January, 1950. He defined the United States defense perimeter as running from the Aleutians through Japan and the Ryukyus to the Philippines — thus excluding South Korea (and Formosa) as essential to United States needs and not guaranteeing her security if she were attacked. While money for military equipment was finally granted to Korea by Congress, the low priority of her needs prevented any equipment from arriving before the invasion.

While on the surface the withdrawal of troops and lack of commitment to South Korea were rational moves to carry out the President's program for economy, in fact three important aspects of the problem were overlooked by government planners.

First, since in the case of a global war there would be no attempt to defend Korea, the Defense Department, preoccupied with the possibility of global war, neglected to make plans to aid Korea if she should be attacked outside of the context of a global war. Thus, there were no war plans in existence for the nation which the United States was shortly going to go to war for.

Second, the State Department failed to consider how the Soviet Union and North Koreans would view a South Korea whose independence was not guaranteed by the United States. It was not realized that South Korea — with no American troops, pledges of support, or apparent interest — might appear tempting to an expansionistic Soviet Union that might want an advance in Asia to offset growing Chinese power. Intelligence sources showed that until 1952 the Soviet Union lacked the power to fight a war with the United States. With this fact in mind, the Department expected Soviet expansion to continue taking the form of internal subversion rather than overt war. Thus, two factors contributed to the Department's planning failure: the failure to imagine the possibility of a limited war — the war that actually occurred two years later — with Russian equipped and trained North Korean troops fighting only in Korea; and the failure to step into Russian shoes and ask if the Russians would really see the sponsoring of a North Korean attack on South Korea as risking war. It would seem that the Soviet Union did not risk a global war by instigating an attack on Korea; and, given the minimum American commitment, they must have believed they were risking no war at all.

Third, both the Defense and State Departments failed to imagine what the loss of Korea would *mean*. When Korea was attacked the United States rushed to its defense — not because of its strategic interest (which was low) nor because of its terrain (which was disadvantageous), but because not to have done so would have destroyed the idea of collective security, encouraged Soviet aggression elsewhere, and damaged American prestige. But these non-strategic factors had been given weight neither in the Defense Department's recommendation to withdraw troops nor in the State Department's lack of formal commitment to defend Korea. Nor were these factors considered by planners in the Soviet Union. The government of neither nation anticipated what the invasion would *mean* to the United States.

Note that the above oversights were not directly caused by any actual constraints operating on the planners. Thus, speaking of the failure to be prepared for the Korean war, Schilling[1] states,

> The difficulty, of course, had been primarily conceptual. The war which the State Department (and everyone else) had not expected the Russians to start, at least until they achieved a nuclear capability, had been World War III, not a satellite attack in Asia.

Nor were the oversights caused by the mechanism which the government uses to create budgets. Summarizing the fallacies in thinking within the government, Schilling[2] states,

> The policy deficiencies of the fiscal 1950 budget were, in short, the results of failures in political conception not the product of peculiarities in political structure.

We assume that most policy failures are failures in conception. To take another example, after assessing the technical problems involved in the Peace Conference following the First World War, Kennan[3] states,

> But I think we should note that all of this operated against the background of a great and persuasive conceptual error, which was an inability to assess correctly the significance and the consequences of the war in which Europe had just been engaged. The meaning the allied statesman had insisted on reading into the war now blinded their judgment of the possibilities of the peace.

Taking the Korean case as an example, we must now consider *why* governmental planners failed to adequately consider the possibility of a limited war, failed to put themselves in the position of their opponents, and failed to envision the meaning a Korean invasion would have.

Perhaps the best way to understand a planning failure is to consider successful planning as a creative act. This allows us to apply what is known about creativity to planning, and it recognizes the fact that a planning failure is not usually a failure in the sense that someone made a mistake or did not try hard enough. Rather, it involves the overlook-

---

[1] W. R. Schilling, "The Politics of National Defense: Fiscal 1950," in W. R. Schilling, P. Y. Hammond, and G. H. Snyder, *Strategy, Politics and Defense Budgets* (New York: Columbia University Press, 1962), p. 211.
[2] *Ibid.*, p. 250.
[3] George F. Kennan, *Russia and the West under Lenin and Stalin* (New York: Little, Brown and Company, 1960), p. 149.

ing of important factors, an absence of creative insight into the structure of the situation one is trying to deal with.

In what follows we shall consider a series of six variables that operate to hinder the attainment of creative insight. The first of these has been called "the climate of opinion."

The Climate of Opinion

At any given time within an organization, there are certain plans that seem realistic and others that seem inconceivable. If a person brings up an idea which the head of the organization is known to oppose, or which the public would never accept, or which persons with power could never agree upon — his idea is not taken seriously. This notion of what things could conceivably be brought about constitutes the "climate of opinion." Just as a group has certain norms or expectations which a member cannot break without experiencing counter forces, so also it has a climate of opinion which one must respect if he is not to lose his reputation for realism. The climate of opinion is the framework in which conflict and consensus can occur. Outside of these limits is the "opinion universe" — a policy wilderness of ideas without advocates, of plans that are never seriously considered because it is believed no political consensus could be achieved about them.

Now, whatever climate of opinion exists creativity may be hindered because of the exclusion of "unrealistic" ideas. Thus, in planning the 1950 defense budget almost every official in the administration shared the assumption that the economy could stand only a fixed amount of government expenditures. Within the Congress, Schilling[4] notes that

> The members of the committee (on armed services appropriations) did not challenge this perspective; indeed, as will be seen they fully shared it. As a result, the committee tended not to see even the theoretical possibility of spending significantly larger sums for defense than those which the Executive had determined the nation should bear.

The "climate of opinion" is built around a sense of what others want and are willing to do. Thus, the general size of the defense budget was determined by what the Executive thought Congress would give, and this was influenced by what Congress thought the Executive believed it needed. When, two years later, the NSC-68 paper finally advocated a higher budget, a key Senator felt that the paper was an interesting

---

[4]Schilling, *op. cit.*, p. 86.

formulation, but his sense of reality made it difficult for him to take it seriously. It is this feeling of what is or is not "realistic" that characterizes the boundary of the climate of opinion and makes it such a restrictive barrier. Presidential decisions help create a climate of opinion. When the President makes a decision, this operates not only to freeze action on certain programs but also to constrain his subordinates' thinking, since it defines certain other programs as impractical. When the President set a ceiling on the defense budget, no practical minded subordinate would propose plans that would violate this budget. While the subordinate has no dissonance about the budget ceiling (for that was the President's decision), he does have dissonance about spending time thinking about things that will be impractical because of the President's decision. In fact, he may be even less inclined to think about problems that would question the decision, because he is not responsible for the decision and can always blame a failure on the constraints set up by someone else's decision.

Now, as a result of this restriction on thinking, governments often make serious errors in judgment. Consider the following very incomplete list of examples which I have selected from Kennan's[5] *Russia and the West.*

1. Germany's judgment that Britain would not declare war if Poland were attacked.
2. Great Britain's judgment that in 1938 the Soviet Union was an available ally against Germany.
3. The Soviet Union's judgment that the Nazi party was not a true revolutionary movement and, hence, could not keep effective power in Germany.
4. The United States' overestimation of Japanese resistance capacity.
5. Britain's and the United States' underestimation of the German resistance movement.
6. The United States' fear that the Soviet Union would make a separate peace with Germany.

It will be observed that somewhat different factors influence each error. Thus, while wish fulfillment played a role in the first three errors, the latter three cannot be attributed to that factor. While the stubbornness of an autocratic leader contributed to the first and third failure, it did not play a large role in the other failures. However, it does appear that in *all cases the judgment was biased in the direction of supporting plans that had been built on the basis of other considerations.*

---

[5]Kennan, *op. cit.*

The climate of opinion about the 1950 arms budget set limits of between $14 and 16 billion on the budget. Schilling[6] suggests that if the Defense Department had been encouraged to develop its initial 23.6 billion dollar budget along with the required 15 billion dollar one, it would have aided rational thinking. For example, it would have shown the different plans which the different budgets could support and would have provided a feeling for what was being sacrificed by choosing the lower budget. He notes that, instead, the $23.6 billion budget was viewed with horror as an indication of the insensitivity of the military for the state of economy. Rather than stimulating a look at the effect of the ceiling, it led to a demand that the military be made more aware of the effects of their program on the economy. The forces generated by the climate of opinion thus prevented what could have been a helpful analysis.

One factor which creativity always has to overcome is the "set" or expectancies the problem solver has. Most government officials were set to meet total war with the Soviet Union, internal subversion by communists, or limited exploitation of a situation such as the Soviet attempts to gain control during the Greek Civil War. To have anticipated the Korean War, an official would have had to break this set.

To break free of one's set, it is often necessary to follow trains of thought that start in an absurd way. A step that is obviously ridiculous must be considered in order to reach another step that will prove to lead to a solution. In 1947, there was danger that the United States might become over-involved in the Chinese Civil War. The State Department was quite sensitive to the possibility that the United States would exhaust its strength in China and become easy prey for the Soviet Union. Now, to break free of the set that large external attacks had to be part of a global war, it might have been necessary for government officials to consider a war with China. This first ridiculous thought might have led to a second thought — that a large external attack might be undertaken in a limited war; and this thought could have been applied to Korea. This type of free thinking was unlikely to occur because, with the Administration engaged in a combat with opponents who *seriously* wanted to intervene in China, one can imagine that anyone who *speculatively* began to consider it was not thanked for his troubles.

The fact that creative solutions often demand that the thinker free himself from practical considerations is one argument in favor of having at least one planning group divorced from operational responsi-

---

[6]Schilling, *op. cit.*

bility. There are several other arguments for this position. A person with operational responsibility is likely to be strongly motivated to get a solution to his problem. While high motivation is desirable and aids some problem solving, Glucksberg[7] has demonstrated that it interferes with the solution of problems that require breaking a set. Thus, the high motivation of government officials may often be detrimental to their achieving optimal solutions. Another consideration involves the fact that an operating group must be a fairly homogeneous group whereas a group without practical responsibility can afford a degree of heterogeneity in personality and philosophy that would produce discordance in an operational group. Since a homogeneous group is more likely to use the same set in approaching a problem, there will be fewer approaches and less likelihood of a creative solution.

Finally, an operational group is more likely to have formalized procedures, and it has been shown[8] that when group procedures are formalized inhibitions are increased and fewer ideas expressed

In general, investigators of creativity agree that the process of getting ideas should be kept separate from the process of evaluating these ideas. An "impractical" group of men should be utilized to get ideas from which a practical oriented group may select those useful for operational plans. Maier[9] has recently suggested additional principles and devices that increase the effectiveness of a group of problem solvers by increasing the exploration of creative alternatives. In every case it would be difficult for an operational group to apply his suggestions, whereas an "impractical" group of men could apply them to arrive at solutions more practical than those currently evolved. A group of "impractical" planners might have avoided the Defense Department's failure to plan for limited wars because of the latter's responsibility to be ready for a global war.

While the climate of opinion prevents the kind of "unrealistic" thinking often needed to obtain a creative insight into the nature of the future, there is a wide range of factors that can be considered within the bounds of "reality." Unfortunately, a different sort of bias, or set of biases, operates to cause planners to uncritically focus on some factors to the exclusion of others.

---

[7]Sam Glucksberg, "Problem solving: Response competition in the influence of drive," *Psychol. Reports,* 15 (1964), pp. 939-42.

[8]C. A. Gibb, "The effects of group size and threat reduction upon creativity in problem solving," *Amer. Psychol.,* 6 (1951), p. 324.

[9]N. R. F. Maier, *Problem-solving, Discussions and Conferences* (New York: McGraw-Hill Book Company, 1963).

Selective Biases

Undoubtedly, there are many biases that repeatedly affect the thinking of most policy makers. Here are some of Schilling's observations, which I have generalized and stated in the form of hypotheses.

1. When an official is reviewing a decision made by others, he will tend to assume that there is a correct answer to the choices that confronted the others — when, in fact, there may be many valid answers depending on one's values and expectations. This assumption of an absolute truth will cause the reviewer to perceive his task to be the checking of the solution to a problem rather than the occasion for exercising his own values.

Thus, Schilling,[10] speaking of the committee reviewing the defense budget, says,

> At least some members seem to have believed that there was a determinate answer to the question of how much to spend for defense. They simply did not see the budget as unavoidably a problem in choice: choice among the values to be served, and choice among the divergent expectations of what would happen if one or another course of action was followed . . . With a perspective of this sort, [a Representative] had no incentive to approach the hearings as an occasion for developing a number of alternatives from which he and his colleagues might choose [therefore] they did not think to ask the kind of questions that would have prepared Congress to take a more effective part in that choice.

Another example of this error is reported by Snyder[11] in his description of the formulation of the defense budget during the succeeding administration. He states,

> [the new President's] abhorrence of conflict in the Joint Chiefs of Staff, and between himself and the Chiefs might also be related . . . to a conception of military policy as a problem in logic, to which there could be only a simple correct solution — a solution to which all reasonable military men would be led unless they were biased . . . a belief that there was only one correct solution to the economy — security equivocation and that this solution would reveal itself simply by the application of reason, if approached in good faith.

This type of mistake may occur because of a reluctance to make an arbitrary use of one's power and a desire to weigh the situation

---

[10]Schilling, *op. cit.*, pp. 133-34.
[11]Glen Snyder, "The 'new look' of 1953," in Schilling, Hammond, and Snyder, *op. cit.*, pp. 523-24.

objectively. Often, as Schilling observes, a congressional hearing "is a political as well as an analytical exercise," and congressmen "are interested in building as persuasive a case as they can for the alternatives they favor." When this occurs, the desire to make a case for one's side restricts the type of questions that are asked, and a congressman may be more interested in generating political pressure for what he wants than in making a searching analysis. It is with the intention of avoiding this type of bias that a congressman may try to search for *the* right solution. Unfortunately, this counter reaction does not achieve the desired objectivity.

2. When an official trying to make a rational choice is confronted with many uncertainties, he will uncritically seize on any constant that is offered and base his calculations upon it.

Thus, the idea that the economy could only stand $15 billion provided a constant that simplified the problem of defense budgeting. The fact that what the economy could stand actually depended on how much sacrifice the public believed was necessary — and, hence, was a variable that could be influenced — was not considered.

Similarly, a proposal that a seventy group Air Force was needed became a fixed point of reference for budgeting in the House, despite the fact that seventy was a rather arbitrary number.

Schilling[12] states,

> If the idea that there was a determinate answer to the size and composition of the defense budget constituted the fallacy of the one right figure, and the idea that the dispute among the services could be eliminated was the fallacy of the 'one right organization,' the idea that $15 billion was all the economy could stand can be considered the fallacy of the 'one fixed limit.' No perspective was more crippling of rational choice . . . [it] had the effect of foreclosing automatically on a number of alternatives which might otherwise have seemed rather desirable.

3. When a team is engaged in a competition, it will neglect major variables which it is responsible for in order to concentrate on the variable it believes will win the power struggle.

Thus, Hammond[13] notes that in the competition for power between the three services, the climate of opinion made it appear that the variable

---

[12]Schilling, *op cit.*, p. 231.

[13]Paul Hammond, "The National Security Council as a device for interdepartmental coordination: an interpretation of appraisal," *Amer. Pol. Sci. Rev.*, 54 (1960), pp. 889-910.

that would decide the power struggle was efficiency of weapons systems in a full scale war. This caused the Air Force and Navy to devote all their attention to trying to prove that they could best handle massive air strikes at the heart of the Soviet Union. The flexibility and selectivity of limited peripheral war was neglected, though it was to prove to be the most important variable.

Similarly, when the Administration was developing the Marshall Plan, the competition for money caused the Administration to focus on what it thought would be a winning case — the preservation of American power. This caused it to completely neglect the development of the United Nations. It failed to consider that a *strengthened* United Nations might administer its aid program.

4. When an official is faced with a choice, he will weigh immediately certain costs more than distant uncertain costs, even when the latter are of much greater consequence.

For example, in 1948, two obvious major problems confronted American foreign policy. The first was occasioned by the collapse of Western Europe and, hence, the absence of foreign governments that could balance Soviet power. The second problem was presented by nuclear armaments with their great destructiveness and relatively low cost. Schilling notes that most officials concentrated on the first problem and ignored the second. He suggests that this was because it was commonly felt that the first problem was more immediate, while the second was in the future; the first problem was more familiar while the second was new; and the first problem was easier, while the second had no apparent solution. As a result, the unexpected rapidity of Soviet development of nuclear weapons took the United States by surprise; and even today, while most people agree that it is dangerous for more countries to develop nuclear weapons, the effort to handle this problem has not been enough to achieve results.

5. When an official is given a piece of information that has implications for planning, he will see those implications that will help him attain his goals and fail to see implications that will create problems.

As an example, consider the congressional reaction to the "Finletter Report," a report that, in 1948, warned that the United States should be prepared for atomic war by 1953 and would need a seventy group Air Force (at the time there was a fifty-five group Air Force). Schilling notes that what captured the attention of almost all congressmen was not the idea that there might be a full-fledged two-way atomic war but the idea that an American one-way atomic war would eliminate the need for a large land army. *This* argument was used to reject the proposed program of universal military training. Any idea that will be attractive to important persons in the government (what they will pay attention to) is likely to reflect common assumptions, preoccupations, and needs — and thus not likely to innovate the new policy that is needed.

All of the above biases select certain features of the situation at the expense of others and, hence hinder effective planning. The "assumption of one correct answer," "seizure of a constant," and "neglect of variables which won't help in the immediate power struggle" all act to limit the number of alternatives that are developed. The "focus on immediate costs" and "failure to see implications" both act to prevent a consideration of problems that need to be solved. We now turn to a different sort of problem in planning — the difficulty of understanding how the situation looks to other governments.

Seeing With the Eyes of the Other

We have already noted how American officials failed to consider that South Korea might look like a very tempting target to the North Koreans or Russians. This failure must have been due in part to officials assuming that the opponents saw the situation in the same way they themselves did. Since they believed that the United States would resist aggression, they assumed the Soviet Union would believe that the United States would resist in spite of overt indications to the contrary. Since they knew that the United States would prevent the South Koreans from invading the North, they assumed the North Koreans would know this and ignore the threats of invasion made by the South Korean leader. Since they saw the South Korean Army as capable of repulsing an attack, they assumed the North Koreans would see the same strength rather than the strong discontent in the South that portended popular support for an invasion. In later chapters, we shall see that the same type of error was involved in the failure to heed Chinese warnings not to cross the 38th parallel. Since — as we saw in the last chapter — American officials are likely to perceive a somewhat different reality than officials from some other nation, it is very difficult for them to anticipate another nation's moves.

Even when there is a common view of an important aspect of reality, the difference in perspective may lead to different conclusions. In reviewing the failure to anticipate Pearl Harbor, Wohlstetter[14] notes,

---

[14]Roberta Wohlstetter, *Pearl Harbor: Warning and Decision* (Stanford, Calif: Stanford University Press, 1962), p. 354.

. . . Japanese and American estimates of the risks to the Japanese were identical for the large-scale war they had planned, as well as for the individual operations. What we miscalculated was the ability and willingness of the Japanese to accept such risks. As Ambassador Grew had said, "National sanity would dictate against such an event, but Japanese sanity cannot be measured by our own standards of logic". . .Similarly, the Japanese completely miscalculated the American response to their action. To have believed that the United States would accept a defeat and relinquish its power in the Far East was a total failure to empathize with the American character.

Needless to say, such failures at putting oneself in the other's shoes are particularly apt to occur when a correct view would disrupt one's plans and threaten one with some unpleasant consequence. In the last chapter, we noted how, in 1914, the German Chancellor did not attend to dispatches warning against counting on British neutrality. As North[15] observes,

It was recognized in Berlin that German military capabilities were inadequate, and the whole "blank check" policy rested on the assumption that the Russians, the French, and particularly the British would not intervene. In this respect the German leaders not only misperceived fundamental attitudes in St. Petersburg, Paris, and London, but persisted — almost to the eve of major war — in the conviction that Russia would be constrained by the British and that the British, in turn, would maintain neutrality.

Let us examine this general type of distortion more closely. It is basically a distortion that permits one to pretend there is no problem.

Pretending

Once upon a time, there was a little boy who hated fat. While his parents were fairly tolerant of his distaste, one day they insisted that he should eat the little bit of fat that clung to the edges of some otherwise lean meat. If he did not, he could have no dessert. So, when his parents were not looking, the little boy removed the bits of fat and threw them under the table! Most strangely, he never considered what his mother would think when she swept up the floor. . . .

In the late 1940's the United States did not *want* to build up its army but it *had* to if it wanted to defend Korea and prevent Soviet

---

[15]Robert C. North, "Perception and action in the 1914 crisis," *J. International Affairs*, 21 (1967), p. 107.

expansion. Consequently, it *pretended* it had built an adequate army in South Korea. It threw its fat under the table by creating a token South Korean Army — and then failed to consider how its opponent might respond. One might generalize this process to hypothesize:

When either a person or an organization is faced with unacceptable alternatives, then an unrealistic third course of action is attempted and thoughts that challenge this action are ignored.

Lewin has observed that when a person is in an avoidance-avoidance conflict, trapped between two negative alternatives, he tries to leave the field of the conflict and often does this by fantasizing. It would appear that when he is forced to remain he may seize on a third alternative that *appears* to avoid the unpleasantness but is actually unrealistic. Once he has committed himself to this panacea an extreme form of dissonance occurs — extreme because contradicting thoughts challenge not just any decision but a decision that appears to be the only one acceptable. This force prevents attention to set-breaking ideas that might provide a solution to the situation. It also provokes a rationale for the unrealistic action — e.g., the person says the action is necessary because of the constraints under which he is operating. This rationale then may get in the way of a real solution. In the case at hand, the administration defined its defensive posture as all that the economy or Congress would permit. By 1950, there was actually some public and congressional support for an increased defense budget, but the President did not seem aware of this fact. As a leading Senator later remarked, "The foreign policy seems to be circumscribed by what they think Congress will give them."

A related distortion involves believing something that is false but which one has to make true in order to *avoid* an avoidance-avoidance conflict. In 1948, the Secretary of State believed that the nation would not sustain a large defense budget yet had to demonstrate its intention to defend Europe. His solution was to press for universal military training and refuse support of the Secretary of Defense's request for a higher defense budget. The Secretary of State kept the idea of universal military training in spite of much evidence that Congress just would not pass the bill. Admission of this fact would have thrown him back into what appeared to be an insolvable dilemma.

Yet another situation that may lead a person to believe that an imagined situation is real, is when something *should* be true. When the President decided to price the program suggested by NSC-68, the Secretary of Defense assigned this responsibility to his Assistant for Foreign Military Affairs. The latter considered the idea of establishing budget requirements by special channels because he knew that the regular channels in the Department of Defense were ineffective. Hammond[16] notes,

> . . . he had been aware of the inadequacies of Army procedures for determining requirements in both world wars. But he decided to use regular channels because he believed that they *ought* to be effective, and this would be one way to improve them. The result was not what he had hoped.

Of course, if the individual or organization becomes aware that in order to escape a dilemma he or it is misjudging the situation, then he or it would not want to continue the misjudgment. It is a rather startling motivational fact that if a basically correct solution will get one into some trouble there will be a force working against the solution. This force may prevent the solution from occurring in spite of the fact that if the person were conscious of what was happening he would definitely judge the correct solution to have been worth the trouble it would cause. The situation is analogous to a repression. If going to a dentist will cause pain and interfere with what one really wants to do, then one may forget his appointment with the dentist in spite of the fact that if one were conscious of the choice he would decide that keeping his appointment was worth the pain and trouble.

To have really considered the possibilities of limited war, to have put themselves in the position of their opponents and seen the opponents' opportunities, to have imagined the possible meaning of the loss of Korea, government officials would have had to think about increasing the defense budget and changing their budget plans. The unpleasantness and seeming impossibility of this prospect created a force that prevented them from putting two and two together and considering certain problems.

Within an organization, pretending that there is no problem is accomplished in a number of different ways. There is, for example, what might be called "semantic slippage." Thus we saw that when the Commander Far East said South Korean forces were adequate to preserve *internal* order he was quoted to the Security Council as saying that withdrawal was justified. Similarly, when estimates of North Korean strength indicated that they would not be strong enough to invade *unless* furnished with much Russian equipment, it was reported that North Korea did not have adequate strength for a successful invasion, and estimates to the contrary were forgotten.

---

[16]Paul Hammond, "NSC-68: Prologue to rearmament," in Schilling, Hammond, and Snyder, *op. cit.,* p. 341.

It has been noted that government officials, like most people, often fool themselves. In his discussion of the First World War peace conference, Kennan[17] observes that the Allies, ". . . had been fighting for different things and pretending, in an endless flow of beautiful phrases, that what they were fighting for was the same thing." And Barrett has observed that while an official often initially recognizes an inconsistency in policy, he usually glosses over this inconsistency with rhetoric for the benefit of the public or the government coalition he is appealing to. The resultant linguistic abstraction reorganizes the official's perception so that he behaves as if there were no inconsistency. In short, the official's political rhetoric begins to fool himself.

In his discussion of the unfortunate decision to cross the 38th parallel to unify Korea, Neustadt[18] states,

> In White House memoranda and in papers for the National Security Council, in intelligence evaluations, and the like, repeated use of such terms as 'the U N objective,' 'the decision of the U N,' 'the U N's purpose to unify,' soon dulled awareness that the new war aim was nothing but a target of opportunity chosen rather casually (and at first provisionally) by the very men who read these words.

Neustadt points out that within a month everyone thought of the "U.N. aim" as the cause of unification rather than as a convenient justification of a fairly low priority American goal. The language used in the bureaucracy to create images for the public had created the same images in the officials themselves.

A different technique for avoiding the confrontation with reality is to ignore any upsetting information that is communicated. Aiding those forces, that prevent communication is the tremendous amount of incoming material. Sorensen[19] notes,

> All Presidents, at least in modern times, have complained about their reading pile, and few have been able to cope with it. There is a temptation, consequently, to cut out all that is unpleasant . . . to require more screening of information, with only the most salient facts filtering through on one page memoranda.

As we saw in the last chapter, when the United States was preparing an invasion of Cuba, officials managed to completely ignore polling

---

[17]Kennan, *op. cit.*, p. 147.

[18]R. E. Neustadt, *Presidential Power* (New York: John Wiley & Sons, Inc., 1960), p. 139.

[19]Theodore C. Sorensen, *Decision Making in the White House* (New York: Columbia University Press, 1963), p. 38.

data that showed an overwhelming majority of Cubans to be currently in favor of the Castro regime.

One of the most serious consequences of avoiding a dilemma by making unrealistic plans, is that the organization is unaware of having a problem and therefore fails to motivate or utilize the insights of those rare individual officials who break through the common set and emerge with a genuine solution of the problem. By systematically distorting information, the organization is unaware of the problem which the insights could have solved. By pretending to have a solution, it prevents necessity from becoming the mother of invention.

Organizational Loss of Individual Insight

In spite of the climate of opinion, selective biases, and the difficulty of seeing what another nation perceives, it must not be supposed that *no* individuals were creative and able to correctly perceive the Korean situation. The man who was the Director of the State Department's Policy Planning Staff (and later became the Counselor to the Department) quite clearly foresaw the probability of a limited war like Korea. It is interesting to note that his insight into the situation may have occurred because he did not believe there was a real possibility of global war. Consequently his thinking was not inhibited by the ceiling on the defense budget; the budget did not have to be raised to accommodate his insight — simply re-allocated.

In order to fully understand why this individual insight did not influence organizational planning we must note some results from an interesting experiment involving the communication structure within a group.

Given an experimental group we may allow all of the members of the group to talk with one another. On the other hand, recognizing the constraints of larger organizations, we may allow each man to talk only to his immediate neighbors (a "circular" communication pattern), or we may allow one man to talk with all the others but the others to talk only with him (a "hierarchical" pattern). The communication structures of these latter groups might then be diagrammed as in Figure 1.

Now when such groups are given problems to solve they behave quite differently. Surprisingly, at first the circular pattern may do better than the hierarchical pattern at solving routine problems because the man at the head of the hierarchy is swamped with information. Since he is at the center of communications he becomes established as the leader of

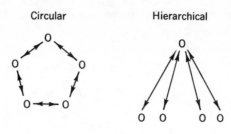

Figure 1. *Patterns of Communication*

the group and only as he learns to handle the situation does the hierarchical pattern become more efficient. Eventually the hierarchical group solves routine problems much more rapidly. However, morale difficulties arise because the other group members become dissatisfied with their minor role in the solution of problems — a difficulty which is not present in the circular pattern.

During one of the experiments with these groups, an interesting phenomenon was noted.[20] Occasionally, an individual group member would break out of the set way of thinking and get an insight into how to solve the problem more rapidly than the group had perceived or even than the experimenter had foreseen. While the frequency of the occurrence of this creative insight was fairly even in the different groups, it was observed that the chance of the insight being adopted by the group appeared to differ. The insight was utilized to solve the problem by three groups with circular patterns but by none of the groups with hierarchical patterns. While not enough occurrences were available for statistical analysis, it would appear that certain communication patterns may increase the group's ability to utilize the insights of its members.

Returning now to the insight of a member of the State Department, we may wish to inquire about the communication patterns within the government. One is at once struck by the extremely poor communications between the Defense Department and the State Department. This poor situation was made particularly bad in 1949 when the new Secretary of Defense prohibited all interdepartmental communication that was not cleared through his office. Since the Secretaries of State and Defense did not care for each other, the communications between the

[20]H. J. Leavitt, reported in Alex Bavelas, "Communication patterns in task-oriented groups," in *Group Dynamics* (second edition), eds. D. C. Cartwright and A. Zander (Evanston, Ill.: Row and Peterson, 1960).

departments effectively went through the President. The situation is diagrammed in Figure 2.

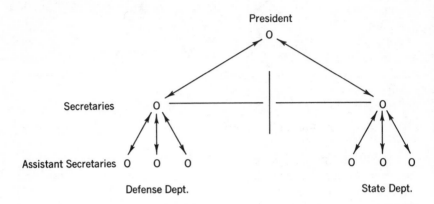

Figure 2. *Government Communication in 1949*

This pattern is, of course, hierarchical rather than circular and may well have decreased the probability of insightful ideas, such as the Policy Planning Director's, from being accepted.

During one of the few opportunities for communication that were possible between the departments (these occurred by outmaneuvering the Secretary of Defense), the Director of the Policy Planning Staff and one of his staff members met several times with the strategic planners of the Defense Department.[21] The Director of Policy Planning outlined the implications of his perception of the probability of a series of limited engagements. He argued that small, highly qualified, mechanical, mobile task forces should be developed in order to contain the Soviet Union. He met resistance from the Defense Department men, who were planning only for global war capability. When the Director challenged the assumptions behind this way of thinking, he was told that defense planners agreed on the need to be able to fight limited wars as well as global ones but felt that budget limitations made it necessary to prepare for either one or the other. In order to be ready for the worst, they concentrated on global war and particularly on the Strategic Air Command. While the Director personally felt that the possibility of a global war was too remote to deserve attention, and while he was sure that limited engagements would occur, he did not have enough people agreeing in order to force a serious consideration of a change in plans.

---

[21]Hammond, *op. cit.,* p. 287.

In such a situation, of course, a lack of communications is particularly harmful. Had the Director had the time to communicate the background his views were based on, and had he had the opportunity to mobilize the potential support of Army and Navy allies within the Defense Department, he might have obtained some shift in thinking.

When a democratic society is truly functioning as such, one has to mobilize support for a plan and develop a working consensus. When communications are open the necessity for consensus makes for good policy — the development of the Marshall Plan is an excellent example. On the other hand, if communications are closed no creative planning gets accepted and the organization is forced into either weak compromises or a dictatorial policy. We shall study this more closely in the chapter on consensus formation. At the moment, we must consider how the pressure of circumstance may force the development of a consensus that would not otherwise exist and that excludes the consideration of important sets of values. The American policy concerning Formosa illustrates some of these problems — problems similar to those which later arose in connection with Vietnam.

Forced Consensus: The Pressures of Circumstance and Momentum

At the Teheran Conference in 1943, it was decided that the island of Formosa should be taken away from Japan and given to China. This decision, of course, failed to anticipate that the government of China might come under communist control. The United States, keeping to its policy of non-intervention in the Chinese Civil War and mindful of the cost of defending Formosa, had decided not to protect Formosa when the government of the Republic of China retreated to that island. This was announced as a decision based on the fact that the United States agreed that Formosa was legally part of China and that the United States had no legal right to intervene in another nation's civil war. But behind this legal-moral position were many other considerations, such as the determination not to commit troops to Asia that might be needed in Europe, the hope that the Chinese communists would eventually recognize the United States as more friendly than Russia, and the knowledge that the military costs involved would necessitate an increase in the defense budget. Thus it was, that in June of 1950 the Chinese communists were poised on the mainland opposite Formosa, ready for what would have undoubtedly been a successful invasion that would have solidified all of China under their rule. At this point the Korean invasion occurred.

In the chapter on small groups, we shall see that when the President of the United States met with his advisors to decide what to do about the invasion of South Korea, the Secretary of State made a number of suggestions. One of these was to interpose the Seventh Fleet between Formosa and the mainland. The next day, the President accepted this suggestion, and United States policy began to rapidly change. Officially, it was stated that the intervention would help prevent the spread of conflict in Asia. This, however, was only a polite phrase to mask the fact that in actuality the move prevented the communist defeat of the Chinese nationalist forces on Formosa and was the same illegal intervention in a civil war that had been rejected previously. Why did the Secretary of State suggest an action that constituted such a policy reversal?

In the small group chapter, we shall see that one reason for the move must have been a felt need for unity within the government. The American Commander in the Far East had repeatedly argued that Formosa was of key strategic significance and had convinced the Secretary of Defense and the Chairman of the Joint Chiefs of Staff that this was so. Furthermore, a very vocal block of opposition congressmen who wanted increased intervention in the Chinese Civil War, were developing a "soft on communism" political theme that had to be checked. Under these circumstances, a defense of Formosa would enhance the unity within the government at a time when unity was essential.

A second factor must have been the consideration of what the Korean invasion might lead to. While the Secretary of State had reconciled himself to the loss of Formosa, he had not considered losing Korea as well. If Korea fell, the saving of Formosa would balance the altered status quo and restore American prestige. If the Korean conflict led to a more general war — and it must be remembered that Soviet intentions were not clear — then Formosa would be an important strategic asset. Both the Secretary of Defense and the Counselor to the State Department urged that Formosa be held. Probably a related factor was that Formosa was the one place where available power — the Seventh Fleet — could be brought to bear upon the situation. It was something that could be done to rapidly strike a successful blow against the communists.

It should be emphasized that the idea of stopping "the communists" may have been (and may still be) a grave conceptual error on the part of the Administration. By labeling a North Korean attack that was inspired or condoned by the Soviet Union "communistic," the Administration justified a blow at China. In announcing the interposition of the Seventh Fleet on June 27, the President stated,[22]

---

[22]Department of State press release.

The attack upon Korea makes it plain beyond all doubt that *Communism* has passed beyond the use of subversion to conquer independent nations and will now use armed invasion and war. *It* has defied the orders of the Security Council of the United Nations issued to preserve international peace and security. In these circumstances the occupation of Formosa by *Communist forces* would be a direct threat to the security of the Pacific area and to the United States Forces performing their lawful and necessary functions in that area. (My italics)

By attributing a *North Korean* attack to "communism," the President justified intervening in the *Chinese* Civil War.

Now, of course, it may be argued that the President was essentially correct in identifying the attack as implicating the Chinese. Certainly, although they did not participate, the Chinese may have known that the attack was going to be launched. There had been a meeting between the Chinese and Russian heads of state. Certainly, too, the Chinese had shown an attitude of belligerence and no indication of wanting to cooperate with the United States.

On the other hand, it would seem that American officials were assuming a much greater degree of unity between China and the Soviet Union than the evidence really warranted. The Americans seemed to have had more faith in the idea of international communism than Chinese or Russian leaders ever had. To perceive Russian aid to China, a meeting between the heads of state, and a treaty for mutual defense as clear indications of complete cooperation in war plans suggest that beliefs were determining American perceptions as much as data were.

The question of whether there was sufficient differentiation between China and Russia in the Secretary of State's and the President's thinking, is an interesting one. There is some evidence that indicates that any stimulus perceived as threatening often remains undifferentiated in the threatened person's mind. For example, simulations of national decision making have shown that during "wars" the decision maker draws fewer distinctions in describing the enemy and tends to perceive others mainly in terms of alliance structures.[23] Furthermore, Gladstone[24] has presented some data that indicate that thinking may become simplistic when one is advocating belligerent policies. Thus, in the 1962 speech announcing the American resumption of atmospheric nuclear tests, the President made seventeen statements of single causal relations and three statements of multiple or developmental causality. In the 1963

---

[23]Michael J. Driver, *Conceptual structure and group processes in an inter-nation simulation. Part One: The perception of simulated nations* (Princeton, N.J.: Princeton University and Educational Testing System, 1962).
[24]Arthur Gladstone, "Separative and Integrative Approaches to Conflict," paper presented at the Amer. Psychol. Assoc. Convention, 1963.

speech announcing test ban negotiations, the corresponding numbers are five and ten. It should also be noted that if the Chinese and Russians had not been perceived as a unit, it would have been difficult to justify the Formosan intervention. The President would then have been placed in the position of either doing something unprincipled or preventing unity within the administration. We have already seen that almost any distortion will be utilized to avoid having to choose between two negative alternatives.

On the other hand, there may have been no simplification of thought processes whatsoever. It is very hard to tell from interviews after the event is over, because the decision maker always stresses all the rational reasons for his choice and has the benefit of hindsight to select which reasons to stress. It may be that at least the Secretary of State simply sensed that the Korean invasion provided a perfect reason to increase the defense budget, that the momentum of events would now permit the defense of Formosa. Had the idea of developing friendly relations with China persisted only because there was not political support for intervening in the Chinese Civil War — or was the Secretary ever really committed to friendly relations with Communist China?

A third big factor in the decision to interpose the Seventh Fleet must have been that it was viewed as a temporary decision. At the time, it seemed that the invasion would be checked fairly easily; and when the idea of Chinese intervention in the Korean War was first brought up it was suggested that the Chinese could be kept out of the Korean War — and perhaps would even work for its early end — in return for an agreement to remove the Seventh Fleet after the war was over and the invaders had been thrown back. It would be easy to remove the Seventh Fleet, if that was desirable, once things had calmed down. Because of this, the full implications of the decision were probably not thought out.

In fact, once the Korean crisis held the prospect of a partial national mobilization, the reason which had originally led the Joint Chiefs of Staff to oppose the defense of Formosa (i.e., limited troops) was removed.* What had before seemed politically undesirable — requiring an effort beyond American capacity — now seemed quite reasonable and easy. Capacity is more psychological than material; and with the focus on repelling an aggression rather than intervening in a civil war, the situation had changed psychologically. In this way, a key decision starts a whole process rolling, a process that builds a momentum of its own, makes possible decisions that were impossible before, and renders impossible what was yesterday's common sense. The decision to aid

---

*It is not clear to me why the Navy could not have protected Formosa.

Korea made possible the decision to intervene in Formosa. In addition, it led to a chain of other "impossible" decisions. Thus, in June, the United States avowed sincerely that its only purpose was to throw the invaders out of South Korea. By August, the United States had declared that it must destroy the North Korean Army. By September, the announced policy of the United States was to unify all of Korea. In June, the President's advisors were reluctant to send planes across the 38th parallel. In August, in spite of the possibility of Chinese intervention, only one man (the Secretary of the Air Force) opposed sending infantry across the parallel. Thus does momentum operate.

We may note that the factors involved in momentum are related to the same factors that prevent creative policy. Once the situation shifts enough that plans are changed and a new consensus is possible, all sorts of new policies are suddenly made possible. While this momentum is related to the *inter*personal structure of consensus, there is a corresponding *intra*personal fact. Once individual men are committed to new group decisions, their own personal attitudes and models of reality shift to maintain an inner consistency; this shift leads to new individual perceptions, which, in turn, lead to new decisions. The shift in group consensus operates as a type of organizational *momentum* — that is, energy is available for new policies, and only opposing forces can slow down the new trend. The realignment of cognitions in the individuals who are involved, creates a type of *hysteresis* — that is, if conditions changed back to what they were, the individual officials would not respond as rapidly as one would expect because of their own internal changes. The new realignment of cognitions would resist the change called for by the reversed conditions. It would be interesting to perform a study where key officials were interviewed *before* a policy was changed in order to study the effect of momentum and hysteresis. One could count the possible ideas that were *not* mentioned by various officials and ask officials which events would have to occur to make them change their judgment. Lags in thinking — such as the time it took to recognize Soviet intransigence in 1945 or Soviet mellowness in 1955 — could then be evaluated.

In physical systems, both momentum and hysteresis refer to difficulties in changing an ongoing process. Momentum refers to the fact that a mass in motion will persist in its motion unless opposing forces resist it. It took energy to set the mass in motion (or to gain a consensus), and the motion (or policy) will continue unless just as much energy is involved in stopping it. Hysteresis refers to the fact that a process may not be immediately reversible because of changes in the internal characteristics of a system. Thus, a simple electromagnet will not lose all of its magnetism when the current is removed, because some of the individual magnets within its core persist in their new realignment. Likewise, an organizational decision may persist after the removal of the forces-holding the consensus together, because the formation of the consensus changed the positions of some of the individual decision makers.

While the decision to protect Formosa with the Seventh Fleet was a reversal of policy, it did not immediately mean that the United States was committed to aiding the Nationalist Chinese for all time. In fact, some officials must have hoped that the United States would withdraw its support after the successful completion of the Korean War. Almost immediately, however, the momentum of the decision began to prevent this. Concern with Formosa's protection, and pressure from the opposition in Congress, led to military aid to the nationalist forces on Formosa. After China entered the Korean War, it became unthinkable to abandon Formosa — it would have been regarded as a pro-communist move; moreover, the opposition party in Congress demanded support for the Chinese nationalists as a price for their own backing of aid to Europe.

Testing Foreign Policy

Hilsman notes,[25]

> Getting a wide variety of people who hold different values to sit down and decide on how to rank those values would be next to impossible; but getting people to agree on a particular policy that serves a mixture of values is done all the time. One group accepts a policy because it serves one value, and another group accepts the policy because it serves another, quite different value . . . The *test* of policy is not that it will most effectively accomplish an agreed-upon value but that a wider number of people decide to endorse it. (My italics)

While we might call the above the "test of consensus," it would be a mistake to assume that this is the only test of policy and that policy can not be evaluated from a value-free point of view. For the real test of policy is not simply that a number of people *think* it will help them achieve their values but whether in fact the policy *does* help them achieve their values. Thus, in spite of the fact that policy is a-rational, we may ask a kind of reasonableness of it. We would like the policy to:

---

[25]R. Hilsman, "The foreign-policy consensus: an interim research report," *J. Conflict Resolution*, 3 (1959), pp. 361-82 (p. 364).

(1) achieve the goals which its supporters hoped it would achieve,* and (2) to achieve these without having unanticipated consequences that damage other values which its supporters hold. If a policy meets these criteria, then it is a "good" policy, whether or not it is good for a particular individual who may not have supported the policy. We may call this the "test of reasonableness." Now let us see how the new Formosan policy meets this test.

At the time, the suggestion to protect Formosa seemed a wise one, and all the President's advisors apparently were in its favor. The new Formosan policy met the test of consensus, of satisfying parties with different values. It ended the domestic deadlock over how to deal with Communist China, and it permitted the nation to act with unity to resist the Korean invasion. Nevertheless, the consensus for defending Formosa was initially forced by the situation, contaminated by confused thinking, and solidified by the sheer momentum of events. Today, the validity of the decision may possibly be challenged.

The interposition of the Seventh Fleet between the mainland and Formosa accomplished its major objective. It prevented Communist China from capturing Formosa and thereby shrinking American power in the Pacific. The problem with the policy was its unanticipated consequences, many of which were harmful to the values of many of the policy's supporters. The major problem grew out of China's reaction. Whiting[26] observes,

> In contrast with the delayed and occasionally diffident treatment of the Korean War, Chinese communist reaction to the June 27th order placing the U.S. Seventh Fleet in the Taiwan Strait was immediate and authoritative. Within twenty-four hours of the Truman statement, Foreign Minister Chou En-Lai denounced the move as armed aggression against the territory of China in total violation of the United Nations charter.

In his history of Chinese-American relations, Tsou[27] notes that American officials somehow thought that the Chinese communists were basically both friendly and weak when, in fact, they had a distrust of America as an imperialistic power and were quite confident of them-

---

*For our purposes, we assume that the supporter is supporting the policy because he thinks the policy will work and will advance his values or self-interest. Practically, of course, a person might support a policy because he thinks it will not work and, hence, will create the conditions for a revolution or a foreign takeover. If he was correct, we would consider the policy to be "bad" policy.

[26]Alan Whiting, *China Crosses the Yalu: The Decision to Enter the Korean War* (New York: The Macmillan Company, 1960).

[27]Tang Tsou, *America's Failure in China* (Chicago: University of Chicago Press, 1963).

selves. Consequently, American officials failed to see what impact the "neutralization" of Formosa would have. Failing to see the action through Chinese eyes, they did not seem to consider that the move would confirm Chinese suspicions that America was an imperialist power that would like to exploit China just as Japan had done. When, three months later, American troops crossed the 38th parallel and marched towards the borders of China, the Chinese entered the war. The troops that had been poised opposite Formosa and prevented from attacking that island by the Seventh Fleet, had been shifted north-wards towards Korea. The entire Chinese Army, which might have been engaged in the Chinese Civil War, was engaged fighting America's troops in Korea.

It might be argued that the strategic value of Formosa was worth the cost of the subsequent war. If the matter ended there, this might be true. However, the action confirmed the suspicious belligerence of the Chinese. As Tsou[28] has observed,

> The unresolved question of Formosa became an obsession with Communist China, [while] on the part of the United States, the initial defeat and subsequent frustrations aroused deep fear and hostility toward the Chinese Communist regime, all the more because of the previous sentimental attachment to China. This fear and hostility has since replaced traditional friendship as the dominant mood in the American attitude toward China. The United States thus reciprocates Peking's phobia and hatred for Washington.

Tsou notes that the policy of encouraging the communist government in China to be friendly was replaced by its opposite — an attempt to isolate Peking, rehabilitate the Nationalists, threaten war, and pretend that the communists would soon be overthrown. He concludes, "Pride in America's moral leadership in China has been replaced by apprehension about Chinese ideological influence in Asia."

In addition to cementing Chinese-American distrust with blood, the Formosan intervention hurt relations between the United States and other countries. For example, many Americans, embittered by India's refusal to send troops to Korea, did not realize that India's reluctance was due to the Formosan intervention and its concern that this move would alienate the Chinese. As a result, some pressure was applied to try to influence India's decision. In turn, Indians began to feel that strings were being attached to American aid.

---

[28]*Ibid.*, pp. 589-91.

Furthermore, the intervention weakened the cause of the United Nations and collective security. Hoyt[29] has observed that while international law was considered in the decision to defend Korea it was conspicuously absent in the decision to defend Formosa.

The decision to help Korea was carried out in accord with the United Nations Charter and was supported by all but seven of the member nations of that body. A study of nations' attitudes toward the United Nations revealed that the Korean stand enhanced its prestige and convinced smaller nations that they had a vital interest in the organization.[30] On the other hand, the Formosan intervention was so unjustified that the United Nations was never consulted. There was almost no support for this aspect of American policy. Since they are based on the idea of national independence, the Charter and the idea of international law were both weakened. As Hoyt[31] notes, "Rather than providing evidence of American insistence upon the Charter principles, it seemed to indicate that the United States was unpredictable in its actions and would depart from the rules when it chose." Certainly, it hardly seems appropriate to charge the Chinese government, which the United States had kept out of the United Nations, with violating a United Nations charter which the United States first violated by intervening in the Chinese Civil War.

Finally, the Formosan intervention greatly weakened the administration's domestic political position and indirectly contributed to McCarthyism. As Hoyt observes, if the Administration had consistently emphasized its adherence to the Charter of the United Nations, it would not have opened itself to the damaging charge that it had appeased Communism in China. The late support of Formosa seemed to indicate that the China lobby had been right all along.

It seems doubtful, that if the President and his Secretary of State had foreseen the above consequences they would have decided on the Formosan intervention. That action met the test of concensus but not the test of reasonableness. However, given the pressure of a situation fairly demanding unity and the use of available power, it may have been psychologically impossible to have looked at the consequences.

It is precisely in such circumstances that it is helpful to have a set of principles to test one's actions against. If the actions do not match

---

[29]Edwin C. Hoyt, "The United States reaction to the Korean attack: A study of the principles of the United Nations Charter as a factor in American policy-making," *Amer. J. Internat. Law,* 55 (1961), pp. 45-76.
[30]Robert MacIver, *The Nations and the United Nations* (New York: Manhattan Publishing Company, 1959).
[31]Hoyt, *op. cit.,* p. 72.

the principles one may resolve to violate the principles; but, at least, one has been forced to take a hard look at the proposed actions. Hoyt,[32] for example, suggests that if the decision makers had looked at the principles of international law, with its assumption of the sovereignty of states, they would have realized what the intervention meant. Noting that there was no discussion of legal justification for the interposition of the Seventh Fleet, he observes, "The President and his advisers had not abandoned their intention to avoid involvement in the Chinese civil war. They hoped to accomplish this by imposing a cease fire on the Nationalists as well as the Communists. In fact, however, such involvement was an inevitable consequence of the decision. Both Chinese governments recognized this. If the legal aspects of the decision had been discussed by the policymakers, the inconsistency of their position in this respect must have become apparent." Since legal principles reflect a view of reality, we may ask if there are any principles with an even broader generality against which policy could be tested for reasonableness.

You will recall that in the last chapter we saw that any valid perception had to reflect the essential structure of the stimulus. We may now assert that while many possible policies may reflect a multitude of different values (and thereby meet the test of consensus), only those that meet the structure of the situation they are designed to cope with will have a chance of success.

Now, when we examine the Formosan policy with this idea in mind — that is, when we ask, "Does the policy reflect the structure of the situation?" — we are at once struck by the inconsistency we have noted before. American decision makers knew that the Korean Invasion was instigated by either North Korea or the Soviet Union. But the protection of Formosa was a blow struck at the Chinese. Here is a situation where country A instigates or supports its puppet B to expand into nation X, and X's protector Y responds by punishing country A's ally C! No matter how good the internal reasons for this decision, it poorly reflects the structure of the situation.

We shall postulate that whenever a decision poorly reflects the structure of the situation there will be unfortunate consequences. Then this can be used as a principle against which a policy can be tested for reasonableness. This is not to say that no persons will like consequences — "it is an ill wind indeed that blows no man some good." It is to say that there will be unforeseen results that will go against the values of most of the persons who supported the decision in the first place. If we are correct, it is not sufficient that a policy merely reflect a consensus and thus mobilize the resources of a nation; it must also meet the struc-

---

[32]*Ibid.*, p. 65.

ture of the situation facing the nation. The situation is somewhat analogous to the difference between novelty and creativity. Some psychologists have attempted to test creativity by giving the subject an object, such as a brick, and asking him to think of all the possible uses of the object. It is argued that the more unusual uses a person can think of, the more creative he is. Such tests are not very satisfactory because they put no constraints on the possible answers. Thus, while we would recognize a use such as "a hot water bottle" as a legitimate answer, if a person says, "as a balloon," we do not consider him creative but simply unrealistic. Likewise, just because compromises have satisfied enough persons, consensus has been obtained, and the nation can act, it does not mean that the action will be a good one, i.e., a reasonable or realistic one.

It is hard to define the characteristics of a policy that does not fit the structure of the situation. It is not that the policy has simply been based on a misjudgment or has proved a failure; sometimes one lacks information, and chance may always play a role in determining an outcome. Rather, policy with poor structure is like a note that is out of key. All the "Gestalt forces" call for one type of event, and another seems out of place — silly. Such a policy neglects causality in such a way that it is bound to cause what it does not want. If one wants to encourage a friendship, it is silly to punish the potential friend for what his friend does — it doesn't make sense. Perhaps some other examples of policies with inherently poor structures will help in defining the idea. The following examples are taken from Kennan's book *Russia and the West under Lenin and Stalin*.[33]

1. In 1917, the Allies were so intent on the war effort that they insisted that the Russian government continue fighting Germany, in spite of the fact that the war was undermining the Russian government's strength. The resulting strain on the government caused its overthrow and the loss of Russia to communism (p. 150). This structure is similar to that involved in killing the goose that lays the golden egg — a product is so desired that the producer is destroyed.

2. In 1919, the weak, hesitant, allied intervention in Russia strengthened the communist government's control (p. 119). The structure here involved meddling in the affairs of another enough to be resented but not enough to insure the desired change. Forty years later, the identical poor structure occurred when the United States supported the invasion of Cuba and probably strengthened the regime of that country.

---

[33]Kennan, *op. cit.*

3. At the close of the First World War, the autocratic regime of the Kaiser was replaced by a democratic government. The French, having suffered heavily in the War, proceeded to punish this new reform government for the sins of its predecessor. This weakened the new government so that it eventually lost control to the fascist government of Hitler (pp. 163-69). Again, we have a structure where the wrong party gets punished.

4. The First World War ended with a peace treaty that surrounded an aggrieved Germany with small new states. Kennan states, "To break up the Austro-Hungarian Empire, to leave Germany united, and then to penalize a new German regime which had no part of the responsibility for the war, was to invite trouble" (p. 164). The structure here consists of putting something you do not wish to lose in front of a party that wants it and believes itself unfairly treated.

5. The allies wished to keep Germany isolated but did not invite Russia to join them in making the Versailles Peace Treaty. This opened the way for relations between Germany and Russia, and an "alliance" resulted at Rapallo (p. 208). The structure here consists of excluding two parties and not expecting them to be drawn together.

6. In the 1920's, the Allies failed to support the Weimar Republic's appeal for economic unity with Austria, but later permitted Hitler to forcefully join Austria to Germany (pp. 218, 320). The structure: the request is denied, the grab is permitted.

7. During the Second World War, the United States and Great Britain perceived the Soviet Union as a permanent friend rather than a temporary ally. This perception, together with an insistence on unconditional surrender, prevented the limitation of Soviet territorial gains (pp. 351, 366). Here one works with a party on the basis of a limited common interest, assumes a much broader range of interests, and omits any precautions.

8. In the years following the First World War, the Allies were so involved with getting reparations from Germany that they failed to perceive the necessity of reconstructing Europe (p. 201). Here the policy failed to adjust to the demanding structure of economic reconstruction in Europe. This mistake was not repeated after the Second World War.

These are but a handful of the many examples of unrealistic foreign policy that could be cited. If a person acted in the above way we might consider him either irrational or unintelligent — but governments act this way all the time. This occurs largely because of the factors we have examined and because of the tendency to be satisfied with any kind of a consensus rather than demanding reasonableness. Many feasible plans have poor structures. Many plans are makeshift things that can temporarily mobilize a nation's energy at the expense of inaccurately reflecting the structure of the situation they are designed to meet. There are always "good" reasons why an administration produces a policy with a poor structure, but there is always a horrible cost that is usually not anticipated.

The reason why a policy must fit the structure of the situation if it is to be successful, is because the other nation's response will be governed by the structure, or their own wishful misperception of it, rather than by one's own wishes. A failure to recognize structure is, therefore, closely related to failing to anticipate what the other will do. That is, one does not stop to think about the situation the other is in or will be placed in by one's own actions. Punishing one government for the mistake of another is, in this sense, connected with failing to anticipate that the punished government will be aggrieved and, hence, misestimating the strength of its response. Earlier, we noted that officials often fail to look at events through the eyes of another nation. The Formosan intervention is a good example of this failure. There was no intent to strike at the Chinese Communists, and the Secretary of State appears to have been somewhat hurt when the Chinese later struck in Korea. But to the Chinese, the interposition of the Seventh Fleet was a blow that confirmed their image of the United States as an imperialist aggressor.

In view of the fact that a government is so different from an individual person — having a completely different policy formation process — it is most interesting to note that in the examples we have examined it does not seem to matter whether the parties involved are persons or governments. That is, it appears as though the properties of good and poor structures are the same for interpersonal and international relations. It is difficult to believe that there are not some differences in the principles that govern the relations between persons and nations, since the actors are so dissimilar in their basic nature;* but if these differences exist, they have not yet been delineated. We shall return to this subject in a later chapter.

---

*One possible reason has been suggested by Sidney Verba. "(Assumptions of rationality and non-rationality in models of the international system," *World Politics,* 14, (1961), p. 114.) He points out that, in the case of foreign policy, " . . . the fact that the decision involves an external power, in relation to which the members of the foreign policy-making coalitions all occupy the same status as citizens of their nation, increases the salience of norms associated with the individual's role within the nation rather than within the sub-system of which he is also a member."

While policy must be the product of some kind of consensus process, it is so evident that *someone* should check this product against the structure of the situation, that the reader may wonder why so many errors occur. To understand this, we must examine the current attempt to plan and coordinate policy so that it will be realistic and consistent. Then the difficulties will be more apparent.

The Attempt to Plan

One factor that greatly affects the amount of consistency in foreign policy, is that very few people are concerned with coordinating one policy with another. Hilsman [34] conducted over two hundred interviews to survey a number of different policy areas. He found that " . . . the bulk of the participants in any particular policy area seem to confine themselves to that area almost exclusively. All participants, in other words, tend to specialize." Thus, a congressman or newspaperman who specializes in foreign aid rarely influences military policy. The only men concerned with all areas are the President, a few of his staff members, the Secretary of State and the head of his Policy Planning Staff, and a few top congressional leaders. Since good coordination would have to begin at much lower levels, there is little close coordination of different policies.

Because of this organizational feature, Verba [35] points out that an amount of stress that might create irrationality in an individual may produce more rationality in organization planning; this may occur because the policy will be made by higher officials who are responsible for the overall system of policy and who will be unhampered by bureaucratic commitments and bargaining. In a similar manner, conflict may help policy. It is the unsettled conflict between groups that brings an issue before the President. Sorensen [36] notes,

> Just as conflict will bring issues to the President, so a lack of conflict may sometimes keep them from him even when he should be involved. For example: Had there been some disagreement between White House and State Department officials on the contents of a press statement on nuclear warheads in Canada, it would have been brought to the President's attention before it exploded in the headlines.

---

[34]Hilsman, *op. cit.*, p. 376.

[35]Sidney Verba, "Assumption of rationality and non-rationality in models of the international system," in *The International System,* eds. Klaus Knoor and Sidney Verba (Princeton: Princeton University Press, 1961).

[36]Sorensen, *op. cit.*, p. 16.

Likewise, had there been some disagreement about the Formosan intervention, the action would have been given more thought.

A second factor affecting rational planning is that, even within the somewhat specialized area of foreign policy, the average person in the State Department, even at the Assistant Secretary level, is so busy handling the problems of the moment that he is unable to think about overall relationships or long range policy. To really grasp this fact and be able to appreciate how the average officer becomes completely absorbed in coping with day to day demands, it is helpful to read Ogburn's[37] brief and concrete description of some events in a typical day in the State Department. This absorption in the current day's work has been noted by Acheson,[38] who writes,

> The central task of a foreign office should be to understand what these forces [of current history] are, to do what can be done to shape them favorably to our interests, and to prepare to deal with them. This should be the task, but it is not. The principal effort goes into dealing with the overpowering present, the present, which like the Mississippi in full flood, absorbs the whole energy and thought of those who man the levees.

The effect of this is often a blinding loss of perspective. Thus, Kennan,[39] speaking of the "interminable wranglings over debts and reparations" during the conferences following the First World War, states,

> Staggering investments of the time of experts and statesmen were expended on them, and to no avail. Even while they were in progress, real life was moving on — the mysterious life of the feelings and attitudes of men, which is all that really counts in politics — was moving on in ways that were in no one's interest, in ways that began to point already to the new tragedies of the Thirties and Forties. Yet people could not see this movement of events — it was obscured from them by the great columns of unreal figures by which they allowed themselves to be bemused.

In an attempt to combat this absence of any time for perspective, the Department of State created a group called the Policy Planning Staff* — a group of about fifteen men who are theoretically freed from the

---

*Now the Policy Planning Council

[37]Charlton Ogburn, Jr., "The Flow of Policymaking in the Department of State," in *The Formulation and Administration of United States Foreign Policy,* ed. H. Field Haviland, Jr. (Washington: The Brookings Institution, 1960).

[38]Dean Acheson, "The President and the Secretary of State," in *The Secretary of State,* American Assembly, Columbia University (Englewood Cliffs, N.J.: Prentice-Hall, Inc., 1960).

[39]Kennan, *op. cit.,* p. 203.

time pressures of daily routine. According to a former director of the Staff,[40] the group was created to be responsible for the identification of long range forces, for the direction of attention to actions that have no short run implications but may be vital in the long run, for the criticizing of existing policy to ensure its integration with other plans, and for the stimulation of similar analysis and review in the other bureaus of the Department. Unfortunately, almost immediately after its inception the members of the planning staff were drawn away from analysis and into current affairs. The Department could simply not forbear from using good men to meet the pressing needs of the moment, and the men themselves were tempted to exert influence on current policy. The men on the staff were caught in a basic dilemma. If they became involved in current policy, they lost time for thinking (and their thinking became biased); whereas if they only thought, their thoughts had little influence on policy. Since general long range planning becomes translated into action by influencing specific current decisions, and since relatively little weight is given to long range considerations, there was a constant force away from planning! It is instructive to read Elder's[41] account of an average day in the life of the Director of Policy Planning. Clearly, involvement with the present greatly encroaches upon thinking for the future; and one begins to understand why the government is constantly reacting — "putting out fires" — without really developing a consistent long range policy. Elder[42] suggests an epitaph; "Entranced with the present and its smaller problems, the future stole on them unaware."

Each Secretary of State makes different uses of the Policy Planning Staff, whose prestige and authority have greatly varied in accord with the degree to which the Secretary has personally valued long range planning and analysis and has cultivated intellectual intimacy with its Director. In combination with this factor, the power of the staff has varied with the power of the Secretary of State and, hence, with the Secretary's relation with the President and whether the President relies on the Secretary, or himself, or some other person or group for the programming of foreign policy. In brief, the role of the Policy Planning Staff — or of any other institutionalized part of the bureaucracy — depends on how the President and his key appointees use the resources available for making foreign policy. While occasionally a person will

---

[40]R. R. Bowie, "The Secretary and the Development and Coordination of Policy," in *The Secretary of State, (op. cit.)*.

[41]Robert E. Elder, *The Policy Machine: The Department of State and American Foreign Policy* (Syracuse, New York: Syracuse Univ. Press, 1960).

[42]*Ibid.*, p. 84.

make more of his office than was anticipated, ordinarily the appointer has the effect on the office — it is upgraded if he appoints a man he particularly trusts and respects.

There is no systematic thinking about this important organizational point and how it relates to the power of bureaucracy. One wonders, for example, what happens when the President has no particular interest in foreign affairs and chooses a Secretary of State with whom he relates well but whose own skill lies in implementing orders rather than initiating policy. Will the bureaucracy of the Department tend to fill the gap and begin suggesting more policy, or will the opening be filled by some Assistant Secretary, or will policy simply not be planned?

In other areas of the government, there is considerably more planning. According to the Brookings[43] report, the Department of Defense engages in much more planning than the Department of State and is critical of the latter's weaker planning emphasis. In part, this difference simply reflects the difference between military operations and diplomacy. The former stresses the coordination of the many factors involved in a complex logistics operation and, hence, necessitates planning; whereas the latter stresses the need for flexibility to meet different situations and, hence, necessitates improvisation. In part, the difference may also reflect the day to day operations of the Department. The Defense Department is usually preparing for a war while the State Department is constantly engaged in diplomacy. Whatever the reasons, a general agreement runs through the various government investigations, that there is not enough planning of foreign policy. Furthermore, with the lack of State Department planning, the views of military planners may be influencing foreign policy to a greater extent than is desirable.

During the Eisenhower Administration there was a concerted effort to use the National Security Council as a device to secure good planning. This proved a failure because of the great tendency to compromise issues between Departments and Agencies rather than to arrive at a creative integration. Acheson has commented how interdepartmental committees tend to get agreements by increasing the vagueness and generality of their statements. And Hammond[44] has pointed out that the formation of the council assumed that persons who were responsible for segments of policy could produce a whole policy. While a President can direct a department head to give up the perspective of his department and take a government wide point of view, few personality types can actually do this. On the contrary, most men are concerned with

---

[43]*The Formulation and Administration of United States Foreign Policy, op. cit.*
[44]Hammond, "The National Security Council as a Device for Interdepartmental Coordination," *Amer. Pol. Sci. Rev.,* 54 (1960), pp. 899-910.

protecting their agency's program and getting the best policy to maximize their own department's interest. While we have no research on the circumstances under which a person will set aside his own responsibilities and interests to consider the interests of the whole, these circumstances would certainly not include the utilization of men who have parochial responsibilities and bureaucratic positions to defend. Such circumstances are not compatible with the exploration of all relevant issues and with a thorough discussion of the problems involved in a given policy.

An alternative to a committee of department heads is a committee of Presidential staff men who have no operating responsibilities and, hence, no role or loyalty conflicts. Unfortunately, as Hammond points out, the problem with such an arrangement would be that such men would lack the reality and the prestige that comes from department responsibilities, and the policy that was formed would have to be implemented by men who had no hand in its making. This general problem of securing coordination — whether to use men with responsibilities and biases, or men with good overall views but no operating responsibilities — has not been adequately studied.

There seems to be little doubt, however, that the work of the National Security Council was along the lines of revising details and compromising between agencies, rather than considering broad problems or proposing new programs. After pointing out that some of the Council's statements were too general to be useful and that others were internally inconsistent, Hilsman[45] states, "In still other instances, discussion in the NSC seems to have substituted for decisions, with the participants satisfied psychologically even though no decision had actually been reached." This abrogation of responsibility, together with the enormous pressure on top level personnel, causes decision making to be made at lower than optimal levels. As Child[46] notes,

> . . . decisions affecting policy are sometimes made by Directors of Offices, and even lower down in the hierarchial scale, in sheer desperation to get things done. The result is that instead of policy being made first, decisions affecting policy have precedence . . .

One might think that compromise could be avoided by introducing fresh new policy. In fact, however, Verba[47] points out that very few

---

[45]Hilsman, *op. cit.,* p. 328.
[46]J. R. Childs, *American Foreign Service* (New York: Holt, Rinehart & Winston, Inc., 1948). p. 42.
[47]Verba, *op. cit.*

alternatives are considered at the beginning of a new policy. Rather, the policy is made as similar as possible to past policy so that past experience can be used. Alternatives are suggested towards the end of the policy making process, when the policy's implications look as though they may injure some of the members of the necessary consensus group. One of the problems is that any new idea from the State Department's Policy Planning Staff, or anywhere else, must fit in with approved current policy. This adherence to precedent presents little room for maneuver in foreign policy. Thus, Elder[48] asks,

> How can a single challenging idea, no matter how well argued, be more than moderately effective against the mountain of consistent detail intricately blended into the approved body of National Security Council policy?

And he answers,[49]

> What is now missing from the policy machine is an appendage which could provide seminal ideas and a continuing challenge to the basic assumptions, goals, and implementations of American foreign policy.

In establishing any such appendage, it should be remembered that innovative ideas have rarely come from within a department. Acheson[50] points out that the Marshall Plan was largely developed by men who had wide governmental experience, and views that were not constrained by the perspective of one department. Policy initiatives, such as the Fulbright program and the Peace Corps, were not initiated within the State Department; and the Point Four Program and crucial aspects of foreign aid were actually often opposed by forces in the Department.

Now let us briefly review the many factors that affect how officials project the future. First, we saw that while planning is constrained by many objective factors, it is often poor because of basic conceptual failures. We noted that these are often not obvious mistakes so much as creative failures. Necessary creativity is hindered by current plans and the climate of opinion, by various systematic biases that select certain features of the situation at the expense of others, and by the difficulty of seeing the situation through the eyes of other nationalities. We suggested that only an "impractical" group of men who are divorced from operational responsibilities can overcome these hindrances to

---

[48]Elder, *op. cit.*, p. 166.
[49]*Ibid.*, p. 613.
[50]Acheson, *op. cit.*

creative conceptualization. We then saw that whatever creative insights are available to individuals, are often lost to the organization because of closed communication channels and the pretense that there is no problem that needs to be solved. Turning from long range planning to those situations where the pressure of events dictates or forces consensus, we noted that such a consensus often produces poor policy. We observed that it is particularly in these circumstances that policy needs to be tested against principles. It was suggested that policy should be tested against the structure of the situation and that no governmental groups currently in existence have either the time or the detachment to do this.

It seems clear that some sort of group is needed to suggest "impractical" policy and to constantly evaluate whether "realistic" policy actually fits the structure of the situation. Such a group should not have any operational responsibilities and should be divorced from politics by operating completely within the administration. Its main job would be to serve a consulting function for the President, his assistant for national security affairs, and the Secretary of State, and to point out to various interest groups some of the long term consequences of the policy that is developing as the result of consensus. In order to insure that the ideas of such a group actually affected policy, it might be necessary to have "middle men" who could operate between such a group and the officials making practical plans.

CHAPTER 4

The Individual's Decision

Perception and planning are important determinants of policy, but ultimately a course of action must be selected and acted upon. The United States does not entrust this selection to the chance roll of a die, or the set program of a computer, or the vote of its citizens, or the consensus of an executive council. Instead, it relies on the decision of an individual. While the President's decisions are constrained by many factors, he is responsible for formulating the best possible policy. If he fails to make decisions, he abrogates this responsibility, and policy becomes determined by fate rather than by his judgment.

It is not at all clear what a decision is. How does it differ from the roll of a die or the majority of a vote? Cardozo,[1] later one of the great judges on the Supreme Court, posed this problem when he wondered about the nature of justice. He asked, "What is it that I do when I decide a case? . . . *Some* principle, however unavowed and inarticulate and subconscious, has regulated the infusion . . . . a choice there has been, not a submission to the degree of Fate". In this chapter we shall examine this question in some detail.

Governmental policy is affected by the conflicts among many different persons and the nature of the consensus they can form. Each of these persons must decide as an individual whether or not to support a given

---

[1]Benjamin Cardozo, *The Nature of Judicial Process* (New Haven: Yale University Press, 1960). pp. 10-11.

policy. Therefore, in the last analysis, it is the conflict *within* each person that will decide policy. In fact, if the decision is an important one the person may seclude himself in an effort to ward off the pressures of the others' thoughts and to come to grips with his own basic values. It is often in these lonely periods that the individual makes his decision. Thus, in the case of the Korean Invasion, as the President rushed back to Washington he retired to think in a private compartment in his plane,[2] and it was at this time that he appears to have made his basic decision to fight. Likewise, after the Secretary of State had talked for a long while with his top advisers, he broke off the meeting and said that he wanted time to think and to write out his position. His specific recommendations — including the interposition of the Seventh Fleet between the mainland and Formosa — came out of this period of thinking by himself. They fit in with the President's decision and became the basis for Korean policy.

I should like to be able to describe exactly what went on in the minds of the President and the Secretary of State: the thinking, with its creative insights and its subtle distortions; the arguments that occurred to each man — and those that failed to occur; the emotions that were provoked by the various alternatives; the subconscious meanings that affected the course of the process but were not revealed until later free association brought them to light; and the final process of commitment as it reflected the impact of each man's personality. Unfortunately, just a bit of this is available; there is no reasonably exact record of any of these important decisions. The major reason for this is that investigators are not fully aware of the subtleties of the decision making process and do not know which questions to ask.

In the other chapters of this work, there is a sufficient amount of historical data to which we can refer our psychological analysis. Here, the basic research material is so limited that, in two-thirds of the chapter, we shall have to work from the mundane data of every day life or simple laboratory experiments. We shall have to take the analysis based on this simple data and work backwards, attempting to hazard a guess at what we might find if we could conduct depth interviews during important political decisions. I hope the reader will not begrudge the time we will spend on what might appear to be peripheral material. It is the best we can do, and I believe the result may be more pertinent than might be imagined. Considering its importance, remarkably little is understood about decision making within the individual. We shall at least be able to raise some scaffolding for future investigations.

---

[2]Harry Truman, *Memoirs,* Vol. one: *Years of Trial and Hope, 1946-1952* (Garden City: Doubleday & Company, Inc., 1956).

The Dynamics of Decisions

Utility models

Many models of the decision making process are "utility models" or modifications of them. A utility model sees the decision maker as attempting to pick the most useful alternative. Imagine the person in a situation where he must choose one of several available alternatives. Each of these alternatives may lead to a whole series of outcomes, some good and some bad. While the decision maker cannot be sure exactly which outcome will occur, he can estimate how likely an outcome is if he chooses a given alternative. Each outcome has a given value for the particular person at the moment of choice. He either wants the outcome (a positive value) or does not care (a zero value) or wants to avoid the outcome (a negative value). Now, a person can calculate the utility of an alternative by multiplying the probability of each possible outcome by that outcome's value and then adding up these possibilities. The person then chooses the alternative with the greatest expected utility.

Thus the decision maker judges:

(I) the expected usefulness of alternative A = (the probability of outcome$_1$'s occurrence if A is chosen $\times$ the value of outcome$_1$) + (probability of outcome$_2$'s occurrence $\times$ the value of outcome$_2$) . . .

and (II) the expected usefulness of alternative B = (the probability of outcome$_3$'s occurrence if B is chosen $\times$ the value of outcome$_3$) + (probability of outcome$_4$'s occurrence $\times$ the value of outcome$_4$) . . .

It is not, of course, implied that the person necessarily consciously calculates the above quantities. It is assumed that, somehow or other, rough estimates are made and combined in the above fashion.

Neither is it necessarily assumed that the person considers *all* possible alternatives or outcomes. As Simon[3] has pointed out, a person may be satisfied with a reasonable level of expected utility; he may choose the first alternative that is *satisfying* to him instead of really trying to *maximize* his expected utility.

Now consider a simple example of the utility model in operation. Suppose that a person is told that if he chooses alternative A: he will have 1 chance in 10 of winning $5.00 and 9 chances in 10 of winning nothing; whereas if he chooses alternative B he has 5 chances in 10 of winning $2.00 and 5 chances in 10 of winning nothing. On the simplest level, we might assume that the utility of the money and the probability

---

[3]Herbert Simon, *Administrative Behavior: A Discussion of Decision-Making Process in Administrative Organization* (New York: The Macmillan Company, 1947).

of winning can be taken as the above values. Then the person could intuitively estimate:

alternative A's expected utility$=(1/10 \times \$5.00) + (9/10 \times \$0.00) = \$.50$

and

alternative B's expected utility$=$

$$(5/10 \times \$2.00) + (5/10 \times \$1.00) = \$1.00.$$

Then, maximizing his expected utility, he would choose alternative B.

It should be observed that both alternatives A and B had positive expected utility. Since an outcome may have negative utility (or cost) it may be true that one or both alternatives have a negative expected utility. In that case, of course, the person will choose the alternative with the least negative utility expected.

In the above example, we assumed that the utility of the money was equal to its market value. We do not need to make that assumption. For example, if our decision maker had only one real desire — to go and see his lover — and if the bus fare was $5.00, then the utility of winning $5.00 might actually have for him the utility of $10.00 and the utility of $2.00 might only have the utility of $1.00. In this case, that of a lover, who must gamble in order to win the desired bus fare, the expected utility of alternative "A" would be $1.00, of "B" $.50, and the person would choose alternative "A".

Now, in a sophisticated model, the probability of an event occurring is actually the *subjective* probability — the probability in which the decision maker believes — rather than the actual objective probability. Thus, in the first example, a decision maker might feel lucky so that regardless of the objective probabilities he feels he has 7 chances out of 10 to win. In this case, he would calculate his expected utilities to be $3.50 and $1.40 respectively and, hence, pick alternative A. Many of the distortions we examined in the last chapter may affect decision making by operating on subjective probability in this way.

An interesting experiment that examines the effect of desire on subjective probability has been performed by Irwin[4]. He assembled packs of cards containing various proportions of marked cards. The subjects were told what proportion of the cards in a pack were marked, then each subject guessed whether or not he would draw a marked card from the pack. This process was repeated with many different packs and under two conditions — for half of the packs, a subject was told

---

[4]Frances W. Irwin, "Stated expectations as functions of possibility and desirability of outcomes," *J. Personality,* 21 (1953), pp. 329-35.

that he would gain a point if he drew a marked card (the "desirable condition"); while for the remaining packs, the subject was told that he would lose a point if he drew a marked card (the "undesirable condition"). Whether the subject guessed correctly did not affect whether or not he gained or lost a point; so the subject's guesses are a good measure of his "hunches" about what would happen — his subjective probability. The results obtained by adding together the guesses of all of the subjects are shown in Figure 1.

It is apparent that, while subjective probability approximates objective probability, there is a distortion introduced by the motivation of the subject. We must note three interesting facts about this distortion: (1) it is greatest when the objective probability is .50; (2) when the objective probability is low, the subjective probability of a desirable alternative is accurate, but the estimation of an undesirable alternative is reduced to nothing; (3) when the objective probability is high, the subjective probability of the undesirable alternative is accurate, but the estimation of a desirable alternative is inflated to certainty.

Figure 1.   *Effect of Desirability on Subjective Probability*

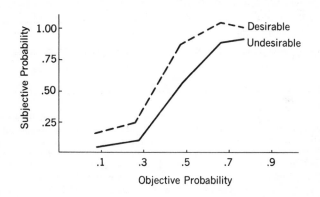

Another set of distortions is involved in the calculations of chance probabilities. Cohen and Hansel[5] have experimented with these and demonstrated the following facts:

1. There is an underestimation of the probability that should be obtained from adding independent probabilities.

---

[5]John Cohen and C. E. M. Hansel, "The nature of decisions in gambling," *Acta Psychologica,* 13 (1957), pp. 357-70.

2. There is an overestimation of a probability that should be obtained from multiplying independent probabilities.
3. There is a tendency to view samples as miniature populations instead of realizing the fact of chance variations.
4. Recent events in a series of samples will be overweighed in one's estimation of the population parameters.

Unfortunately, there have not been any studies of probability estimation in governmental decisions. Numerous examples of discrepancies between subjective and objective probabilities exist. We have noted that, Hitler judged that Britain would not declare war if he invaded Poland, and most Western statesmen in 1938 overestimated the likelihood of the Soviet Union joining an alliance against Hitler. Contrariwise, both American and British officials underestimated the resistance movement in Germany during the Second World War, and American officials were inordinately afraid that the Soviet Union would cease fighting Hitler. It would be interesting to see how the distortions reflected in Figure 1 interact with cognitive dissonance and political reality to produce real errors in judgment.*

Various attempts have been made to predict the actual choices of persons when the utility of a given amount of money has been established prior to the choice situation. However, the difficulties involved in measuring utility have restricted the application of the utility model, and for our purposes it simply provides a heuristic framework for the

---

*I would like to note two interesting problems that have not yet received much experimental attention.

1. If there is a given objective probability that a desired act will result in an undesired event, what is the subjective probability of the undesired event? Further, if the undesired event occurs and there is a certain objective probability that one can nullify its bad consequences, does this affect the subjective probability of the undesired event? For example, if a nation wished to cheat on a nuclear test ban treaty and there was actually a 20 per cent chance of it being caught, what would this percentage appear to be? If it were caught but had a 50 per cent chance of escaping a penalty, how would this affect the looks of the percentage? We know little about how such probabilities interact. (I am indebted to Thomas Lough of the Arms Control and Disarmament Agency for posing this interesting problem.)

2. There are several indications that if a person must take risks on essentially chance events, he will develop superstitions — that is, he will believe the chance is not really chance but can be known or controlled. When an essentially chance event is assumed to be determined, a number of distortions are introduced. For example, as information accumulates about an originally unknown system one will be more influenced by recent events whereas one should take all the information into equal account. Likewise, one may fail to add and multiply probabilities correctly. Does this occur regularly when officials attempt to interpret the actions of other nations?

statement of some important observations. Using the model Simon[6] has pointed out that a decision is harder to make if the alternatives have equal utility, or if they involve unacceptable outcomes or unknown probabilities. Likewise, while a decision may be easier to make if one has more information, getting this may cost time, money and loss of momentum, hence, it may be more useful to make the decision in the absence of the information. The model also reminds one to search for any factors that will affect the utility of an outcome and to specify the factors that influence the discrepancies between subjective and objective probability.

It is possible to conceptualize important decisions in terms of the utility model. For example, one can think of the President's decision to keep a ceiling on the 1950 defense budget as a rather calculated choice of that alternative. There is no doubt that the President did attempt to weigh the probability of continued Soviet expansion and the probability of an economic or political disaster, and that these possible outcomes had calculable negative utilities (costs). As a rough approximation of the decision, it would not be too distorting to outline it as follows:

Expected Utility of Alternative$_1$ (keep the ceiling) = [probability Soviet expansion $(2/10) \times$ utility of Soviet expansion $(-1,000)$] + [probability of economic disaster $(1/10 \times$ utility of economic disaster (-300)] = -230.

Expected Utility of Alternative$_2$ (increase arms budget) = [probability of Soviet expansion $(1/10 \times$ utility of Soviet expansion $(-1,000)$] + [probability of economic disaster $(8/10) \times$ utility of economic disaster (-300)] = -340.

Looking at the decision in this way, we would say that the President chose alternative$_1$ (keeping the ceiling) because it had a higher expected utility (in this case, a lower cost).

Furthermore, we may consider that some important factors that influenced the decision, did so by affecting variables in the utility model. Thus, the director of the budget decreased the expected utility of alternative$_2$ by increasing the probability of economic disaster. And the bias we have observed in subjective probabilities may have operated to artificially lower the already low objective probability of economic disaster in alternative$_1$.* Now, of course, nobody actually obtained the utilities and probabilities which we have inserted in the model, but

---

*Remember that low negative probabilities are perceived to be lower than they actually are, whereas high negative probabilities are perceived accurately.
[6]Simon, *op. cit.*

measurements could have been made, and they probably would have shown values similar to those we have estimated.

The need for other models of decision making

While the utility model is easily conceptualized and allows us to get a grip on the decision making process, it does not seem to match a closer inspection of what actually occurs when a person is making a decision. In assuming that each outcome has a given value the model says nothing about how an outcome happens to have that particular value and implies that the association is reasonably stable. We shall see that this is not so; rather, the value of an outcome depends on the *meaning* of the outcome and, hence, on the goals of the person and on the context in which it is perceived. Likewise, the model implies that the estimation of likelihood of an outcome is reasonably stable and does not fluctuate as the person turns from one outcome to another. Finally, in picturing a person as weighing the alternatives before him, the model draws our attention away from the formation of the alternatives — an aspect of decision making that may hold the key to how the decision is made.

If we take a closer look at the 1950 budget decision, we can see how the above factors may be important; for the President does not, in fact, seem to have confronted the decision in the way we conceptualized it. It appears that he went about it as follows: The President believed that the government should not engage in deficit financing, and he took some pride in the fact that he had been able to reduce the national debt in the two preceding years. He also believed that the United States had to maintain its Armed Services in order to discourage further Soviet expansion. However, he did not ask how much money this would take. Rather, he allotted as big a chunk of money for defense as he could without giving up his idea of reducing a small amount of the national debt. Now, the Secretary of Defense claimed that more money was needed for defense. Had the money been relatively available the President would have given him more. But the Director of the Budget said that the money was not available. Since the Secretary of State did not support the estimate of the Secretary of Defense, the President determined that the latter's estimate was more a result of interservice wrangling than sophisticated judgment. He therefore determined that there was enough money for defense — and certainly as much as he could afford without giving up his belief in sound fiscal policy.

Thus, rather than choosing the alternative with the most utility the President created the best alternative he could in order to satisfy *all* his interests. He had to compromise a bit and not reduce the deficit as much as he would have liked, he had to resist some pressure from the Secretary of Defense, he had to distort probabilities a bit by perceiving the Secretary of Defense's judgment to be quite biased — but basically he was satisfied and not in conflict. His decision was not really a choice between two hard alternatives; it was the creation of the best course of action which he could achieve under the circumstances.

Returning now to the utility model, we might postulate that the model only applies when a person is confronting alternative means to achieve a given end — for example, the maximization of monetary gain. That is, if the various outcomes are not valued for themselves but for their use attaining an end, a sort of market value can be assigned to them. This will be relatively constant so that some alternatives will be "worth" more, probabilities of occurrence will not be unduly distorted, and there will be no need for a person to create an integrative alternative. However, when the person is confronting alternative ends we must construct a different model to explain his actions.*

To see why a utility model will be applicable when the decision is between alternative means but not when it is between alternative ends, we must examine the differences among "means," "ends," and "interests." We may define "means" as actions or objects that allow ends to be attained. For example, a match or a lighter may be a means to smoking a cigarette. Means have the property of substitutability; that is, a person is indifferent to what means he uses, as long as his end is efficiently attained and some other end is not violated. Means have no intrinsic value; they are only useful in attaining ends. The utility of different means depends on the relative usefulness of each means in helping a person reach his end or goal. Money is an example of means *par excellence,* for it is worthless in itself but is a means to a variety of ends. This is why most experiments with the utility model have used monetary alternatives.

An "end," or goal, may be defined as a desired state of affairs that governs a person's actions until it is attained. For example, smoking a cigarette or helping another person *may* be an end. "Ends" have the property of emotionality; that is, a person has a specific emotion in

---

*In a similar fashion, the utility model will hold if a person has a rule to apply to a situation, but not if the person must create a new response. For example, a rule for action might be: if situation A occurs, do x; if situation B occurs, do y. Here the person in effect has one end that will be best met by x means if situation A occurs, and by y means if situation B occurs. His only decision (which may be a hard one) is whether A has occurred or B has occurred. We considered such detection problems in the chapter on perception, and the reader can now see that Swet's detection model is essentially a utility model.

connection with any end. The different emotions may be defined in terms of the different states of affairs that can be desired. Thus, fear may be defined as a desire to escape an object, admiration as a desire to be like an object, and so forth. The desired state of affairs or the object involved has value. The value of an end is dependent on the strength and centrality of the interests it serves. While ends vary in value, it is difficult for a person to substitute one end for another.

"Interests" may be considered as dormant concerns that become active whenever an event may affect them. For example, if a person has an "interest" in another person (perhaps, is in love), he has a dormant concern about the other that becomes activated if the other is threatened or if he sees a chance to give something to the other, etc. The activated concern may then lead to the "end" of protecting or helping the other. Interests have the property of belongingness; that is, a person possesses interests. Indeed, Chein* notes that a person's self is composed of many different interwoven interests so that if a person changes his interests he changes his self. "Interests" also have centrality. A peripheral "interest" (such as a liking for spaghetti) is usually called an attitude, while a central "interest" (such as love for another person, or one's self-respect) is usually called a sentiment.

The relationship between interests (or self) and end is quite different from the relationship between end and means. The latter is quite straightforward. Given an end, the person searches for the most useful means to fulfill his valued end and *selects* this means. As we have noted, one means may be easily substituted for another with little objection. The former is more complex. At any moment of time, the person may be in a situation that affects many of his interests. He must coalesce or focus these interests on one particular end that satisfies as many interests as possible. For example, a person may be in a situation that activates an interest in food, an interest in a friend, and an interest in relaxing. This pattern of interests may focus on the end of having dinner with his friend. The person must create an end that satisfies many interests. The fact that an end must serve many different interests is one of the reasons why one end is not substitutable for another. The interrelations among means, end, and interests may be diagrammed as in Figure 2.

Now consider how a conflict between two possible ends must differ from a conflict between means. In a simple conflict of means, there is just one end (for example, to make money) and a conflict between two alternatives, each of which may provide the means of accomplishing this

---

*cf. Isidor Chein's concept of "perpetuated motives." ("The Image of Man," *Jour. of Social Issues,* 18 (1962), pp. 1-35.)

Figure 2. *The relationships among means, end, and interests.*

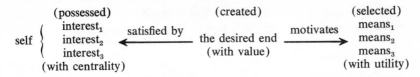

end (for example, two different possible bets). In this case, the utility model applies and tells us that a person will choose the alternative means that has the greatest expected utility — that is most likely to provide the best means to satisfy his end. This type of conflict rarely exists in a pure form because, even when there is only one major end, each of the possible means often has some intrinsic value as well as some utility — that is, the means are also ends, and these ends may be in conflict. As Verba[7] has observed,

> . . . individuals do not have a clear set of value preferences that exist independently of the situation and can be matched against a variety of alternatives to see which gives the best value outcome. Instead one's values depend in part upon the situation one is facing and what is attainable in that situation. In actual policy decisions, as Lindblom points out, means and ends are not isolated from each other and handled independently.

However, this simple "utility conflict" is a useful approximation whenever a person perceives a situation in such a way that only one of his major ends is operative. Many business decisions fulfill these conditions, since the profit motive is usually predominant. However, even in these cases, other ends may become relevant; and in most political decisions, the mixture of important conflicting ends necessitates a more complex model.

Many important decisions involve conflicts between ends. The person is confronted with alternatives involving outcomes that advance some of his interests but hinder others. Such a conflict cannot be settled simply by choosing the end that satisfies the most interests, because other interests will remain unsatisfied. In a conflict between ends, any worthwhile end will satisfy some interests but not others. Even when one end is much more valuable than another, a person hesitates to sacrifice the lesser end, because it too satisfies some of his interests and is emotionally involving.

---

[7]Sidney Verba, "Assumptions of rationality and non-rationality in models of the international system," *World Politics,* 14 (1961), pp. 93-117.

Since a person will not want to give up either end, we may tentatively surmise that the person will try to form an alternative that will satisfy all of his interests or at least cope with them. Until he can do this, he will be incapable of making up his mind and acting. Note that our model now emphasizes the formation of a new end rather than the act of choosing.

Creating a viable end

A small number of investigators have attempted to carefully examine some of their own decisions in order to specify what occurs during the decision process. Schuetz[8] has added his insights to those of Dewey and Bergson to give us an excellent summary of how a person makes a decision. Their description of the process essentially involves four factors:

First, each alternative is projected into the future so that one can imagine all the possible outcomes it may lead to. Thus, Dewey states, ". . . . each conflicting habit and impulse takes its turn in projecting itself upon the screen of imagination. It unrolls a picture of its future history of the career it would have if it were given head."

Second, one reacts to this picture of the future — the outcomes may look attractive or repulsive, may cause satisfaction or annoyance. The weighing of an outcome is determined by evaluating it against some pre-existing frame of reference — one's interests and whether the outcome is an advance or retreat, relative to one's present position.

Third, one returns from this projected trip into the future and begins to consider another alternative — projecting what its possible outcomes might be. However, as Bergson and Schuetz note, one's self has changed in the process of exploring the previous alternative — one has grown older and enlarged his experience. Hence, the new alternative, or the old alternative one is re-exploring, do not appear in the same light; new outcomes are imagined and may be reacted to in different ways.

Fourth, there eventually emerges a preference that permits one to act. Dewey points out that this choice ". . . is the emergence of a unified preference out of competing preferences." That is, the alternative that is finally enacted must somehow provide some satisfaction for many of one's interests. One cannot force the choice. While one can side with one of the alternatives, one cannot proceed until the others get a fair trial. Until all the demands are met in some fashion, one cannot *intend* to carry out one of the alternatives.

---

[8]Alfred Schuetz, "Choosing among projects of action," *Philosophy and Phenomenological Research,* 12 (1951), pp. 161-85.

This commitment process is an intriguing one. As Bergson indicates, one should not think of an ego hesitating between alternatives and finally choosing one of them. Rather, the ego ". . . lives and develops by its very hesitation until the free action detaches itself from it like too ripe a fruit."

Let us carefully examine an example of decision making in order to see how the above conceptualization applies and whether we can add to it. Unfortunately, we do not possess careful introspection from a President or a Secretary of State making an important policy decision, but for our present purposes an ordinary citizen making a trivial decision will furnish all the material we need. In the example which we shall consider, a person was trying to decide whether to buy a cast iron stove or a sheet metal stove to heat his summer cabin in Maine.

Initially, the person decided on a cast iron stove because it looked more handsome and rugged, would hold heat longer, and was not as hazardous as the sheet metal stove. However, when he tried to purchase a cast iron stove, he found that the price of new stoves was too high (about $50.00), and that the few second hand stoves available were the wrong shape or size. Thus, budgetary and asethetic interests blocked the action. A friend then urged him to purchase a sheet metal stove; this could be done for only $5.00. The friend argued that such a stove was not dangerous in the summertime when it would not be crammed with wood. Furthermore, the sheet metal stove was more useful in the summer since it would rapidly take the chill off the cabin and would not retain heat into midday. In spite of all the arguments for a sheet metal stove, the person could not bring himself to buy such a stove because of its poor looks. He associated the handsome ruggedness of a cast iron stove with the coast of Maine and the character of its people. He had a strong interest in having the stove "fit with its surroundings." Finally, however, he brought himself around to also liking the sheet metal stove. He accomplished this by stressing the fact that Maine lobstermen often used sheet metal stoves in their cabins on the offshore islands. Thus, the sheet metal stove came to represent the hardy ingenuity of the Maine lobstermen and took on an "it's not handsome but it sure works" quality where the ugliness of the stove actually added to its charm. The sheet metal stove was immediately purchased. Note that by changing the meaning of the looks of the stove, the interest in a handsome stove was bypassed so that a decision could be made.

The next day, the person discovered a second hand cast iron stove that had the exact shape and size he had desired, and cost only $10.00! Had he seen this stove before he purchased the sheet metal stove, he would have been overjoyed and would have bought it immediately. As it was, he noticed all the rust that would have to be scraped off, he thought of the time it would take to return the other stove, he remembered that a cast iron stove was not really as useful for summer heating. Still — the stove was exactly what he had wanted, and it was so much better looking. But Maine lobstermen used sheet metal stoves. He stood in indecision. His wife, who was mainly concerned about the relative safety of the two stoves, supported the idea of purchasing the cast iron stove. The old farmer selling the stove praised its iron — "they don't make them like this nowadays" — and came down to $9.00. The person then remembered that this type of stove was used in logging camps. He worked his imagery around to again support the ruggedness of the cast iron, log taking stove. With some feeling of effort, he bought the stove.

Still, he could not really shake off the imagery supporting the sheet metal stove. It was really more useful in the summer; and, although he set to work to clear the rust off the cast iron stove, he hedged his decison by thinking that he could always keep the other stove and sell the cast iron one if it did not prove useful. Fortunately, the battle between the two stoves was settled by a friend who took one look at the sheet metal stove and said exactly the right thing. "Why," he said, "that doesn't look like a stove, it looks like a chemical toilet." This remark dealt a mortal blow to the image of the sheet metal stove. It *did* look like a chemical toilet. The looks of the sheet metal stove had always been its weakest point, and the reinvigoration of the interest in looks made it no longer possible to argue that its ugliness added to its charm. The stove was immediately returned to the store, and the cast iron stove was regarded with pride — although it should be noted that there were still some lingering doubts about its functional quality, until it proved itself by heating up the cabin "just as quickly as a sheet metal stove would have done."

Note that the decision between a sheet metal and cast iron stove was not simply one about which stove would have the most utility, but one that involved a conflict of interests. If the person had simply wanted to efficiently heat his summer cabin at the lowest possible cost, the sheet metal stove would have had the greatest utility. If the person had simply wanted the stove that looked nicest, the cast iron stove would have had the greatest utility. But it is apparent that the person had interests in an efficient, inexpensive, nice looking stove that also fit in with its surroundings and with his image of himself as a hardy, independent, ingenious person. Faced with the fact that neither alternative could satisfy all of his interests, the person attempted to maximize his interests by adjusting the meaning of each alternative. Each alternative, then, picked up a cluster of meanings and accordingly became more or less attractive. As we have seen, the cluster of meanings may shift fairly rapidly to affect the value of the alternative.

Now we may observe all the factors suggested by our conceptualization of the decision making process. The person imagined owning each of the stoves and thought of many different possible outcomes — the sheet metal stove looking bad, the cast iron stove fitting his image of Maine, the cast iron stove not heating quickly enough, the sheet metal stove being a fire hazard. To each of these outcomes there was a reaction of distaste or pleasure, and in the course of exploring an alternative, the person emerged with changed attitudes. We may also add the observation that biases or inclinations were present — at first, in favor of the cast iron stove; later, slightly in favor of the sheet metal stove. We should note that the bias could not force a decision until all the opposing arguments were considered.

However, perhaps the most interesting aspect of the account is the large amount of activity invested in the commitment process — activity spent in insuring that the ultimate decision would satisfy most of the relevant interests. The person was obviously working hard to make one of the alternatives solid enough so that a decision could be made and he could act. Thus, when he was trying to build up the alternative of buying the sheet metal stove, he countered the idea that it was a fire hazard by thinking of how he could place asbestos at strategic places. Likewise, the poor looks of the stove were converted into a virtue by tying them into an image of himself as a practical man who could sacrifice looks for utility. Later, confronted by the fact that the other alternative had new arguments in its favor, he again had to work actively so that a new decision could be reached. Thus, he got assurances of help in scraping the rust off the cast iron stove, he had to tear down the image of the sheet metal stove, and he built up the meaningfulness of the cast iron stove by imagining it in a lumber camp.

We must, therefore, amplify on our conceptualization of the commitment process; there is much activity behind Bergson's ripening fruit. First, we must recognize the existence of an emotional bias or indication that often seems to exist for one of the alternatives. Then, there are forces compelling us to pay attention to arguments which we would like to ignore and which prevent us from reaching a decision. Caught between these forces, a person actively attempts to answer the opposing arguments within him. He tries to provide a means of handling objections; and, above all, he attempts to change the meaning of outcomes so that interests that cannot be met will not be as salient and can be circumvented by the promotion of substitute interests. Until the person can cope with all the arguments in some fashion or other, he cannot make up his mind.

The function of meaning and emotion

The above example is one in which the person had some difficulty in making up his mind. It may be objected that decisions are often relatively easy to make and that a decisive person does not usually go through the conflict we have described. In such cases, we note that the person finds it relatively easy to set priorities so that the decision is governed by some central principle. For example, the President made his decision to limit the 1950 arms budget on the principle that the national debt should not be increased. Nevertheless, I believe that a close examination of such decisions will always reveal the process we have just observed in "slow motion." That is, when we are decisive we simply rapidly structure the meanings of the outcomes in a way that meets most of our interests and prevents opposing interests from "having a good argument." Furthermore, this is often accomplished by somewhat distorting the meaning of the situation.

Now that we are alerted to these features of decision making, let us quickly review the President's decision to put a ceiling on the 1950 defense budget. Note that the President mobilized a number of his interests behind the idea of a ceiling — interests such as his fiscal interest in reducing the national debt, his political interest in preventing the Republican opposition from reducing taxes, and his personal pride in being an effective administrator. He met his opposing interests — adequate defense against communist expansion — by believing that the defense budget was adequate and that the Secretary of Defense was not exerting enough leadership in stilling interservice rivalry. To cap it off, he probably believed that the ceiling would force the defense department to function more efficiently and would thus help both his interest in reducing the debt and his interest in effective defense.

We must emphasize that in this view of decision making we do not view the person as having a hierarchy of values and making his choice by selecting the alternative that meets his highest value. On the contrary, the person mobilizes his interests to support an end, and the commitment to that end decides what will be valued.

In creating an alternative that meets his momentary interests, a person must cope with a number of constraints that insure his attention to crucial side interests. He is, in fact, in a whole network of important relationships. Some of the most important of these are his various roles and the responsibilities these entail. The President, for example, is making decisions primarily as President. That is, he cannot decide on the basis of what is in his best personal interest; he must think in terms of what is best for the entire nation. While, of course, he will have a very personal view of what is best for the nation, all his thinking (or at least communications with others) must be argued in terms of what is good for the nation rather than what is good for himself.

We shall examine some of the constraints this poses later in this chapter. The relationship of an individual to this office is not a simple one. He may be in touch with the desires of his constituents or arbitrarily impose his own values. He may accept his authority and make decisions or simply work with past rules. In the next chapter, we shall see that how an individual fills his role is a function of differing personality dynamics. President Roosevelt, for example, filled the office in quite a different way than did President Truman.

The President is also in the position of being the head of his political party and, perhaps, also the head of his personal family. He has his own personal financial interests, his own personal ambitions, and his own reference groups. Finally, he may have a responsibility to some personal ideals and to the dictates of his own conscience.

In trying to formulate an alternative that can cope with whatever interests are momentarily salient, a person comes up against emotional forces that prevent the violation of any of the above latent interests and encourage their observance. If he begins to abandon his responsibility for the nation or fails to follow his personal conscience, he may feel ashamed or guilty. If he fails to act, he may feel depressed. If his decisions fit his image of himself and the nation, he may feel proud or elated. These emotional forces are often overlooked because the felt emotion, like the top of an iceberg, is but an indication of the emotional power that underlies the current of thought and sways decisions. To get an inkling of the forces involved, it is usually necessary to imagine a decision other than the one that occurred. Imagine the President deciding *not* to intervene in the Korean War. Before the Korean Invasion, the President was proud of being a man who was successfully reducing the national debt, but if he had maintained this image of himself instead of defending Korea his pride would have turned to shame. If other national needs had forced him not to resist, he might have become depressed. Given his interpretation of the invasion as a blatant act of Soviet aggression, if he had yielded to political considerations he would have felt quite guilty about not intervening. He would never have forgiven himself for the responsibility of thus encouraging an aggressor.

To say that emotions guide us in the making of most important decisions, is not to imply that these decisions are "emotional." On the contrary, the majority of decisions are cool, rational affairs based on hard logical reasoning. *But,* all that reasoning is an attempt to create an alternative that will satisfy one's interests without disturbing an underlying structure of highly emotionally charged relationships. Even group decisions are strongly affected by underlying emotional elements. Within a group a common emotion may suddenly make a new consensus possible. Thus in assessing the unanimity within the State Department that made it possible to change American policy and quickly intervene in Greece and Turkey in 1948, Jones[9] mentions the feeling of pride. He states, "During those weeks of tough decisions and hard-headed thinking, emotion — proceeding from a realization that world power was at that moment changing hands — was not far from the surface." Contrariwise, one of the main forces the Department had to overcome was the emotion of resentment in persons who did not want to have to decide to support autocratic governments.

Since a person must attend to the emotional consequences of his decision he will act on an alternative only if it "feels right" to him. Thus, his anticipation of the positive and negative emotions which stem from his important relations to others, guides him in his choice. He cannot act until he manages to formulate an alternative with a meaning that satisfies his diverse interests and his emotional relationships.

With all of his various interests clamoring for recognition and a number of important emotional relationships demanding attention, the person does not make a choice as much as he supervises some very active processes. In order to act, he must take the reality of the situation that confronts him and *give it a meaning* that both fits the objective structure of the situation and meets his interests and emotions. When the stove buyer gave the sheet metal stove a meaning of efficiency, he mobilized his interest in a useful stove and his interest in his own image as a practical person; later, when he gave it the meaning of a chemical toilet, he mobilized his aesthetic interests against it. When the President placed a ceiling on the defense budget, he gave his action a meaning of efficiency not only for the nation's financial welfare but also for the long range welfare of the defense department. The reader should note this close connection between the decision process and the perceptional process. From a functional point of view, they are completely intertwined, for the decision we make must be congruent with the meaning we give to a situation.

---

[9]Joseph Jones, *The Fifteen Weeks* (New York: The Viking Press, 1955), p. 130.

The possibility of error

Just as a perception or a plan may or may not fit the objective structure of a situation, so a decision may be more or less correct. Just as a consensus may permit the nation to act without guaranteeing the realism of its plans, so the fact that a person may formulate an alternative that mobilizes his interests and permits him to act, does not guarantee his decision to be correct.

When an individual makes a personal decision, he enhances some of his interests more than others and this, in a sense, helps define what his strong interests are and establishes his identity. When the President makes a presidential decision, he promotes what he sees as the nation's interests and thus helps define what the national interests are. There are two possible errors that can be made: First, in his endeavor to mobilize his own or national interests, the person may give an incorrect meaning to the situation. Second, in his endeavor to stay in touch with the objective situation and yet act, the person may fail to establish certain interests which he really should have.

Speaking quite generally, both of these errors seem to be seriously affecting post-World War II policy. First, as we shall see in Chapter 8, the President has frequently been able to make effective decisions only by giving a situation the meaning of "stopping communism," regardless of the objective structure of the situation. Second, as we shall note in Chapter 9, no American President has really established a national interest in international law.

Factors preventing decision change

We have noted that in order to act — to make the decision — a person must both perceive the situation in a way that supports the decision and arrange the meanings of the various outcomes that might occur. As soon as he acts (and not before), these perceptions and meanings become frozen in the form that supports the decision — just as a verbal label fixes the way we perceive a form. While there may be thirty variables involved in the decision, perhaps only seven can be held in the mind at one time. These seven are organized in an ideal way when the decision occurs and fixes them. The freezing acts to prevent a different perception of the situation or its meaning and, hence, a revision of the decision.

In addition to this "freezing" factor, Lewin[10] has noted that the very fact of acting has placed the person in a new position — a position with

[10]Kurt Lewin, *Principles of Topological Psychology* (New York: McGraw-Hill, 1936), p. 29.

its own perspective. The person now perceives new facts and becomes concerned with new problems that change the whole focus of his concern.

Once the President had acted to send ground troops into Korea, he was in the position of having to wonder how far these troops should go — a whole new set of problems occupied his attention. He was no longer a man reducing the national debt but rather a man stopping Soviet aggression. Such a man would hardly decide to reverse the decision to commit troops.

A further conservative factor stems from the fact that, once a decision is made, other decisions are based upon it. Cardozo[11] has noted the importance of this fact in judicial decisions. He states,

> Until the sentence was pronounced, it was as yet in equilibrium. Its form and content were uncertain. Any one of many principles might lay hold of it and shape it. Once declared it is a new stock of descent. It is charged with vital power. It is the source from which new principles or norms may spring to shape sentences thereafter.

Now, if the primrary decision is questioned the whole structure of decisions and actions may have to be changed. Hence, there is much resistance against changing the initial decision. The resistance may abate if a solution to the problems handled by the other decisions can be presented so that the person sees that the whole structure will not be vitiated if the initial decision is changed.

Still another factor that works to prevent a person from changing a decision is his own set of reactions to his post-decisional conflict. While a person may have temporarily dealt with the forces opposing a decision and formed a course of action that permitted a decision in spite of pre-decisional conflict, these opposing interests are still present and may create post-decisional conflict. These opposing forces may be compounded by the fact that the decision may have actually led to certain unfortunate consequences. This post-decisional conflict must be handled: wronged friends must be compensated, guilt must be expiated, and dissonance in general must be reduced. The very process of compensating, expiating, and making up good reasons for the decision, may solidify the decision. A person with post-decisional conflict is alert to many means of reducing dissonant thoughts. For instance, in the decision for the cast iron stove, the person had some dissonance about his final choice of the cast iron stove because of the idea that it would not heat as quickly. This dissonance was reduced — first, by seizing on the idea

---

[11]Cardozo, *op. cit.*, p. 22.

that the sheet metal stove looked like a chemical toilet; second, by observing that the cast iron stove really did heat quickly because its stove pipe radiated heat. The pressure to reduce dissonance acts as another force against considering elements that might lead to the decision being changed.

As we noted in Chapter 2, Festinger[12] has proposed that all ideas conflicting with a person's decision are sources of discomfort. If there are many arguments in support of a decision and few that are opposed, the "dissonance" is low and has little effect. If the decision is a "close one" and the relative number of opposing arguments is high, then the person will be on the alert to seek favorable and avoid unfavorable ideas. When dissonance is high, a person will distort reality to provide new arguments for a decision made on quite different grounds. Festinger has observed that dissonance is lessened if a person can psychologically separate himself from his action, either by admitting a wrong choice or by denying responsibility for the action. In line with this point is the fact that after the Korean decision the President continually insisted that there *was no choice* except to fight in Korea.

These factors that prevent an individual from changing his decision, are one aspect of the fact that organizational decisions are hard to change. In the last chapter, we noted how an organizational decision tends to persist for two different reasons: First, because of a momentum factor, in that difficulties of obtaining a consensus give pause to anyone who thinks of trying to change the consensus that is working at the moment. Second, because of a hysteresis in the system, in that each individual in the organization changes when he makes his individual decision to join the consensus, and changes in a way that resists a reversal of the decision.

Distortions in the decision process

We have seen how the individual attempts to formulate an alternative that will meet all of his values so that he can overcome restraining forces and act. In many cases, at least one of the elements being considered will prove resistant to the favored alternative and to any kind of rational manipulation. In the case we considered in some detail, the fact that the sheet metal stove would heat and cool more rapidly made it more functionl for taking the chill off the cabin, and, hence, resisted the dominant idea of buying a cast iron stove. There was no way this

---

[12]Leon Festinger, *A Theory of Cognitive Dissonance* (Stanford, Calif.: Stanford University Press, 1957).

fact could be changed. In such cases, the person may begin to distort reality so that commitment can occur — i.e., so he can make up his mind and proceed. Thus, in our sample case, the person imagined the cast iron stove in a lumber camp in *winter*. He focused his thoughts about this image — in which the cast iron stove was decidedly superior — and conveniently overlooked the fact that he was buying a stove for summer use. This distortion permitted him to make a decision that was in accord with the majority of his needs.

Little is known about exactly how distortions occur. We have indicated how interests keep pressing to be represented in a decision and how they will not permit the person to ignore them and commit himself to an alternative that will damage them — no matter how favorable the alternative is in other respects. In order to make a decision and stay in contact with reality, the person must either accept the situation as unfavorable to some of his interests and respectfully postpone the actualization of those interests, or permanently give up some of his interests. The alternative is to distort reality or his course of action so that he fools himself into believing the damaged interests have actually been represented. Two questions immediately confront us: *when* is one able to accept the situation or give up interests rather than fool himself, and *how* can one fool oneself?

We know that the President was able to give up his interest in balancing the budget in favor of resisting Soviet aggression, and we do not detect a distortion in this process; that is, the President does not seem to have thought that he would not have to give up his budget. However, the President did not really give up his interests in saving American lives. Rather, he (1) put off the commitment of troops and (2) told himself that in the long run his action would save lives; he also seems to have (3) underestimated the number of American lives that would be lost.

Likewise, the stove buyer was able to give up his image of the sheet metal stove as "ingenious and looks be bammed" without making any distortions, but was unable to give up his interest in a stove that was efficient, and had to delude himself by imagining the cast iron stove in winter.

Perhaps distortion is more likely when interests cannot be postponed and have to be completely given up. It may also be true that distortions occur when the unfulfilled interests are particularly strong or linked to the very interests that sway the decision.

How does one manage to fool oneself so that the demands of the unfulfilled interests are overlooked? Why were the unfulfilled interests strong enough to prevent a straightforward decision but not able to refute such obvious errors as large underestimates of casualties and the turning of summer into winter? Let us take a microscopic look at a portion of yet another decision to see the distortion process at close hand.

A graduate student who lives in the city close to his university, gets a chance to rent a charming house in the country with the additional room which his growing family requires. The rent is about the same as he is currently paying. He is biased towards moving — if he passes up the chance he will regret it — but is prevented from commitment by a series of factors: (1) his best friends are in the city; (2) he has an image of himself as a scholar busy at a university, and this image conflicts with being "comfortable" in the country; (3) commuting expenses would add $30 a month to his budget; and (4) the commuting trip into the city takes an hour and fifteen minutes during non-rush hours.

The first argument was easily handled by imagining how he could invite city friends to visit in the country over the weekend. The second argument was initially met by imagining spending long hours at the university. The third argument was largely overlooked — the student kept forgetting that commuting costs money. Whenever he added up the relative costs of the two living arrangements, his wife had to bring up the commuting cost. She would then think of how they could save some money by sponging a free meal off her parents, who lived near the country house. In spite of the fact that this could hardly save $30 a month, the idea somehow enabled the commuting cost to be momentarily forgotten. If the thought re-arose, the $30 a month was translated into "it's a *little* more money." On the rare occasions when this did not work, the student decided he would ride to work in a car pool — thus cutting almost all the commuting costs.

The fourth argument, the length of the commuting trip, proved the stickiest. First, the fact that the trip was one hour and fifteen minutes in non-rush hours, was slightly changed to "it's an hour's commute." Then the student decided he could work on the trip — could read or learn a required foreign language. He knew he could not read on the bus, so he visualized taking the train into work or working late and sleeping on the bus. Notice that he could neither work nor sleep well if he joined a car pool; but the idea of a car pool was not considered except when commuting expenses confronted him, at which time he overlooked that he could not work or sleep in the car pool. In spite of this maneuvering, the student knew he was not going to like commuting. He told himself, "People spend forty or fifty minutes coming in from suburbs that aren't half as nice as the country." Finally, he began to question coming into work every day. At this point, the second argument — that of being a scholar — arose again. This argument was met by the idea that he could study in the country house. It is interesting to note a failure to plan for certain contingencies at this point. For example, the student had a small lively boy who would have made studying at home impossible except on nice days when he could have been shuttled outside. Needless to say, in the student's fantasy the days were nice ones.

Finally, the objections were chopped down to a manageable size, and the student was almost ready for commitment. At this point, he utilized his wife to start the process. Since he knew she also had a bias to make the move, he asked her to imagine going and then pulled back a little, saying "Maybe we should make a list of pros and cons." The sight of her disappointment catapulted him into the decision. It is interesting to note how often a decision is helped along by asking for the advice of a friend whose advice we know will be in the right direction.

Note that distortions occurred by a sort of shuttling process. When a problem is posed, the person counters with an argument that exposes another problem — but one that is not salient at the moment. By moving rapidly, the person prevents the opposition from making a case. There are so many factors which the person can manipulate, that he befuddles the opposition so that commitment can occur. A sort of "divide and conquer" principle is used, each argument of the opposition being answered by an argument that is good but not consistent with the arguments used in other places.

It is interesting to note that this same shuttling process — with a lack of regard for inconsistency — is the same tactic we use in defending a decision that is criticized by somebody other than ourself. In making the decision to enter the Korean fighting, the President may have used a similar kind of distortion process in order to cope with arguments against using ground forces.

In practice, it may be difficult to distinguish between "distortion" and simple variations in the estimate of reality or interpretation of facts that occur before any decision is made. However, in principle the distinction is clear; a distortion always constitutes a departure from the real structure of the situation, a structure that is accurately reflected in a number of different interpretations. In practice, a distortion is often accompanied by some uncalled-for emotional reaction. Thus, during the Korean decision, the President flared up when one of his advisers mentioned that political factors should be considered, and this probably indicates some distortion tension. Likewise, the Secretary of State seems to have felt that the Chinese Communists had betrayed him by entering the Korean War, and this suggests that some distortion was present in his difficult decision to recommend interposing the Seventh Fleet between the mainland and Formosa.

By using a distortion technique such as "shuttling," the various opposing arguments are contained and prevented from unifying; however, their voices are not completely stifled, and the person must make use of his temporary advantage by committing himself in some way that changes the situation to provide further support for the decision. As we have mentioned, once a stove is actually purchased or armed forces have been sent and suffered casualties, there are new reasons that solidify the decision and commit the decision maker.

In order to remember the sequence of processes in a decision, it is useful to distinguish carefully among "bias" (or inclination), "decision," and "commitment." We can use "bias" to refer to the initial emotional predisposition a person may have towards the favored alternative. While this bias usually provides the basic structure for the decision, it can be substantially changed or even replaced by another bias. We can use the term "decision" to refer to the moment when the alternative is developed enough and the opposition silenced enough to permit the first action to take place — that is, the person "accelerates," or changes direction. This action then begins to "commit" the person to his decision. "Commitment" may be used to refer to the effect of a number of factors that make a decision non-reversible. "Commitment" occurs when the decision itself is made a part of the person's self and the person is willing to suffer the loss involved if the outcome is unfavorable. A decision or change in action may be made without commitment, but until commitment is present the person cannot channel his energy into a fully concentrated effort. Nor can he experience either triumph or defeat.

The Decision in the Context of the Organization

We have already noted that, insofar as the President is performing in his role as President, he makes decisions in what he believes are the national interests rather than his personal interests. The fact that the individual is making his decisions as part of an organization, influences both his decisions and the behavior of the organization.

Presidential decisions

While the basic decision making process is the same, there are special factors that influence a presidential decision. Theodore Sorensen,[13] who

---

[13]Theodore C. Sorensen, *Decision-making in the White House* (New York: Columbia University Press, 1963).

was one of President Kennedy's close aides, has given an excellent summary of these factors. Sorenson points out that presidential decisions are unique in their volume, importance, and difficulty. The nature of the presidential office — the fact that it is a court of last resort — means that the President is confronted with numerous, important, difficult decisions. Easy decisions that do not involve conflict between different interest groups, are settled before they reach the President.

In any important decision, there are constraints that restrict the formation of desirable alternatives. The President, in particular, may be limited by laws, by the necessity of having his alternatives accepted by important co-workers in the executive branch, accepted by the men who must carry it out, accepted by Congress, accepted by public opinion, and accepted by other nations. There are promises, traditions, and precedents that are difficult to break, and any innovation may involve the formation of a new consensus and the creation of new governmental machinery. And, of course, there is a fantastic amount of information which a President should know and that simply cannot be known by one man. The President can spend his resources to alter these constraints and allow action, but the fact that his resources are limited is yet another constraint — there is only so much money, manpower, time, credibility, patronage, etc., available. Therefore, he must set up priorities and choose wisely in order to accomplish the things he deems most urgent.

Within the limits of these constraints, the President must formulate a course of action that satisfies many different political groups. Sorensen[14] notes,

> Politics pervades the White House without seeming to prevail. It is not a role for which the President sets apart certain hours. It is rarely the sole subject of a formal presidential meeting. It is instead an ever-present influence — counterbalancing the unrealistic, checking the unreasonable, sometimes preventing the desirable, but always testing what is acceptable.

The President is in office because he managed to put together an effective group of supporters, and he must continue to maintain support. As a politician and as the head of his party, it is his proper job to reconcile the many different interests that support him.

But he is also the President of *all* the persons in the nation. The office entails a role that makes him responsible for all persons, even the ones

---

[14]*Ibid.*, p. 44.

that vote against him. He cannot choose what he would personally like, because he must choose in his role as President. He is responsible for representing everyone.

The President must try to put all these interests together. Each decision involves many variables that merge and cut across almost all of the nation's major policy areas. Whatever he does will affect everything else. If he appoints a given man to one position, he cannot utilize him elsewhere. Some groups will be pleased, others annoyed, the country may be advanced at the expense of his party, the appointment may increase the chances of some vital program but decrease the possibility of an important bill passing. And each decision involves not only conflicting ends but uncertainty — the appointment *may* have the above effects, but it might also have the opposite effect from what was intended. And yet the decision, and many more of them, must be made. Needless to say, he tries to build a course of action that will maintain his flexibility.

Furthermore, the decisions are important and the responsibility great. Sorensen[15] reminds us,

A President knows that his name will be the label for a whole era. Textbooks yet unwritten and school children yet unborn will hold him responsible for all that happens. His program, his power, his prestige, his place in history, perhaps his re-election, will all be affected by every decision. His appointees, however distinguished they may be in their own right, will rise or fall as he rises or falls. Even his White House aides, who see him constantly, cannot fully perceive his personal stakes and isolation. And no amount of tinkering with the presidential machinery, or establishment of new executive offices, can give anyone else *his* perspective.

He cannot take a vote and do what the majority wants. He himself must integrate and decide. He must lead; his decisions *define* what the national interest is. When a person undertakes such responsibility, when he decides properly, he is quite alone, quite isolated.

The President's decisions, then, are most analogous to the important decisions which any person in authority makes. A surgeon deciding whether to operate, a parent deciding how he should raise his child, or a manager deciding how to run his office, are all in the position of having to reconcile different ends and take the responsibility for a decision which only they can make. It is unfortunate that such decisions have not been been studied in more depth. In the absence of such studies

[15]*Ibid.*, pp. 83-84.

we can only apply what we have learned from the minor personal decisions we have considered. To do this, let us consider the presidential decision to fight in Korea.

Because of Korea's low strategic significance, the President's strong desire to keep a balanced budget, and the fact that Korea was a poor place to fight and was not under announced American protection, the utility of resisting an invasion seemed low. Most officials in Washington, the Commander of the Far Eastern Forces, the allied governments, and the Soviet planners, expected that the President would decide not to fight in Korea. This predictive failure may have been based on the calculation of utility with a failure to examine the President's basic interests.

While at first glance the Korean Invasion might appear to be a simple matter, it can be perceived in a number of different ways. In the previous chapter, we noted how both American and Russian officials failed to anticipate the President's decision because they knew that South Korea was not valued by the United States for either its economic or military significance. Using essentially a utility model, they assumed that the value of one outcome — losing Korea — would remain at a reasonably constant low value. They failed to see that the *meaning* of the outcome could shift so that it would become very important to prevent Korea's loss. However, even with our knowledge that the value of an outcome depends on its meaning and that this meaning will be formed to allow the decision maker to mobilize his interests, the prediction of the decision is not a simple one. To the extent that one had an interest in the containment of communism, one could perceive that it would be foolhardy not to resist the invasion. In this case, one would see that, if the invasion were not resisted, Soviet desires would increase and Soviet officials would learn that planned aggression was a useful way of getting what they wanted. One would also note that Oriental leadership respected power and might begin respecting the Soviet Union more than the United States. And one would see that small nations all over the world might become afraid to stand up to Russian threats since they could not count on American support. Furthermore, the prestige of the United Nations would decline and the idea of collective security would be lost.

On the other hand, to the extent that one had an interest in saving American lives and treasure, one could perceive the invasion so that it would be foolish to resist. One could see that the Soviet Union believed that Korea was a special case, since in terms of a global conflict it had no strategic significance, and since the United States had indicated that it had no formal obligation to defend Korea. Thus, there was no danger of further aggression in any area which the United States did care about — Korea was an isolated instance. One would also see that South Korea was hardly a democratic nation that had to be defended. And one would note that the South Korean government had constantly pressed the United States to give them the strength to invade North Korea so that they could force unification on the country. Thus, one would see the Korean Invasion as part of a civil war and, hence, view the invasion as quite different from a Munich. One would also see that American forces were too weak to successfully resist the invasion, that a mountainous peninsula in Asia was the last place to commit American troops that were needed elsewhere, and that there was a good chance of the intervention failing since the North Korean offensive was rapidly winning the entire peninsula. One would see that one would have to abandon a balanced budget and risk the start of a world war in order to defend an undemocratic nation of no strategic importance.[16]

Now, if one held the first set of perceptions, the utility of fighting would be high; but if one held the second set of perceptions, the utility would be low. Since the President had an interest in *both* stopping Soviet expansion *and* saving American lives and treasure, how could one predict which set of perceptions he would develop? One sees immediately that one would have to imagine different meanings that could be given to the situation and which of these meanings could account for both sets of interests. To do this, one would have to know the President's tolerance for somewhat inexact meanings and the set of emotional relationships that would be called into play.

In fact, the basic bias of the decision — the initial preference for an alternative that involved resisting the invasion—appears to have stemmed from the President's private thought as he flew back to Washington. In his memoirs[17] he notes, "I had time to think aboard the plane. In my generation, this was not the first occasion when the strong had attacked the weak. I recalled some earlier instances: Manchuria, Ethiopia, Austria. I remembered how each time that the democracies failed to act it had encouraged the aggressors to keep going ahead. Communism was acting in Korea just as Hitler, Mussolini, and the Japanese had acted ten, fifteen, and twenty years earlier. I felt certain that if South Korea was allowed to fall, communist leaders would be emboldened to override nations closer to our own shores. If the communists were permitted to force their way into the Republic of Korea without opposition from

---

[16]These arguments, pro and con, have been summarized from William Reitzel, Morton A. Kaplan, and Constance G. Coblenz, *United States Foreign Policy 1945-1955* (Washington: The Brookings Institution, 1956).
[17]Truman, *op. cit.,* p. 33.

the free world, no small nation would have the courage to resist threats and aggression by stronger communist neighbors. If this was allowed to go unchallenged it would mean a third world war, just as similar incidents had brought on the second world war. It was also clear to me that the foundations and the principles of the United Nations were at stake unless this unprovoked attack on Korea could be stopped."

Note how this way of thinking, so adaptive to the interest in checking communist expansion, already began to incorporate the President's other interests, his concern for American life and treasure. For, clearly, a third world war would mean an even greater expenditure of both; and, hence, the alternative of fighting in Korea meant serving these interests as well.

Still, the possible outcome of a war in terms of loss of American life and its inflationary impact on the economy, created a negative force that hindered any immediate decision. Since the President was biased (in the sense of preferring) an alternative that resisted the aggression, he worked to reduce this negative force in several ways. First, with the help of his Joint Chiefs of Staff, he reduced the probability of serious losses or disruption of the economy by minimizing the strength of the North Korean forces and underestimating the size of the American force that would be required. Second, he handled the possibility that the war might escalate into serious proportions by stressing that, if it did, it would eventually come anyway in a worse form if the aggression were not countered. Third, with the help of his Secretary of State, he initially formulated his alternative in a minimal way by conceiving of helping the South Korean Army with equipment and air and sea support.

Perhaps even more important in permitting decisiveness and insuring the President's peace of mind, was a complete dismissal of the idea that Soviet expansion might be different from German or Japanese expansion, that the government in South Korea might not be worth saving, and that the people of Korea might be better off under a unified communist rule. Thoughts of this nature caused no doubts in the President's mind because they were not there.

Growth of a decision in the organization

When a person holds an office in an organization, his decision is affected by the interests of other important office holders; and full organizational commitment cannot occur until these interests are met in some way.

While the core of the President's decision — his initial perception, his inclination towards resistance, and the initial workings towards a course of action that would meet all of his values — seems to have taken place on his plane trip to Washington, this core was not a full commitment. It was still liable to challenges that could force revision of the favored alternative: challenges that might come from other interests which he remembered or from the arguments of others. The initial perception with its favored alternative is at the core of a decision; it contains the decision as a seed contains a tree, but many forces influence its growth.

In the case of the Korean decision, forces began to operate on the President as soon as he stepped off the plane at Washington. He was met by the Secretary and Undersecretary of State and the Secretary of Defense. Reportedly, when the President expressed a determination to prevent the invasion's success, the Secretary of Defense expressed his relief, while the Undersecretary of State urged caution. That night, the President met with a group of his advisers, a meeting which we shall consider in Chapter 6. At the close of the meeting, the President ordered that the American Military Commander of the Far East be authorized to start a crash aid program to the South Koreans, that the United States Naval and Air Forces cover the evacuation of American citizens, that the Joint Chiefs of Staff prepare orders to make some United States forces available (if this were requested by the United Nations),* and that the Seventh Fleet be ordered to proceed to Japanese waters (from the Philippines).

On the next day (Monday), the President was encouraged by the news editorials, most of which argued for action. The American delegate to the United Nations reported that there was a strong support from the United Nations delegates for sterner measures to be taken. The President conferred with the Chairman of the Senate's Committee on Foreign Relations and said that he wanted to review all possible alternatives before involving the nation in war — Korea was a hard place to fight in, but he was not going to tremble and surrender American rights.

The Senate Republican Policy Committee recommended that the United States should give maximum aid but not let the fighting develop into a war. Most officials in Washington thought that, in view of the low strategic value of Korea, the risks from American intervention were too great. There was an atmosphere of "apathetic fatalism."** (This, of course, was not true among the top decision makers, who had met the night before and had a consensus to resist).

---

*According to President Truman's memoirs. Paige states that he finds no evidence of these orders prior to the next night's meeting.
**For comments on the atmosphere, see the June 29, 1950, editions of *The New York Herald Tribune* and *The Christian Science Monitor*.

Monday evening, the President again met with his advisers: it was reported that the capital of South Korea was falling and that South Korean units were unable to resist the North Korean offensive. It was clear that a decision was needed immediately. The President asked the Secretary of State for his recommendations — the ones which we noted were drawn up in solitude. These were that the United States (1) order its Naval and Air Forces to give full support to the fighting south of the 38th parallel, (2) that the Seventh Fleet be ordered to protect Formosa, (3) that the Philippines be strengthened, (4) that military assistance to Indo-China be accelerated, and (5) that these actions be reported to the United Nations.

The Secretary of Defense said that he had nothing to add. The consensus was that Soviet reaction to American Naval and Air Forces was possible but not probable. The advisers felt that the Soviets would be surprised by American intervention and would have no plans to counteract it.

It was felt that the Chinese would not intervene since their troops were disposed towards Formosa and South-East Asia. The Secretary of the Army was concerned about how the American public would react if the Russians did counter the intervention, but this did not become a serious question.

As we have seen, the President's perception led him to consider that a failure to intervene would be appeasement. He believed that one appeasement led to another whereas American firmness in Greece and Berlin had prevented further aggressiveness in those areas. He therefore approved all five of the Secretary of State's suggestions. His advisers were in unanimous approval. In just one hour the meeting was over. The President stated,* "Everything I have done in the last five years has been to try to avoid making a decision such as I had to make tonight."

On Tuesday, the President and Secretary of State briefed fourteen leading congressmen on the action that had been taken. There was no criticism of the action. The news of the action was released to the public. The major public reaction was one of relief and unity. The candidate whom the President had defeated in the 1948 election telegraphed his support. The Senate agreed with the action.

On Thursday, the Secretary of Defense told the President that American air support was hindered by distance, weather, poor liaison, and restriction of activity to south of the 38th parallel. He recommended

---

*According to Beverly Smith "Why we went to war in Korea" *Saturday Evening Post,* (Nov. 10, 1951), p. 80.

that planes be permitted to cross the 38th parallel, that the United States establish a port-airfield in Korea and defend it with troops, and that some American Army signal and transportation units be employed.

These recommendations were sobering ones. While the President had decided to resist the invasion, he had not decided to get *that* involved in the process. His initial bias to fight now had to contend with the arguments of other interests. The desire to "hit them back" and prevent the success of the invasion now had to contend with the desire to avoid committing forces to Korea that might be needed elsewhere. For no matter how much the President believed in discouraging aggression, he also believed in the necessity of defending Europe. As we shall see, this basic conflict continued to play a major role in decisions about Korea and ultimately led to a decision to limit the forces in Korea and accept a forced withdrawal if necessary. Even then, and even now, the conflict between interests elsewhere and interests in Asia continued. As Bauer, Pool and Dexter[18] have documented, the passage of an act, the acceptance of a budget, and even an agreement to go to war, do not signal the end of ongoing controversy. It is never long before the same basic issues return to be fought out anew on a slightly different battlefield.

While the President was worried about getting so committed that American forces could not handle situations that might arise in other more important places, and the Secretary of State was concerned about possible involvement with Soviet forces, the recommendations were accepted — but with the caution that if Soviet forces began to intervene the American forces were not to take the offensive against them. Thus, it appears if the Soviet Union had suddenly committed troops in force, the invasion might not have been resisted with large numbers of ground troops. There were practical limits to the inclination to resist. Of course, the United States might have decided to strike elsewhere in retaliation, but the hard fact of the matter was that its military forces were not really prepared to do much of anything. Had this situation arisen, the different perceptions which we noted in Chapter 2 might have led to a serious split within the administration.

Early Friday morning, the commander of the American Far Eastern Forces contacted the Army Chief of Staff and said that Korea would fall unless the United States committed two infantry divisions to Korea. He said they were needed immediately. The Chief of Staff contacted the Army, who contacted the President at 4:57 A.M. The President,

---

[18]Raymond Bauer, Ithiel de Sola Pool, and Lewis A. Dexter, *American Business and Public Policy* (New York: Atherton, 1963).

who was already up, approved the use of one regimental combat team immediately. He met with his advisers at 9:00 A.M. The President authorized the Far Eastern Commander to use all the forces at his disposal (then four divisions) but reminded him that the security of Japan was still basic. Thus, the President, consistent with his bias, decided to risk American lives in order to halt the invasion. While he could not risk Japan in order to repel the invasion, balancing the budget had finally become a memory rather than a keystone.

It should be noted how the President's perception and inclination hardened into resolution with the press of events *and the support of his advisers, the Congress, the public, the press, and his allies.* Had these elements not supported his earlier tentative moves, the later moves might not have been made. The President's first reaction was the core of his decision, but the opinions of his advisers and the reaction of the Congress were wind, sun, and rain that affected the final product. While this particular decision could best be described as a gradual hardening of resolution, we must not forget that the initial reaction of stopping the invasion was tempered into the resolution of trying to stop the invasion without weakening European defenses.

It must not be thought that all initial reactions harden into a decision. The President's basic bias may even change if the actions that flow from it cannot occur because of lack of support. For example, on Thursday evening, the President of the Republic of China offered 33,000 troops for the Korean fighting. The American President's first inclination was to accept these troops. He wanted to have U. N. troops from all nations fighting in Korea, and of course it would help the sparse American troop situation. The Secretary of State advised against this, pointing out that it would seem strange to have the natural defenders of Formosa fight in Korea while the United States defended Formosa, and that the troops would probably have to be re-equipped. The President was still inclined to accept the troops but waited until Friday morning to bring up the matter with his advisers. The Secretary of State argued that the troops would increase the probability of Chinese communist involvement in the fighting, and that the President of the Republic of China would use the occasion to remove troops of questionable loyalty from Formosa and would try to gain a foothold in the mainland China with American support. The Defense Department also advised non-acceptance of the troops. They argued that the troops would have to be completely re-equipped for the fighting, that American transportation would have to be used to convey them, and that this transportation was scarce and could be better used in the conveyance of American troops. The President reluctantly accepted this advice and declined the offer. His perception of the offer does not seem to have changed, but his advisers changed the action that started to flow from it.

It is worthwhile to note the gradual involvement of the United States into the Korean conflict. As late as Monday night (when the decision was made to give full naval and air support to the South Koreans), because of the continuous underestimation of the seriousness of the situation, not one adviser recommended that American ground troops be committed. Some said they did not wish ground troops committed. It was mentioned that if troops were committed some mobilization would be needed to meet commitments elsewhere. Also, there was full accord that the United States should do only what was necessary to repel the invasion. The worsening military situation caused the United States to gradually become involved in a deeper commitment. And later, having been forced to partially mobilize and having spent so much in lives and money, the United States could not resist crossing the 38th parallel to try to unify Korea — with the disastrous consequences of a much worse war with China.

The gradual involvement of the United States raises an interesting question. If the American decision makers had known at the outset that ground troops and a mobilization would be required, would they have still decided to resist the invasion? If the decision had been approached in terms of short range interests, there would have been great psychological impediments to giving thousands of American lives to prevent the invasion of a relatively worthless piece of real estate. But the decision was approached in terms of principle. The final decision was that communist aggression had to be resisted with whatever forces could be spared from the European theater. Given this fact, it is possible that the invasion might have been resisted even if the full costs could have been foreseen. On the other hand, we saw in the last chapter that early low cost decisions build up a momentum that makes later high cost decisions much easier to make. While experimental evidence is lacking, it would seem that a costly decision is much more apt to be made if a less costly decision (based on the same premises) is made at an earlier date.

Risk taking in the group

There is a general feeling that, while an individual official might be willing to take great risks, the process of consultation and group decision will produce a more moderate, conservative policy. However, some recent experimentation shows that, under some conditions, group decisions may encourage more risk than individual decisions. In a study by Wallach *et al.*,[19] students were given twelve situations to evaluate. For example, they considered a man with a heart ailment who had to curtail his life unless he underwent an operation that would either cure him or prove fatal. Each student indicated how good the chance of success would have to be before he would recommend the operation. Following this judgment, the students met in groups of six, discussed the same situation, and came to a group consensus on the level of chance of success they would require before recommending the risky alternative. Finally, the students were asked to again give their individual opinions — immediately and a week later. In almost every case, groups demanded less chance of success (advised more risk) than their members had required when acting as individuals. This effect was retained so that a week later the individuals advised more risk than they had previously.

The experiments show that the group member who was perceived as being most influential was generally a member who had advised more risk when he was acting as an individual.

An experiment by Marquis[20] used the same general procedure with executives in a training program. Executives considered the same twelve situations as individuals and then met together as a group. However, this time the leader of the group was appointed beforehand. The leader was told that he should run the group discussion, make his own personal decision, and be prepared to defend his decision against the leaders of other groups. The experimenter appointed a leader whose individual risk taking recommendations were closest to the middle of the group he was to lead. In other words, the experimenter insured that the leader be average on "propensity to risk taking" and that the leader realize he was responsible for the final decision. In spite of these precautions, the groups again recommended more risky courses of action than the individual members of the group had previously recommended.

In attempting to explain results such as the above, Kogan and his associates[21] state, "Where there is group discussion to consensus, we would suggest that each member, by drawing support from the others, begins to feel that his fate rests with the group; therefore, greater risk taking is warranted." While there appears to be some merit in this suggestion, it is not clear exactly when it can be applied. Not all group situations have produced greater risk taking; indeed, sometimes the

---

[19]Michael A. Wallach, Nathan Kogan, and Daryl J. Bem, "Group influence on individual risk taking," *J. Abnorm. Soc. Psychol.*, 65 (1962), pp. 75-86.
[20]D. G. Marquis, "Individual responsibility and group decision involving risk," *Industr. Mgmt. Rev.*, 3 (1962).
[21]Wallach, Kogan, and Bem, *op. cit.*, p. 271.

group is more conservative than its individual members.[22] In the realm of foreign policy, for example, it seems clear from Sorenson's[23] account of the Cuban missile crisis that the group exerted a conservative influence which it failed to exert during the consideration of the "Bay of Pigs" invasion of Cuba.

In order to see how a group making foreign policy may take an inordinate risk, let us examine the decisions involved in crossing the 38th parallel and invading North Korea. To understand the first decision to cross the parallel, we must realize that there was a difference between the private and the public decision. The public decision occurred on October 7, when the General Assembly voted that Korea should be unified, and on the following day, when the United States troops crossed the 38th parallel. The private decision occurred, or began to occur, in early September when the amphibious attack on Inchon was under consideration. It was clear that, if the attack should succeed, the Commander of the United Nations forces would need new directions. A National Security Council paper, initialed by the President on September 11, stated that *if* there was no indication or threat of entry of Soviet or Chinese troops in force, then operations should be extended north of the 38th parallel with the plan of occupying North Korea.

At the start of the war, the Secretary of State had clearly stated that his nation's purpose was only to restore the land seized from South Korea. Several forces caused this policy to be reversed. In meeting the North Korean Invasion, lives and money had been expended — more than had been anticipated — and psychologically it seemed proper that the resistance should be rewarded. Then, it was argued that if North Korea were allowed to remain a separate nation, it might launch another invasion at some future date. It was pointed out that the 38th parallel was an artificial line drawn only five years before and intended to be only a temporary division of responsibility between Russia and the United States; before 1945, Korea had been a unit, and it was better for it to be a unit again. The congressional opposition's sentiment for a more aggressive policy in the Far East was probably a factor, particularly in view of the desire for a unified non-partisan foreign policy. And, of course, a sweeping victory in Korea would help the administration in the forthcoming congressional elections, whereas a stop at the parallel might furnish the opposition with a weapon. Still another factor may have been the South Korean leader's intransigence and his determination to unify Korea at any cost. Finally,

[22]Allan Teger and Dean G. Pruitt, "Components of group risk taking," *J. Exp. Soc. Psychol.,* 3 (1967), 189-205.
[23]Theodore C. Sorenson, *Kennedy* (New York: Harper and Row, 1965).

the fact that troops were in Korea, supply lines were functioning, a unified chain of command was in operation, and political prestige was being gained created a momentum that worked to broaden the war.

One wonders whether this decision would have been made as easily if its makers had had more confidence in the forthcoming amphibious landing. The role of uncertainty in the path *before* the decision, has not been investigated experimentally. One would suspect that any misgivings about a decision can be handled by reference to the fact that the decision may not have to be acted upon. Therefore, the fact that the decision may nevertheless commit one to a course of action will be overlooked. We will hypothesize:

When it is not known whether a decision will have to acted upon, the decision makers will make decisions that are objectively more risky.

The amphibious attack of September 15 was a success but not an unqualified one, since portions of the North Korean forces managed to evade the trap and slip back across the parallel into North Korea. By September 22, this pattern was clear and the President's advisers were for pursuing these troops — if no complications arose. The mood of optimism generated by victory, called for further bold acts; time and again in history, the victorious have not known when to stop. On September 27, the Commander of the United Nations forces was informed that his objective was the destruction of all North Korean forces and that he was authorized to cross the 38th parallel — *provided* that when the occasion arose there was no entry of Soviet or Chinese forces, no announcement of intended entry, and no threats of entry. On October 1, South Korean units began to cross the parallel, but American and other troops waited for a decision by the United Nations.

While the decision makers had initially conceived of the issue as one of liquidating all North Korean forces, they were aware that the public, Congress, and the United Nations conceived of the issue as one of crossing the 38th parallel. In addition, the administration felt that the United Nations should provide for the occupation of North Korea. Therefore, on September 21, the President stated that the matter would be brought before the General Assembly. The resolution that was presented to the Assembly carefully avoided commitment in case of Soviet and Chinese intervention and was mainly devoted to creating machinery for Korean reconstruction. The war aim was thus not spelled out but rather assumed by the implication that military action would produce a unified Korea. While the Assembly did not give final approval to unification until October 7, it was clear that it would do so. In fact, nations with troops in Korea had agreed to cross the parallel back in late September. On October 8, the full advance into North Korea was begun.

Notice that the consideration of public opinion and concern for the reactions of other nations had unfortunately established a de facto commitment to unify Korea. This now created a force that somewhat limited the administration's freedom of action.

It should be observed that the orders that reached the United Nations Commander on September 27 specified that authorization to cross the parallel was contingent on the absence of Soviet or Chinese threats to enter the war. This contingency was stressed because the main goal of saving South Korea would be accomplished and the secondary goal of uniting Korea was much less important than the avoidance of an all out war with China or Russia. As we have seen, the administration was determined not to become involved in such a war over Korea. But, after the United Nations' decision to unify Korea, it was no longer so easy to make unification contingent on the Chinese reaction.

Imagine an official who was really worried about Chinese reaction to the invasion of North Korea. One can see him cautiously insist that the decision to invade be made contingent on the absence of Chinese threats. But he cannot argue against presenting unification to the public and to the United Nations. His argument would somehow appear irrational. The best he can do is to word the United Nations' resolution cautiously. Yet this public presentation would begin to commit the nation to the very course of action he fears. Thus, psychological forces cause him to take each step of the process leading him to what he fears.

Now let us examine the Chinese reaction to the parallel crossing. For the first two months of the war, most Chinese statements had hit at the Formosan intervention. On August 17, the American Ambassador to the United Nations stated that all of Korea should be assured freedom and that the United Nations should be able to travel throughout all of Korea. Three days later, the Chinese Foreign Minister protested that the Chinese were interested in Korea and should be involved in any considerations on that country's future. The Chinese, perhaps under some Russian pressure, began to change their view from Formosa to Korea. As early as July, when it became apparent that American forces could prevent the fall of all of South Korea, Chinese troops began shifting northward; but Whiting[24] states, ". . . the emergence of China as one of the actively interested parties in Korea appears linked with the vain effort by [the Soviet delegate] to arrange negotiations to end the 'civil war' between [North and South Korea] under Security Council auspices." The sudden turn of the war, caused by the successful amphib-

---

[24]Alan Whiting, *China Crosses the Yalu: The Decision to Enter the Korean War* (New York: The Macmillan Company, 1960), p. 86.

ious landing on September 15, must have brought matters to a climax within the Chinese government.

In mid-September, the General Assembly debated an Indian proposal to admit China to the United Nations. The American government, opposing admission in order to keep congressional unity, asked the Commander of the United Nations forces to gather all the material he could that implicated China in the Korean War.

If the invasion by North Korean troops was instigated by an outside power, it was instigated by Russia rather than China. The Soviet Union had considerable control over the communist government of North Korea, and Chinese influence had been excluded. The Russians furnished equipment, direction, and training for the North Korean troops. However, it is probable that the Chinese knew the attack was coming. They did release about 12,000 ethnically Korean troops who had been fighting in the Chinese Communist Army and were thus made available to aid the North Korean invasion. This was probably done largely as a favor to the Soviet Union, although the Chinese might have felt that Russian control over South Korea would decrease support for Chiang Kai Shek and check Japanese ambitions. Evidently, the Chinese completely overlooked the possibility that the United States would react by intervening in Formosa. As we have said, all governments are prone to blind spots when good sight would put them in a difficult conflict.

On the 18th, the Commander of the United Nations forces in Korea charged that China had aided the North Korean invaders by releasing contingents of Korean troops to serve in the invasion. On the 19th, the Indian proposal was defeated thirty-three to sixteen with ten abstentions. On the 22nd, the Chinese government replied that it would always "stand on the side of the Korean people."

On September 23, an official Chinese newspaper argued that the Chinese were against American imperialists because of their support of Chiang Kai Shek, their refusal to recognize China in the United Nations, and their rearmament of Japan. And as troops fought in Seoul, Peking launched a "Hate America" campaign in its newspapers.

The Chinese government asserted that China would always stand by North Korea and made several different charges against American planes that had strayed North of the Yalu River and had strafed and bombed Chinese territory. In a cable to the United Nations, the Chinese Foreign Minister said that the General Assembly must accept some responsibility for the extension of the war into North Korea.

In spite of these angry murmurings, there were as yet no real threats of Chinese entry into the war. Then, on September 24, the Indian Ambassador to China reported a disturbing conversation with the acting

Chief of the Chinese Communist General Staff. The General had stated that the Chinese would not permit the United States to reach the Yalu. When troops reached the 38th parallel, the Chinese Foreign Minister made a public speech, on September 30, in which he said, "The Chinese people absolutely will not tolerate foreign aggression, nor will they supinely tolerate seeing their neighbors savagely invaded by the imperialists." The following day, he again stated that China could not stand aside if the parallel was crossed. On October 1, South Korean forces poured across the parallel and the Commander of the United Nations forces broadcast an ultimatum to North Korea in which he demanded unconditional surrender. That night, the Chinese Foreign Minister summoned the Indian Ambassador to a conference. On October 3, the Indian Ambassador informed his government that the Chinese Foreign Minister had told him that[25] ". . . if the United Nations forces crossed the 38th parallel China would send in troops to help the North Koreans. However, this action would not be taken if only South Koreans crossed the 38th parallel." This message was immediately relayed to Washington. Messages of a similar nature came from American embassies in Moscow, Stockholm, and London and from other allied and neutral channels.

Now there was a concrete Chinese threat, and a second decision had to be made: should Korea be unified or not? As Neustadt demonstrates, the central decision makers failed to really make this decision. Instead, they gave the decision to the Commander of the United Nations forces. He was told,[26] "In the light of the possible intervention of Chinese Communist forces . . . you should continue the action as long as, in your judgment, action by forces now under control offers a reasonable chance of success." In view the fact that the last thing the administration wanted was to become involved in a major war with China, this reversal of the cautious preceding decision was risk taking indeed, although decision makers may not have perceived it as such.

We shall pursue the reasons for the Chinese decision to enter the war* in Chapter 9 (the section on maintaining communications). Here,

---

*The last attempt by the Soviet Union to achieve a compromise in the Security Council and prevent the unification of all of Korea, failed on October 3. On the 10th, the Chinese Ministry of Foreign Affairs warned the country of mobilization, and on October 14, troops began to cross the Yalu under cover of darkness. By November, 200,000 Chinese troops had entered Korea without American knowledge. (It should also be noted that, on October 7, the invasion of Tibet was begun.) In spite of increasing information that left less and less doubt about Chinese intentions, the idea that the Chinese had entered the war in full strength was resisted until their trap was sprung.

[25]R. E. Neustadt *Presidential Power* (New York: Wiley, 1960), p. 135.
[26]*Ibid,* p. 137.

however, let us examine the factors involved in the American risk taking.

As we have seen, there were many pressures for trying to unite Korea. These had resulted in the decision to cross the 38th parallel, and doubts — such as fear of becoming embroiled in a war with China — were handled by placing a restriction on the decision, a restriction that the decision would hold only as long as there were no threats of Chinese entry into the war. If the Chinese threat had come immediately, it might have had its desired impact and the decision might have been reversed. Unfortunately, several weeks passed before serious threats were received. In the interval, the American leaders had become committed by telling the American people about the "necessity" of unifying Korea, and having the United Nations vote on occupation plans.* In addition, they had become privately committed, and the dissonance about the decision had caused them to think of all the advantages that would follow from the reunification. It is important to note that nobody is to be blamed for the time delay — the Americans could hardly have announced their decision before the amphibious landing was successful, and the Chinese could not be expected to make a concrete threat until there appeared to be a realistic intention of crossing the border.

It will not surprise the reader to learn that the cognitive imbalance created by the Chinese threats was deftly reduced by a series of ingenious defenses. Thus, the Foreign Minister's public warnings were seen as a bluff intended to influence the current discussion on Korean unification at the United Nations. The warnings from the Indian Ambassador were dismissed because he "had in the past played the game of the Chinese Communists fairly regularly, so that his statement could not be taken as that of an impartial observer." The 300,000 Chinese troops in Manchuria were ignored because they could somehow not get across the Yalu. The fact that the Foreign Minister could be trying to influence the United Nations without necessarily bluffing; the fact that good ambassadors usually are sympathetic to nations they are dealing with — without necessarily "playing their game"; the fact that with initiative and darkness a river can be crossed; the fact that there were no other diplomatic channels open to the Chinese — that there was no other way for them to deliver their threat if they had been serious — these facts were not considered.

The argument in favor of seeing Chinese threats as a bluffing tactic, was bolstered by reference to the fact that China had made threats after

---

*Note that this lack of flexibility was precisely why the Counselor to the State Department argued against involving the United Nations in Korea.

the Formosan intervention which she had not carried out. In this connection, Whiting has made two important points on the interpretation of threats. He[27] states, "Whereas references to the 'liberation' of Taiwan had become *less* specific following the U.S. move of June 27, the references to Korea had become *more* so." Furthermore, whereas Formosa was separated from Chinese forces by seventy miles of water, "Given the absence of troop movement into Manchuria from July to September and the subsequent increase of forces there from 180,000 to at least 320,000 troops, the Nieu-Chou warnings were visibly strengthened by military dispositions."

It is interesting to note that while the threats of the Chinese Foreign Minister and the intelligence reports of Chinese troops moving toward the Yalu alarmed neither the United Nations Commander in Tokyo nor the President in Washington, they did alarm the Eighth Army Headquarters in Korea. According to Marshall, the headquarters believed that the Chinese would enter the war, and accurately forecast the order of battle along the Yalu River. Marshall[28] states,

> But so delicate was this subject itself at the merest mention of Chinese intervention in the official reports, our South Korean ally had a tremor phasing into paralysis. The psychological impact upon the field agents was tremendous; they acted like men hexed and their interest in their work dropped to zero. If the periodic report took a pessimistic tone, the effect on the Koreans was such that officers had to be sent forth to calm them with assurances that the words were probably exaggerated . . . The group of American advisers serving with the South Korean divisions reported that troops had become highly nervous, with signs of demoralization increasing. The Defense Minister, Shin Sung Mo, urged that the advance towards the Yalu be halted. With some mental reservations, intelligence therefore took a more conservative tone.

As we have seen before, many forces prevent accurate communication and create a gap between field and center.

The conceptualization of the Chinese threats as a bluffing tactic was probably partly determined by the fact that the decision makers were in a potential avoidance-avoidance conflict. If they did not invade North Korea, they would lose prestige publicly; if they did invade, and if they took the Chinese threats seriously, they would step into a war they wanted to avoid. Had they been in this conflict, we would predict that they would do something unrealistic — failing to anticipate the conse-

---

[27]Whiting, *op. cit.* pp. 110-111.

[28]S. L. A. Marshall, *The River and the Gauntlet* (New York: Time, Inc., 1953), p. 7.

quences of their action. As it was, in order to stay out of the conflict, they did not take the threats seriously. Their interpretation of the threats as bluffs was, of course, only partially reassuring. In order to handle what doubts were left, they (1) shifted the responsibility for evaluating the strength of the Chinese to the Commander of the United Nations forces* and (2) ignored the consequences of what would happen if the Chinese did enter the war in full strength.** In this way, they did not have to seriously consider their evaluation of the threats as bluffs. We have seen how a graduate student who wished to live in the country used "shuttling" tactics and distortion to handle disturbing facts. If one argument against the decision became too strong, he shuttled to some other consideration of the situation without regard for consistency. In deciding to go ahead with their plans to unify Korea in the face of Chinese threats, government officials probably used similar tactics. If arguments built up to take the threats seriously, the decision makers begin thinking in terms of weak Chinese forces that could be handled by the United Nations forces. If arguments begin to build up for larger estimates of the Chinese force, the decision makers shuttled back to the idea that the threats were bluffs, and/or distorted the width of the Yalu river.***

Now, in the case at hand there was a *group* of decision makers, and we must ask why the members did not correct each other's oversights and distortions instead of collaborating in an optimistic view of the situation and perhaps taking more of a risk than an individual would have taken. It appears that the individuals involved supported each other's beliefs in a manner that increased risk taking. Let us see how.

The President viewed the Chinese as puppets controlled by the Soviet Union. Since he knew the Russians were not prepared for a world war, he thought that they would not encourage the Chinese to intervene in Korea. He failed to see that, by encouraging the Chinese to enter the war, the Soviet Union would not really risk a global war.

One would think that the President might have been cautioned by his Secretary of State, who neither thought of the Chinese as a Russian puppet nor believed that the Chinese would be dissuaded by the fear of bombing. However, the Secretary of State had different reasons for the same optimistic belief in Chinese non-involvement. He viewed the Chinese Communists as fairly independent of Russia and interested in their

---

*We shall examine a similar abrogation of responsibility in Chapter 7.

**The general overconfidence in the might of American arms and general under-estimation of the Chinese, undoubtedly facilitated this process.

***It should be noted that if the parallel were to be crossed, it had to be done before the North Koreans could regroup their forces. The resulting time pressure probably contributed to the propensity to take a risk.

own national welfare. He appears to have miscalculated the effect which crossing the parallel would have on the Chinese. Since his own policy was to "let the dust settle" with the Chinese Communists, he stressed Chinese problems with Russia and ultimate friendliness with America. He did not anticipate how upset the Chinese would be by the intervention in Formosa or the parallel crossing. In fact, the Chinese had a more negative perception of the United States than he realized, and American acts far outweighed any verbal assurances of good will. The Secretary of State was later to state that the Chinese authorities could not possibly have misinterpreted the intentions of the United States. In fact, they probably did exactly that. To the Secretary of State, the Chinese could gain no advantage by intervening. Russian pressure in the North, the possibility of American friendship, and the tremendous improvements needed internally, dictated a policy of non-intervention. Hence, the Chinese threats must have been a bluff.

In evaluating the Chinese warnings, the President has said that he relied on the United Nations Commander's estimate that the Chinese would not enter Korea. The latter stated that this estimate was based on his belief that allied air superiority could destroy half of the Chinese troops as they tried to cross the Yalu, and on the fact that the optimal time for intervention was past. But behind this estimate lay the Commander's assumption that he would be able to bomb China proper and, hence, his judgment that the Chinese would not risk intervention.

Had the President been aware that the Commander's estimate was based on this latter factor, he would hardly have relied upon the estimate, since he knew that he probably would not bomb China. As it was, the President relied on a Commander whose estimate was based on the Chinese looking at *his* policy, whereas in fact the Chinese were looking at the President's policy and may have guessed that they would not be bombed.* The resultant was a three ring circus of the President looking towards his Commander, his Commander looking at the Chinese, and the Chinese looking toward the President. Later, the Commander (who had been accused of illusions of grandeur) would appear quite paranoid and believe that the British had secretly told the Chinese that the United States would not bomb the Chinese if they intervened.

While the President, the Commander, and the Secretary of State had different reasons for their optimism, the fact of their optimism supported each other's willingness to take risk. Neustadt notes that none of the President's advisers reminded him of the possible dangers relative to the benefits. Since there was agreement, there simply was nobody to urge caution; and no one bothered to challenge the other's assumptions.

---

*We shall examine the point more closely in Chapter 7.

We may hypothesize:

When group members advocate different alternatives, the group will behave more conservatively than the average individual member. When the situation is such that only one alternative is advocated, the group will take greater risks than the individual.

Challenges Confronting the Decision Maker

It will be observed that while the organization may constrain and temper the decisions of its members, responsibility for decisions ultimately rests on the individuals who are involved. It is the individual who gives meaning to an event and must cope with his emotions.

As he attempts to create a viable alternative without distorting the situation, the decision maker may be faced with a number of different challenges that may tax his strength and integrity. We shall examine three of these: the problem of stressful conditions, the tension of making a difficult decision, and the difficulty of maintaining his principles.

The effect of stress

Stress or crisis — times when unanticipated threats to important interests force swift decisions [29] — may create tensions that force distortions in the decision making process. In the last chapter, we mentioned that a person's thinking may become less differentiated under stress; furthermore, a person may become more prone to seizing on a constant to reduce uncertainty and to increase the relative importance of immediate as opposed to long term costs. Stress may lead a person to assign to the situation any meaning that will allow him to act.

Various experimental studies suggest that the effects of stress are most noticeable when a person is responsible for the decision making. For example, Brady [30] has shown that, when monkeys are threatened with severe electric shocks, ulcers develop in those animals that can make decisions preventing the shocks but not in those animals that simply receive the same number of shocks.

While stress is almost always debilitating at high levels, it may be facilitating at low levels. From animal and human experiments that utilize painful shocks to interfere with learning and performing tasks, the conclusion has been drawn that stress increases effectiveness up to a point and then begins to hinder it. Where this point is, depends on the

---

[29] This definition has been explored by Charles F. Hermann, *Crises in Foreign Policy Making*. Doctoral dissertation, Northwestern University, 1965.
[30] Joseph V. Brady, "Ulcers in 'executive' monkeys," *Sci. American*, 10 (1958), pp. 3-6.

nature of the task. In general, if the task is a routine one that relies on well established habits, a greater amount of stress is facilitating than if the task is a novel one that requires complex judgments.

Field studies have shown that personality is also important in determining the level of stress that is most beneficial. Thus, I have shown that student pilots with low test anxiety scores obtain higher flight grades when they are exposed to the stress of bad tempered flight instructors, whereas students with high test anxiety scores do quite poorly with these instructors but perform quite adequately with mild mannered instructors.[31]

The most comprehensive stress experiment has been reported by Berkun and his associates.[32] After experimenting with several devices for realistically creating high degrees of stress, they used the following technique. A solitary soldier was stationed in a remote bunker. While his comrades were wiring in some explosives in a nearby canyon, he was instructed to complete the wiring of a remote control circuit and then to throw a switch to put the circuit into the line. The instructions were slightly ambiguous. When the soldier completed the wiring and threw the switch, an explosion rocked the bunker. In a moment, an intercom informed the soldier that someone had been badly hurt. The only way aid could be summoned was by a telephone in the control cabin. When the soldier attempted to call for aid, he found that the phone was dead! Instructions telling what to do in order to repair the phone were available on the phone. As the soldier completed each step in the instructions, an automatic device timed his problem solving. At the end of forty-five minutes, a psychologist interviewed the soldier about his experience. The behavior of the soldier in this stress condition was compared with the behavior of soldiers in two control groups. Soldiers in one of these control groups were simply asked to repair the phone as a test. Soldiers in the other group believed they had to repair the phone in order to call for additional rations for the entire work party.

We must note that only soldiers were used who were classified by the Army into its two highest categories of mental and physical fitness. The soldiers in the experimental condition were constantly monitored and, after the experiment, given a detailed explanation with several individual and group discussion periods in order to insure that there would be no bad after effects from this experience.

---

[31]Joseph de Rivera, "The prediction of anxiety in student aviators," U.S. Naval School of Aviation Medicine, Pensacola, Fla., 1957, Project No. NM 16 01 11.

[32]Mitchell M. Berkun, *et al.,* "Experimental studies of psychological stress in man," *Psychol. Monogr.,* 1962, whole number 534.

In the experimental condition, the soldiers repeatedly ignored a placard on the front of the phone, that specified that if the operator could not be reached a circuit failure should be assumed, and repair instructions followed. They continued to try to get the operator, usually until the intercom suggested that perhaps the phone was out of order. The time taken to begin repairs was significantly longer than for soldiers in the control groups. Evidently, in the stress condition, the men could not bring themselves to believe a fact with such dire implications. As we shall see later, this fact has an interesting parallel in the German high command's failure to believe that the Russians were mobilizing before the First World War.

When the soldiers started to read the repair instructions, they had difficulty in concentrating and were bothered by thoughts of the injured man's condition, the necessity for hurrying, and concern over their personal responsibility for the accident. Many had to reread the instructions and even then would overlook major steps. Confusion was also manifested in such statements as, "It said to take this panel No. 2 off and change over the wires underneath it, but I found the panel and it was screwed down so I decided I'd better leave it alone" and "I tried to get that inner cover off but it was screwed down and I couldn't get the screws out. There was a screwdriver on the shelf by the set, but I didn't think about using it."

Real progress was not made until the soldier could forget everything but following the instructions — until the goal of simply repairing the set became dominant. Times taken to make various repairs were always longest in the stress conditions and shortest in the control group which was not even concerned with getting rations. The investigators summarize, "Besides reporting having felt stressed, the men who had an emergency to cope with, the men who had a real reason to perform — these men were the most ineffectual in the situation."

There have not been any studies on the effects of natural stress on top American decision makers although there is anecdotal evidence of its impact. We shall note several examples of the effects of stress when we consider emotional breakdown in the next chapter. Reporting on the Cuban missile crisis, Sorenson states,[33]

As the exhaustive and exhausting deliberations of that long October week went forward, however, the limits of time did become more pressing. For all of us knew that, once the missile sites under construction became operational, and capable of responding to any apparent threat or com-

---

[33]Theodore C. Sorenson, *Decision-making in the White House* (New York: Columbia University Press, 1963) pp. 31, 76, 30.

mand with a nuclear volley, the President's options would be drastically changed.

The hardest-working man may be too busy and out-of-touch with the issue at hand, or too weary to focus firmly on it. (I saw first-hand, during the long days and nights of the Cuban crisis, how brutally physical and mental fatigue can numb the good sense as well as the senses of normally articulate men.)

And Sorenson cites the President as saying, "If we had to act in the first twenty-four hours, I don't think . . . we would have chosen as prudently as we finally did."

One might suppose that top statesmen are so highly selected that the probability of breakdown under stress is minute. Nothing could be farther from the truth. In the first place, minor breakdowns occur all the time. During the Korean crisis, the President appears to have refused to consider the political consequences of his actions. This was a minor breakdown that had costly repercussions later when the General commanding the U.N. forces was permitted too much discretion in the field. Some of the poor decisions we have considered may well have been partly caused by a desire to rush the decision in order to reduce mounting tension. Distortions of reality that serve the function of keeping emotional balance, occur frequently. And of course the control of what information is brought to one (the prevention of information that would be disturbing, and the avoidance of problems that would introduce too much strain) are mechanisms that protect the decision maker — at the cost of his functioning.

Perhaps the most dramatic breakdown of rationality in decision makers has been described by North.[34] As Austria-Hungary began to press its demands on Serbia, German leaders underestimated Russian hostility towards Austria-Hungary until a crucial "threshold point" was reached. After this point, the German leaders "misperceived Russian moves undertaken to deter Austria as moves specifically theatening to Germany." As tension mounted, the Kaiser began to misread cables, to see all messages as evidence of hidden hostility. As a result of a conversation with the British Foreign Minister, the German Ambassador telegraphed:

The British Government desires now as before to cultivate our previous friendship and it could *stand aside as long as the conflict remained confined to Austria and Russia.* But if we and France should become involved, then the situation would immediately be altered, and the British

---

[34]Robert North, "Perception and action in the 1914 crisis," *J. International Affairs,* 21 (1967), pp. 103-22.

Government would, *under the circumstances find itself forced to make up its mind quickly.* In that event *it would not be practicable to stand aside and wait for any length of time* . . . If war breaks out it will be *the greatest catastrophe* that the world has ever seen.[35]

In the margin of the report, the Kaiser notes, "This means they will attack us," and at the end he notes,

England reveals herself in her true colors at the moment when she thinks that we are caught in the toils and, so to speak, disposed of. That common crew of shopkeepers has tried to trick us . . . England alone bears the responsibility for peace and war, not we any longer . . .[36]

North states,

Previously the Kaiser and his colleagues had persistently misperceived British, French, and Russian attitudes and interest. Now, in the course of a few hours, they swung to the other extreme: exaggerating British, French, and Russian hostilities and grossly overreacting. In the consequent high tension, moreover, they were unable to see any alternatives to large-scale war.[37]

The German Kaiser, scribbling on the margin of a diplomatic report from St. Petersburg, wrote

The net has been suddenly thrown over our head and England sneeringly reaps the brilliant success of her persistently prosecuted purely anti-German world policy, against which we have proved ourselves helpless, while she twists the noose of our political and economic destruction out of our fidelity to Austria, as we squirm isolated in the net. . . if we are bled to death, England shall at least lose India.[38]

North notes,

Perceptions of its inferior capability did not deter a nation like Germany from going to war. The Kaiser's desperate response to the events that were engulfing him suggest the behavior of a decision maker under stress so severe that any action is preferable to the burden of the sustained tension.[39]

---

[35]*Ibid.,* p. 113.
[36]*Ibid.,* p. 114.
[37]*Ibid.,* p. 115.
[38]*Ibid.,* p. 115.
[39]*Ibid.,* p. 118.

While stress often produces distortion and top decision makers are often under stress, most decisions are reasonably well controlled. How does the decision maker manage to control himself so that he produces clear, penetrating thinking rather than a random emotional behavior? How does he usually manage to avoid acting like a child who "goes to pieces" under frustration? While sometimes he purchases control at the expense of distorted thinking, ulcers, or nervous breakdown, often he manages to legitimately cope with tension.

Several different processes seem to be involved in the legitimate controls of tension. One of the most important seems to be the same commitment process we found to be at the heart of decision making. A person who is genuinely interested in what he is doing — who is being himself — is able to conquer his emotionality. For example, a person who commits himself to politics or teaching finds a source of strength that enables him to gradually overcome his fear of talking before large groups of people.

C. S. Lewis[40] describes the inverse of this process in his brilliant discussion on cowardice. He shows that a man who is faced with a dangerous or fatiguing situation, may intend to do his duty but starts vaguely thinking of things he could do to make himself safer or less burdened. He may begin by merely hoping that certain plausible things will happen, and his ordeal will soon be over. In order to avoid the worst possible eventualities, he begins to imagine a series of expedient measures — all within the framework of performing his duty. The effect of this thinking is to build up a subconscious will that the worst *shall* not come to the worst. The resolution to bear the crisis becomes a resolution to bear it for a reasonable period. The man believes that he has something (plans, expectancies, etc.) to fall back on, and when the plans and expectancies fail and terror comes, this subconscious buildup betrays him into an act of cowardice or loss of control. Lewis notes that the only way to avoid this emotionality is to have nothing to fall back on except one's self and its faith.

This process must not be considered contradictory to the process of "emotionally working through" the bad results that may occur. As Janis[41] has noted, psychological preparation can reduce the emotional impact of a disaster that would otherwise be overwhelming. He notes that the German Ambassador to the United States in 1916 effectively attempted to keep the United States from entering the First World War

[40]C. S. Lewis, *The Screwtape Letters* (New York: The Macmillan Company, 1960).
[41]Irving L. Janis, "Decisional Conflicts: A Theoretical Analysis," *J. Conflict Resol.*, 3 (1959), pp. 6-27.

in spite of lack of support from his government. The ambassador was able to handle himself well in the face of several crises such as the torpedoing of American ships, censures from his own government, and the devastating exposure of a German telegram advocating a Mexican attack on the United States. Janis suggests that the Ambassador retained his composure by emotionally preparing himself for the worst.

A third important process in the control of tension is the use of abstraction to avoid elements that would be too upsetting. Later, we shall examine some of the dangers in this process. But here we must note how it enables rational thought to proceed. When the surgeon cuts into human flesh, he sees only a small exposure of skin isolated from the rest of the patient's body by gauze and cloth. When the President considers war, he also, at times, isolates his act from the deaths that will be involved. Similarly, when a person is in a role, he isolates his considerations from many factors that are pertinent to other aspects of his life. In his role as President, the President does not consider his needs as a father.

Lastly, we must note the importance of support from other persons. The decision maker's family and close friends may provide emotional support and love that enable him to face odds that would otherwise overwhelm him. If this support is suddenly taken away, the decision maker may flounder until he can find a substitute. Certainly this was the case after the death of Woodrow Wilson's first wife.

The difficulty of making a decision

While a person in office has a responsibility to make decisions, it is often easier for him to do nothing. Of course, there are situations in which it is better to let time take its course; but a frequent error seems to lie in a failure to decide. Not only does it take energy to make a decision and thus intervene in the flow of events, but also it is often difficult to reconcile different interests, and one must overcome his fear of making the wrong decision.

James[42] points out that in a difficult decision one is balanced between the tension of doubt and the necessity of action that call out for an immediate decision, and the dread of the irrevocable that argues for postponement. Often a person may impose a deadline on himself — such as agreeing to make a speech on a given date — so that the decision will be forced by a certain time.

---

[42]William James, *Principles of Psychology* (New York: Dover Publications, Inc., 1950).

In 1947, Europe was in a desperate condition with its people under-fed and freezing, and with a worsening economy. The Soviet Union was prepared to encourage communism. But numerous domestic interests, such as the demand for lower taxes, made American action difficult. Jones[43] notes that the President could have tried to muddle through with stop gap measures and postponed the crisis to let the next administration deal with the basic issues. Instead, he chose to accept responsibility and exercise this power. "The situation itself, gigantic, inexorable, was crushing in its compulsiveness. But as is evident from history, men in authority may act to deal with compelling situations, or they may just rock along and see what happens; they may act boldly and decisively, or they may act timidly, partially, ineffectually." Whenever a person fails to confront a situation and make a decision, he abdicates his office, passes up his chance of influencing events, and lets the dice of fate take control.

Making a decision often requires one to judge what is most important, to gauge whether the situation will permit the advancement of one interest or another interest, and to set priorities accordingly. Jones[44] notes that, in late February of 1947, a crisis arose in Greece and Turkey; American aid was required in order to meet the American interest of checking Soviet expansion. At the same time, preparations were being made for an international conference in Moscow where the future of Germany was to be decided. Here, there was an interest in reaching an accommodation with the Russians. News of aid to Greece and Turkey would offend the Russian government, and the President's message to Congress advocating this aid would reach Moscow at the beginning of the conference. The Secretary of State had to decide what to do. He judged that the Russian government was more interested in expansion than in cooperating with the United States; hence, he went ahead with the aid request, possibly sacrificing his position at the conference. In order to do this, of course, he had to accept the situation as one in which the Russians were intransigent.

It is sometimes said that if a person does not decide, then that in itself is a decision. For example, when the President did not choose between the established budget and the increases proposed in NSC-68, he actually favored the economy drive, since that was the present governmental policy. However, while it is true that a failure to decide will influence events, the failure to decide is not a decision psychologically, and the person has failed to be himself. The only exception to this

---

[43]Joseph Jones, *The Fifteen Weeks* (New York: The Viking Press, 1955), p. 100.
[44]*Ibid.*, p. 109.

occurs when a person decides to leave the office — *then* he has truly decided not to decide.

It should be noted that every person is frequently faced with the problem of deciding or failing to decide. Acheson[45] has noted, "In cases like Korea the mind tends to remain suspended between alternatives and seek escape through postponing the issue. The problem itself becomes the enemy." The same person may be able to decide sometimes and unable at other times. Thus, President Truman was able to decide to meet the needs of Europe and to resist the invasion of South Korea; but, as we shall see in Chapter 7, he was unable to decide whether or not to advance in North Korea when Chinese troops began to enter the war.

It is often easier to avoid decision and fail to use one's power. This is often demonstrated by a leader's passively accepting public opinion rather than working to change it. Such was the case in the failure to increase the 1950 arms budget. Schilling[46] notes,

> There was no suggestion . . . that the people might be willing to pay more taxes and still retain their incentive to work or invest if they were persuaded that the gains to security were worth foregoing the alternative uses to which they or the government could have put the money. . . . The problem was not the capacity of the economy to carry larger expenditures, but rather the ability and desire of the administration to undertake the task of persuading the taxpayers and their representatives that the gains from larger expenditures would be worth the costs.

Public opinion is sometimes as much an excuse as a real impediment to action. It can be established by decisions as much as it can influence decisions. (For example, the German opinion in favor of the reunification of Germany was affected by American decisions encouraging this opinion.) Indeed, Neutsadt's[47] central thesis is that the President should structure his decisions so that they teach the public his view of the situation. And often a leader succeds in doing this.

Thus, in 1947 the President rejected the congressional and public opinion in favor of decreasing taxes and the feeling of fatalism about Europe, and worked to explain the situation as he saw it. His leadership

---

[45]Dean Acheson, "The responsibility for decision in foreign policy," *Yale Review,* 44 (1954), p. 7.

[46]W. R. Schilling, "The politics of national defense: fiscal 1950," in Schilling, P. Y. Hammond, and G. H. Snyder, *Strategy, Politics and Defense Budgets* (New York: Columbia University Press, 1962), pp. 102, 213.

[47]R. E. Neustadt, *Presidential Power* (New York: John Wiley & Sons, Inc., 1960).

got the nation committed to a program of European aid and out of a "psychological barrel of its own construction." With respect to public opinion, surely Jones[48] is correct in stating that, "There is no substitute for courageous leadership. Most men are prisoners of their own limited conception of what is possible . . ."

In the chapter on consensus formation, we shall see that it is easier to maintain a consensus than to create a new one — particularly when the participation of the general public is needed. We shall also note the general ignorance of the public and some of the irrational factors that affect public opinion. Almond[49] states,

> The American foreign policy mood is permissive, it will follow the lead of the policy elites if they demonstrate unity and resolution . . . The problem of contemporary foreign policy is not so much one of mass traditions and resistances as it is one of resolution, courage, and the intelligence of leadership.

A failure to assert effectively one's power to change the opinion of others is often due to self-doubt. Analyzing the failure to convince the President of the necessity of lifting the ceiling on the defense budget, Schilling points out that the Secretary of Defense failed to develop an economic as well as a military argument against the ceiling. His opponents *had* tried to justify the ceiling on military as well as economic grounds; they argued that, if the ceiling was exceeded, the Congress would cut military funds at a later date and thus introduce an instability that would eventually hurt the military. The Secretary of Defense could have found economists who would have disagreed with the premises of the Budget Bureau or even argued that exceeding the ceiling would be beneficial to the economy. This would have weakened the position of his opposition. Schilling[50] observes, "The trouble was that the Secretary of Defense was himself more than half persuaded of the validity of the Budget Director's reasoning."

The problem of maintaining principles

There are many situations in which a President or any other person must compromise in order to retain power and put together a working consensus that will accomplish some of his ends. However, in other decision making situations the person must maintain his principles at

---

[48]Jones, *op. cit.*, p. 260.
[49]Gabriel A. Almond, *The American People and Foreign Policy* (New York: Harcourt, Brace & World, 1950).
[50]Schilling, *op. cit.*, p. 201.

the potential expense of good will and his power. It is not clear exactly what distinguishes these situations, but the person feels that he must maintain his principles regardless of the consequences. His own integrity seems to depend on his deciding along the lines of his principles. If he fails to do so, he will have sold his soul — given up some central interests more important than his political interests. Such decisions cannot be made on the basis of calculations; they are a crucial fact of behavior, and their impact is often quite extensive. The heroic act, the planting of a standard which others may or may not observe, is of this nature. It is in this sense that we must understand Washington's famous remark, "Let us plant a standard to which the wise and the just may repair. The affair is in the hands of God."

Kennedy[51] has presented a number of case histories that illustrate men risking political careers for principles. For example, Senator Edmund Ross sacrificed a promising career in order to vote against the impeachment of President Andrew Johnson. Jahoda[52] has analyzed this case and pointed out that Ross' independent behavior cannot be explained in terms of the groups he cared about (most of whom wanted impeachment), nor in terms of a personality trait (he was neither free from anxiety nor a "defiant person"). Rather, we can only explain his behavior as stemming from the fact that "he cared very much about the issue at stake" — had "an emotional and intellectual investment in the issue." Ross saw that if the President was impeached for what were essentially political reasons, the office of the Presidency would be so weakened that it would destroy the balance of power in the government. Since he cared for the government (and his own self-respect), he sacrificed his career.

This type of decision may be much more frequent than we realize. When President Truman was organizing the 1948 Nomination Convention, he had to decide whether to press the civil rights issue. While he may have considered whether the northern city vote or the southern vote would be more crucial to his re-election, this must have been quite uncertain. In his memoirs, (Vol. 2, p. 84) he states,

> I did not discount the handicap which the loss of a 'Solid South' presented as far as my chances of winning the election were concerned. I knew that it might mean the difference between victory and defeat in November. I knew, too, that if I deserted the civil-liberties plank of the Democratic party platform I could heal the breach, but I never

---

[51]John F. Kennedy, *Profiles in Courage* (New York: Harper & Row, 1956).
[52]Marie Jahoda, "Conformity and Independence," *Human Relations,* 12 (1959), pp. 99-120.

traded principles for votes, and I did not intend to start the practice in 1948 regardless of how it might affect the election.

The decision to risk good will or power for one's beliefs is often present in quite inconspicuous circumstances. Consider the following case: The development of NSC-68 was hampered by the Secretary of Defense's commitment against an increased defense budget and his prohibition of contacts between Defense and State Departments. The only official exempt from this restriction was a close friend — his assistant for Foreign Military Affairs. If this man had been the spokesman for the Defense Department, he would have had to represent the viewpoint of the Secretary of Defense. Consequently, he allowed *someone else* (a member of the Joint Strategic Survey Committee) to become the spokesman for the department. This permitted the committee to bypass the economy viewpoint of the Secretary of Defense and freshly explore the problem with military professionals to develop a new position. Hammond notes, "This was perhaps the most important decision made in connection with NSC-68." The assistant for Foreign Military Affairs knew that an open meeting might have results that would jeopardize his friendship with the Secretary of Defense, but it appears that he risked that valued friendship in order to do what he believed was best.

The essence of this particular dilemma lies in the fact that the person in authority may have a broader perspective than his colleagues or those he represents. The opinion of those who are not responsible is sometimes inaccurate and unreasonable, with no concern for the future or insight into what can or cannot be achieved. Yet a leader who bucks this opinion risks complete rejection. A preliminary study by Langenbach and Miller[53] illustrates the type of experiment that can be constructed to investigate a leader's resistance or submission to the opinion of others. In their study, students were appointed or elected to the leadership of a five man group that had to solve a series of three problems. The leader was told his followers each had a copy of the problems, would work on them separately, and then communicate their answers to each other. If all the group members could agree on the correct answers, and if their time was faster than a previous group's time, each student would receive three dollars. If the group could not reach and agree on the correct solutions, each member could still win seventy-five cents if the group could bring itself to agree with any three arbitrary solutions. The followers (actually stooges) each communicated their solution to

[53]Edward R. Langenbach and Whitney Miller, "A leader's decision to plan for a long range reward as a function of being elected vs. being appointed to his position and tough vs. tender group pressures," unpublished paper, Dartmouth course, 1962.

the leader, who had the responsibility of checking the solution and turning it in to the experimenter. The leader had the authority to change the solution of his followers if he found it in error. The followers had the right to remove the leader from his office (and end his chance to win any money) if three of the four became dissatisfied with his actions.

Each of the problems given to the group was constructed in such a way that the leader, with his overall view, could have an insight into the problem which his followers could not possibly have. For example, the first problem required each of the followers to match a shade of green with one of eight possible shades on a color chart. Only the leader could see that the followers could not agree on a correct answer because each of their charts was labeled differently! Because they could not agree on the correct answer, the followers decided to agree on an arbitrary answer and win the lesser amount of money; they communicated this decision to the leader. The leader was now in the dilemma of having to either accurately reflect the opinion of his followers and neglect his own insight into the problem and the group's ultimate good, or assert his power and give his own answer at the possible expense of losing his office. As the experiment progressed, the notes from his followers became more exasperated and, in half of the cases, became "tough" and threatened to remove the leader.

The reactions of the leaders varied considerably. It has been shown that difficult decisions take more time to make, and we may therefore use the time which each leader spent in deliberation as a measure of the extent of his conflict. On any given problem, this time ranged from as little as twelve seconds to as much as nine minutes. Of the twenty-two leaders, seven showed little conflict, five showed considerable conflict but succeeded in resisting the group's pressure, and ten eventually gave in the demands of their followers. Those leaders who were appointed to office seemed less under conflict than those who were elected. (While concerned with the group's anger, they were not as worried about what their duty was.) However, there was no significant difference in terms of the number of leaders who submitted. On the other hand, only three of the eleven leaders who were under fairly weak protest, capitulated; whereas seven of the eleven leaders who were actually threatened with removal, submitted to the group's demands. It is interesting to note that the time it took to decide to give in to the group, was much longer than the time taken to decide to resist. Sometimes a leader gave in because he had wasted so much time trying to decide that he no longer had a chance of winning. On the other hand, once a leader had decided to resist, he felt committed to doing his best so that a later threat of removal was not enough to make him change his convictions.

Can society be arranged so that a leader is encouraged to be courageous and to do what he believes is best for his society? Janis[54] has
pointed out that if a person's acts are contrary to the desires of his group,
the person must either: persuade the group he is correct; or compensate
for his actions by sacrificing for the group in some other area — thus
demonstrating his loyalty; or psychologically detach himself from the
group (lose interest in having its approval). Consequently, Janis suggests that an organization will encourage free action if it (1) gives its
leader high status and power, making the leader less vulnerable and
encouraging persuasion and compensation, and (2) has traditions that
allow for cohesiveness in spite of heterogeneous opinions (for example,
the tradition of a loyal opposition, the tradition of allowing a disposed
leader to keep his citizenship, etc.)

I know of only one experiment that has varied an organizational
factor in order to examine its effects on the freedom of the organization's leader. Kersey and Rowe[55] worked with the appointed leaders
of four man groups. Each leader played a game* against another person
in order to try to win money for his group. Each gave its leader
general instructions about how to play the game, but the details were
left to the leader's discretion. Half of the leaders and groups were told
that if the leader did not follow the group's general instructions *and*
if the leader lost money, the leader would be fined. The remaining
leaders and groups were told that if the leader did not follow the
group's general instructions, there would be no penalty. Which leaders
would feel freer to exercise their own judgment, even if it went
against the group's instructions?

The results show that the leaders who were fined were more independent of their groups. Evidently, the fact that if they failed they would
be punished, relieved them of guilt and group pressure and allowed
a freer reponse. Perhaps if the fine had been severe the results would
have differed, but the experiment shows that penalty *may* increase rather
than decrease freedom of action. Given a conscience, the democratic
leader may have more psychological freedom than the absolute dictator.

Another interesting trend (which was not statistically significant
because of the small number of groups) was that the groups that
could not invoke a penalty against their leader, were the groups that

---

*A two person, non-zero sum game of the "Prisoner's dilemma" variety.

[54]Janis, *op. cit.*

[55]Eugene Kersey and Nicholas Rowe, "Degree of co-operative attitudes of authoritarian and democratic group leaders as a function of penalties in a two-person
game," unpublished paper, Dartmouth course, 1962.

tended to instruct their leader to play more aggressively. They tended to want him to compete rather than cooperate with the opposing players.

As the individual attempts to cope with stress, make a difficult decision, and maintain his principles, his personality manifests itself in many ways. His identity is bound up in the interests and emotional relationships which the decision must satisfy; his character is reflected in how he copes with the pressures of reality and the ways in which he distorts it. In the next chapter we shall consider a few of these numerous relationships between decision making and personality.

CHAPTER 5

The Personality of the Decision Maker

One may ask whether personality is really an important determinant of decisions when a person is acting in his official capacity. If we examine an official behavior, it is clear that much of it is governed by the duties of the office the person holds, by the power of his office, by the objective situation that confronts him and with which he must cope, and by the knowledge that is available. Nevertheless, the same behavior is also a product of the individual's personality. The office gives him the responsibility for making certain decisions, but whether he actually makes those decisions may depend on his "decisiveness." The office gives him certain powers, but whether he enlarges the power of the office may depend on his "assertiveness." The objective situation will influence the decisions of any man, but his personal view of the national interest and his own personal interests will also shape the decision. Knowledge must be available for it to be taken into account, but *how* a person goes about making the decision (his personal style) also influences what is taken into account. Therefore, we must insist that the personality of official decision makers is always an important determinant of their decisions and, hence, of the nation's policy. The fact that President Truman quickly "sized up" situations in terms of principles with moral implications, affected his decisions to hold down the national debt, to fight in Korea, to promote civil rights, and (as we shall see) to hold the Soviet Union to a strict version of the Yalta Agreements. Area is a product of both length and breadth; decisions are a product both of

facts such as role, power, the situation, and knowledge, and of the
fact of the individual's personality.

The Description of Personality

There are many important facets to personality. For example, consider the following variables, all of which came up during a two day
conference on decision making.[1]

First, there are the various preferences a decision maker may have:
1. He may prefer high, low, or moderate risks. Independent of this,
   he may prefer to risk high or low amounts.
2. He may prefer to search for problems and control his agenda, or
   he may prefer to let the external world set his agenda and to wait
   for the problems to come to him.
3. He may have a preference for innovation or for proven methods.

Then, there are his abilities:
1. He may or may not be able to take large amounts of information
   into account.
2. He may or may not be able to resist the pressure to reduce
   discrimination in a crisis.
3. He may or may not be able to easily restructure his ideas.

There are the "problems" he has:
1. He may equate a difference of opinion with a threat to his own
   power.
2. He may have an icy detachment.
3. He may have a furious temper.

There are the various rules he uses:
1. Rules for what is to reach his desk.
2. Rules for what must be decided first.
3. Rules that are quite specific, e.g., subordinates are permitted to
   err one time, but only one time.

And there is his general style:
1. He may make his rules explicit or never state them.
2. He may evaluate a proposal on its intrinsic merit (and, if it has
   merit, arrange the situation to suit the proposal), or he may
   evaluate a proposal on whether it would be practical to do in the
   existing set-up.
3. He may innovate within the existing framework, or he may try
   to change the "game's" rules, or he may try to play an entirely
   different "game."

---

[1] A "Project Michelson" conference led by Thomas Milburn.

4. He may lead with a democratic, authoritarian, or laissez-faire style.
5. He may delegate authority or assign parts of a problem to different people in order to maintain control.

Typical stylistic differences between President Johnson and President Kennedy are reflected in a *Newsweek*[2] article that quotes advisers who knew both men:

> ... where Mr. Kennedy picked only carefully selected brains, his successor tends to seek the views of everyone around, regardless of expertise on the problem at hand.

> With Kennedy, you knew 90 per cent of the time whether to sign the letter yourself or clear it with him first. If we ever get above 50 per cent in guessing right with Johnson, I'd be happily surprised.

> Delegate authority? No, the [new] President is more likely to ask three people to do the same thing, and then see what he likes best.

There are so many preferences, abilities, rules, and styles that it is difficult to know how to describe the behavior of a decision maker with some economy. Furthermore, it is not clear how to relate these individual differences in behavior to the deeper facets of personality they may reflect. According to Neustadt[3], President Franklin Roosevelt had a "competitive theory of administration." That is, he delegated incomplete authority to ambitious men so that they would compete with each other for more power, and he put men of clashing temperament or outlook in charge of organizations whose authority overlapped. In this way, information and decisions were constantly pushed up to him. Exactly how was this choice of administrative behavior related to Roosevelt's personal enjoyment of power?

We know that individuals differ in the ease with which they make decisions. How may such a behavioral difference be related to stylistic variables such as the number of factors a person considers in making a decision, the extent to which he uses rules, and the ways he can distort reality? Individuals differ a great deal in exactly *how* they come to a decision. Whereas Secretary of State Acheson seems to have considered many different aspects of a situation before forming an alternative, President Truman seems to have had a few basic principles which he applied to whatever situation was at hand. Such differences in the style of decision making would seem to be actual aspects of the personality that should relate to temperament and many other factors.

---

[2]The Austin-Boston Axis, *Newsweek*, (January 13, 1964), p. 19.
[3]R. E. Neustadt, *Presidential Power* (New York: John Wiley & Sons, Inc., 1960).

How can we best conceptualize personality; what variables would be most efficient to use?

Unfortunately, we cannot answer the above questions because of our basic ignorance about many of the dynamics of personality. It is clear, however, that we would like to have personality variables that are useful in explaining a number of different decision making behaviors, that remain relatively constant over time, that relate to other aspects of the decision maker's behavior, and that are useful in describing the behavior of more than one person.

Because it is not yet clear which variables will have these characteristics, it would be a disservice to present a simplistic view of personality. Rather than attempting to systematically show all the ways in which personality affects decision making, I believe it will be more profitable to describe a number of different approaches to dealing with personality, and to show how each of these yields variables that may be applied to the behavior of a decision maker. The reader who understands these approaches will have a basic grasp of the array of available techniques. He will then be in a better position to study whatever aspect of personality is of particular importance to the behavior he is trying to predict or understand. After examining these approaches, we will take time to sketch the portraits of three important political leaders whose careers were somewhat marred by aberrant personality factors.

Although psychologists are just begining to focus on aspects of personality that have bearing on decision making, they have developed a number of different approaches to measuring personality. We may divide these into three major categories: the "nomethetic" approach, which begins with a classification interest and imposes this interest on all persons in order to classify them; the "ideographic" approach, which begins with individuals and attempts to objectively describe their individuality; and the "phenomenal" approach, which attempts to understand individuals subjectively in terms of processes which all men have in common.

The Nomethetic Approach

Since the nomethetic approach is by far the most widely used approach, it should be understood by the reader so that its legitimate uses can be appreciated and its limitations kept in mind. We shall briefly consider the various different sub-divisions of this approach. Then we shall see how the approach can be applied to decision making behavior and why the other two approaches are more useful for our particular purposes.

The nomethetic approach may be subdivided into the "operational," the "conceptual," and the "complex description" approaches.

In the operational approach, one develops a personality test that will distinguish between different groups of persons. In this approach, one first decides which groups he wishes to distinguish. For example, one might want to distinguish between persons who can learn to fly and those who will not be able to,[4] or between persons who will be prejudiced against minority groups and those who will not be prejudiced,[5] or between persons who are diagnosed as hysterics, depressives, or schizophrenics.[6] These groups become the focus of the personality test.

Second, one manufactures hundreds of items that may reflect differences in the groups. For example: "I like to ride motorcycles," "strangers cannot be trusted," "someone is trying to control my thought," etc. Third, one gives these items to persons who are in the criterion groups and selects all those items that actually discriminate between the groups; that is, any items that are answered differently (on the average) by members of the different groups. Fourth, one tries the items again to see if they "hold up" in their ability to discriminate. Fifth, regardless of *why* the items work and of whether or not they "make sense," one uses them in the test. By simply adding up how a person answers the items, one can guess which group the person belongs to. There are, of course, elaborate statistics involved in the above procedure, but this is the basic idea.

In the conceptual approach, a different procedure is followed. Rather than beginning with groups of persons who differ on some criteria of interest, one begins with a concept that captures an important aspect of behavior. For example, the investigator may be struck by the fact that some persons seem to have a need to achieve, a desire to personally accomplish difficult tasks. Or he may note how some persons seem to have so strong a need to be approved of that it always causes them to engage in behavior that is socially desirable. Or he may see that some persons seem relatively detached from others and enjoy manipulating them. With his concept in mind, the investigator devises some way to measure the tendency he is interested in. In the above example, the need to achieve[7] has most often been measured by showing a series of pictures to a person, having the person tell a story about each picture,

---

4cf. "The Biographical Inventory," U. S. Nav. Sch. Av. Med., Pensacola, Fla.

5cf. T. Adorno, E. Frenkel-Brunswick, D. Levinson, and R. Sanford, *The Authoritarian Personality* (New York: Harper & Row, Publishers, 1950).

6cf. S. R. Hathaway and P. E. Meehl, *An Atlas for the Clinical Use of the MMPI* (Minneapolis: University of Minnesota Press, 1951).

7David McClelland, J. W. Atkinson, R. W. Clark, and E. L. Lowell, *The Achievement Motive* (New York: Appleton-Century-Crofts, 1963).

and then scoring these stories for themes that involve achievement. Need for approval or social desirability[8] has been measured by asking a series of items having a socially approved answer (such as "I like to gossip at times" — True or False), and then counting all the socially desirable answers which the person gives. Detached manipulation[9] has been measured by culling a series of statements from Machiavelli's book on power and asking the person whether he agrees or disagrees with the attitudes that are expressed.

In order to validate his measuring device and show the power of his idea, the investigator arranges some social situations in which he believes his variable will be important. In the above cases, we might expect that if persons are given a moderately difficult task (such as a crossword puzzle) those with a higher need to achieve will perform better. Given a situation where there are pressures to conform, we would expect more conformity from a person who cares about being socially desirable. If we ask a person to manipulate another person's behavior, we might expect that someone who likes Machiavelli will do a better job than someone who is opposed to manipulation. In fact, it has been shown that when the above variables are measured in the way we have discussed, a person's behavior in the above situations can be predicted with better than chance accuracy.

Finally, as his test proves its worth in some situations but fails to predict in other situations, the investigator may modify his test or qualify what he believes it is measuring. Since his prediction is by no means perfect, he may also seek to improve his prediction by adding other variables that may influence or predict the person's behavior in the situation. For example, he may discover that some of the persons who appeared to have a strong need to achieve actually had a need to avoid failure and, therefore, he might add "test anxiety" as a predictor variable.

Whereas in both the operational and conceptual approaches the investigator is working with *a* personality variable that interests him, in the "complex description" approach he works to describe individuals in terms of many variables. There are several different ways to do this:

1. Capitalizing on operational variables, he can describe a person with a *profile* of several different test scores. For instance, a person

[8]D. P. Crowne and David Marlowe, *The Approval Motive* (New York: John Wiley & Sons, Inc., 1964).

[9]Richard Christie and F. L. Geis (eds.), *Studies in Machiavellianism* (New York: Academic Press Inc., 1968) (in press).

could be described as one who has a seventy per cent chance of completing college, who is slightly above average in prejudice, who answers questions as depressives rather than schizophrenics would do, and so forth.[10]

2. A test may be built of items that force the person to choose between different activities (e.g., going to the theater or sketching a dog, or solving a mathematical puzzle or going to a natural history museum, etc.). The activities may be scored in an operational way (e.g., professional artists prefer one, while accountants prefer another)[11] or a conceptual way (e.g., one is related to the appreciation of beauty, while the other is related to the discovery of truth).[12] In either case, the relative preferences for various types of activities are added up and result in a *listing,* or profile, of the person's interests or values.

3. A description may be created by inter-relating the answers to many different items in a way that reveals the factors that underlie the pattern of responses which persons give. An individual may then be described by indicating how *pertinent* each of these *factors* is in accounting for *his* behavior.[13]

Using these methods (with variants and combinations), and a variety of measurement techniques, psychologists have created a barrage of tests that describe various aspects of personality and may be utilized to predict individual differences in almost any conceivable aspect of behavior. In order to see how this approach to personality measurement may be applied to decision making behavior, we shall consider the attempt to predict individual differences in one important aspect of that behavior: the propensity to take risks.

The prediction of risk-taking behavior

That there are wide individual differences in risk taking is shown by some naturalistic data gathered by Cohen.[14] By stationing an observer at a dangerous corner, he noted 1,189 instances in which a pedestrian

[10]S. R. Hathaway, P. E. Meehl, *op. cit.*

[11]L. W. C. Strong (ed.), *The Strong Vocational Interest Blank, Research and Uses* (Minneapolis: University of Minnesota Press, 1960).

[12]G. W. Allport and P. E. Vernon, *A Study of Values* (Boston: Houghton Mifflin Company, 1931).

[13]R. B. Cattell, *Personality: A systematic, theoretical and factual study* (New York: McGraw-Hill Book Company, 1950).

[14]John Cohen, *Chance, Skill, and Luck* (Baltimore, Md.: Penguin Books, Inc., 1960).

looked up at approaching traffic and then decided to cross the street or wait for a safer moment. The data is presented in Figure 1.

Figure 1.   *Percentage of pedestrians who crossed a street when an approaching vehicle was x seconds away*

Seconds which vehicle took to reach crossing	Percentage who crossed
1	0.0
2	0.5
3	11.5
4	25.7
5	21.4
6	21.8
7	11.2
8	0.4
9	4.6
10	1.5

Some pedestrians are obviously much more cautious than others. While Cohen could not administer personality tests to the pedestrians, he did note each person's age and sex. He found that persons whose ages ranged from sixteen to thirty took greater risks than those from thirty-one to forty-five, and that men took greater risks than women.

Similar results have been found in the laboratory. Wallach and Kogan[15] asked undergraduates and a number of persons whose age was seventy, to estimate the likelihood that various events would occur. Each person estimated how many chances there were in a hundred that the event would occur. Each also stated how confident he was in his judgment. In general, when a person's confidence was high, his judgments were more extreme; that is, the person would guess that out of a hundred chances there were nearly zero chances or close to a hundred. The investigations showed that young persons were more extreme than old persons, even when confidence was held constant. As in Cohen's study, the young men had more confidence than the young women as well as than the older persons. The older men were also more cautious than the young men on a different test that involved advising a fictitious person to take risks in order to gain a greater payoff.

Of the personality variables which we have mentioned, the one that has been used most successfully in risk taking studies has been the need

[15]Michael A. Wallach and Nathan Kogan, "Aspects of judgment and decision-making: Interrelationship and changes with age," *Behav. Sci.,* 6 (1961), pp. 23-36.

for achievement. We have noted that it is possible to obtain a measure-ment of a person's "need to achieve" by scoring a person's stories for achievement themes, and we stated that differences on this test often relate to how well a person performs on simple tasks. Now, in any situation where achievement is possible, there is also the possibility of failure; and unless one has a relatively high need to achieve, one may avoid a feeling of failure by choosing very easy tasks or by choosing very difficult tasks which one cannot blame himself for failing. But a person whose need for achievement outweighs his fear of failure must choose a task in a medium range of difficulty where he has the best chance of worthwhile accomplishment. Similarly, such a person would prefer intermediate risks in a gambling situation, whereas a person with a low need to achieve might be content with low winnings or might try for improbable but high winnings.

Atkinson[16] has reported a series of studies that confirm these expecta-tions. Children with high scores on "need to achieve" stand at inter-mediate distances when they play ring toss; students with high scores play shuffleboard by standing neither as close nor as far as students with low "need to achieve." Similarly, when college students were asked what grade they would settle for in order to be excused from the final exam, those with high need achievement scores were more likely to choose grades in between the maximum and minimum grade which they believed they might obtain if they took the exam.

When persons were asked to choose between bets with the same expected positive value (for example, one chance out of two in winning thirty cents, or one chance in eight of winning $1.20), Edwards[17] found that, on the average, persons had a preference for bets involving one chance in two and a relative preference for bets whose chances were seven in eight rather than one in eight. Analysis of individual dif-ferences shows that persons with high "need to achieve" scores have a relative preference for the one-in-two bets, while persons with low scores prefer the seven in eight or even the one-in-eight.

Scodel *et al*[18] have confirmed the above finding by giving men money to bet on dice throws and then observing which bets they chose. The probability of winning ranged from three-in-four to one-in-eight. Again,

[16]John W. Atkinson, "Motivational determinants of risk-taking behavior," *Psy-chological Review*, 64 (1957), pp. 359-72.

[17]Ward Edwards, "Probability preferences among bets with differing expected values," *Amer. J. Psychol.*, 67 (1954), pp. 56-57.

[18]Alvin Scodel, Philburn Rotoosh, and J. Sayer Minas, "Some personality correlates of decision making under conditions of risk, in *Decisions, Values and Groups*, Vol. 1, ed. Dorothy Willner (New York: Permagon Press, Inc., 1960).

men with low need achievement scores tended to choose the extreme bets, while high "need achievers" chose middle odds. It should be noted that since high "need achievers" desire success, they may be thinking of desirable results and, hence, have a higher subjective probability of success (c.f. Figure 1, Chapter 4 on page 109). On the other hand, persons concerned with avoiding failure may be concentrating on undesirable outcomes and, hence, have a lower subjective probability of success.

Need for achievement is probably but one of many personality variables that can be related to risk taking behavior. For example, the risks which a person will take may be related to how much confidence he possesses. One interesting approach to the study of confidence has been reported by Block and Peterson.[19] They asked fifty-three military officers, whose ages ranged from twenty-eight to forty-five, to judge which of two lines was taller. The investigators varied the difficulty of the discrimination and asked each person to report how confident he was after each judgment. They then divided the men into three groups: an over-confident group that reported high confidence in discriminations which were below their threshold, an over-cautious group whose confidence was low even when the discriminations were easy for them, and a "warranted confidence" group whose confidence shifted appropriately with the difficulty of the discrimination. A staff of eight men who knew the officers, independently described each officer by indicating which of seventy-six items best described him.* Some of the results are shown in Figure 2.

Figure 2. *Items which were most likely to be used to characterize the officers who were:*

Overly Confident	*Overly Cautious*	*Warranted Confidence*
rigid	introspective	self-reliant
narrow range of interests	concerned with self	socially perceptive
pedantic and fussy	self-indulgent	
lacks insight into self		

The above results suggest that confidence may be related to many aspects of one's personality. The most comprehensive study of this possibility has been reported by Kogan and Wallach[20]. They admin-

---

*A q-sort was used. Those items listed were significant at the .01 level.

[19] Jock Block and Basil Peterson, "Some personality correlates of confidence, caution, and speed in a decision situation," *J. Abnorm. Soc. Psychol.,* 51 (1955), pp. 34-41.

[20] N. Kogan and M. A. Wallach, *Risk Taking* (New York: Holt, Rinehart & Winston, Inc., 1964).

istered twelve different personality scales (including scales of defensiveness and anxiety) to a variety of persons, and then presented each
person with ten different betting situations (some involving skill, and
some chance). On the final bet, a person could bet all of his winnings
against dice throws of varying probabilities. The investigators then
looked for consistent betting styles and the relation of these styles to
personality variables. In one sense, the findings are rather disappointing.
The average person did not show consistent styles related to personality
factors but rather tended to respond in a situationally specific manner.
For example, if a risky strategy was not working, the person would
switch his strategy. This lack of consistency — or sensitivity to the
situation — seemed most true when the person did not have consistently
"poor" scores on the various personality tests. Thus, the authors[21] state,

> In making a risky or conservative final bet, the 'least disturbed' sub-
> group for both sexes is significantly influenced by amount of prior
> winnings; the larger these winnings, the more conservative the final
> bet. No such relationship is obtained for the high test anxious-high
> defensive individuals, whose risk or conservatism on the final bet
> depends on whether risk or conservatism is their preferred strategy in
> other decision-making contexts.

Because healthy individuals do take risks in accordance with their
individual aims and perception of the situation, and because personality
tests and laboratory risk taking experiments work on the basis of
averages, we are ill prepared to predict the behavior of *a* normal
individual in *a* situation in real life. For instance, we have seen that
several experiments have shown that older persons take less risks
on the average, and that persons with high need achievement *tend* to
prefer moderate risks to either large or small risks. Let us examine the
behavior of General MacArthur who, at age seventy, was the Commander
of the United Nations Forces in Korea and had an undeniably high
need to achieve. The details in the account below are taken from
Leckie's[22] history of the Korean War.

Specific Instances of Risk-taking

As the summer of 1950 progressed, the North Koreans swept down
the peninsula to eventually capture all but the tip of Korea, where
thousands of Americans doggedly (and almost unsuccessfully) held a

---

[21]*Ibid.,* p. 191.

[22]Robert Leckie, *Conflict, The History of the Korean War, 1950-53* (New York:
G. P. Putnam's Sons, 1962).

perimeter about the port of Pusan. The Commander of the United Nations forces knew he would gain a limited number of new troops — perhaps two divisions. How should he deploy them? The strategy that was most obvious, most conventional, and perhaps most conservative, would be to pour the new troops into Pusan and attempt to break out from the North Korean vise. However, the Commander conceived of using his reinforcements to make an amphibious landing far behind the bulk of the North Korean forces. Specifically, he decided to land at Inchon — the port of Seoul, half way up the Korean Peninsula. He reasoned that this would cut the North Korean supply lines, confront the enemy with a two-front war, capture a badly needed port (Korea's second largest), and strike a psychological and political blow by leading to the rapid recapture of the South Korean capital.

The trouble with this bold conception was its extreme risk. For this reason, his headquarters and the Joint Chiefs of Staff adamantly opposed the plan. The navy was horrified. Inchon was about the worst conceivable place to attempt a landing. There were enormous tides — the second highest in the world — with an average twenty-nine-foot rise. The port was surrounded by mudbanks that ran out six thousand yards from the shore and could be cleared by LST's only when the tide was at least twenty-nine feet high. An adequate tide in the daylight hours only occurred about twice a month and meant the landing would have to occur on September 15, or wait until October 11 or November 3. The LST's would then have to be left stranded on the mud. Furthermore, the channel into the harbor was extremely restricted, with no space for the bombardment ships to maneuver, and the tidal current in the channel would necessitate anchoring the ships within range of a shore battery.

The marines were horrified. On September 15, the tide was not high enough until 5:30 p.m., which, with sunset at 6:43 p.m., would leave about one hour for troops to land and fight inland over a high sea wall and directly into an oriental city of 250,000 persons with all of its buildings undoubtedly armed to the teeth.

The army was horrified. The amphibious assault would require marines who were being used to help hold the tenuous line about Pusan. The Chairman of the Joint Chiefs of Staff had been an opponent of amphibious warfare and of the marines as a separate service. The commander had to go through him to convince the President to give him control of the marines he would need for the landing.

A final fact that enhanced the risk of a landing at Inchon, was Wolmi, — a highly fortified island which rose 350 feet and commanded the entire port area. The island would have to be captured in order to secure the invasion's flanks. This could be done, but it would necessitate a bombardment for several days and thus give up any element of last minute surprise! If one adds to these factors a general ignorance of the enemy's disposition of troops and the possible presence of mines, one gets a general feeling for the degree of risk involved.

On August 23, the Joint Chiefs of Staff came to Tokyo to dissuade the Commander. About nine top ranking military leaders were present at the meeting. There was an eighty-minute briefing on the proposed landing. During this briefing, the Commander quietly puffed on his corncob pipe and occasionally interrupted to ask a question. At the conclusion of the briefing, the Commander of the Seventh Fleet said, " . . . the best I can say is that Inchon is not impossible."[23] The Army Chief of Staff presented all the objections to Inchon. Furthermore, he stated that he believed Inchon was too far away from Pusan to have the desired effect. He advocated landing at Kusan — one hundred miles closer to Pusan and with fewer natural obstacles. The Navy Chief of Staff seconded this suggestion.

The Commander of the U.N. forces waited a moment while tension grew in the room. Then he began to speak, quietly at first, then dramatically. He knew, he said, all the drawbacks to Inchon; but he reminded the group of Wolfe's success in attacking Quebec from an "impossible" position. The very arguments against the attack would insure its success, because the enemy would not really be prepared. Furthermore, the boldness of the attack would capture the oriental imagination, and the troops that landed at Inchon would be an anvil against which the General at Pusan could hammer the North Koreans. He argued that Kusan was not far enough behind the enemy to cut their supply lines and that they could simply back up and reform into a single front above Kusan. He argued that landing at Inchon would save 100,000 lives. Then the Commander remarked how the status of the marines would never again be in doubt, and he reminisced about some landings during the Second World War. He stated,

"The Navy has never let me down in the past and I am positive it will not let me down this time. I realize that Inchon is a five-thousand-to-one gamble, but I'll accept it. I am used to those odds." Then he paused, and his voice sank to a whisper as he said, "We shall land at Inchon, and I shall crush them."[24]

---

[23]*Ibid.,* p. 132.
[24]*Ibid.,* p. 132.

This dramatic presentation of his arguments and confidence convinced all those present except the Naval Chief of Staff. The next day, he spent another hour and a half with the Commander of the U.N. forces, emerging persuaded and saying, "I wish I had that man's confidence."

Here we have an example of a man with high need achievement rejecting the moderate risks and pay-off of a landing at Kusan for the extreme risks and pay-off of a landing at Inchon. Here is a man, seventy years old, who not only rejected the conservative strategy of breaking out of the Pusan perimeter but also created a high risk and fought to get the troops and the support to carry it out. How can we account for his behavior?

One way would be to see the Commander as mentally unstable. Certainly the risks were almost inordinate; and later, after his retirement, the Commander was to make statements that might have reflected a tendency towards paranoia with delusions of grandeur. However, the Commander's risk taking and confidence do not appear to have stemmed from any divorcement from reality. The Commander was aware that he was taking a risk, and he had some doubts to overcome. His doubts seem to have been highest *after* he had convinced his opposition. He knew he was assuming that the harbor would not be heavily mined, that the tide could be surmounted, that the enemy would not station many reserves by Inchon, that Japan would remain orderly while its occupation forces were being used in the invasion, and that the landing would successfully break the supply lines and morale of the enemy near Pusan. It was not shutting his eyes that answered his doubts, nor only charisma that silenced his opposition.

After the first phase of the landing operation had been successfully accomplished (for the Commander's assumptions held, though a passing hurricane nearly destroyed his plans), doubts as to the follow-up were again appropriate, and the Commander was again open to doubts. For example, the day after the landing, the Americans began an offensive to break out from Pusan. When the enemy held firm, the Commander began considering a second landing at Kusan, thus indicating that he did not have an inflexible faith in the success of his plan of deep envelopment and an unshakable confidence at the wrong time.

Abandoning a hypothesis of mental instability, we might attempt to account for the Commander's behavior by applying the utility model. But would it really be accurate to say that he chose the bet with the greatest expected value? Or should we say that of bets with equal expected value, his personality led him to choose the one with the greatest risk and greatest pay-off? As we saw in the last chapter, a decision cannot be accounted for so easily. The Commander created the alternative on which he bet, and we must explain this in terms of the meaning which he gave to the situation in order to actualize his interests.

The heart of the Commander's risk taking lay in his perception of the situation he confronted. Inchon *was* the only port where he had a chance of destroying the enemy with a single dramatic blow. The alternative *would* have eventually involved a bloody frontal assault on the enemy. This was the meaning which the Commander gave to the situation. He was a professional military man who had an interest in clean tactics and the winning of battles without a blundering loss of life. He was also a person with an interest in the dramatic. These and other interests made him seek a dramatic blow that would beat the enemy. Once he had found one, he decided to act. Here the Commander had to draw on his confidence to convince himself and others. For him, it would have been a weakness to hold back, and therefore the Commander temporarily silenced all his doubts.

We can see the same processes at work in the next risk which the Commander took, but in this case distortions seem to have operated and he appears to have accepted a bet with a lower expected value than was objectively necessary. After Inchon, the victorious United Nations forces swept up the Korean peninsula until, within sight of their goal, they met with new resistance from Chinese forces. When these forces suddenly pulled back, Chinese intentions became unclear. The Commander of the United Nations forces had to decide what to do. His most conservative choice would have been to concentrate his forces and dig into a defensive position. A moderately risky strategy would have been to concentrate his forces and advance slowly. The high risk strategy was to keep his forces dispersed and launch a full scale offensive. The Commander did the latter, walked into a Chinese trap, and suffered extremely heavy losses. Let us examine some of the factors that may have contributed to his poor judgment.

First, the Commander had poor intelligence information. Aerial reconnaissance failed to find masses of Chinese troops, and the Commander's intelligence accordingly estimated from sixty thousand to seventy thousand men. Actually, of course, the troops simply hid in the daytime, and there were 300,000. As we have noted, this intelligence failure was another case of persons seeing what they believed they would see.

Second, it is possible that the Commander projected his own uncertainty onto the Chinese. Cohen has suggested that, in 1941, American intelligence was uncertain that the Japanese would attack and, projecting, thought that the Japanese were uncertain about whether they would attack. The Commander may well have thought that the Chinese were undecided about whether to attack and would be convinced by a bold move.

Third, dissonance reduction may have been an important factor. The Commander, having assured the President that the Chinese would not dare to intervene, was fully committed to securing North Korea. To suddenly act as though they might, would have provoked quite a cognitive reorganization. He never seems to have seriously asked what the Chinese were doing in Korea in the first place if they had no intentions of fighting.

Fourth, as Simon has noted, the imagination is quite limited in giving the possible consequences of an action the weight they should actually have. To the extent that the Commander did intellectually visualize a trap, he may not have emotionally realized the consequences.

Fifth, we have noted that when a person is fearing failure, he may take extreme risks because psychologically the failure will be lessened. It is conceivable that at this point in time the Commander did fear failure or at least could no longer tolerate the uncertainty involved in whether an attack was forthcoming.

Sixth, the Commander's values were such that if the Chinese had attacked, he would have bombed and blockaded the Chinese mainland. He believed the Chinese would fear this massive retaliation and, hence, be deterred from intervention. He never stopped to think that the President, with his values, would not order such a retaliation, and that the Chinese might be considering what the President would do rather than what *he* would do. This egoism would not have been so disastrous if the President had made his own decision about what to do rather than leaving it to the Commander (a classic example of bad structure!).

The combination of the above factors and the Commander's interests and confidence led him to give the situation a less dangerous meaning. As a result, his risk taking was not as appropriate as it was in the Inchon landing. Note that in either case do nomethetic variables, such as need for achievement or age, account for the risk taking behavior.

While a relatively small number of personality tests and methods associated with the nomethetic approach have been applied to the study of risk taking, it is safe to say that *none* of these tests or methods would really help us in our endeavor to understand a particular case of risk taking. However, it would be unfair to criticize the nomethetic approach to personality measurement for this deficiency. All of the methods which we have reviewed are really designed to *compare* one individual with another rather than to catch the *essence* of *an* individual's personality. The probability that a person will learn to fly an airplane, or the extent to which an individual has a need to achieve, are measures of how that individual compares to other persons along a dimension that is imposed on the individual because it is of interest to the investigator.

A profile of an individual's test scores or an indication of what factors apply to him, is not really a description of *him;* it is a description of how he compares or contrasts with other individuals on a multitude of abstract dimensions. A list of a person's interests or values is a labeling or sorting rather than a portrait of the person. The interest areas or values are arbitrary abstractions that provide a frame of reference against which the real person can be placed and compared to others.

This is not to say that personality tests based on the nomethetic approach are of no value. If one is interested in a given dimension such as pilot success, need for achievement, or whether a person can adapt to a given psychological environment, then a well designed personality test can predict *on the average* what a given person will do, and it can predict this far better than a good man's intuition. But when it comes to accurately describing the personality of an *individual,* the best battery of personality tests is a poor substitute for a skillful biography. When a scholar attempts to describe Leonardo da Vinci or Josiah Gibbs or Abraham Lincoln, his portrait is subjective and uses variables that may have nothing to do with most men. He may even have to invent new variables to do justice to the individual he sees. It would be inconceivable to describe da Vinci without referring to his ability to visualize complicated interrelations between parts, to describe Gibbs without referring to his capacity to think without stimulation from others, or to describe Lincoln without referring to his charity and his internal struggle with his desire for power.

The Ideographic Approach

The "ideographic" approach attempts to deal with the individuality of a person by beginning with the individual, having him produce a number of responses, and then examining the pattern of these responses *within* the individual. This pattern may then be described in its uniqueness, or a person may be related to a class of individuals with a similar pattern — thus, *typed* in some way. In principle, this method can be used with any kind of responses. For example, Allport and

Vernon[25] have worked with a variety of "expressive" responses, such as the area a person fills when he writes, voice intensity, writing pressures, etc. Often, however, the investigator works with responses or items that have some theoretical or systematic significance. Thus, Stephenson[26] asks the person to describe himself by arranging statements into piles ranging from "most true" to "least true" of himself. These statements may be carefully worded to reflect dimensions such as introversion and extroversion. If a person consistently chooses certain items he may be typed as an "introvert" or a "Pickwickian," according to whatever essential character structure has been built into the items. Using a somewhat different technique, the person may be asked to rank order which basic needs most characterize him. Using this method, Stein[27] has shown that within a given population of persons a number of basic patterns or types can be distinguished. Some of these types are more successful in certain given situations, whereas others are more successful under different circumstances.

While, to date, the ideographic approach has not been used much in the study of decision making behavior, we may expect its use in an increasing number of studies on politicians. This is because the approach easily lends itself to the observational data which one can obtain even when unaccessible officials will not furnish the more common "self-descriptive" and "projective" data. Thus, Shneidman[28] has analyzed the frequency of different kinds of logical errors made by Kennedy and Nixon in their series of television debates. And, working with the transcripts of press conferences during the New York City subway strike, Hermann[29] has shown how a number of measures of verbal behavior reflect the degree of stress which the individual negotiators were under.

In a sense, too, the ideographic approach is usually involved in the writing of a case history. That is, one starts with the individual, describes his life as a series of responses, examines the pattern, and classifies. In the latter half of this chapter, we shall consider three such case histories of political leaders.

---

[25]G. W. Allport and P. E. Vernon, *Studies in Expressive Movement* (New York: The Macmillan Company, 1933).

[26]William Stephenson, *The Study of Behavior* (Chicago: University of Chicago Press, 1953).

[27]Morris Stein, *Volunteers for Peace* (New York: John Wiley & Sons, Inc., 1966).

[28]E. S. Shneidman, "The Logic of Politics," in L. Arnos and M. A. May (eds.), *Television and Human Behavior* (New York: Appleton-Century-Crofts, 1953).

[29]Margaret G. Hermann, "Indirect methods of assessing defensive behavior and effect in stress," (Princeton, N.J.: Educational Testing Service).

In spite of the fact that the ideographic approach begins with the individual person, the investigator may soon find himself looking for patterns that are similar to those of other individuals. Thus, in common with the nomethetic approach, the ideographic approach examines the person "from the outside" and uses descriptive labels to *type* rather than *understand* his behavior. If the nomethetic approach measures personality by imposing fixed categories on the helpless individual, the ideographic approach hopes to capture his essence by its *reflection* in an objective mirror of his behavior.

The Phenomenal Approach

The phenomenal approach attempts to grasp the personality of the individual by describing the situation the individual is in and the decisions he makes, from a *subjective* point of view. This is only possible to the extent that there are essential dimensions that are common to all men and allow them to "put themselves in each other's shoes." Some biographies do this, but in a non-systematic way. The problem with using biography as a method is that the ordinary biography is so interested in the individual that it neglects to systematically relate one individual to another. Because of this, it is an uneconomical method of description that fails to capitalize on the insights in past biographies. The phenomenal approach attempts to be subjective in a systematic way. In the following analysis we shall attempt to capture uniqueness and yet relate individuals to each other by describing how they achieve certain essential functions.

For example, for any person to be happy and successful, he must arrange what he does so that his unique abilities can be used. Thus, we may expect an artist or a scientist or a politician to pursue his work in a way that will allow him to maximize his own talents. Regardless of the unique personality of a given politician, we may expect that this consideration — the maximum use of his ability — will affect the coalition of voters he tries to put together in order to be elected, the staff arrangement he chooses to employ, and the type of problem he will try to solve while he is in office.

Thus, President Eisenhower's talents at compromise are reflected in the coalition between the conservative and liberal Republicans that elected him, in the fact that he constantly attempted to get his staff and cabinet to take the position of the entire government rather than the position called for by their individual roles, and by the fact that he was particularly interested in solving the problem of reconciling the conservative and liberal elements within the Republican party and the positions of the Soviet Union and the United States.

While each man's principal ability is a rather unique talent, we can predict that when any man makes a decision, he will attempt to maximize the opportunity to use his particular ability.

A man of strength can build his career around whatever abilities he possesses. He is free to capitalize on the best within himself and to build his appeal to whatever groups of people he can pull together to vote for him. But certain abilities are clearly of great use in the Presidency. We are familiar with tests of spatial ability, mechanical comprehension, and verbal intelligence; but the abilities mentioned by historians and political scientists are of a subtler nature, viz., good judgment when presented with alternative proposals, a sense of timing (when it would be wise to introduce a given measure in the light of congressional and public opinion, for example), the ability to make decisions and bear the weight of vast responsibility without over-worrying, good judgment of the character and abilities of men, a sense of where power lies, organizational ability, a large amount of energy, and a charismatic personal charm. Little progress has been made in measuring such abilities or trying to define their essential natures.*

Another function common to all individuals is the learning that occurs while the individual is in office.[30] Thus, Jones notes that when Harry Truman first became President, he tried to avoid some of the tremendous responsibility inherent in the office. Specifically, he tried to select able men whom he trusted and let them perform various important jobs with no control from his office; he left them free. In a short time, he learned that while he *could* delegate all his duties in this way, he could *not* escape the responsibility for what happened. Consequently, he soon began to exercise more control over how decisions were made.

---

*We do not have civil service exams or selection tests for the Presidency. Have we simply been lucky in generally getting good men? Sorenson, in essence, suggests that the nomination and election procedure is a good selection test for the presidency, because in order to win the election the candidate must have the same abilities he needs as President, e.g., organizational ability, energy, judgment, the ability to win support, etc. If this is true, it would suggest that we get a poor President only when the selection test — the election — has failed to measure these abilities. This should happen only if the winning candidate did not have to campaign — for example, if he possessed such overwhelming popularity that there was essentially no contest. Of course such a man could possibly make a good President, but there would be no guarantee of this, and all the weaker Presidents should come from this category. Ratings of the different Presidents are available; it would be interesting to see if the poorer ones did not, in fact, have to campaign hard.

[30]I am indebted to Glenn Paige for this suggestion.

Similarly, Sorensen[31] has observed that President Kennedy learned a number of things from the disastrous "Bay of Pigs" affair that helped him to handle the Cuban Missile Crisis.

To date, no one has made a study of the types of things that are learned in an important office. Nor have there been any studies of which models a President utilizes in learning how to behave in office. We know, for example, that President Truman was an admirer of Andrew Jackson. What effect did this have on his conception of the Presidency and how he learned to fill the office?

A number of psychologists have begun to describe individual personalities in terms of functions that are common to all men. Thus, Bühler[32] has pointed out that the development of any personality can be understood as a series of *crucial decisions* which a person makes; and Kelly[33] has suggested that each individual should be understood in terms of the *dimensions* of the world he creates about him. Jahoda[34] has emphasized the importance of focusing on what governs an individual's *interests* and has suggested[35] that a variation of Kelly's "repertory grid" method could be employed to arrive at the dimensions underlying interests. Using this method, the person would be asked to choose a person, a job, an issue, a game, etc., that interested him, and a corresponding person, job, issue, game, etc., that he was familiar with but did not care about. By asking him to categorize what was different about the two persons, jobs, etc., the investigator might be able to discover regularities that characterized the individual's interests. Erikson,[36] amplifying on Freudian theory, has described personality as the resultant of a number of crucial stages in development. Each individual passes through these stages and learns — or fails to learn — trust in others, independence, and other crucial relationships. Erikson has applied his scheme to the life of Martin Luther[37] and thus produced a biography

---

[31]Theodore C. Sorensen, *Kennedy* (New York: Harper and Row, 1965).

[32]Charlotte Bühler, "The goal structure of human life," *J. Humanistic Psychol.,* 1 (1961), pp. 8-19.

[33]George Kelly, *The Psychology of Personal Constructs* (New York: W. W. Norton & Company, Inc., 1955).

[34]Marie Jahoda, "Conformity and independence," *Human Relations,* 12 (1959), pp. 99-120.

[35]Jahoda, personal communication.

[36]Eric Erikson, *Childhood and Society* (New York: W. W. Norton & Company, Inc., 1950).

[37]Eric Erikson, *Young Man Luther* (New York: W. W. Norton & Company, Inc., 1962).

that could be related to any other biographies based on common functional stages.

Note that the above ways of conceptualizing a personality, all examples of the phenomenal approach, rest on the premise that the common function being used as a base — crucial decisions, thought categories, interests, developmental stages — is a fundamental process that is important in understanding any man. In the nomethetic approach, whether or not a person can learn to fly or has a high need to achieve is a specific question put to a general man and giving an average prediction. But if Erikson's stages are fundamental, then how a person passes through the stage in which he may learn to trust others, is a general question asked of a specific man and having an exact answer. If one is using nomethetic variables, to say that a person is an introvert or has a high need to achieve is a reification, because introversion and need to achieve are abstractions that are imposed on the person. On the other hand, the phenomenal statement that a person is interested in Mozart's music and can trust others, is a direct description of the person.

The function of emotions

In the last chapter, we asserted that when a person makes a decision he is guided by the operation of underlying emotions. If we are correct in our assumption that emotions are fundamental processes with common functions in all men, then the way in which an individual accrues an emotion would be an ideal way to describe his personality.

As an example, we may consider the emotion of confidence. The primary function of this emotion is to enable the individual to commit himself to a decision or to a view of reality. Thus, the Commander of the U.N. forces needed a great deal of confidence to decide to land at Inchon and to convince his opponents that his view of the situation was correct.

Any good President must have a high degree of self-confidence while he is in the Presidential office. He must be able to decide and press forward with all his strength. The Presidents who have been judged as strong, such as Woodrow Wilson and Franklin Roosevelt, probably also would have defended Korea; whereas weak Presidents, such as Harding or McKinley, might have wavered.

Sorensen[38] gives two examples of how decisions may be met. Reportedly, Franklin Roosevelt said to a friend,

---

[38]Theodore C. Sorensen, *Decision Making in the White House* (New York: Columbia University Press, 1963), p. 42.

At night, when I lay my head on my pillow . . . and I think of the things that have come before me during the day, and the decisions I have made, I say to myself — well, I have done the best I could — and I turn over and go to sleep.

Reportedly, Warren Harding said to a friend,

I listen to one side and they seem right, and then . . . I talk to the other side and they seem just as right, and there I am where I started . . . God, what a job.

How a President (or any person) achieves the confidence which he needs, differs from individual to individual and is an important aspect of his personality. President Truman appears to have drawn his confidence and strength from the office of the Presidency rather than from any particular belief in himself. He had always been loyal to his party; and when he became head of the party, he could expect loyalty from others. He expected others to obey and respect him, not because he was Harry Truman, but because he happened to be in the office and was doing his duty. He did not think that he was *the* best person to be President or that his decisions were necessarily correct; but he did know that somebody had to make them, that he was that somebody, and that others should obey him as, in the past, he had obeyed and respected others in the office.

On the other hand, President Roosevelt did not obtain strength from the office as much as from himself. He had a tremendous confidence in himself; he did not *fill* the office, he *was* the office, and he enjoyed power for its own sake. Whereas Truman did not see his personality affecting decisions, Roosevelt did. Psychodynamically, one has the impression that such basic self-confidence often stems from quite a close relationship with the mother. This was true in both the case of President Roosevelt and General MacArthur.

According to the Georges'[39] analysis, President Wilson derived his strength from his relationship with an attentive but autocratic father. His competition with his father created a drive for power that had to be masked in the service of some idealistic cause. Thus, Wilson had tremendous confidence and energy whenever he could serve some ideal.

Since the strength of these three Presidents came from different sources, we would expect them to be prone to different but corresponding weaknesses. This certainly appears to be the case. Thus, President Truman was prone to back up his subordinates to an extent that was indiscriminate and led some of them to become too independent. This

---

[39] Alexander and Juliette George, *Woodrow Wilson and Colonel House, A Personality Study* (New York: The John Day Company, Inc., 1956).

weakness would seem to stem from his own reliance on the governmental hierarchy as the basic source of his strength.

President Roosevelt's strong inner confidence led him to disregard the advice of State Department officials that would have forced him to change his views and, hence, would have weakened his confidence in his own judgment. To defend his confidence he failed to consult all the persons who could have contributed to a wise decision.

President Wilson's downfall came at the hands of Senator Lodge, who adroitly played on Wilson's inability to compromise. The Georges suggest that this inability was due to Wilson's struggle with his father. That is, if Wilson had "given in" to Senator Lodge's demands, it would have been analogous to "giving in" to his father, and the effect would have been to undermine his basic source of strength. Thus, in all three cases, the individual's greatest weakness seems related to his source of strength. That is, his weakest actions seem determined by forces designed to prevent an undermining of his confidence.

We have used the emotion of confidence as an example of how one could describe individuals in terms of the common function of achieving a necessary emotion. We could also describe each person in terms of how he achieves, or fails to achieve, security (which functions to preserve the individual's identity so that he can "be himself" in awkward or threatening situations); how he maintains his pride; how he avoids anxiety; and so forth. The ways in which a person accomplishes these feats are often related to specific patterns of behavior. Thus, a person may maintain his pride by constantly seeking to achieve. But another person who also has a high "need to achieve" may be avoiding anxiety or showing gratitude, etc.

For some purposes, it will suffice to know whether or not the person is concerned with achievement. But to really understand the person, one needs to know the conditions for his emotions. One is then in the position of knowing not only whether achievement or something else is important, but also why it is important and how this may change.

The extent to which General MacArthur had a generally high need to achieve does not help us to predict that he would attempt the Inchon landing. To do this, one would have to know about his emotions. The fact that he had an internalized confidence in his beliefs, tells us that in order to predict his behavior we can look at his beliefs, since he will act in accordance with them. The fact that he was a professional military man who took pride in winning wars with decisive strokes and had contempt for blundering actions that killed masses of men, gives us these beliefs. By thus describing the individual in terms of functions such as confidence and pride, we can generate explanations for unique events.

Earlier, we noted that descriptive elements should be economical so that they do not become multiplied beyond comprehension. In this connection, it is interesting to note that most of the common functions we have discussed seem related to one another. Crucial decisions are usually the ends of critical developmental stages and often involve an emotion, such as the determination of an object of admiration. Likewise, the interests of a person seem to grow out of this process. Just as interests may be determined by a variation on a method for determining the categories in which a person thinks, so they may also be determined by inquiry into emotions. Thus, we can ask a person what he admires, what aspects of his life satisfy him, what he would be ashamed of, etc. That is, since we can conceive of emotions as ends necessary to advance a person's interests, we can work through the person's emotions in order to discover what his interests are.

The advantage of this procedure is that a person can more readily answer a question about his emotions than one about his interests. Once we know which persons or actions he admires, is ashamed of, etc., we may search for what aspects of the person or action are crucial to the interest, by varying characteristics of the person or action and seeing whether the emotion remains or vanishes. For example, if a person admires someone who is a famous general but is only impressed by a similar person who is a famous pianist, we can hypothesize that his investment is governed more by military values — such as being ready to die for one's country — than by aesthetic values — such as expressing oneself with integrity.* This can be checked by exploring other objects of admiration, and the objects of other emotions.

Such interrelations as the above give us hope that these functions are fundamental and will be able to provide an economical description.

Emotional breakdown

While we have focused on common functional processes, there are also common "breakdowns" that may be phenomenally understood. While high government officials usually keep their emotions under

---

*In the last chapter, we distinguished several different problems that confront the person in power. It is noteworthy that President Truman particularly admired men who solidified power, whereas President Kennedy particularly admired men who maintained principles. Thus, in his book *Mr. Citizen*, Truman lists eight famous Presidential decisions which he admired. All of them, like Washington's putting down the Whiskey Rebellion, involved the courage to assert or protect the power of the federal government. On the other hand, in *Profiles of Courage*, Kennedy cites case after case of Senators who did what they thought was best in spite of pressure from their constituents. Their courage consisted of standing for their principles at the expense of their power, rather than the courage of taking the responsibility of solidifying power. This difference between the two presidents may be important in understanding many of their decisions.

control, there are lapses. Tension is often close to the surface and some-times crops through to cause problems. We can observe this in the President's behavior during moments of the Korean crisis. At the beginning of the invasion, when the President arrived in Washington National Airport, he was tense and wore a look of "grim determina-tion." When the photographers begged for "just one more picture," the President (who usually gracefully acquiesced) abruptly cut them off, saying, "that's enough, we've got a job to do." Similarly, as Sunday night's meeting drew to a close, an adviser said that he would like to discuss the political aspects of the situation; the President abruptly snapped, "We're not going to talk about politics; I'll handle the political affairs."

Several months later, John Hersey was present at a meeting between the President and his staff. Hersey noted that the President was pre-occupied throughout the meeting. After the ordinary business of the meeting was handled, the President brought himself to tell his staff some news. That morning he had been notified that massive Chinese intervention in Korea had suddenly occurred. As the President outlined the immediate actions which would have to be taken, he kept his feelings hidden. Then Hersey[40] notes:

> . . . he paused for a few seconds, and suddenly all his driven-down emotions seemed to pour into his face. His mouth drew tight, his cheeks flushed. For a moment, it almost seemed as if he would sob. Then, in a voice that was incredibly calm and quiet, considering what could be read in his face — a voice of absolute personal courage — he said, "This is the worst situation we have had yet. We'll just have to meet it as we've met all the rest."

After a brief discussion of working plans, the President began to sign documents. While doing this, he said,

> Well the liars have accomplished their purpose. The whole campaign of lies we have been seeing in this country has brought about its result. I'm talking about the crowd of vilifiers who have been trying to tear us apart in this country. . . . We can blame the liars for the fix we are in this very morning. It's at least partly the result of the vicious, lying campaign. What has appeared in our press, along with the defeat of our leaders in the Senate, has made the world believe that the American people are not behind our foreign policy — and I don't think the communists would ever have dared to do this thing in Korea if it hadn't been for that belief.

---

[40]John Hersey, "Profiles: Mr. President II — Ten o'clock meeting," *The New Yorker,* (April 14, 1951), pp. 38-55.

After signing the papers, the President's mood changed again — his voice became confident and personal as he said,

> We have got to meet this thing just as we've met everything else. And we will! We will! Let's go ahead now and do our jobs as best we can.

Then, with another sudden shift in mood, the President recovered a measure of his usual exuberance and closed the meeting with a typical,

> Well! If none of you gentlemen have any more non-controversial items, I'll declare myself satisfied, and the meeting can adjourn.

It is not surprising that the President became emotional; it would leave us rather dismayed if he had not. But we must note his displacement of aggression when he blames "the liars" for the Chinese attack. In fact, the President had been getting a relatively favorable press, and the nation had supported the Korean campaign. In the last chapter, we saw that the attack was basically the administration's own fault. This momentary displacement of blame may have helped him to recover emotionally.

Another example of an "emotional outcropping" is provided by the Secretary of Defense's reaction when he first read a summary of NSC-68 and saw that it challenged his budgeting policy. Hammond[41] notes,

> The abruptness and severity of his reaction startled everyone present, even though there had been forebodings of it. He questioned the authority under which the study was made. He charged [his assistant for foreign military affairs] with failure to perform his duties . . . and all present . . . with scheming to underlie his politics . . . He pointed out that the paper conflicted with established policies, and he indicated his contempt for it. The scene ended almost as abruptly as it had begun with [the Secretary of Defense] storming out into [the Secretary of State's] office to talk the matter over privately, leaving surprise, anger, humiliation, and dismay behind.

It must not be supposed that emotionality is reflected only in outbursts; in the last chapter we saw how the emotionality associated with stress could directly affect decision making. Defensiveness is yet another symptom. In reviewing the Eisenhower administration's defense budget

---

[41]P. Hammond, "NSC-68: Prologue to rearmament," in W. R. Schilling, Y. Hammond, and G. H. Snyder, *Strategy, Politics and Defense Budgets* (New York: Columbia University Press, 1962), p. 324.

policy, Glenn Snyder notes that the President pressured the Joint Chiefs of Staff into ratifying his defense budget program. He states,[42]

> . . . it is somewhat less clear why the administration should have felt such a strong compulsion to secure unanimous approval of that program by the Joint Chiefs of Staff, in view of the President's tolerance of repeated instances of deviation by his subordinates in non-military policy areas. One possible explanation is that the President felt his own prestige to be most deeply involved in military affairs. Disagreement with his own program by one or more of his highest military subordinates would have tended to undermine that prestige and would have cast doubt on his own military wisdom.

Still another evidence of tension is found in exaggerated precautions. Jones states that President Roosevelt had been deeply bothered by Wilson's failure to lead the United States into the League of Nations. He determined that this error should not be repeated and became so committed to this end that he failed to speak frankly. Speaking only of the advantages of world government and avoiding the trials and tribulations, he failed to educate the American people on the responsibility they would incur in the post-war period. Thus, says Jones, "Fearing a repetition of 1920, Roosevelt actually retarded the genuine, informed acceptance by the people of the very thing he so fervently desired — our full participation in world affairs."*

Uncontrolled emotions are also behind many of the distortions in perception and thinking that we observed in Chapter 3. These distortions may be viewed as protective devices to preserve the decision maker from negative emotions. Thus, when thinking is dulled and blurred by rhetoric, the thinker is fooling himself with words designed to fool others. His thinking is wishful in nature and simplifies the dilemma so that disturbing emotions are avoided. Likewise, choosing unrealistic alternatives or believing false ideas is usually a product of avoiding the emotional disturbance of an avoidance-avoidance conflict with no good realistic choices. And part of the restricting influence of the prevailing climate of opinion is due to the emotionality that may be produced if one thinks outside of its limits.

While occasional emotional disturbances are easily understood, there are more serious disturbances that tax the power of the phenomenal

---

[42]G. H. Snyder, "The 'new look' of 1953," in Schilling, Hammond, and Snyder, *op. cit.,* p. 523.

*J. M. Jones, *The Fifteen Weeks* (New York: The Viking Press, Inc., 1955), p. 102.

method. A reaction such as schizophrenia can be grasped subjectively*
but is far beyond the scope of this book. Therefore, in considering
some examples in political leaders, we shall use more of a case history
approach. The reader will note many phenomenal variables in the
second of these case histories.

Aberrant Personality

In the last chapter, we considered the transient emotionality associated
with stress. A person can usually recognize such emotionality in himself if it is called to his attention, and he usually wishes to cope with it.
Unfortunately, there is also the more permanent emotionality associated
with unconscious ideas that may be repressed and disowned by the decision maker. Hence, various neurotic and psychotic phenomena occur.
While we are all affected to some degree by these unconscious problems,
some persons have been affected to a more noted extent. We shall very
briefly consider some problems reflected in the actions of Stalin,
Wilson, and Forrestal.

Stalin

Let us consider Stalin's personality as it is portrayed by Kennan.[43]
It is impossible to divorce a person's personality from the situation he
is in. What we mean by personality is that, in a specified situation, the
person will react in a particular way. Therefore, it is useful to contrast
Stalin's behavior with the behavior of another person from the same
culture and faced with similar problems. Kennan contrasts him with
Lenin. There is no doubt that both men were hostile to the Western
capitalistic world, that each enjoyed power and was capable of the
most ruthless cruelty when it served his own ends. However, Lenin
was the founder of a movement, and his central purpose was to bring
this movement to fruition. He had a brilliant mind and ruled his
followers with their respect and love. Feeling secure, he could run the
government with its needs rather than his needs in mind. He had created
Leninism, and once he was in power, he had little fear of changing it;
that is, he was fairly open to suggestions. Knowing all this, his subordinates could devote all their energy to their professional problems,
confident that if they solved them they would be rewarded.

---

*See, for example, Hannah Greene's *I Never Promised You a Rose Garden* (New
York: Holt, Rinehart & Winston, Inc., 1964).

[43]George F. Kennan, *Russia and the West under Lenin and Stalin* (Boston: Little,
Brown and Company, 1960).

Kennan's thesis is that Stalin, on the other hand, was a man who was wracked with a sense of inferiority — a man whose main motivation became the maintenance of his power and who eventually became quite unbalanced mentally. Stalin's background was quite different from that of the more cosmopolitan Bolsheviks, who initially held much more power than himself. He felt himself to be on the outside of their circle, and he resented the men who made him feel inferior. Once in power, his deepest fear was that somehow he would succumb to the power of this idealistic group that might build up its strength outside of Russia. While his main ambition was to protect his own position rather than that of his country, he concealed this by manufacturing external enemies for Russia that would justify measures actually taken on his own behalf. That he was *really* afraid of the power of external socialists rather than of external capitalists or fascists, is shown by his destruction of independent communist forces and his lack of preparation for the German invasion.

Because of these fears, a diplomat dealing with Stalin could never be sure whether a proposal was rejected because it was not in the best interests of the Soviet Union, or because it was not in the best interests of Joseph Stalin. In fact, dangers to himself and to his country became confused. Kennan[44] notes,

> Unlike Lenin, who could view objective reality as something apart from himself, Stalin was able to see the world only through the prism of his own ambitions and his own fears.

The consequences would have been severe enough had Stalin been an anti-social personality who simply placed his own power above the good of his party and country. But Stalin became mentally ill, and his suspiciousness reached the point where he began to see ulterior meanings in innocent remarks. Kennan describes a crisis beginning in 1932 with the growth of opposition to Stalin's ruinous agricultural policies. His wife's mother was living with them at the time and was a transmitter of complaints from the peasantry. Stalin ordered the woman to live elsewhere and shortly thereafter had a public argument with his wife. That night, his wife either committed suicide or was murdered. Shortly afterward, Stalin wanted to kill some oppositional elements. At the moment, he was blocked; but within a few years, using masterful timing and "dosage," he managed to combine the exploitation of differences in his followers with some key assassinations,

---

[44]*Ibid.*, p. 258.

insuring his own power. He was then in a position to kill off his opposition. This means of control seems to have fascinated him, and he developed a technique of execution, finding that the executed were innocent (shortly after their death) and charging the executors with treason, etc. In this way, during the 1936-38 purges, he killed 1,108 of the 1,966 members of the Seventeenth Party Congress. In all, it is estimated that about half a million persons were killed in the course of these purges.

The differences between Lenin and Stalin should be particularly stressed, because they are so similar in their desire for power and we sometimes tend to group all of the power hungry into one class. In contrast to Lenin, Stalin ruled with fear, manufactured false dangers and ignored real ones, suspected his friends and placed confidence in Hitler, took as his diplomatic goal the protection of his own position, and killed far, far more of his countrymen than was necessary to maintain his power.

Stalin is, of course, an example of extreme aberration. But there are many other examples in history. All nations should arrange their political systems so that such careers are aborted. This is particularly important in this day of nuclear weapons. One does not feel confident that either Stalin or Hitler would have hesitated to begin a nuclear war if it were the only way to save their power.

Let us now examine another aberration of power that, while nowhere as serious in its consequences, demonstrates a different sort of difficulty that can arise.

Wilson

Woodrow Wilson has been the subject of many biographies; we shall consider the psychologically oriented portrait of the Georges'.[45] It is based on Freudian theory and Lasswell's work on power as a compensation for feelings of inadequacy. They point out that Wilson's brilliant father took an exceptionally strong and not altogether benevolent interest in his son's upbringing.

> Dr. Wilson was noted for his caustic wit. This he directed not only at his contemporaries but at his young son as well. Tommy never retorted and he never rebelled. Instead, he accepted his father's demands for perfection, tried to emulate him, and interpreted his stinging criticisms as humiliating evidence that, try as he might, he was inadequate.[46]

---

[45]George, *op. cit.*
[46]*Ibid.*, p. 6.

His recollections indicate that he had early fears of being stupid, ugly and unworthy of love. When Wilson was young, he showed several signs of resenting the intense pressure he was placed under. For example, although he was quite intelligent and the family was very literate, he failed to learn to read until he was eight years old — a detail that must have considerably upset his erudite father. At some point, however, Wilson "fell into line." The Georges note,

> There is not a shred of evidence that he ever once openly rebelled against his father's authority. Instead, he submitted and became an extravagantly devoted son. It was a devotion which lasted throughout his life.[47]

Now, while Wilson's father must have been a strong, likeable man and a devoted father, he seems to have been concerned more with fostering his idea of what his son should be like than he was with loving what his son was. Under these circumstances, we should expect the son to have harbored some resentment. When he did not, we suspect a repression of strong feelings of rebellion. The Georges observe

> All his life long, he shrank from reflecting about his inner motivations. The very idea of such self-examination made him uneasy. He once wrote in a letter that he had always had an all but unconquerable distaste for discussion of the deep things that underlie motives and behavior. He believed the solution to personal difficulties was rigorous self-discipline.[48]

The Georges' thesis is that Wilson's life was affected by an unconscious effort to solve his repressed problem with his father. There were three aspects to this unsolved problem: (1) a persistent feeling of being unworthy of love; (2) the fact of submission to his father's will, which in fact reinforced his feeling of unworthiness, which in turn made it harder for him not to submit; (3) the fact that in his family and in his country the desire for power was viewed with suspicion. Each of these affected the solution he attempted.

First, Wilson kept having to prove to himself (and his father) that he was worthy of being loved. He was compulsive about this; that is, after any of his numerous achievements, he seldom felt genuine pleasure. He was not capable of relaxing, because no achievement could give him what he really wanted — a feeling of being worthy. Consequently, he kept striving for greater achievements and more power. Also, he was overly dependent on the approval and love of personal friends.

---

[47]*Ibid.,* p. 9.
[48]*Ibid.,* p. 11.

A friend could not disagree with him, because such a disagreement unconsciously implied that he was not worthy of love.

Second, he was constantly fighting the fact that he was unconsciously submitting to his father's demands and, hence, could not bear the thought of submitting to any other powerful man's demands. He could not tolerate another power challenging his authority; he *had* to win, for a defeat meant the annihilation of his will.

Third, Wilson could not openly compensate for his inner unworthiness and submission by striving for power and domination. Accordingly, these strivings were masked by his ideals. While, of course, these ideals were quite sincere, they also served the function of justifying or purifying his unconscious desire to dominate his father. The Georges observe,

> For him the problem always was to decide what was right and then cleave relentlessly to it. Instead of considering beforehand what would be his maximum and minimum goals, he tended to formulate only one position which was, in effect, both his maximum and minimum stand. He then endowed this position with moral attributes in order better to mobilize his own emotions and energies in the struggle on its behalf. This approach as a negotiator — and indeed as a college president and political leader — had certain advantages in that the stubbornness with which Wilson pressed for his maximum goals and the skill with which he drew a moral dichotomy between his own position and that of his opponents often culminated in brilliant successes. However, it also had some fatal disadvantages. For when his opponents reached the stage where they would no longer capitulate — and often Wilson did not offer them a gracious way out — his inflexibility led to a complete impasse and ruled out compromise solutions which might preserve a good part of his program. Wilson thus habitually abdicated important responsibilities of political leadership, self-righteously but unrealistically relying on public opinion to vindicate him and force his opponents to surrender to him. It was characteristic of the man to structure every major executive position he held into an inexorable moral battle.[49]

From these elements, the Georges are able to account for many of the facts in Wilson's life, such as his tremendous ambition, his dependence on friends, and his search for moral crusades. Often, even specific details can be explained; as the Georges note,

> He seemed especially drawn to projects which he could conceive of in terms of liberating human beings from their masters — a goal sanctioned

---

[49]*Ibid.*, p. 256.

culturally and perhaps peculiarly appealing to one who had never himself cast off the yoke of parental domination.[50]

These details often have importance for political events. Thus, as we noted in the second chapter, Kennan explains Wilson's decision to impose harsh terms on Germany as a result of the German attempt to dominate his idealized Russia.

Perhaps the most important event in Wilson's life explained by the above formulation, is his failure to persuade Congress to join the League of Nations. The Senator who led the opposition to the League saw that he could not win enough support to defeat Wilson's basic plan. He knew, however, that Wilson would brook no interference with his authority. Therefore, he proposed some amendments to the American treaty, amendments that would not cripple the League but would weaken it and could be passed over Wilson's opposition. He was fully aware that the amendments would not accomplish what he wanted, but he knew Wilson would refuse to accept them. He was correct. Wilson's authority was threatened, and he essentially defeated himself by refusing to accept the amended treaty. Interestingly enough, this whole pattern was a striking repetition of an occurrence in Wilson's previous presidency of Princeton University, where he had a self-defeating power struggle with a Dean who challenged his authority.

An important aspect of Wilson's defeat with the League of Nations, was his failure to listen to his chief advisor, Colonel House. The Georges note,

> One of the most disastrous consequences of Wilson's personal insecurity was his inability to consult about matters which had become emotionally charged for him except with those whose ultimate approval he could count, or with those who, in the last analysis, were not in a position to exert pressure upon him to adopt their views.[51]

House was well aware of Wilson's need for approval and agreement, and his own personality and conscious management of Wilson makes a fascinating story. Here we can only note that House felt the League was so important that he had to risk alienating Wilson by giving him advice which he knew would not be welcome. Unfortunately, the advice did not take, and their relationship did deteriorate.

The Georges are careful to note how Wilson's behavior was a function of the situation he was in as well as his personality. When Wilson

---

[50]*Ibid.*, p. 117.
[51]*Ibid.*, p. 119.

had a small degree of personal involvement in a task and did not link success with his need for self-esteem, he could be extremely skillful in handling the situation. He could be very flexible, select political goals that were ripe for development, and be both shrewd and inventive in his leadership. It was only when the situation related to his unconscious problems that he became inflexible. Of course, on the other hand, Wilson's degree of success was related to the political situation of the times — a situation that called for the idealistic political reforms and strong leadership that fitted Wilson's personal needs. But the American system of government, with its potentially strong legislative checks on Presidential power, eventually placed Wilson in the type of power conflict that generated an effective opposition to his will — the very situation he was least able to handle.

Whenever we know something about an individual's personality, whether it be a comparative measure or a description of some function, and want to predict his behavior, we must take into account the nature of the situation he will be in. Thus, Stein's[52] work on the assessment of Peace Corps workers, shows that different types of personalities are most productive in different situations. General MacArthur would probably have failed as a President of the United States in 1948, but he was a success in heading the Japanese occupation. Rovere and Schlesinger[53] note,

> If Ridgeway can fill his shoes today, it is still no proof that McArthur did not do a unique job in the early years of the occupation. For then the overpowering need was for faith, for a *mystique,* for a moral revival in the midst of moral collapse. The powerful and dedicated figure of MacArthur filled that need, as probably no other American general could have filled it. He was the universal father-image in a season of terrible spiritual crisis. But the spiritual crisis came to an end, and so did the desperate need.

The very importance of the individual's personality depends on the situation he finds himself in. If a person is placed at the hub of a communication network, he will become the group's leader; that is, the situation will force leadership upon him, regardless of his personality. But if there is no hub, if everyone in a group can talk freely with everyone else, then (as Guetzkow[54] demonstrates) personality

---

[52]Stein, *op cit.*
[53]Richard Rovere and Arthur Schlesinger, Jr., *The General and the President* (New York: Farrar, Straus & Giroux, Inc., 1951).
[54]Harold Guetzkow, "Differentiation of roles in task-oriented groups," in *Group Dynamics*, ed. D. Cartwright and H. Fander (Evanston, Ill.: Row, Peterson, 1960).

factors, such as individual differences in the desire for "ascendance," will govern who seizes leadership of the group.

Forrestal

Let us now look at another person, with a different set of problems, in a different situation. James Forrestal, the United States' first Secretary of Defense, a figure in some of the interactions we have described in this book, has not yet received the study which the future will bring. We are indebted to Arnold Rogow[55] for gathering and presenting the material on which the following account is based.

While we do not have satisfactory material on the details of Forrestal's childhood, it appears that, unlike Wilson, his mother exerted the stronger influence in the household. Rogow portrays Forrestal's father as a self-made immigrant, a successful contractor who was proud of his commission in the National Guard but who deferred to his wife at home. Mrs. Forrestal, who came from an established second-generation home, was a devout Catholic, had a commanding physical presence, and was a rather hard disciplinarian. The older of the three Forrestal boys took to her, while the second took to his father and entered and successfully managed his father's business. Jim, the third son, six years younger than his nearest brother, seems to have been unable to accept his father for a model or his mother's wishes for him to become a priest. While his position in the family and the genesis of his conflict is uncertain, it appears that he may have scorned his father's weakness and resented his mother's strength. In any case, it is evident that by the time he was sixteen he was striking off on his own with a fairly clear rejection of his family — though not of many of the positive things they valued.

Forrestal clearly had an extremely high need to achieve and the ability to do it. He decided on his own initiative to go to college and build himself a successful career. He chose Princeton because, he said, he wanted to meet "people who counted for something." At Princeton he became an amateur boxer, joined one of the best private eating clubs, became Editor of the daily paper, and was voted the man most likely to succeed.

We must note three interesting facts of his Princeton life: First, Forrestal did not want to take any financial assistance from his family (though he did take a little), stayed away from home, never discussed personal problems with his parents or brothers, left the Catholic Church,

---

[55]Arnold A. Rogow, *James Forrestal* (New York: The Macmillan Company, 1963).

and was actually perceived by some friends as an orphan; that is, he severed all close personal ties with his family. Second, in spite of this rejection of his family, he retained many of the attitudes and values he had learned from his family. He respected work and was proud that a "Mick" had been successful at a rich Ivy League college Third, he withdrew from Princeton six weeks before graduation! The surface reason for his withdrawal was a conflict with one of his Professors, who told him that he would flunk a required course, regardless of his exam grade, if he did not attend the lectures. Behind the conflict lay Forrestal's problem with powerful authority figures — and possibly a wish to punish himself for his rejection of his family.

Forrestal's life at Princeton foreshadowed his future. He had a meteoric career. Since he admired bright, tough, successful Wall Streeters, he joined an investment banking firm and quickly rose from a bonds salesman to the manager of a district office, to the head of the sales department, to a partnership and vice-presidency of the firm. He was regarded as the "boy wonder" of Wall Street, engineered tremendous coups — such as buying Dodge motors for his firm and merging it with Chrysler — made himself a millionaire, and became President of the firm.

The other aspects of his life held true as well. Though Forrestal enjoyed and was enjoyed by other persons, he did not seem capable of forming a deep emotional attachment. He married at age thirty and had two sons; but he wanted no strings attached to himself, saw little of his children, and (later) was virtually separated from his wife. He was fair and understanding, but not affectionate. While he enjoyed his wealth and liked to be with prominent people, he was scornful of the values of rich, "useless" people. In short, as before, he retained many of his old values in this new situation.

A friend of Forrestal has beautifully summarized the dilemmas that were confronting him. On the one hand, Forrestal had "embraced the American dream and found it wanting." He had left his parents with their high values to become a success in a society that "saw the Racquet Club as a social Nirvana."

> . . . the tragedy was that Forrestal was aware of it all. He lived his life as a conflicted man, walking a tight rope held taut by a concept of original sin at one end, the American dream of success and recognition at the other. Deeply sensitive, uncertain, afraid of intrusions upon his soul, he solved his dilemma by becoming a caricature of the Rational Man. Functioning almost entirely on a rational level, he could never allow himself to enter the world of childhood, for to do so would have meant

shedding the self-woven cocoon by which he protected his vulnerability. Above all, Forrestal was vulnerable. He smothered himself in his own highly developed art of self-protection as few men have.[56]

Remembering these factors — the ability, the tremendous drive to achieve, the conflicting values (with his scorn of weakness and resentment of strength), the fear of emotional attachment — let us see their effect on Forrestal as, in 1940, at the age of forty-eight, he left the business world to conquer the new and challenging world of government.

Forrestal initially entered the government as an assistant to President Roosevelt, but he found that this job did not give him the scope and independence his drive required. Consequently, he soon accepted the newly created office of Undersecretary of the Navy and built this job into the most influential office in the department as he financed the build-up of the wartime Navy. In the process, he fought off a power bid by the Chief of Naval Operations. Rogow observes that Forrestal had difficulty with other authorities and tried to relieve the tension that was often present by a sort of labored camaraderie.

In 1944, Forrestal became the Secretary of the Navy. As the war drew to a close, he viewed the mood of victory with dismay. He was suspicious of communism, believed that the United States should fight hard to establish control over as large an area as possible, and fought against demobilization. It is not clear whether Forrestal had insight into the nature of the forthcoming struggle (he was quite familiar with communist ideology) or whether his desire for power led him to perceive the situation in the way he did. Probably both of these factors were important. In any case, he began a personal war against communism and used his office to begin an investigation of communist activities within the United States.

Forrestal was, of course, quite opposed to former Vice President Wallace and his sympathies with the Soviet Union. It is characteristic of Forrestal that when President Truman complained of Wallace's critical speeches in foreign countries, Forrestal asked Truman why he did not deny Wallace a passport! Forrestal seemed to have no appreciation of the many arguments against such a move. Truman merely replied that it would expose the administration to criticism. It is this type of exchange that led Forrestal to devaluate the President. *He* would rather have taken the criticism than risk the failure of a policy which the nation required. Had the President answered in terms of principles, Forrestal might not have been so ready to perceive him as

---

[56]Cited in Rogow, *op. cit.,* p. 326.

weak. We must note, however, that Forrestal may well have been subject to unconscious forces that led him to categorize authority figures into either weak characters (as he perceived his father) or strong rivals (which he resented and could not deal with in a relaxed way).

A similar example of Forrestal's insensitivity and lack of emotional attachment, is revealed in his stand against the establishment of Israel. Forrestal was, of course, reflecting his role as defender of the nation's military power. He was afraid that the Arab nations would refuse to sell oil to the United States and allow the Soviet Union to become established in the Middle East. He also, correctly, foresaw that American troops might have to be sent to the area. Though Forrestal had a legitimate position, he could not see any arguments on the other side; and, with his usual scorn, he perceived only election year politics interfering with national security. He kept up a strong lobby for putting national security above politics until he was virtually ordered to desist. Forrestal's error was in part based on his listening only to military and oil men who were convinced that the Jewish forces would lose to the Arabs. However, his judgment may also have been influenced by his general indifference to Jewish suffering. While he was not prejudiced against individual Jews — he promoted the first Jewish admiral over the protests of a prejudiced Naval selection board — his upbringing and his jobs in Wall Street and the Navy led him to view Jews as somewhat "different." His lack of emotions probably prevented him from empathizing with the cause involved.

It should be noted that Forrestal consistently fought for what he believed, regardless of the political consequences. On the more liberal side of the ledger, he backed David Lilienthal's appointment as chairman of the Atomic Energy Commission in spite of conservative opposition.

When President Truman pushed for the unification of the armed services, Forrestal predictably fought for the Navy's power. He argued that the proposed job of Secretary of Defense was too big a job to be efficient. Fighting the Secretary of the Army, Forrestal succeeded in weakening the unification bill and strengthening the Navy's relative power. Typically, he fought hard and was prepared to resign if necessary. Ironically, Forrestal became the victim of his own strategy, for when the Secretary of the Army declined the job, Forrestal found himself the new Secretary of Defense, forced to play a hand that he had purposely made weak. Of course, Forrestal promptly began legislation to strengthen the office, but this was to take several years to accomplish.

The stage was now set for the tragedy that was to follow. Forrestal found himself in an historical situation that was not compatible with his personality. Forrestal's tense drive and his toughness had been needed in the war years; now, despite his incisive warnings, the nation wanted to return to normality. His own maneuvers had made his position as Secretary weak and had exposed the most vulnerable side of his personality: his inability to deal authoritatively with other powerful men. An excellent example of this is the following conversation that reportedly took place in the first war council meeting between the new Secretary and his Chiefs of Staff:

FORRESTAL: "I expect each of you gentlemen to attend each meeting of this body."
EISENHOWER: (then Army Chief of Staff): "I presume if we are out of town we can send our deputies."
(Silence)
FORRESTAL: "I expect each of you gentlemen to attend each meeting of this body."
EISENHOWER: "I had to break a very important engagement to get here this morning."
(Silence)
FORRESTAL: "I expect each of you gentlemen to attend each meeting of this body."[57]

We have seen how Forrestal was unable to convince the President that the arms budget should be raised. This further weakened his influence over the defense establishment. We have noted how he began to perceive the President as putting politics before national security and how their relationship deteriorated.

Forrestal had a considerable political following of his own. He had a charismatic appeal and essentially represented what could have been a conservative wing of the Democratic party. He was, in fact, perhaps closest to being a liberal Republican. He considered the idea of running for governor of New York, or Senator, but instead talked with the Republican Presidential candidate (Thomas Dewey) and may have had an agreement to stay on as Secretary of Defense if, as was expected, Dewey was elected. Forrestal, of course, did not actively campaign for Truman. We do not know what would have happened if Dewey had been elected and Forrestal's position had grown stronger. As it was, Forrestal was placed in an impossible position. By January of 1949, he was becoming quite depressed. He was not satisfied with his performance as Secretary of Defense. The budget was too low and he had not really achieved unification of the services (an impossible

----

[57]*Ibid.,* p. 284.

task, given the low budget). He was exhausted and began to regard himself as a failure.

We have noted that when a person is making a decision, he clusters meanings about the alternative he favors; we have seen that this bias may shift rapidly, as when the person shifted his preference for a cast iron stove to a sheet metal stove and back again. In a similar manner, a person clusters meanings about his self, and Forrestal's feeling of worth and confidence rapidly shifted to meanings of failure and worthlessness. His self-definition underwent a serious change. In March, the President asked him to resign. Leaving office precipitated the depression and paranoia that had been building up. The events that followed — Forrestal's reaction as he started to leave and realized he no longer had an official car, the help of his friends, the psychiatric diagnosis of involuntary melancholia, the unfortunate error in judgment that allowed him to jump to death — are carefully chronicled by Rogow.

We must note that, according to Rogow, Forrestal first showed signs of being sick in the spring of 1948. He had loss of appetite and weight, some insomnia, a feeling of chronic fatigue, and a number of nervous habits. As time progressed, his mind wandered from discussions at meetings, and he began to postpone trivial decisions. He began to fret and worry over decisions, wrote eight drafts of a minor speech, and grew incapable of making up his mind. There were also isolated incidents of memory slips and mistakes in identity. These facts have not been integrated into an analysis of his activities, such as the formation of the 1950 arms budget.

By the end of 1948, Forrestal believed he was being followed by communist and Zionist agents. He also felt that his phone was being tapped. When the President learned of this, he believed that Forrestal was probably correct and asked the Chief of the Secret Services to investigate. The investigation revealed that Forrestal was extremely forgetful and suspicious and had been accumulating a quantity of sleeping pills. In spite of all these signs of mental disturbance, most persons assumed that Forrestal was simply showing signs of exhaustion. Torre and Glaser[58] have noted that this kind of assumption also prevented the recognition of Foreign Secretary Castlereagh's illness.

Rogow observes that in the context of the developing cold war, it seemed reasonable to be anxious, insecure, and suspicious. But because of his "exhaustion," men began withholding decisions from him, having

---

[58]Mottram Torre and William Glaser, *The effect of illness on diplomatic intercourse,* Monograph No. 1, (New York: Research Institute for the Study of Man, 1963).

meetings without him, and so forth. This must have contributed to his feeling that his authority was being undermined and that people were being secretive.

While the three leaders we have examined in some detail have all reflected fairly uncommon psychological problems, lesser problems are probably quite frequent. Men in high office usually enjoy power and, as Lasswell[59] has pointed out, power is often a compensation for a basically low self-esteem. Unconscious problems always interfere with the making of any decisions that involve those problems. Times of stress are likely to demand powerful leaders and thus increase the possibility of aberrations. When we remember that strokes, doses of tranquilizers, and many other medicinal drugs have psychological side effects, we may well be puzzled by the fact that less provision is made for detecting and helping psychological problems in public officials than in private industrial managers.

In 1947, Forrestal could have resigned voluntarily, but by late 1948, he did not have the strength to face the loss of esteem and the new life he would have to create. His agony was prolonged. No one realized how ill Forrestal was until it was too late. He could have been helped. As Rogow[60] notes, it is well to name a super carrier after Forrestal, but "perhaps the most lasting tribute to James Forrestal would be a massive effort to reduce the incidence of physical and mental breakdown in political life."

---

[59]Harold Lasswell, *Power and Personality* (New York: W. W. Norton & Company, Inc., 1948).
[60]Rogow, *op. cit.*, p. 351.

CHAPTER 6

Interpersonal Relations: The Small Group

The Formation of Groups

When a job needs to be done, the chances are that a group will form to do it. We may study this process by examining the formation of the group that met in order to deal with the invasion of South Korea. You will recall that when the United Press received news of the invasion from an alert reporter in Korea, it asked the Public Affairs Officer of the Bureau for Far Eastern Affairs for confirmation of his dispatch. This was an established procedure, and it was natural for the public affairs officer to then contact the Assistant Secretary for Far Eastern Affairs. By an "established" procedure, I mean a procedure that is dictated by the positions men hold and the roles they are expected to play. The press is *supposed* to contact the Public Affairs Officer. From our knowledge of the positions, roles, and norms, we would predict that communications would flow the way they did. If they did not, we would be surprised and would look for an explanation. For example, an exception might be caused by a "status incongruity" — where the person filling a position has been given more or less status than others believe he deserves. Established procedures help to determine group formation. We would be surprised if the Assistant Secretary for Far Eastern Affairs was not included in a group that formed to meet an invasion in the Far East.

When the Assistant Secretary was phoned, a "chance" factor became introduced into the group formation process. Since the Assistant Secretary of State happened to be at a dinner party with the Secretary of the Army, the latter also heard the news. When he called the Secretary of Defense, he was delegated the responsibility of following the invasion and, after stopping by the Pentagon, he went to the State Department and became part of the group that was developing there. Of course, we must note that such "chance" factors often reflect the factor of personal friendship since friends are more apt to be in contact with one another and are more likely to be confided in.

As soon as the Assistant Secretary for Far Eastern Affairs received the additional information contained in the Ambassador's cable, he notified the Secretary of State — an established procedure — and the Assistant Secretary for United Nations Affairs. This latter move can be considered neither as a completely established procedure nor as due to chance; it forces us to recognize another factor involved in group formation. We know that the Assistant Secretary for Far Eastern Affairs was a strong supporter of the United Nations and probably thought of using that organization to help solve the portending conflict. The Assistant Secretary for United Nations Affairs would provide support for such an idea, and we would guess that this was one reason why he was quickly brought into the group. Certainly, it is true that shortly after the Assistant Secretary for United Nations Affairs arrived at the State Department, he spoke on the phone with the Secretary of State and mentioned that both he and the Assistant Secretary for Far Eastern Affairs thought that the United States should react to the invasion through the United Nations, perhaps by calling the Security Council to an emergency session. While the Secretary of State was not as committed to strengthening the United Nations,* he accepted this recommendation and suggested it to the President when he phoned him later that night. When the President concurred, the group completed the initial arrangements to begin responding via the United Nations.

The "need for support" factor may also help to account for the inclusion of the Ambassador at Large, who was a strong supporter of the United Nations. We conceive of this factor as including not only the need to gather support so that one's views will be accepted but also the need to gather support for the implementation of these views. When a leader is dependent on others to furnish money, time, or commitment, he will wish to include them in the decision group.

While the State Department's Counselor would not have supported going to the United Nations,** it would have been natural to call him

---

*The antipathy of the Secretary of State was reflected three days later when, at the end of a briefing for leading congressmen, the President had to prompt him, "But Dean, you didn't even mention the U.N."
**He later argued that becoming involved with the United Nations restricted the nation's freedom of action.

because he was an expert on Soviet intentions. How, then, can we account for his *not* being called? Although the Counselor was at a summer cottage where there was no phone, another key man without a phone was notified by using the State Police Service. Furthermore, when the Counselor finally arrived in Washington (still unnotified) the following afternoon, the Secretary of State asked him to come to a dinner meeting with the President — but somehow his name was not included on the guest list and, hence, he could not attend. To explain these oversights, we must invoke another factor — the rejection of a group deviant.

The rejection of deviancy

Group rejection of a deviant has been produced experimentally by Schachter.[1] He introduced a confederate into each of several groups that were discussing problems in juvenile delinquency. The confederate was instructed to argue for a solution that deviated from the solution advocated by the majority of the group. Faced with this deviancy, each group would try to convince the arguer that he was wrong. At first, the deviant would receive a great deal of attention; but when this failed to bring him around, the group would begin to ignore him completely. At the close of the meeting, the experimenter asked each member of the group to indicate those members whom he would like to see included in his group for the next meeting. The man who had persisted in arguing against the group was usually not included — the group rejected the deviant.

While, in the above experiment, the deviant was actually a confederate, the observation of untampered groups has shown that, as time passes, one member often begins to play the role of a deviant. That is, he tends to consistently raise objections to the policy or solutions favored by the rest of the group. One might suppose that this type of behavior would come from a rather obnoxious character with little real ability, and often the group seems to perceive him in precisely that way. In fact, the role is usually played by an assertive person who is a potential leader of the group, a man who may have lost out in the struggle for leadership but who could take over the leadership of the group if the opportunity arose.[2] In a sense, then, deviancy is one kind of reaction to a status incongruity. While an uncontrolled deviant can be destructive to the group's goals, usually the role is functional and the deviant fulfills a real need by continually challenging assumptions

---

[1]Stanley Schachter, "Deviation, rejection, and communication," in *Group Dynamics* (2nd edition), ed. D. C. Cartwright and A. Zander (Evanston, Ill.: Row, Peterson 1960).
[2]I am indebted to Albert Hastorf for this observation.

and keeping the group on its toes. In the chapter on perception, we observed how useful such a "devil's advocate" could be. Unfortunately as Schachter's experiment demonstrates, this is often not appreciated and the deviant is likely to be rejected.* Rejection produces a more homogeneous group that smooths interpersonal relations but prevents a wide range of views that may aid problem solving if the conflict is tolerable.

Now let us see how these observations may apply to the case at hand. The State Department's Counselor was a brilliant man with strong views of his own. He had served in the American embassy in Russia and had been influential in formulating American policy towards that country. He would have enjoyed directing his country's foreign policy and, while this was not a real possibility, he undoubtedly could have if the circumstances had been different and he had been appointed Secretary of State. In such a situation, we would predict that the Counselor would begin to take on the role of State Department deviant; and this is precisely what seems to have occurred. For example, a day after the group we have been examining secured the President's approval to respond via the United Nations, the Counselor volunteered to brief a number of allies on the situation in Korea. In this briefing, he presented the American decision to intervene in Korea as justified by the unique responsibility of the United States, rather than as a defense of the charter of the United Nations. That is, he presented his own views rather than the group's views. The group reacted by preventing him from giving any more briefings. The Counselor could not understand this intransigency — the allied ambassadors had responded very favorably to his presentation!

This egocentricity is quite natural in a person who is in the position of a deviant. Since he has confidence in his own view of the situation but lacks the security of group support, he tends to shut himself off from the group's feelings and react vehemently to the actions of those who have the power to implement a different view. One test of a good group leader is his ability to tolerate and make constructive use of his deviant. It is a tribute to the Secretary of State that he was able to utilize the Counselor for his ideas without losing control over decisions or becoming threatened. Undoubtedly, the secure position of power which the Secretary enjoyed because of his excellent personal relations with the President helped him in utilizing the great abilities of a man who was a potential rival. He did not need to reject the deviant.

*Murray Horwitz has noted that rejection is most apt to occur if the group feels that the deviant is not giving the other members as much respect or consideration ("weight") as they feel is their due.

The Assistant Secretary for Far Eastern Affairs was in quite a different situation. Without the power of the Secretary, and trying to advance an idea which he knew the Counselor would oppose, he may have perceived the Department's deviant as a competitor and developed a need to reject him.

We may further specify our views about the nature of deviancy and the response to it by postulating: (1) If circumstances allow the deviant to become a group leader, he will undergo an apparent personality change. He will begin asserting his views in a reasonable way with tolerance for the views of others, and he will no longer be argumentative, stubborn or extreme in his views. (2) The more secure the power position of a group's leader, the more the leader will be able to utilize the talent of the group's deviant.

These two hypotheses are good examples of current thinking in social psychology. Note how the behavior of an individual is seen to result from the structure of the situation rather than from his personality. The postulate asserts that *anybody* who is in the described situation will react in the proscribed way. Characteristics such as argumentativeness and cooperativeness are seen as products of the situation rather than as character traits.

Expansion of the group

Returning now to the factors involved in the formation of a group, we may note that the five factors which we have specified — established procedures, the chance factor, personal friendship, the need for support, and the rejection of deviants — are sufficient to account for the formation of the group that first met, on Saturday night, to consider the Korean crisis. The following day, the situation in Korea grew worse and the President, who was in Missouri, decided to interrupt his plans and return to Washington. He asked the Secretary of State to assemble a group of advisers for a meeting that night. From his own department, the Secretary asked his Undersecretary, the Assistant Secretaries for Far Eastern and United Nations Affairs, and the Ambassador at Large. He also asked, from the Defense Department, the Secretary of Defense, the three service secretaries, and the Joint Chiefs of Staff. While no new factors were involved in the formation of this larger group, we should note that the group was built on the earlier group and that the inclusion of the Assistant Secretary of United Nations Affairs reflected the need for his support to implement the earlier decisions to respond through the United Nations. With minor exceptions, this larger group remained the decision-making group throughout the next five crucial days.

Restricted resources

The above factors are sufficient to account for the various groups that formed in the course of making the 1950 defense budget and the document titled NSC-68. However, one group that was crucial in the development of the Marshall Plan forces us to introduce an additional factor — the limitation and use of available personal resources.

It will be recalled that, in 1947, the administration found it necessary to seek funds for the aid of Greece and Turkey. When the Undersecretary of State perceived that it might be possible to obtain funds to aid additional countries, he directed the State-War-Navy Committee to study the problem of where else aid was needed and how it should be given. He selected this committee because it had an efficient secretariat and was the only group that integrated the different departments — although its function had hitherto only involved policy in occupied enemy countries. This committee proceeded to form an ad hoc group to study the problem. As Jones[3] points out, one might expect that there would have been considerable competition to serve in this important group, that its work would be closely directed and its report eagerly awaited. This was not the case. In part because the committee's Chairman was not widely known and had little authority, in part because the State Department representative was a newcomer, and in general because high officials were too busy, the committee found it difficult to get high ranking officials to serve in the group or give it much attention. Faced with these circumstances, the representative from the War Department suggested that the committee give up trying to get prestige and rank in the group, and concentrate on getting young, low ranking officials who were known to be interested in the aid problem, hard working, and filled with ideas. This procedure was successful, and the group that was formed did excellent work — work that became the foundation upon which higher officials later built the Marshall Plan. Thus, in this case, the factor of limited personal resources was met by forming a group from newly discovered resources.

Pervasiveness of the small group

It is important to note how pervasive small group meetings are. Because of the necessity of assuring the representation of different

---

[3] J. M. Jones, *The Fifteen Weeks* (New York: The Viking Press, Inc., 1955).

factions, there are even more group meetings involved in running the government than in running a large business. Committee meetings are the cement of a bureauocracy and even high level decisions are preceded by at least one, and usually many, meetings of small groups of men. While the size of these groups varies, they rarely exceed fifteen men. For example, there were six *major* meetings *within* the executive branch during the week of the Korean crisis. Four of these groups had from twelve to fourteen members, and the other two had six members. During the Cuban missile crisis, there were fifteen members in the major group meetings. It is also worth noting that the Soviet Union's Presidium has from twelve to fifteen members.

In a crisis situation, such as the Korean Invasion, there may be only one group of men directly involved in the decision process. The pressures of time and secrecy and the fear of getting bogged down by objections from different interests, may result in a decision that has involved few consultations outside of this immediate group. The rest of the administration, the bureaucracy, the Congress, and the public may be presented a fait accompli. This is not to say that the reactions of these larger elements of the society are not carefully considered by the decision making group, nor that feedback from these elements is not important in governing subsequent decisions. Nevertheless, the decision itself may be directly influenced by only one small group of men.

The Group Meeting

Since a small group of men may hold the fate of the entire nation in their hands, one wonders how they act in their meetings. What forces shape their discussion, what is the meeting like, does their group behavior follow the same rules which other groups obey? While no social scientist has tape-recorded an important meeting of government officials, enough details have emerged from memoirs and interviews so that some meetings can be partially reconstructed.* These reconstructions are aided by a knowledge of group processes which we have derived from group meetings that have been observed and experimented with.

As we have seen, the Secretary of State assembled a group of twelve other advisors to meet with the President the day after the invasion of Korea began. The group met at the living room of Blair House at

---

*Transcripts of important meetings are sometimes on file in the government archives. These are usually not available to the researcher.

about 7:30 p.m. and held a preliminary conversation as they waited for dinner to be served. The Secretary of State reported that the Security Council had passed the essential parts of a resolution that had been presented by the United States.* The resolution noted an attack by North Korea, called for a ceasefire and withdrawal to the 38th parallel, and asked for members to render assistance in the execution of the resolution. One of the participants later reported, "One of my most vivid recollections of the Sunday meeting is of the President sitting in sort of a window seat saying, to no one in particular, 'We can't let the U. N. down; we can't let the U. N. down.'"

The Secretary of Defense and the Chairman of the Joint Chiefs of Staff had just returned from Tokyo (there had been no hint of the invasion while they were there) and wanted the group to hear a memorandum concerning the Chief of Far Eastern Forces' views on Formosa. Intelligence had reported that the Communist Chinese were ready to invade Formosa and had been so for the past ten days. Although Formosa was considered part of China and current American policy was to avoid intervening in the Chinese Civil War, the Chief of Far Eastern Forces argued that the island was of great strategic significance and that the United States should aid in its defense. The Secretary of Defense considered Formosa to be of strategic importance, and he asked the Chairman of the Joint Chiefs of Staff to read the memorandum to the group.

Shortly after 8:00 dinner was announced and the President requested that all discussion be postponed until after the meal. As soon as the table was cleared, the group settled down to business.

The President stated that he had an open mind, had not made any decisions, and wanted to hear everything his advisors had to say. He said that he was not planning to make any quick decisions. He then asked the Secretary of State to open the discussion with a detailed picture of the situation. The Secretary first reviewed the information which supported the idea that an all-out invasion had been launched. Then he gave a detailed account of the meeting of the Security Council and reported that a note was being delivered to Moscow requesting a disavowal of responsibility for the invasion. He concluded by offering some suggestions for action. These were that more military equipment be furnished to South Korea, that American planes cover the evacuation of citizens, that the Air Force be authorized to destroy North Korean tanks and planes interfering with the evacuation (and

---

*At the time, the Soviet Union was boycotting the Security Council and thus could not exercise a veto.

therefore slow up the invasion), that consideration be given to what further assistance might be given under the Security Council resolution, and that the Seventh Fleet be ordered to prevent a Chinese Communist invasion of Formosa.

Personal conflict and group unity

This last recommendation, concerning Formosa, was quite radical since it involved a shift in the nation's policy to avoid intervention in the Chinese Civil War. To fully understand what lay behind this recommendation, we must digress from the group meeting for a moment and examine the background of the group. The principal schism in the group of assembled men was between the Secretary of State and the Secretary of Defense. There had been a number of disputes between the two men, such as the conflict over whether the State or Defense Department was to have jurisdiction over South Korea. In this dispute, as in most, the President had finally decided in favor of the Secretary of State. The President clearly felt close to his Secretary of State, considered him loyal, had confidence in his judgment, and usually supported him in any conflict. As we have seen, it was the Secretary of State rather than the Secretary of Defense who first talked with the President about the Korean Invasion; neither man even knew that the Secretary of Defense had returned earlier in the day from his trip to Japan. In addition to the tension created by various interdepartmental conflicts, the two Secretaries obviously disliked and distrusted each other personally. Reportedly, the Secretary of Defense undercut the Secretary of State whenever he could. He supplied ammunition to hostile Senators and frequently dropped remarks, such as "I'll keep asking what his China policy is until I find out." The conflict between these two cabinet members helps to account for several events that occurred.*

One of the many disputes between the Secretaries had been an argument about how to deal with Formosa. Both the State and Defense Departments** believed Formosa to be strategically significant, but this belief may have meant more to men charged with maintaining the nation's defenses than to men concerned with over-all foreign relations. Since Formosa belonged to China and the remnants of Chinese Nation-

---

*It would be interesting to study the effects of other cases of conflict between cabinet members, such as the classic dispute between Hamilton and Jefferson in Washington's cabinet.
**State Department" and "Defense Department" are, of course, abstractions — in fact, individuals in each department had varying views, and the stated view is really the consensus in the Department or the position taken by the Department rather than the common views of the individuals in it.

alist Forces had retreated to the island, the State Department had to consider how support for Formosa and, hence, intervention in the Chinese Civil War would affect the Chinese Communist government, a government which many hoped to encourage to be another Yugoslavia — communist but autonomous from Soviet control and not unfriendly. In spite of these desires, a number of persons in the State Department wanted the Defense Department to station troops on Formosa and guarantee its defense. The Defense Department, however, felt that its forces were too limited for it to commit troops to Formosa. It believed that the State Department should give diplomatic and monetary aid to Formosa in the hopes that this aid and a small military mission would suffice to defend the island. The State Department completely disagreed with this judgment — it was believed that this type of action would be insufficient to defend Formosa and would result in a further loss of prestige for the United States. The support would only serve to damage relations with Communist China and interfere with relations with India, Indonesia, and Indo-China. Consequently, the State Department opted for no support rather than the little support which the Defense Department was willing to grant. A group of Senators supported the policy urged by the Defense Department, and this forced the conflict up to the President — who ruled in favor of the State Department. Thus, at the time of the Korean Invasion, the policy of the United States was to keep out of the Chinese Civil War and thereby let Formosa fall to a Communist invasion that was anticipated in the very near future.

Why did the Secretary of State decide to recommend interposing the Seventh Fleet between Formosa and the mainland, thereby changing the policy of non-intervention? In the chapter on decision making, we noted that one factor may well have been the desire to have unity in a time of crisis. The recommendation was one on which both departments could agree, and, hence, it helped reduce the division between the two Secretaries; it was also one that would gain the support of the segment of Congress that had been so critical of the administration's China policy. While it has often been observed that a group tends to unify to meet a crisis, the precise conditions under which this occurs have not been specified. There are times when a group shows its weakness and shatters under the impact of a crisis. Here, we seem to have an instance of pulling together in spite of various personal animosities. The cohesion of the group was aided by the fact that the group members had no real role conflicts, everyone present shared a common responsibility for national security, and all the advisers felt they were under some pressure to agree so that the President could act with decisiveness. The force towards unity manifested itself in several other events that occurred, such as the fact that three days later the Secretary of Defense publicly praised the Secretary of State for the fine job he was doing.

After the Secretary of State had presented his recommendations, the President called on each of his advisers in turn to comment on the recommendations and to contribute further suggestions. He first asked the Secretary of Defense to present the views of his department. The Secretary said that he had no recommendations to make. This failure to either make suggestions or present a clear view of the military situation, and the Secretary's general lack of participation in the meeting, may be partly accounted for in terms of the Secretary's resentment of the relation between the President and the Secretary of State. He evidently felt that since the Secretary of State had wanted responsibility for Korea, and since the President had favored his request, the Secretary of State could now stew in his own juice for a while. While this resentment may seem rather childish, we human beings are often childish, and even high officials are humans. We must note that within four days it was clear that American forces were going to be deeply involved, and the Secretary of Defense left his resentment and began to take the initiative in describing the situation and making recommendations.

Differences of opinion

When the President called on the various members of the Joint Chiefs of Staff, they presented no prepared or coordinated estimates of the military situation but did discuss the difficulties involved in fighting on the narrow and mountainous Korean Peninsula. They also examined whether a commitment was possible in view of American responsibilities in other areas. There was still unanimous agreement that Korea was of no strategic importance in a global war. There was a general feeling that information on the progress of the fighting was too limited to be sure of anything other than the seriousness of the situation. On the one hand, the North Koreans had gone from ten to twenty miles beyond the 38th Parallel and were only twelve miles from Seoul. On the other hand, there were reports that the invasion was slowing down and meeting increased resistance. The group's consensus was that the attack would probably be contained. In general, there was a complete overestimation of South Korean strength and a complete underestimation of North Korean strength. We have already seen how the Ambassador's report and various military estimates, which could have corrected this illusion, had been filed away and forgotten; it is important to note that all fourteen of the men present shared this illusion of relative South Korean strength.

There was a general discussion of the intentions of the Soviet Union. There was no doubt in any minds that the invasion had been inspired and controlled by the Soviet Union, but the implications for general Soviet strategy were unclear. It was believed that the Soviet Union was still not ready to risk a global war but that there was a possibility of the invasion being succeeded by attacks in Iran or Yugoslavia or coordinated with the Communist Chinese invasion of Formosa or with an expansion into Indo-China. The possibility of a guerilla uprising in the Philippines was also considered, and there was some concern that the Soviet Union might attempt to land troops in Japan (since there was still no peace treaty and they could invoke the right of belligerency). It is interesting to note the many possibilities which the group brought up; and it should be observed how this adeptness involved treating the Soviet government as though it were a rational opponent. In view of all these possibilities, the President ordered a worldwide intelligence alert to check on other communist moves.

As we saw in the perception chapter, each member of the group perceived Soviet intentions in a slightly different way. The President saw another Munich, with the Russians gambling on the United States doing nothing — the strong attacking the weak with the fate of the United Nations at stake. Others saw a probing for a soft spot, an attempt for an easy limited victory with no willingness to risk an all-out war, a specific reaction in order to counter increasing Chinese power and American influence in Japan. Still others saw the attack as a possible diversionary move and noted that Korea was a poor place strategically for American arms. The differences in these perceptions were not really apparent to the members of the group and do not appear to have created real conflict in the group. To a large extent, this absence of conflict was due to a group consensus that the aggression had to be met in some way. Every member of the group shared the common experience symbolized by the word "appeasement," and no one perceived the situation as a local civil war in which it would be unwise to intervene.

In part, however, the absence of conflict seems to have been facilitated by a bit of distortion that masked differences in perception. All the advisors may have felt some pressure to agree so that the President could act decisively and meet the crisis as the leader of a unified group. Thus, the different perceptions did not really permit an agreement as to the extent to which the United States should become involved in the fighting. At least one advisor believed that ground troops should not be committed to Korea. Yet there was no realization in the group that there were differences in perception. The advisors came away from the meeting with different feelings about what had really been decided. For example, the Assistant Secretary for Far Eastern Affairs felt that the meeting was really a preliminary discussion based on meager information. For him, intervention was not a foregone conclusion and there was no commitment. For others, such as the Ambassador at Large, the meeting had reached a core of resolve — to not permit the aggression to succeed, at any cost. It would also appear that the President was not fully aware of these differences in opinion. One has the feeling that *his* opinion, to do whatever was needed to meet the aggression, had already been shaped by his perception of the situation. It appears that this influenced both what his advisors said and what he heard them say. We know, from laboratory studies, that when a group is placed under pressure to solve a problem, it creates forces to insure conformity and agreement. Evidently, in some circumstances this can lead the membership to distort what one another perceives so that the realization of differences is blurred. The conditions under which this occurs are not clear.

While the differing perceptions did not create much conflict, the masking of differences may have hindered a serious discussion of the proposal to defend Formosa. Also, the differences might have become serious if the Soviet Union had resisted the American intervention.

After talk about Soviet intentions, the discussion moved on to consider the relative capabilities of the United States and the Soviet Union. While the former appeared to be stronger, the President asked for a check of comparative military strength, a check on probable Soviet intentions, a study of what countermeasures were available if the Soviet Union intervened openly in the fight, and a worldwide intelligence alert to spot any other communist moves. The President also asked the Joint Chiefs of Staff to prepare an estimate of the measures that would be required to neutralize Soviet bases in the Far East; he questioned each of the Chiefs about the strength and disposition of United States forces in the Far East.

There was considerable disagreement over how much intervention might be required. Reportedly, the Army representatives felt that the South Korean Army might be able to repel the invasion by itself, while the Navy and Air Force believed that the superior North Korean airpower would prevent this. The Navy argued for a fly-over to show American support, while the Air Force wanted to engage in strategic bombing in North Korea. The Navy opposed bombing because of the civilian damage it would cause. No one foresaw the tremendous amount of support that was to be required. Both Air Force and Navy argued for tactical air support; but the Air Force wanted units based on South Korean fields, whereas the Navy pointed out that this would require troop support and that, therefore, carriers were to be preferred. The Navy and Air Force Chiefs of Staff felt that American naval and air power could prevent the South Korean defeat. (There was a constant overestimate of the effect which air power would have.) The Army Chief of Staff and the Chairman of the Joint Chiefs of Staff (an Army man) felt that infantry might be needed.

In spite of these disagreements, the President later recalled that in the course of the conversation, there emerged ". . . the complete, almost unspoken acceptance on the part of everyone that whatever had to be done to meet the aggression had to be done."[4] However, as we have suggested, this statement seems to reflect the President's own determination more faithfully than it reflects the opinions of all of his advisers — several of whom would probably have put definite limits on how much should be done to meet the aggression.

The President announced that there would be a crash program of military aid and that the naval and air units would be used to cover the evacuation of American citizens. He also believed that American pilots should have wide discretion in attacking North Korean planes and tanks. However, the Chairman of the Joint Chiefs of Staff asked that this not be authorized in the orders to the Far East, since he thought that the pilots would get the idea without being told and might give authorization a broader interpretation than that intended. The President asked the Joint Chiefs of Staff to prepare orders to make American forces available if they were requested by the United Nations. He decided that the Seventh Fleet should be ordered to Southwestern Japan, where it would be closer to both Korea and Formosa, but said that he wanted to sleep on the recommendation to blockade Formosa. Thus, all but the last of the Secretary of State's recommendations were immediately put into effect. Tentative plans were laid to meet again the next evening and the group broke up at about 11:00 p.m.

As one thinks about the meeting we have just described, it is almost as interesting to note what was *not* discussed, as what was. For example, while there was an obvious concern about risking American lives, at no time and in no subsequent meetings was there any consideration of *Korean* deaths. While there was an evident concern for the desires of

---

[4]Harry S. Truman, *Memoirs,* Vol. One: *Years of Trial and Hope, 1946-1952* (Garden City: Doubleday & Company, Inc., 1956).

the Korean government, there was no consideration of what the Korean people might desire.

Likewise, while there was a manifest concern for public opinion, there was no discussion of international law and how it might be furthered or subverted by different American actions. This is not to say that the officials present were at all callous or lawless persons; the discussion did not occur, because *it was nobody's job* to represent the concerns of the Korean people or of international law.

During the succeeding days of the crisis, substantially the same group met almost every day. At each meeting, the group took account of the increasing military news and the public reaction to the decisions made in the previous meetings. In general, the military news grew increasingly worse, the public response to each additional American involvement was positive, and more and more involvement was decided upon. During these meetings, the group behaved in approximately the same way as it did in the meeting we have just examined.

However, it must not be supposed that all important group meetings are conducted in the same fashion. The above meetings reflect the personal style of the President and the fact that a crisis was at hand; and, while the meetings illustrate a number of points described by researchers in group dynamics, we would have to look at other meetings in order to illustrate various other points. For example, Bales and Slater[5] have shown that a group often evolves two different types of leaders — a "task leader," who concentrates on getting the group to solve the problem it is confronting, and a "process leader," who concentrates on smoothing interpersonal relations and maintaining unity within the group. This differentiation is not apparent in the meeting we have examined. This may be due to the crisis atmosphere of the meeting or the ad hoc nature of the group. On the other hand, it may be an artifact caused by interviewers' neglecting interpersonal relations and reconstructing the meeting in only problem solving terms. That governmental groups do sometimes show a distinction between task and process leadership is evident from Hershey's[6] description of a Presidential staff meeting that occurred a few months later. Here it is clear that the President played the role of "task leader" and that his advisor

---

[5]R. Bales and P. Slater, "Role differences in small decision-making groups," in T. Parsons, R. Bales, *et. al.*, *Family, Socialization and Interaction Process* (Glencoe, Ill.: The Free Press, 1955).

[6]John Hersey, "Profiles: Mr. President II — Ten o'clock meeting," *The New Yorker* (April 14, 1951), pp. 38-55.

for press relations was the group's "process leader." Let us now consider in more detail the leadership of the group that met to handle the Korean Invasion.

Group Leadership

It should be noted that during the entire meeting — and all the subsequent meetings — there was no doubt about who was the leader of the group. The President opened the discussion by indicating he had a decision to make, and he conducted the discussion by calling on people to speak. Later, when someone wished to speak, he went through the President. At times, the President would ask that certain information be gathered. At the end of the meeting, he announced his decisions and closed the meeting — he was completely in charge.

Pressure from the leader

Most experiments on group problem solving have dealt with groups whose members have approximate equality; these groups develop leaders, but the leaders do not have much formal authority. Working with such groups, Hamblin[7] has experimentally shown that group members are more willing to accept directive leadership when a crisis exists, and this dynamic fact may have contributed to the complete acceptance of the President's authority during the Korean crisis. However, in the Korean case, we have a group where there is one acknowledged leader who cannot be challenged when he asserts his formal role and who cannot be replaced (unless he were impeached). We need experimental studies of such groups, for there may be slightly different dynamics. For example, in such a group everyone must develop a sensitivity to what the leader is thinking, and there must be great pressures against elaborating a train of thought which the leader is obviously opposed to. One incident that occurred during the meeting we have been considering illustrates the type of pressure involved.

Towards the end of the meeting, the Undersecretary of State (formerly Director of the Bureau of the Budget) said, "I'd like to talk about the political aspects of the situation." Reportedly, the President snapped back, "We're not going to talk about politics. I'll handle the political affairs." As we have noted, there does not appear to have been a process leader to smooth over this exchange. The Undersecretary of State did not speak again during the meeting and does not appear to have been present at subsequent meetings of the group.

---

[7]Robert L. Hamblin, "Leadership and crises," in Cartwright and Zander, *op. cit.*

Furthermore, months later when the President and his advisors debated the wisdom of pursuing the invaders back into North Korea, no one brought up the question of politics. This was a serious omission, for, as Neustadt[8] has observed, the considerations of politics would have dictated caution and averted the disaster that followed.

It must be observed that while the President's authority hindered communication, it pulled his advisors together. A weak leadership might have permitted the development of disputes with resultant disunity and lack of action. The President did not permit his advisors to fight among themselves; he insisted on setting the stage for reaching a decision rather than for obtaining a weak compromise. Nevertheless, since a strong leader is bound to exert a normative force that inhibits the expression and development of ideas contrary to his own, he must go out of his way to encourage his group to act freely. As Sorenson[9] observes,

> Even the most distinguished and forthright advisor is usually reluctant to stand alone. If he fears his persistence in a meeting will earn him the disapprobation of his colleagues, a rebuff by the President, or (in case of a 'leak') the outrage of the Congress, press, or public, he may quickly seek the safety of greater numbers.

The President in office during the Cuban missile crisis conducted group meetings without creating as much pressure for agreement. He was in a different relation to his advisors and they were free to speak up and even hold a straw vote. Nevertheless Sorensen states,

> [The President], learning on his return . . . that the deliberations of the NSC executive committe over Cuba had been more spirited and frank in his absence, asked the committee to hold other preliminary sessions without him.

Distance between leader and group

We have indicated that a good leader should both provide an opportunity for unpopular ideas and exert his strength to insure a decision. Such a feat is possible only when he maintains the appropriate amount of "distance" between himself and his group. In fact, Fiedler[10] has argued that good leadership is contingent upon the leader having

---

[8]R. E. Neustadt, *Presidential Power* (New York: John Wiley & Sons, Inc., 1960).
[9]Theodore C. Sorensen, *Decision-making in the White House* (New York: Columbia University Press, 1963), pp. 62, 60.
[10]Fred Fiedler, *Leader Attitudes and Group Effectiveness* (Urbana, Ill.: University of Illinois Press, 1958).

a moderate "distance" between himself and his key associates.* He suggests that "distance" is a function both of the leader's approachability and aloofness and of the relationship between leader and men. Thus, a moderate distance may be secured by having either an approachable leader who rather dislikes his key associate, or an aloof leader who likes his key associate.

According to this analysis, we can estimate the distance between a leader and his key associates if we have a measure of how much he likes them and a measure of how aloof the leader is. The former is easily obtained by giving the leader a sociometric rating scale. Fiedler believes that the latter, the leader's aloofness, can be measured by asking the leader to rate a worker he likes and a worker he dislikes on such traits as friendliness, confidence, intelligence, etc. Given such a task, some leaders assume that there is little similarity between those opposite persons they are rating. That is, they see the person they like as having characteristics quite different from those of the person they dislike. They have a low Assumed Similarity between Opposites (ASO). Others assume that the liked and disliked workers are actually quite similar to each other. They have a high ASO. Leaders with high ASO purportedly are less aloof and keep less distance between themselves and their key associates. They hesitate to reject somebody as basically different from themselves and believe that there is a common core of goodness in each person. Leaders with low ASO purportedly keep more distance and see a disliked person as basically different from themselves.

Using these measures — sociometric ratings of liking and ASO — Fiedler has tested many groups: tank crews, basketball teams, surveying teams, management in farmer cooperatives, etc.; and he has often been able to show that a moderate distance is most functional. That is, when the leader likes his key associates, the group is more effective if the leader has a low ASO score.**

I have gone into this analysis in some detail because it appears that the basic idea of optimal distance between leader and key associate might be fruitfully applied in studies of government. For example, contrast President Truman with President Eisenhower. President Truman

---

*Of course, some tasks (such as military field operations) may require a large distance, whereas others (such as group therapy) may require a small distance. It is also possible that there are different kinds of "distance" operating in interpersonal relations.

**Unfortunately, this research is marred by the absence of an independent measure of distance between leader and key man and by a tendency to ad hoc explanations. Fiedler's more recent work proposes a much more elaborate theory. cf. "A contingency model of leader effectiveness." In Leonard Berkowitz (ed.) *Advances in Experimental Social Psychology:* (New York: Academic Press Inc., 1964).

characteristically behaved as a man with a low ASO score; that is, he assumed that people who did not think as he did were basically different from himself. President Eisenhower would appear to have had a high ASO; that is, he continually assumed that there was one truth and that all men of good will could get together to find it. His attitude implies that all people, whether they are liked or disliked, are basically alike. We would, therefore, expect that President Truman would have a more optimal distance with associates whom he liked, while President Eisenhower would be more effective when he was dealing with an associate he did not particularly like. For example, President Truman's relationship with his Secretary of State does seem to be characterized by a more optimal distance than President Eisenhower's relationship with his most liked and influential cabinet member, his Secretary of Treasury. On the other hand, as we saw in the last chapter, President Truman's relations with his disliked Secretary of Defense were hindered by the great distance between the two men. Note also that an analysis in terms of distance might help us understand why Eisenhower was such an effective commander of the Allied forces in Europe (a position that must have required the sympathy with diverse views which only a man with high ASO could give) and yet was a relatively ineffective President (a job which may require the distance which a good judge must keep).

Procedures for conducting a meeting

Often, meetings are conducted in quite a different way from the one we have described — a crisis situation where President Truman essentially *directed* a discussion with the aim of helping *himself* to make a decision. Neustadt's[11] description of one of President Eisenhower's regular cabinet meetings, shows the President *guiding* a discussion with the aim of having the *group* make a decision or reach a consensus. This difference in technique probably reflects both the non-crisis nature of the situation and the "high ASO" nature of President Eisenhower's personality. President Eisenhower wanted his associates to rise above the particular concerns of their department or job and consider the common good of the nation. He saw his own role as helping them reach a consensus on this basis, and he conducted meetings accordingly.

Neustadt is quite critical of Eisenhower's procedure and demonstrates that it hindered his effectiveness as a leader. He argues that the President is the only person responsible for the entire nation and that this

---

[11]Neustadt, *op. cit.*

responsibility cannot be delegated to others whose jobs require them to represent special interests. Both Eisenhower's ideal and Neustadt's criticism have merit; the one stresses the need for a person to rise above special *interests* to accept responsibility for the whole, while the other stresses the need for a person to be true to the *responsibility* entailed in his representing a part. Which view a person accepts determines his whole style of interaction with others. We may note:

1. Some members of a group, possibly those who would register a high ASO score, may be more comfortable when they consider the needs of the entire organization; whereas others may feel at ease only when they stick to the responsibility of representing their sub-group.

2. Some organizations — perhaps the American government — are designed to function when most positions are filled with men advocating special interests; other organizations — perhaps the American Army — are designed in a way that requires each man to keep the entire organization in mind.

3. Some procedures, such as parliamentary procedures, may be useful when individual responsibilities are expected to conflict; others, such as the procedure used in a Quaker meeting, may be useful when each individual is expected to keep the welfare of the whole in mind.

A related procedural topic is the relative advantages of asking advisers to write a "consensus text" or an "alternative text." In the former, preferred by President Eisenhower, advisers are asked to arrive at a consensus of opinion. In the latter, preferred by Secretary of State Marshall, advisors are encouraged to develop opposing points of view. The consensus text encourages a spirit of compromise and a search for common solutions. The alternative texts method prevents the masking of different opinions and gives the leader a maximum amount of choice. It would be interesting to examine when each of these procedures is most useful in surmounting the climate of opinion — preventing the organizational loss of insight we noted in Chapter 3.

It should be observed that all of these procedures may have psychological consequences. For example, the consensus text, or a meeting designed to get consensus, creates tensions when a participant is forced to compromise his position. On the other hand, alternative texts, or a meeting designed to help the leader decide, may encourage splits in the group and charges of favoritism. The writers of a consensus text have a more nearly equal status with each other and the leader; they all share responsibility. The participants in an alternative text are definitely at a lower status than the leader and do not have the same burden of responsibility. On the other hand, they may actually have a greater *access* to the leader. Different persons will react in different ways to these facts. Certainly, using either procedure, leaders should be more aware of the possible dangers inherent in the technique they use. They may then be more sensitive in spotting unfortunate incidents and in building safeguards.

Administrators usually like to obtain consensus from the group they are working with. Often, disagreement bothers them and they do not like to recognize that different persons may have conflicting power interests. This is understandable, since such differences can only be solved by "political" rather than "administrative" procedures. However, if different interests are not recognized, certain problems can result. An example of this sort of hazard is a misunderstanding that developed during the 1952-56 administration.

Rather than externally impose a budget limitation on the Joint Chiefs of Staff, President Eisenhower made an attempt to internalize the choice — to make the Chiefs responsible for considering economic as well as military factors in their budget deliberations. This worked for some of the Chiefs but not for others. Snyder[12] has noted that the Navy Chief of Staff reasoned that many considerations besides military ones should influence the defense budget, and felt that the consideration of economic factors was appropriate. On the other hand, the Army Chief of Staff had a much stronger professional commitment, believed in a sharp distinction in roles, and felt that the administration should be responsible for non-military considerations. He felt that saddling the Chiefs with economic considerations was a political gimmick. In his 1954 State of the Union speech, the President stated, "The defense program recommended in the 1955 budget . . . is based on a new military program unanimously recommended by the Joint Chiefs of Staff . . . " The Army Chief of Staff, who did not at all agree with the recommended military program, felt "nonplussed"; and his harsh testimony before the House Appropriations Committee later revealed his true sentiments and embarrassed the President.

The misunderstanding of the Army Chief of Staff's views by the President, Secretary of Defense, and Chairman of the Joint Chiefs of Staff, arose because the Army Chief of Staff passively accepted the game but refused to seriously play any role but the professional military role. Since the Army Chief of Staff had agreed to force cuts for 1957,

---

[12]Glen Snyder, "The 'new look' of 1953," in W. R. Schilling, P. Y. Hammond, and G. H. Snyder, *Strategy, Politics and Defense Budgets* (New York: Columbia University Press, 1962).

the others assumed that he would approve a phasing out of forces beginning with a sharp down-turn in 1955! Second, he did not have the opportunity to express his disagreement in an alternative text or a split paper — but he was essentially under orders to produce a joint consensus text paper and, hence, indicated his passive acceptance. Third, in order to provide a basis for the budget discussion, a set of hypothetical conditions was assumed. In the context of these assumptions, the Army Chief of Staff could approve of the budget. But he didn't really believe the assumptions; and, under the "real conditions," he didn't approve of the budget.

In experiments on attitude change, it has often been noted that if a person feels that the communicator wants him to change his attitudes or is manipulating him, then he will resist the communication. We might, therefore, expect to find that the Army Chief of Staff's resistance was related to a perception that he was being manipulated. It is, therefore, interesting to note that while the other Chiefs felt they had been given a degree of real choice, the Army Chief of Staff felt that " . . . incessant pressure was brought to bear on me, seeking to persuade me to make my views conform to a preconceived politico-military party line."[13]

Ways of controlling the group

Any of the procedures we have discussed may be conducted in different ways. For example, a meeting designed to achieve group consensus may be conducted in either a democratic or an autocratic way. An attempt to delineate several of these different ways to lead the group has been made in the classic experiments of Lippitt and White.[14] They make the following distinctions:

1. *Authoritarian.* The policy is determined in advance by the leader; procedures are dictated one at a time so that future steps are uncertain and members cannot seize the initiative; the task to be worked upon and the co-workers are dictated by the leader; the leader remains aloof from the group; the leader praises and criticizes individuals personally rather than in terms of specific actions. When leaders are trained to follow this style, they give more orders, praise and criticism. The orders often go against the

---

[13]M. B. Ridgeway, "My Battles in War and Peace," *Saturday Evening Post* (January 27, 1956), p. 46.

[14]Ralph White and Ronald Lippitt, "Leader behavior and member reaction in three 'social climates,' " in Cartwright and Zander, *op. cit.*

wishes of the group members, and the praise and criticism is personal in nature.

2. *Laissez-faire.* The policy is determined completely by the individual members of the group; information is supplied by the leader whenever it is requested; the leader does not participate in the group's work; the leader neither praises nor criticizes group members. Leaders following this style give out much information but do not exercise any influence or apply any pressure. The responsibility is placed completely on the group.

3. *Democratic.* The policy is determined by a group discussion in which the leader actively participates; procedures are outlined in advance, and alternatives are made clear; the leader does not participate in work assignment; the leader is objective in his praise and criticism of specific acts. When leaders are trained to use this style, they tend to use "guiding suggestions" rather than "orders."

The distinction between a "guiding suggestion" and an "order" is not sophistry. An "order" concerns only what the leader wants to do, whereas a "guiding suggestion" also takes into account the purposes of the group member. Thus, in leading a group of boys who are carving wood, an order might be, "Now I want you to first sharpen the knives," whereas the equivalent guiding suggestion would be, "That's a knife sharpener so that you can have sharp knives to carve with."

Lippitt and White have run a number of experiments in which the adults in charge of boys' clubs tried these different ways of leadership. In the most refined version of these experiments, four adult leaders were trained in each of the three ways of leading. These men each met with a group of five boys, a club, after school. The leaders shifted both group and way of leadership every six weeks, until each club had experienced each of the three ways of leadership. The behavior of the leaders and the reactions of the boys were observed during every meeting, and interviews with the boys and their parents established the feeling of the boys towards their group and the nature of their relations with their parents.

The behavior of the groups often differed markedly under the different leadership conditions. Groups under autocratic leadership tended to show a large amount of either aggressive or submissive behavior. When the group became aggressive, members often dominated each other and were hostile towards each other and destructive toward property. At times, scapegoating was observed to spontaneously occur. When the group became submissive, the boys became dependent on the leader's opinon and did not show the normal amount of spontaneous behavior, or many individual differences. The groups also showed a lack of zest and interest in work, a higher drop-out rate, and an explosive release of tension when the leadership shifted to a laissez-faire or democratic way. When an outside observer questioned each of the twenty boys as to whom they preferred as their leader, the boys did not prefer any one of the four men but did tend to like whichever man had happened to use the democratic way with their group; and nineteen preferred whichever man had used a democratic way, to whichever man had used an authoritarian way.

When the groups were under laissez-faire leadership, the above difficulties were not present. On the other hand, not much work was performed, and what was performed was of poor quality. Most of the time was spent in playing.

Under democratic leadership, much more work was performed. Not as much time was spent in working as under autocratic conditions, but the work was more original and continued when the leader left the room. There was also more group unity under democratic leadership. That is, a greater number of boys would gather in a sub-group, and there was more use of the word "we," more mutual praise, and a greater readiness to share property.

We must be careful not to overgeneralize from these experiments. The findings are limited to adults directing small groups of boys who have been reared in a democratic society. We cannot, therefore, be assured that they would apply to situations where adults are directing adults, or where the group members have been reared in different traditions, or where the "group" is a whole society. On the other hand, the experiments have a value that extends far beyond helping adults direct small groups of boys — these experiments attempt to develop a definition of "democratic leadership" that would apply to any type of group in any society. By carefully pointing out aspects of the democratic way, and by contrasting it on the one hand with authoritarianism and on the other with a laissez-faire attitude, Lippitt and White help us to formulate a definition of democracy so that we can recognize it and become sensitive to different ways of leadership.

When we try to apply these distinctions to the governmental groups we have been working with, we meet one serious problem. The definition which Lippitt and White offer seems limited to situations where there is no serious conflict between the leader and his group. The leader of a boys' club wants only a happy and productive club; and, hence, his goals do not tend to conflict with those of the boys. In the government and in many other enterprises, there are times when the leader has a definite goal that does conflict with the goals of at least some members of his group. We are not told how a democratic leader behaves in this important situation.*

Now, it may be argued that a truly democratic leader will take a vote and follow the wishes of the majority of the group. In actual practice, however, few leaders do this. In many groups, such as those led by the President, it is recognized that the decision and the responsibility for it lies entirely with the leader; and even in those groups where the group as a whole makes and is responsible for a decision, a real *leader* takes the responsibility of trying to get his group to do what *he* thinks is best; and, consequently, he does not take a vote unless he thinks he can win it. This is not to say that voting is functionless; on the contrary, it forces the leader to recognize the desires of members of his group.** However, this suggests that the essence of democratic leadership lies in the leader's concern for the needs of his group rather than in the procedure of voting. Thus, in a conflict situation, the "democratic" leader realizes that others have a different view, tries to take this view into account, and feels sorrow when he cannot. That is, he has a real concern for and valid perception of each group member's needs and values.

It may be objected that this description fits a "benevolent dictator" as well as a "democratic leader." To distinguish between them, we must add a proviso. The democratic leader sets or accepts some limit on the means he employs to realize his end. These limits may vary with the leader and the situation; they may consist of operating within a framework where a majority vote must be obtained in some way or other, or they may consist of a resolve not to abolish a legitimate opposition party or kill a recalcitrant member of the group. Whatever the limit is, there is some limit to what the leader will do to stay in power, regardless of how confident he is in his vision of what is best for his group.***

The reader may or may not accept these gropings towards a definition of democratic leadership. He may, for example, wish to reserve the term "democratic" for the leadership White and Lippitt describe and use other terms to distinguish a "caring" leader from a callous one. What is important is the realization that it is necessary to develop viable distinctions between different ways of controlling a group, dis-

---

*He may simply avoid having a meeting!

**It also forces the members of the group to make up their minds .

***Note that this limit on means only applies within his group. It does not necessarily affect his dealings with persons outside the group.

tinctions that hold even when the leader's vision conflicts with the goals of some members of the group. If we do not develop such distinctions, we are liable to confuse ways of leadership with the procedure the leader uses. For example, Eisenhower's procedure of obtaining a group consensus may seem more democratic than Truman's procedure of using the group to help him make his own decision. These are dangerous confusions. Obtaining a group consensus may be done in a legitimate democratic way, but it may also be used as a very devious device to manipulate a group into thinking it has made a decision which it has not in fact made. Having a group help the leader make a decision, may be done in an authoritarian way — using the group members and ignoring their values — but also in a democratic way — recognizing the individual needs and capacities of each member. We need to sharpen these distinctions if we are ever to improve group leadership.

Advisement

Distorting influences

No matter what his method or style, a leader such as the President or Secretary of State must have good advisors who give him honest advice. The first biasing that occurs lies in the choice of these advisors, who are often selected from a group of men who believe in what the leader believes. Then, unfortunately, there are a series of factors that work against an advisor's frankly presenting his ideas. In the chapter on perception, we observed how information is filtered by considerations of what others want to hear and by attention to what one personally thinks is important. These factors are also important in the transmission of advice. We have already noted how advisors hesitate to make suggestions that go contrary to the leader's train of thought, and later we shall see how this factor contributed to the disaster in North Korea.

A related distortion pressure stems from the advisor's need to present a good image to others so that his power as an advisor will be maximal. Thus, Sorensen[15] states,

> Still others may address themselves more to their image than to the issues. The liberal may seek to impress his colleagues with his caution; idealists may try to sound tough-minded. I have attended more than one meeting where a military solution was opposed by military minds and supported by those generally known as peace-lovers.

---

[15]Sorensen, *op. cit.*, p. 62.

A third hindrance stems from role conflicts within the advisor. If, for example, the advisor is also the head of a department, he must consider the effect his advice will have on the power of his own department. After all, his department has its own aims, clientele, and personnel problems; it has its own congressional relations to worry about. Therefore, the advice from a department head is shaped not only by the department's specialized perspective on events but also by the department's bureaucratic power interests. A fourth hindrance arises if the advisor has some political power of his own and desires to further his ambitions by building a viable political program. His advice may then be contaminated by his own needs for power. These conflicts of interests are minimized when the advisor is not in a department and has no political following, when he is simply a member of the President's staff. On the other hand, such an advisor has neither the power to influence the active operations of a department nor the responsible perspective of someone from the department.

The first two factors — the fear of the leader's opinon and the fear of presenting a poor image — create pressures on the advisor that are quite similar to the conformity pressures that have been studied by Asch[16] and by Deutsch and Gerard.[17] Their experiments clearly demonstrate that the expectancies of others, particularly when a group goal is at stake, create pressures that cause the average person to distort his own personal judgment and make incorrect statements which he believes the group will respect. The third and fourth factors, however, involve the search for power for one's group or one's self and create a different kind of pressure to distort. We have no studies that have investigated the circumstances under which these power pressures would cause a person to make incorrect statements or offer poor advice. It would seem possible to devise experiments based on this issue. A person could be placed in a conflict between offering good advice at a cost to his own power and offering poor advice without such a sacrifice — (or with a gain in power). One might think that if the poor advice would actually lead to the injury of others, most persons would forsake their own ambitions. However, it is not at all clear when this would be true. One's own immediate interests are often more compelling than group interests that will affect oneself indirectly, and there are all kinds of rationalizations available to soothe away misgivings.

---

[16]S. E. Asch, "Effects of group pressure upon the modification and distortion of judgments," in Cartwright and Zander, *op. cit.*

[17]Morton Deutsch and Harold B. Gerard, "A study of normative and informational social influences upon individual judgment," in Cartwright and Zander, *op. cit.*

Choice of an advisor

Given these distorting influences, it is not strange that a leader is much more apt to accept advice when there is a bond of attachment between himself and his advisor. This bond, which is composed of respect, trust, affection, and the ability to communicate, will only form between the leader and *some* of the persons who might be advisors by virtue of their position. Whether or not the bond forms, is influenced by personalities, social ties, and occupational background. For example, it has been observed that some Presidents seem to favor the advice of politicians, while others prefer generals, businessmen, or intellectuals.

During the period 1945-1952, the same President had four different Secretaries of State. His relations with the second were rather acrimonious and hindered by a sort of power struggle. Jones[18] states that the President regarded his third Secretary as a "perfect man." He had complete confidence in him and was awed by him — never relaxing in his presence. The Secretary, on his part, was always perfectly correct, loyal, and courteous — but dry and brief. With his fourth Secretary, the President had a comfortable and relaxed relationship. The President trusted him and backed him up, and the Secretary returned his loyalty and was completely frank in his advice.

A study of the history of relations between Presidents and their Secretaries of State has led Acheson[19] to hypothesize:

> If a President chooses a man of greater political stature than himself to be his Secretary, and if he does this in the belief that the appointment will add to the power of his administration, or will placate a rival's resentment, or will prevent his rival from doing more harm outside of the organization, then the President will be disappointed, and the relationship will have to be terminated or revised.

From his personal experience, Acheson points out that the President and his key advisors have to spend a great deal of time together working on frustrating problems that are sure to provoke controversy and that involve the acceptance of distasteful measures. In such circumstances, the advisor is a potentially unwelcome visitor; and the need for mutual respect, trust, and affection is a necessity. Acheson[20] concludes, " . . . a President's best guide is a sense of confidence in his appointee and a

---

[18]Jones, *op. cit.*

[19]Dean Acheson. In Don K. Price (ed.), *The Secretary of State* (Englewood Cliffs, N. J.: Prentice-Hall, Inc., 1960).

[20]*Ibid.,* p. 35.

belief that the man can help him more than others . . . " It would be interesting to do a historical study on this point, since Fiedler's theory of optimal distance suggests that the above statement would only hold true if the President tended to have a fairly aloof personality. Certainly, if the President might grow too close to his Secretary, it is conceivable that a certain amount of coolness in their relationship would help organizational efficiency. It is also not clear what the optimal relationship would be if the Secretary were more of a briefing officer and administrator rather than an initiator of policy in his own right.

In the chapter on personality, we observed how different Presidents have quite different styles of decision making. Fenno[21] shows how these stylistic differences affect how a President uses his advisors in the decision making process. Thus, Hoover, who kept tight executive control, initiated group discussions in order to explore the consequences of various alternatives which *he* proposed. Wilson, absolutely inflexible once he had broodingly made a decision, invited a rather free controversy before the decision. And Eisenhower, who liked to reach his conclusions in the process of talking to others, used his advisors to talk out his thoughts.

Each President expects different things from his advisors. Fenno notes that while Coolidge relied on Stearns for emotional support, he would not accept any advice from him — a quite different situation from the dependent relationship we observed between Wilson and House. Coolidge, Truman, and Eisenhower believed it was a virtue to delegate authority, while Wilson and Roosevelt liked to keep important decisions in their own hands. Whereas Truman relied heavily on various men who served him as Secretaries of State, backed up their authority, and expected their loyalty; Roosevelt kept his own council, constantly undercut the authority of his Secretary of State, and did not really expect a great deal of loyalty. A detailed study contrasting these various interpersonal relationships would be most interesting.

The acceptance of advice

While the bond between advisee and advisor is an important factor in governing the acceptance of advice, there are other elements that need to be considered. Sorensen[22] has pointed out that the rejection of advice may be a difficult task: advice that comes from a man who is going to have the responsibility of carrying out the decision has to be

---

[21]Richard F. Fenno, *The President's Cabinet* (Cambridge, Mass: Harvard University Press, 1959). (cf. "Dimensions and types of presidential influence" in Chapter 1.)
[22]Sorensen, *op. cit.*

seriously considered. If a man has committed his prestige and his advice is not taken, a dangerous enemy may result. If the public image of a cabinet member is involved and his advice is not taken, then his authority will be undermined. If an outside advisor has been used to gain support for one's position, then his advice must be followed or that support will be lost.* On the other hand, when there is conflicting advice, someone's cannot be taken; and, as we have seen, most advice is not motivated by a pure concern for the leader's position and responsibility. Consequently, the leader must use his own judgment in the acceptance and rejection of advice. He has his own vision of what the situation is and what will work. Let us see if we can state some of the conditions under which he will decide to accept a piece of advice.

1. When a problem is perceived and the decision maker has not yet formed a policy, he is open to suggestions. Thus, we saw how the Assistant Secretary for United Nations Affairs successfully suggested to the Secretary of State that the Security Council be called to an emergency session. This began the procedure of always directing the United States response through the United Nations.

2. When a problem is perceived and the decision maker has a policy, a suggestion that implements this policy will be accepted. Thus, when the Commanding General of the American forces in the Far East suggested that American ground troops be committed in order to save South Korea, this commitment was made. Likewise, when the Navy Chief of Staff proposed a blockade of Korea, this was immediately accepted.

3. When a problem is perceived and the decision maker has an opinion but is not yet committed to a policy, a trusted and close advisor may make an opposing suggestion and get it accepted *if* he has support from other advisors. For example, when the President of the Republic of China offered 33,000 troops to fight in Korea, the President of the United States was fully inclined to accept this offer. The Secretary of State advised against this. He argued that acceptance would alienate our allies, might provoke Communist China to enter the war, and would weaken the defense of Formosa at the very time the Seventh Fleet was being sent to protect it. The President was still inclined to accept the aid but checked with the Defense Department. They too were against acceptance, since it would divert logistic support away from

---

*These facts are added reasons for picking advisors who will give the advice one would like to get.

superior U. S. troops. The President reluctantly abandoned the idea.

It is not clear how frequently an advisor can make suggestions that go against his superior's opinions without endangering his position. This clearly depends on the closeness of their relationship, the depth of trust involved, and the superior's personality. The Georges'[23] description of Colonel House's relation with President Wilson, indicates that House had a great influence over appointments and policy with Wilson, who almost always accepted his suggestions; yet House could not risk the liberty of going against the President's formed opinion. This was basically due to the fact that President Wilson took such opposition personally. When House finally felt it imperative to offer advice that went against the way the President was dealing with Congress on the League of Nations, the President completely rejected him as an advisor.

4. When a policy is being implemented and a problem with the policy is not perceived, a suggestion to modify the policy may be accepted if the advisor pushes hard enough. For example, the Counselor to the State Department felt that if the Soviet Union countered the American intervention in Korea, then the United States should not automatically go to war but should regard the situation as a new one and make a new decision. This idea was supported by the Undersecretary of State but rejected by the Defense Department and the President — that is, they saw the problem as essentially one of resisting aggression whether or not there was Soviet intervention. The next day, the Counselor argued, on the Assistant Secretary level, that all government personnel should be told that if Soviet troops appeared, they should withdraw until further instructions were received from Washington. This maneuver succeeded in getting the question debated at higher levels. That afternoon, a senior Ambassador arrived from abroad and strongly sided with the Counselor. The next day, the Secretary of State asked that a directive be sent to the Commanding General of the United Nations forces to guide him in the event of Soviet intervention. The President approved this and asked the Secretaries of State and Defense to collaborate on its writing. By persisting, the Counselor had won his point. However, while the Counselor was successful on this particular point, he was not able to change

[23]Alexander and Juliette George, *Woodrow Wilson and Colonel House, A Personality Study* (New York: The John Day Company, Inc., 1956).

the perception of the majority of advisors (that the invasion was another move in the Russian game of expansion) to his perception (that the invasion was a local move to offset Chinese power gains).

Getting persons to accept advice is part of the business of diplomacy, and it would be interesting to see to what extent a "history of advice taking" would help us refine the statement of the above conditions. It might also be profitable to conduct experiments or simulations that investigate the taking or rejection of advice under different conditions and with different personalities. For example, an interesting series of experiments has centered about the conditions under which a problem solving group will accept a solution proposed by one of its members. In these experiments, the member is actually a confederate who has been given the correct answer. In this way, one may show that a solution proposed by a high status person is accepted when the same solution from a low status person is rejected. It may also be shown how the timing of a suggestion is important. Thus, Bavelas[24] has shown that if a solution is advanced too soon, it will often not be picked up by other group members who are too busy saying what *their* views are. And Hollander[25] has demonstrated that members who have conformed to the group's procedural norms are more likely to have their solutions accepted. It also seems probable that if a group is "set" on one solution to a problem, it will be quite resistant to a different solution, even if the latter seems obviously better to an outsider.

Maneuvers of the advisor

It is a rare advisor who has only the interests of the President at heart. He has his own values, responsibilities, and desire for power. Consequently, he has many motives to have his advice accepted, and he frequently maneuvers for a favorable position so that his advice will be difficult to refuse. If he is the Secretary of a department or the director of an agency, he has independent power which the President must consider. If he takes the responsibility of implementing a decision, or if he commits his prestige to a position, he forces the President to seriously consider his advice. He may also attempt to maneuver the President into a position where he is more likely to accept the advice. Schilling[26] describes two such maneuvers by the Secretary of Defense, who, in 1948, tried to get the President to accept his reconsideration for a further increase in the defense budget.

---

[24]Alex Bavelas, personal communication.
[25]Edward Hollander, "Competence and conformity in the acceptance of influence," *J. Abnorm. Soc. Psychol.*, 61 (1960), pp. 361-65.
[26]Warner Schilling, "The politics of national defense: fiscal 1950," in Schilling, Hammond, and Snyder, *op. cit.*

The first of these occurred during a group meeting called by the President to consider the recommended budget increase. Present were the President, the Secretaries of State, Defense, and Treasury, the Director of the Bureau of the Budget, and two Presidential staff advisors. The Secretary of Defense arrived after the group had listened to an effective presentation of the view that the budget should not be increased a second time. Seeing this, the Secretary of Defense stated that he had asked for the meeting so that the group could hear why the President had decided to increase the defense budget the first time! This maneuver called for the President to play his role as guardian of the National Treasury; it resulted in the President taking a neutral stance and asking for the opinion of his Secretary of State.

Defeated by lack of support from the Secretary of State, the Secretary of Defense attempted a second maneuver later in the year. He created two different budget proposals. The lower of these was based on a war plan that relied so completely on an air offensive from Britain that it was almost absurd. The higher budget was based on a balanced war plan. By presenting the President with this choice, he sought to compel him to weigh more carefully the costs of rejecting the higher budget. Schilling observes,

> Whether or not [the Secretary of Defense] had plotted this carefully, the choices he was trying to create afford a good example of how a President's subordinate might design alternatives which, in rational terms, have the appearance of free choice but which, politically, are decidedly rigged in advance.

It is interesting to see how this maneuver failed. When the Secretary told the President that he would formally present these two budgets, the President did not appear struck by the absurdity of the first war plan and was not receptive to the role of receiving alternative budgets. He told the Secretary of Defense that he wanted the higher budget held in reserve because its presentation would be interpreted as a step towards preparation for war. While it appears that the maneuver failed because it was too subtle to influence a mind that was already made up, the President's response illustrates a counter-move that could be purposively employed. Later, we shall examine such strategies in more detail.

The Dynamics of a Permanent Group

While many groups, such as the one that gathered to meet the Korean invasion, are ad hoc groups which disband as soon as their mission is over, others are of a permanent nature — miniature societies which outlast their individual members and have their own dynamics.

In Chapter 8 we shall consider some of the organizational and management problems of the State Department "Society." Here we shall consider some aspects of such a society's dynamics. A good description of these may be found in Fenno's account of the House Appropriations Committee.[27]

The enforcement of norms

The group that constitutes the Appropriations Committee is one of the most powerful Committees in the House of Representatives because it controls the flow of money and, hence, can reward or punish various administrative programs. The Committee is proud of its image of being the hardest working group in the House. In spite of its large size — it is the biggest committee and has from forty to fifty members — it is an extremely cohesive group. Thus, in the period from 1947 to 1961, only two men left the Committee voluntarily. As Back[28] has demonstrated, such high cohesion enables a group to apply strong pressure upon its members to obey its norms, and this certainly is the case in the House Appropriations Committee.

There is a consensus in the Committee that its job is to be the guardian of the Federal Treasury — that it is valuable to cut budgets down to the bone. While members are placed in some role conflict when they are ruling on appropriations that affect their own district, the Committee's ideology assigns top long range priority to budget cutting and makes constituency service a permissible short range exception. The norms of the Committee, which is divided into subcommittees, are quite clear and may be stated as follows:

1. Each member should become a specialist in some program area. This is how he can earn power and respect.
2. No member should interfere with another member's work. For example, one should not attempt to amend a bill that is put out by another subcommittee.
3. Each member should maintain subcommittee unity. He should be willing to compromise his personal position for the sake of unity and should not question the group's decision later in full committee. Likewise, no matter how negatively a Committee member feels toward the Committee's recommendations, he should not write a minority report or speak out against the recommendations

---

[27]Fenno, Richard F., Jr. "The house appropriations committee as a political system: the problem of integration," *Amer. Pol. Sci. Rev.,* 61 (1962) pp. 310-324.

[28]K. Back, "Influence through social communication," *J. Abnorm. Soc. Psychol.,* 46 (1951), pp. 9-23.

on the floor of the House unless he has specifically reserved that right previously in the Committee.

4. There should be minimal partisanship in the Committee. The ranking minority member must always be consulted by the Chairman; and, unlike proceedings on the floor of the House, votes should not be biased by party affiliation.

New members are selected with these norms in mind. Usually, the new member has already spent a couple of terms in the House and is regarded as "the kind of man you can deal with" or "a fellow who is well-balanced." When a first term congressman is selected, his reputation is carefully checked. The following quote[29] is revealing:

> The Chairman I guess did some checking around in my area. After all, I was new and he didn't know me. People told me that they were called to see if I was — well, unstable or apt to go off on tangets . . . to see whether or not I had any preconceived notions about things and would not be flexible — whether I would oppose things even though it was obvious.

In addition to this selection procedure, there is an intensive socialization period lasting from one to four years. The newcomer has to learn the norms and how to compromise. Liberals must learn to perceive budget padding, conservatives to grant the necessity of certain programs. The newcomer to the Committee is expected to work hard and keep quiet. He has little opportunity to speak. At some hearings conducted by his subcommittee, one newcomer made the mistake of deliberately asking as many questions as his subcommittee Chairman. He reported the following counteraction:

> In the hearings, I have to wait sometimes nine or ten hours for a chance; and he hopes I'll get tired and stay home. I've had to wait till some pretty unreasonable hours. Once I've gotten the floor, though, I've been able to make a good case. Sometimes I've been the only person. . . . He's all powerful.[30]

The socialization process is aided by the application of rewards and punishments. An obedience to norms is rewarded by choice assignments and, later, by the opportunity of playing a role on the floor of the House. Disobedience is punished — by raised eyebrows, by not

---

[29]Fenno, "The House Appropriations Committee as a political system" *op. cit.,* p. 313.
[30]*Ibid.,* p. 322.

being sent on a trip to Europe, by a change in subcommittee assignment, by not being given anything to do. As a successful newcomer stated,

> The first year, you let things go by. You can't participate. But you learn by watching the others operate. The next year, you know what you're interested in and when to step in. . . . For instance, I've become an expert on the_____program. The Chairman said to me, 'This is something you ought to get interested in.' I did, and now I'm the expert on the Committee. Whatever I say on that, the other members listen to me and do what I want.[31]

It is interesting to see what is rewarding to a Congressman of moderate seniority. The following poignant quotation is from a man who had learned the norms and was now asking to be given a role on the floor of Congress for the Committee:

> When you perform well on the floor when you bring out a bill, and Members know that you know the bill, you develop prestige with other Members of Congress. They come over and ask you what you think, because they know you've studied it. You begin to get a reputation beyond your subcommittee. And you get inner satisfaction, too. You don't feel that you're down here doing nothing.

The bases of power

It should be noted that the rewards of prestige and inner satisfaction, and the various punishments, are not applied to teach a functionless norm. One factor that helps the attitudes of members of the Committee to change as they learn to conform to the norms of the group is that each member learns that the norms are valuable, that the norms within the group are his source of power outside of the group. The specialization, bipartisanship, tolerance, and compromise give the Committee a unity that contributes to its power. And the Committee is powerful — eighty-seven per cent of the Committee's recommendations are accepted by the House, and each administrator in any of the executive departments of the government must pay heed to the feelings of the Committee if he wishes his budget approved.

Fenno points out that the powerlessness of the newcomer leads him to view his Chairman as wielding an absolute power by virtue of his position within the Committee. The newcomer fails to perceive that

[31]*Ibid.,* p. 321.

the Chairman's power and his "idiosyncrasy credit"[32] is actually based on his obedience to most group norms. The experienced member views the power of the Chairman as a grant from the Committee, a grant contingent upon the Chairman's following Committee expectations. He knows that if a Chairman violates these expectations his senior colleagues will threaten a negative committee vote and thereby force conformity.

This observation points up the fact that current definitions of power do not adequately reflect the norms operating on the powerful and the socialization they have undergone. Most work on power emphasizes that a person with power can influence the behavior of others through the application of rewards and punishments which he controls, and through the charismatic influence which he may exert. However, as Homans[33] has indicated, a person gains power over others at the price of allowing others to influence himself. Perhaps more should be said about the granting of this power — of the expectations that govern its use and the training process that insures that these expectations are appreciated by the one in power. Of course, the powerful sometimes escape control — often for considerable periods of time — but, eventually, counter-forces always seem to reestablish the group's control over the leader.

The government as both a permanent and an ad hoc group

One can view the government as a permanent group with certain fixed relations between the President, the Cabinet, the Joint Chiefs of Staff, Congress, etc. From this view, one notes the checks and balances that have been institutionalized between the Executive, Congress, and the Judiciary, and the relative power and prestige of different departments and agencies within the Executive. One may talk of the relative status of different positions that grant certain powers to the incumbent and demand certain duties, and it is possible to examine the flow of communication, orders, and individuals from one position to another. However, one soon realizes that such a view omits a set of important variables — the unique interpersonal relations that characterize any particular administration or Congress. It is when we consider the government as an ad hoc group formed at a particular moment in history, that we are sensitized to the tremendous importance of inter-

---

[32]Edward Hollander, "Conformity, status, and idiosyncrasy credit," *Psychol. Rev.*, 65 (1958), pp. 117-27.

[33]G. C. Homans, *Social Behavior: Its Elementary Forms* (New York: Harcourt, Brace & World, Inc., 1961).

personal relations. With this viewpoint, we see an administration forming about a small group of men who can work closely with the President. We see that one President has a close relation with a man who
is Secretary of State, another with his Secretary of Treasury, a third
with his Attorney General, and a fourth with his Secretary of Defense.
Likewise, each President will rely on certain staff members whose judgment he respects and on whose loyalty he can count. The men closest
to the President form a nucleus, an in-group, which is at the heart of
policy formation.

It is apparent that there are a number of powerful men who are
not a part of this in-group. Some of these men are basically friendly
towards the position of the in-group and have within the administration
important positions that have been given to them because of their
ability and the confidence they inspire, or because of political services
they have rendered. Others have serious disagreements with the
in-group's position or personal antagonisms with some of its members.
These men are either given powerful positions by the in-group in an
attempt to contain their opposition and provide for a degree of unity
that would otherwise be lacking, or they have attained their position by
elections or appointments which the in-group does not control.

In order to implement its policy, the in-group must deal with some
of these other sources of power. When a man is basically friendly, or
when the issue is fairly straightforward, there are few problems; but
if the in-group wishes to follow a policy that is at all controversial,
communication problems usually erupt. These are due to the fact that
the in-group's relations with dissident powers are strained to begin
with. The persons involved are usually not friends and often have little
in common. Because of this, when the in-group becomes involved in a
controversial policy, it cannot easily explain its stance to the hostile
powers it must work with to carry out the policy. In this situation, the
in-group attempts to find envoys who are mutually trusted and have a
foot in each camp. These envoys attempt to mediate the differences
that arise and to achieve an integrated program of action. Unfortunately,
they are faced with very basic differences in opinions and must cope
with each side's mistrust of the other's goals. The outcome of this
conflict between the in-group's policy and the dissident powers who
are involved in its implementation often determines how the nation
actually behaves. In the next chapter, we shall examine this process in
some detail.

CHAPTER 7

Interpersonal Relations Commands and Communication:

The ability of a complex organization to translate decisions into appropriate actions depends on a clear line of authority and responsibility leading to the execution of orders. A poor organization may have two head men or a poorly defined chain of command that prevents everyone from knowing which official is responsible for which actions. But at the moment we are not concerned with these problems; we are concerned with the fact that men in the best of organizations always have the power to be somewhat independent of their superiors, and, for reasons of politics and because of the scarcity of good men, "subordinates" can actually become quite independent from the main organization.

In the chapter on perception, we saw how each person constructs his own view of reality. When the implementation of a decision depends on a person whose views differ from those of the decision maker, both parties are placed in a most delicate situation. The implementor may be torn between his loyalty to the organization — which requires him to obediently carry out the decision — and his own deep seated convictions that a different policy would be wiser. He knows that he has the possibility of revolting and establishing himself as a rival decision maker. On his part, the decision maker may be torn between his desire to back up his implementor and excuse certain deviations from policy and his desire to replace him with a more sympathetic person — in spite of the costs involved in such a removal. In this chapter, we shall consider an example of this situation: the relation between the President and the Commander of the United Nations Forces in Korea.

In the course of describing this interaction, we shall observe not only a failure to cooperate with orders but also an honest failure to interpret orders correctly and a failure to give orders. We shall see how all of these failures stemmed from the conflict between two powerful psychological worlds and the intractability and lack of communication that constituted their interaction.

Both the President and his Commander represented large groups of Americans who held different opinions; indeed, we might view the conflict between the two men as an excellent example of how conflicting domestic forces mold foreign policy. From this viewpoint, we would note that the Democratic administration held beliefs that would have eventually led them to recognize the communist government of China, while the Republican opposition held beliefs that might have led to a war against the communistic forces on the Chinese mainland. Under the catalyst of the Korean War, these beliefs clashed to produce a compromise policy — a commitment to defend the Nationalist Chinese forces that had retreated to Formosa. While this compromise appears to be an accurate reflection of the amount of power the United States had to expend in Asia (it was a good deal easier to defend Formosa than to challenge the communists on mainland China), neither party was completely satisfied, since the intervention prevented good relations with Communist China yet failed to seriously hinder the power of that regime. It is as though American foreign policy were determined by some inexorable law requiring the maximum extension of power rather than by the rational arguments made by each side.

Nevertheless, it would be a serious mistake to assume that foreign policy *has* to be the result of a-rational compromise. To view America's China policy as the *inevitable* result of compromising the different opinions of powerful political forces, is to ignore the individuals who shaped the conflict by their actions and who had the potential freedom to produce a more integrated policy — a policy that utilized the best in each group's thinking. It is for this reason that a complete explanation of foreign policy must begin with a description of the world of each individual leader and include the psychological forces that hinder or facilitate the communication between them and, hence, affect whether policy is a weak compromise or a creative integration. A description of the conflict between domestic forces must include the communication problems engendered by the different personalities and situations of the key leaders. Only with such an approach can we envisage how misunderstandings can be averted and opposing viewpoints can be creatively resolved.

Different "Worlds": General MacArthur and President Truman

The Commander of the United Nations Forces in Korea was not only in charge of a campaign. He was also the Commander in Chief, Far East and therefore the head of all United States army, navy and air forces in Japan, the Philippines, the Ruyuku's, Mariano, Guam, etc. Informally, he was the center of a nucleus of high ranking generals and admirals.[1] Furthermore, he was the Supreme Commander for Allied Powers in Japan and, since Japan was an occupied country, he was the ruler of 83,000,000 Japanese people. All important decisions were cleared by him, all diplomatic relations went through his office; and since his occupation was a successful one, he had the confidence of the Japanese people. Finally, he was high in the conservative circle of the American Republican Party. He had been President Hoover's Chief of Staff and, as a strict constitutionalist, had often argued with President Roosevelt. During the Second World War, he had been for an Asia-first strategy and had won the support of many Republicans who were hostile towards Roosevelt and preferred a national war against Japan to an internationalist effort against Germany. Indeed, in both 1944 and 1948, there were strong movements to nominate the General to be the Republican Presidential candidate. When we think of the support he had and the responsibilities he held, it seems safe to say that his power was second only to the President's. Indeed, if the country's traditions had been different and if the General had been so inclined, he might have had enough force at his disposal to capture control of the American government.

One might inquire why a man with such power who held opinions known to be different from the administration was given more power by being appointed Commander of the United Nations Forces. While the President later saw this as a mistake, at the time it must have seemed the natural thing to do — for the General had control of the American forces in the Far East, and it was natural that this control should be extended. He was a man of known capability (having successfully run a difficult occupation) and it was assumed that he could handle this next problem competently. To have bypassed him would have been a noticeable blow at him and hardly a thing calculated to win bipartisan support for a coming military operation. Finally, it was not foreseen that the Korean military operation would grow to such a a size that it would substantially add to his power and create situations where differences of opinion would get out of hand.

---

[1]Morris Janowitz, *The Professional Soldier* (New York: The Free Press, 1960).

There can be little doubt of the Commander's great abilities. He was the son of a famous general who recognized and encouraged his predilection for a military career, and he had a mother devoted to his greatness. He was an outstanding cadet in intelligence and leadership, a Captain of the Corps. By 1918, at the age of thirty-eight, his initiative in supporting the organization of a division of National Guard troops and his skill and bravery in combat operations led to his appointment as a Brigadier General. After the First World War, he became Commandant at West Point and successfully updated training at that institution. Finally, he became Chief of Staff under President Hoover and was retained in that capacity by President Roosevelt for a year longer than the normal tour of duty (he was a good defender of military budgets). It is interesting to note that while he and Roosevelt had several fights — after one budget fight, MacArthur vomited on the White House steps — their personalities were similar enough so that they could communicate to some extent with each other.[2] In 1935, at the age of fifty-five, it appeared that MacArthur had reached the zenith of his career and had nowhere left to go. In this position, he accepted an appointment to become the military advisor to the Philippine government. With the advent of the Second World War, his career was reactivated. After what may have been poor tactics in the Philippines, he became a great commander of all the American forces in the South Pacific theater of war. While he was not powerful in Washington, his success in the Pacific led to his designation as the head of the Japanese occupation force, where he performed an outstanding job in the difficult task of reviving and democratizing Japan.

It is difficult to be objective about the Commander. Perhaps the fairest sketch is given by Gunther.[3] He notes,

> A great deal of both truth and nonsense has been written about the Supreme Commander, and few people realize what an intricate character he is. I asked one illustrious Japanese what he thought of him. The answer was one of the few quick, sure answers I ever got from anybody in Japan. 'Not a simple man.'

The commander was a man of great charismatic appeal; he attracted loyal followers who practically worshipped him and severe detractors who thought he was an arrogant imbecile. The former proclaimed his

[2]Douglas MacArthur, *Reminiscences* (New York: McGraw-Hill Book Company, 1964). Cf. p. 101.

[3]John Gunther, *The Riddle of MacArthur* (New York: Harper & Row, Publishers, 1950).

genius, while the latter charged the former with being afraid to disagree with his opinions. The truth of the matter seems to be that the Commander was a complex person who had great confidence but little security — a combination that often appears as "arrogance." The Commander defined himself as a soldier. His confidence gave him the strength to fully commit himself to this definition so that he became a man of character who projected a powerful image. His lack of security caused him to cling to this definition of himself even when it was inappropriate. His confidence enabled him to create a world — a vision of reality — that could inspire men and direct difficult decisions. His lack of security prevented him from being able to enter the worlds of other men and to understand disagreement. Consequently, in order to interact with the Commander, one had to accept *his* definition of himself and of the situation. If one could, one discovered a brilliant and decisive man; if one could not, one was rejected and one rejected in turn. Perhaps his most objectionable quality was his habit of issuing communiques that paid more attention to his image of reality than to the facts which they were supposedly reporting. This habit perhaps reflected the fact that he was a man who would brook no rivalry or criticism. He kept careful control over his publicity and was jealous of his image. The Commander felt a destiny, and he had the capacity to attract and to recognize bright young men. However, if these men began to want credit for themselves and to build up an image independent of the Commander's, they ran into trouble.

The Commander was essentially quixotic; he created a portrait of himself and a picture of reality and then acted as though these pictures were reality. It was this that gave him his sense of honor, his feeling of destiny, his fearlessness in battle. Sometimes the results were wonderful; for when his pictures were valid, they became reality and enriched it. At other times, the results were disastrous; for when his picture was poor, the Commander had no way of correcting it — he could not step back from his picture, because of his insecurity. Psychodynamically, it is interesting to note that both his strength of confidence and his lack of security probably stemmed from the unusually close relation he had with his mother. In *Reminiscences,*[4] MacArthur gives us a poem which his mother wrote to him in an hour of trial at West Point. The first two lines read:

> Do you know that your soul is of my soul such a part
> That you seem to be fiber and core of my heart?

---

[4]MacArthur, *op. cit.,* p. 25.

Such a comradeship must have given MacArthur much inner strength of character. On the other hand, it may have prevented a sense of independent identity. He had to have a *perfect* record and could tolerate no criticism of himself. Otherwise, it seems, his sense of identity would be shattered by separation from his mother.

The world which the Commander created was essentially an aristocratic or traditionalistic one, and this influenced the manner in which Japan was occupied. The Commander was a very remote figure and, as Spanier[5] notes,

> At times . . . it seemed as if the General were a mid-twentieth-century spiritual descendant of such Viceroys of India as Clive or Warren Hastings, ruling an Asian people in the imperial tradition of Western benevolent despotism.

However, this world was also a contemporary one, fully aware that colonialism was over. Listen to the Commander in his well known "farewell" speech to Congress,[6]

> In this situation it becomes vital that our country orient its policies in consonance with this basic evolutionary condition rather than pursue a course blind to the reality that the colonial era is now passed and the Asian peoples covet the right to shape their own free destiny. What they seek now is friendly guidance, understanding and support, not imperious direction; the dignity of equality and not the shame of subjugation. Their prewar standard of life, pitifully low, is infinitely lower now in the devastation left in war's wake.
> World ideologies play little part in Asian thinking and are little understood. What the people strive for is the opportunity for a little more food in their stomachs, a little better clothing on their backs, and a little firmer roof over their heads, and the realization of the normal nationalist urge for political freedom.

The Commander's land reform program is a model yet to be emulated in other nations. Mixed in with his neo-traditionalism was a kind of messianic visioning.

> Europe is a dying system. It is worn out and run down, and will become an economic and industrial hegemony of Soviet Russia. . . . The lands touching the Pacific with their billions of inhabitants will determine the course of history for the next two thousand years.[7]

---

[5]John W. Spanier, *The Truman-MacArthur Controversy* (Cambridge: Harvard University Press, 1959), p. 66.
[6]MacArthur, *op. cit.,* p. 401.
[7]Quoted by Spanier, *op. cit.,* p. 67.

While the Commander's feeling may have been correct, and, as we shall observe later, the Commander's personality and the world he created were made to order for the needs of Japan in 1945, one has the feeling that the Commander would have perceived whatever place he was stationed in to be the center of future world power. In any case, he recommended that Asia rather than Europe should be America's first concern in the Second World War. When this recommendation was rejected, the Commander condemned the strategy of emphasizing Europe as inspired by the Russians and the British. He could not seem to appreciate the views of others, to take their perspective, perhaps because it would remind him that he was not *the* center. Under the stress of having these other views prevail, of having European interests take precedence over Asian interests, the Commander withdrew to his Far Eastern outpost. The President repeatedly asked him to return to the United States for a visit, but the invitations were always declined. For fourteen years — until he was recalled — the Commander did not see the United States. One suspects that the Commander preferred the psychological world he had built for himself and did not want it shattered by the less idealistic world of the mainland United States. He had built up his own organization, which was so removed from Washington's control that, as one High State Department official said, "It was like communicating with a foreign government."

One of the strong points of the Commander's personality was that his confidence gave him the ability to become deeply involved in whatever job he was doing. Being involved in the reconstruction of Japan, the Commander became aware of Japan's need for raw materials and food from China and of the usefulness of the potential Chinese market. These factors, combined with his conviction of the future potential of Asia, made him quite critical of the administration's policy towards China. As we have already seen, he strongly argued that Formosa should be defended.

The psychological world of this man was, then, an intricate one built on a fundamental confidence in himself that permitted him to get deeply involved in whatever he was doing and imagine it to be the entire universe. Some flaw, however, perhaps a deep insecurity, prevented him from understanding that other legitimate worlds existed. He believed his country should place Asia above Europe and that those who believed otherwise were the dupes of foreign powers.

We may summarize some of the major cognitive elements of his world as follows:*

---

*In doing this, and indeed throughout this entire chapter, I am indebted to aspects of Spanier's excellent work *(op. cit.).*

1. Asia was basically more important than Europe because she would be the power of the future. Communism and not the Soviet Union was the main enemy.
2. The United States could easily gain control over China at the present time.
3. If it failed to do so, it would lose its chance, for China's strength would grow relative to the United States.
4. Communism was an evil form of government, whereas the Chinese Nationalists would preserve freedom for China.
5. If the United States did oppose communism in China, the Soviet Union would not intervene.
6. If the Soviet Union did intervene, the United States might as well fight a world war then as later.
7. It was fundamentally immoral to sacrifice the lives of citizens without the nation making an all-out effort to help them.
8. The United States should keep control over its foreign policy and not allow other countries to influence its actions.

It should be noted that each of these ideas is in balance — is compatible with and does not contradict any of the other ideas. Also, each idea reflects beliefs and underlying values with which it is in balance. For example, one reason the Commander felt Asia to be more important than Europe was that he perceived Asians to have a will and stamina that Europeans lacked. He appreciated their views of sacrifice and death and must have agreed with Linton's[8] remark, "They can outlast us." This perception of and value for Asian acceptance of sacrifice is, in turn, related to the Commander's feeling that all United States citizens should be prepared to sacrifice themselves in a united war effort and to his basic acceptance of a possible nuclear war. These ideas, beliefs, and values were, in turn, balanced with facets of his personality and his psychodynamics. Thus, as we have noted, the Commander's personality was characterized by a confidence that could allow him to ignore Europe's present power in order to focus on the future power of Asia. He personally valued sacrifice. And, psychodynamically, he would have had to be at the center of the world's stage — since he was in Asia, this was compatible with his perception of "Asiatic virtues" and potential Asian power.

This cluster of ideas, beliefs, values, personality characteristics, and psychodynamic forces — this world — conflicted with another quite different world — that of the President.

---

[8] Ralph Linton, *The Tree of Culture* (New York: Alfred A. Knopf, Inc., 1955), p. 572.

President Truman was the son of a mule trader who became a grain speculator and died broke. In such circumstances, Harry Truman had a difficult time developing a career. While MacArthur's mother was telling her son that he would become a famous general, Truman's mother was proudly hearing the Baptist Circut Rider tell her what a sturdy boy her son was. At age thirty-eight, MacArthur was a brigadier general; Truman was sinking deeper in debt with a failing clothes store. His political history has been well portrayed by Steinberg.[9] When Truman decided to run for county judge, he had to get the support of the Pendergast machine. In spite of these very dubious auspices, Truman managed to do as good and honest a job as was possible; and several years later, when Pendergast needed a man with a good reputation, he promoted Truman into the United States Senate. There, he was virtually boycotted by President Roosevelt, who was out to get Pendergast. However, after the machine's demise, Truman won reelection on his own (in a race even closer than his later presidential race with Dewey) and began a committee to investigate defense contracts. His skillful, energetic work with this committee gave him some national prominence, and one of the men he had patronized became Democratic National Committee Chairman and worked him into the Vice Presidency. While he became President upon Roosevelt's death in 1945, as in the case of his Senate appointment, Truman really became established as a political power when he won the Presidency on his own in 1948.

The President's personality was completely unlike the Commander's. He lacked the latter's self-assurance, and he seems to have often been on the verge of feeling inferior to some of the high powered, confident men he dealt with. On the other hand, whereas the Commander was essentially a-political because he did not really perceive the worlds of others and lacked the skill to anticipate their reactions, the President was fundamentally secure in his role as a professional politician and at ease in the midst of differences in opinion and power.

If the Commander was a modern Don Quixote, the President personified Sancho Panza. He epitomized the virtues and vices of commonness. He was a friendly but decisive person, completely at ease with the average man and with no pretentions. On the other hand, his lack of refinement cost him respect, and he had a limited amount of perspective and discrimination. One cannot read his *Mr. Citizen*[10] without liking his openness and respecting the way he has led his retired life. On the debit

---

[9]Alfred Steinberg, *The Man from Missouri* (New York: G. P. Putnam's Sons, 1962).

[10]Harry S Truman, *Mr. Citizen* (New York: Bernard Geis Associates, 1960).

side, one is likely to be bored by his lack of depth. While he lacked the self-assurance to exert a charismatic leadership, he was able to dedicate himself to an organization and exert leadership through its offices. Thus, he had served his party and government loyally; and, now that he happened to have the job of the Presidency, he was psychologically capable of expecting loyal service from his subordinates. We should also note that the President, like the Commander, was fundamentally a man of principles rather than expediency.

The reader will note that since the Commander tended to draw authority from his image and the President from his position in the organization, there were potential seeds of conflict between them on this ground alone. For example, in a situation like this, certain orders would have to be neglected by the Commander if his image were not to be undermined (and, hence, his authority destroyed), while these same orders would have to be obeyed if the position of the President (and, hence, his authority) were not to be challenged. It is difficult for Don Quixote to be Sancho's squire. But, quite apart from these authority problems, it was difficult for the two personalities to communicate with each other. President Roosevelt was enough of an aristocrat to be able to appreciate the Commander's world, and he had enough confidence to openly argue with him. The Commander was forced to recognize him as a worthy opponent. One feels that President Truman was never able to really understand the Commander's style of life and that, of course, the Commander was unable to appreciate the rich strength of Truman. By themselves, these factors might have been of little consequence, but the President's view of the world included a completely different perspective on Asia.

The President's world had the following cognitive elements:

1. Europe was basically more important than Asia because of her ties to America and because she currently had more power.

2. The United States would have to expend all of its strength to control China, and this would leave Europe vulnerable to the major enemy, the Soviet Union.

3. The Chinese could be used in the future to counterbalance Russian power.

4. Time was on the side of the United States — time to arm, to gain more allies, to give rise to discontent in the Soviet Union.

5. The source of trouble in Asia was the poverty of her people and the ravages of colonialism. Social change was needed, and communism would provide it; whereas the Nationalists had been either unwilling or unable to do so.

6. Asians in general would perceive aid to the Nationalists as an imposition—a form of colonialism; and since the Nationalist leader's

only hope was to provoke a major war between the United States and China, one should minimize involvement with the Nationalists.

7. The United States did not currently have the strength to fight both China and Russia, nor did the people of the United States want to fight in an all-out war.

8. An all-out war was immoral.

9. It was necessary to have allies; to keep them, one had to take their views into consideration.

Note how each of these thoughts is compatible with the others and with the President's other beliefs, his values (such as his value of social change), his personality (one of whose characteristics was a respect for power and status), and his psychodynamics (which involved a concern for the opinions of others).

I have tried to be fair to both the world of the Commander and the world of the President. The reader will note how each is internally consistent and belongs to a man of character; he can also see how they are incompatible.

Now, it might be thought that if these worlds bumped against each other, they would begin to change and to meld into each other to form larger, more veridical worlds. Ideally, the best in each world would be maintained, while weaknesses would be disregarded. In fact, this process does not seem to occur. To see why, we must observe several important factors that serve to bind diverse clusters of ideas into a world in the first place, and that also act to prevent interchange between worlds.

First, there is the interdependency of all the elements. To date, there have been no direct studies demonstrating the interdependency of ideas, values, and personality by showing that when a person changes an important idea, the person's values or personality also changes, and vice-versa. However, McGuire[11] has demonstrated that if a person changes one idea, other interrelated ideas will change in order to retain logical compatibility. Several studies have shown that if an idea changes, related attitudes will change[12], and a number of studies have demonstrated correlations between certain ideas and personality variables.[13] It seems likely that to really change the Commander's view of the importance of Asia, one would also have to change either his perception that Asians

[11]William J. McGuire, "Cognitive consistency and attitude change," *J. abnorm. soc. Psychol.*, 60 (1960), pp. 345-53.

[12]Cf. Roger Brown, "Models of Attitude Change," in T. Newcomb (ed.), *New Directions in Psychology* (New York: Holt,, Rinehart & Winston, Inc., 1962).

[13]See, for example, the relation between prejudice, dominance, and rigidity in T. Adorns *et. al. The Authoriatarian Personality* (New York: Harper & Row, Publishers, 1950).

were capable of more sacrifice or his value of sacrifice. And one could scarcely begin to do either without changing where he was stationed or his basic personality.

Second, there is the fact that a person is usually a member of a group of men who believe in somewhat similar ideas. As we noted in the chapter on perception, the beliefs of one's group determine what a person considers normal or usual and, hence, furnish a base line from which the individual judges all other ideas. Since a person is dependent on his group for both ideas and emotional support, the group helps structure what reality appears to be. The men surrounding the Commander all held similar ideas — although, of course, for slightly different reasons — and the men surrounding the President all agreed on their (different) set of ideas. Both men's attitudes were, then, anchored in the social reality of their respective groups.

Third, each set of ideas leads logically to certain actions. In the case at hand, these were to become involved with or stay detached from the Nationalist Chinese. After a person is publicly committed to an action, he builds up a public following that supports the action for its own reasons. Once this occurs and persons expect one to advocate the action, it is difficult to change one's advocacy because the public will feel betrayed. This, in turn, creates a cognitive dissonance that prevents the person from changing the ideas behind his action. This problem may be compounded when a two-party political structure exists that tends to dichotomize issues.

Fourth, the arguments of the other group always lack the force of one's own arguments because they come separately and seem impractical in the light of the action advocated by the combined force of all of one's own arguments. Thus, the Commander's advocacy of a blockade of China was viewed as impractical by an administration who believed in working with allies (who would reject any such blockade). In turn, their rejoinder that the British opposed such a blockade and that *they* held Singapore and controlled most of Western trade with China, must have seemed callous to a Commander who was directly responsible for troop losses and who opposed any dependence on foreign alliances.

Finally, when a person from one group debates with a member of the other group, he does not present all of his arguments because he knows that some would evoke disagreeable emotions and dislike, or could be used against him politically. In the second chapter, it was noted that the President did not tell his Secretary of Defense some of his reasons for imposing a ceiling on the arms budget. In a similar manner, we shall see that the President never really told the Commander some of his arguments for minimizing support to the Nationalist Chinese.

These five factors that operate to polarize opinion into segmented clusters are only offset when a number of integrative forces occur. These occur to the extent that: some persons have a foot in each group because of personal friends or marriage; or the groups are united by common membership in a larger group (as when the power of both groups is dependent on the existence of their nation); or a pluralism insures that the members of one group are divided on many independent issues (as when an admiral in the Commander's group teamed up with an admiral in the President's group to form a "navy group" opposed to more air force power). While these forces are usually sufficient to prevent differences in opinion from sundering the country, they do not appear strong enough to insure adequate cross-fertilization between groups. The President's group and the Commander's group acted as though they were separate species rather than opposite sexes with the capability to unite and create a decent offspring.

The Interpretation of Orders

The meaning of an order, like the meaning of any communication, is dependent on the context in which it is embedded. Hence, the decision maker must try to formulate his order so that it will have the meaning which he desires in the context of his implementor's world. Likewise, the latter must try to anticipate what the decision maker *really* wants him to do from his knowledge of the decision maker's world. Any discrepancy between the world of the decision maker and the world of the implementor is, therefore, likely to cause problems in the issuing and interpretation of orders.

At the close of the first Presidential meeting that dealt with the Korean Invasion, the President announced that American pilots should have wide discretion in attacking North Korean forces. However, the Chairman of the Joint Chiefs of Staff requested that this be omitted from the orders, since he was afraid this might be given too broad an interpretation, and he felt that the pilots would get the idea anyway. The Army Chief of Staff was in charge of communications to the American Commander, Far East. He had to convey the sense of the conference — that American airplanes were to be permitted to attack North Korean tanks and planes — without actually saying so. The complete text of his orders has not been released. One version of the orders is that the Commander Far East was told that in order to assist in the evacuation of United States dependents and noncombatants, he could take air and naval action to prevent the Inchon-Kimpo-Seoul area from falling into enemy hands. The exact wording of these orders is of interest because, the following night, Washington learned that pilots were limiting their mission to protecting the evacuation and were *not* striking at North Korean tanks and planes! The Far Eastern Command had not "gotten the idea."

It appears that while the orders were slightly ambiguous, the average person would have interpreted them correctly. However, the Commander Far East was so conscious of the differences between Washington and himself that he did not think that the United States would intervene to prevent the Korean Invasion. His Naval Commander commented,[14] " . . . I felt that we should oppose the aggression, but I didn't think we would . . . as a consequence, we had no plans for this type of war." When I say that the Commander Far East was conscious of the differences between himself and Washington, I do not mean to imply that he had any real understanding of the President's world. He simply perceived that it was an alien world. When clearer orders arrived on the following day, the Commander was surprised and commented that the intervention was a complete reversal of American Far Eastern policy. He could not understand the intervention as following naturally from the way the President saw things; he had to think of it as a *reversal* of policy.

The reader must not suppose that misunderstanding is dependent on *large* differences between the worlds of the decision maker and his implementor. Even if the worlds are basically alike, differences in perspective introduced by the fact that one man is at the center and the other is in the field, create enough discrepancy to cause problems. To this extent, the misinterpretation of orders is analogous to the misperception of intelligence reports. Just as intelligence reports can be given interpretations that make them fit the hearers' preconceptions, so orders can be interpreted to mean what the hearer believes he will be told. Historically, this is not an uncommon occurrence. One dramatic example is the misinterpretation that contributed to the beginning of the Boer War. In this case, the General in the Field had been sent off with instructions to prepare a surprise attack. His Prime Minister obtained some new information, changed his plans, and telegraphed, "Do not attack." The General believed that the Prime Minister really wanted him to attack but could not politically afford to have the responsibility laid on his shoulders. Hence, he interpreted the telegram to mean, "I cannot tell you this — but attack!" The resulting "Jameson Raid" had most unfortunate consequences.[15]

---

[14]Malcolm W. Cagle and Frank A. Manson, *Sea war in Korea* (Annapolis, Md: U. S. Naval Institute, 1957), p. 31.
[15]Philip Kerr and Lionel Curtis, *The Prevention of War* (New Haven: Yale University Press, 1923).

It will probably not surprise the reader that when Washington sent the Far Eastern Commander his next orders, they leaned over backwards in the opposite direction. The decision reached by the group in Washington was to clear *all* targets *south* of the 38th parallel for attack by air and naval forces. This was conveyed to the General, but one high official — determined that this time there should be no misunderstanding — told the General, "Your mission is to throw the North Koreans out of South Korea." Shortly after this, when the General saw that his forces were not having as great an impact as was expected, he decided to order attacks *north* of the 38th parallel without consulting Washington. When Washington complained, the Commander justified his action as being within the authorization of a field commander carrying out of his order to throw the North Koreans out of South Korea! The Commander, remember, thought that at least part of Washington had reversed its Far Eastern policy.

It is worthwhile to note that a number of individual interpretations influence the communication of an order, just as a chain of individual decisions influences incoming information. In the above case, the President made a decision and instructed his Secretary of Defense to communicate it. The latter delegated this to the Secretary of the Army who, in turn, had most communications relayed by the Army Chief of Staff to the Commander Far East. While, in this case, all of these men were present at the same group meeting and several helped frame the orders, the chance for distortion is obvious.

If one remembers that the distortions inherent in interpreting orders may combine with the distortions involved in perceiving incoming communication, one can understand the numerous communication failures that occur in rapidly changing situations. This is the reason that most battles are a tragedy of communications errors. Bavelas[16] has designed an interesting demonstration that shows the inherent difficulties of the situation. He takes a photograph of a chess board in the middle of a game. Cutting up the photo into smaller pieces, he distributes these areas to individuals, each of whom thus represents a man in the field with his good perception of a limited area of conflict. These men relay their views to a higher authority, who has a chess board which he sets up to reflect the actual situation as he pieces it together from incoming reports. The higher authority sends orders to the "men in the field" to carry out specific moves in order to try to win the game with a competing team. Bavelas shows that within relatively few moves, the higher authority's picture of the situation as reflected on his board bears little

---

[16]Alex Bavelas, personal communication.

relation to the actual state of affairs on the main board. Time after time, the higher authority makes a slight error of interpretation, this error results in a command that does not make complete sense to the man in the field, and this man makes the move he thinks is wanted by the higher authority. His report back of the ensuing situation naturally makes little sense to the higher authority, who then makes a larger error of interpretation, which leads to an even less applicable order — and so the circle continues.

The only correction for such cycling errors is, of course, adequate feedback as to how an intelligence report or order has been perceived. Such feedback is necessary even within a face-to-face group. For example, the committee that prepared the document that became NSC-68, initially had a bad communication problem. The representatives from the State Department believed that the committee was supposed to produce a new outlook on the defense preparations of the United States, whereas the main representatives from the Defense Department thought that the committee was supposed to work within the frame of reference set by the budget ceiling. No one was really conscious of the resultant communication failures until the representatives from the Defense Department produced a paper that gave a low estimate of the capabilities of the Soviet Union. When the State Department representatives attacked this optimism, it was discovered that the Defense Department representatives was not really convinced of what he had said but had thought the group wanted to be limited by the budget ceiling. His discovery that the State Department was really interested in a serious reappraisal opened the way for a now fruitful discussion. The inadvertent feedback provided by the State Department corrected his initial interpretation of their attitude.

While sometimes, as in a crises situation, there is not enough time for feedback, and often the necessity for feedback is not realized, the major factor hindering adequate feedback is the inherent difficulty in providing it. For a simple command such as "rudder right five degrees," a simple repetition of the command suffices. More complex orders must insure that the command has been understood. While a simple order such as "report to the commanding officer of x airbase" does not specify exactly how the order should be carried out, it is quite easy for the recipient to indicate that he understands the end result that is desired. When, however, the order is as complex as "throw the North Koreans out of South Korea," important aspects of the order are embedded in the issuer's world; and, unless the implementor understands that world, he is likely to make mistakes in carrying out the order. Left to himself, for example, the Far Eastern Commander would certainly have bombed mainland China — something the administration had to specifically prohibit. For such complex orders, a mere repetition of the order does not indicate sufficient understanding of the issuer's intentions and qualifications. Instead, the implementor must demonstrate his insight into his superior's world by being able to deduce how the decision maker would want him to act in new circumstances. If he cannot do this, the decision maker is forced to laboriously spell out details and put restrictions on the implementor's freedom to innovate — restrictions that may result in feelings of irritation and distrust. Matters are made even more difficult if the decision maker is not really sure of what he wants. Often, this becomes clarified only as the situation progresses.

The Clash between the Different Worlds

The worlds of the President and the Commander began to clash long before the Korean War. In 1945, for example, the Commander released a non-authorized statement about reducing the Japanese occupation forces; in response, the acting Secretary of State told reporters that the Commander was merely an instrument and not an architect of policy. The resulting dispute was bitter enough so that direct communication temporarily ceased between the Commander and the State Department. Subsequently, the Commander furnished ammunition for the Congressional group that attacked the administration's China policy, and we have noted how he repeatedly declined invitations to return to the States for a visit. At one point, the Secretary of the Army had to intervene in order to prevent the Commander from approving a bill from the Japanese Diet that was clearly contrary to the administration's declared economic policy for the occupation. However, on the whole, the Commander followed instructions; and while there were often difficulties, they were outweighed by the advantages of the Commander's ability and the bipartisan support that was gained by utilizing a prominent conservative in such a post. The Korean War reopened old issues and created many opportunities for conflict.

Initially, it appears that the Commander believed that there was a reversal in foreign policy, a reversal that entailed a decision to battle communism in Asia. He did not understand that the President's decision to fight in Korea was initially pointed specifically at an aggressive act rather than communism in general. In his defense, it must be pointed out that the decision to defend Formosa by interposing the Seventh

Fleet must have contributed to his confusion since it fit in with his conceptualization; after all, the Chinese had not attacked South Korea. While the administration carefully *called* this measure a "neutralization," it must have been clear to the Commander that it was *actually* more of a "passive defense" of Formosa. It was this confusion — the administration *partly* differentiating between the Korean War and the Chinese Civil War and the Commander perceiving only one war, a fight against communism — that lay behind the ensuing dispute.

In fact, there was no reversal of policy. Rather, the stimulus of the Korean Invasion and the need for compromise and flexibility was leading the administration to extend the policy of "containing" Russia to a policy of "containing" communism in general. The Commander did not really understand this. To him, there was no reason for a *passive* defense of Formosa. Now that the administration had decided to fight communism in Asia, it was silly not to back Chiang to the limit and ridiculous to give the enemy a sanctuary by not striking the mainland.

It will be recalled that on the suggestion of the Secretary of State, the President had decided to temporarily prevent the invasion of Formosa (and attacks on the mainland) by interposing the Seventh Fleet but, with the Commander's concurrence, had decided to decline the offer of Chinese Nationalist troops. A State Department Aide's memoir of June 29[17] indicates that the Nationalists were told that while their offer was appreciated, it would not be accepted: "In light, however, of the threat of invasion of Taiwan . . . it would be desirable for representatives of General MacArthur's Headquarters to hold discussions with the Chinese military authorities on Taiwan . . . ." The decision to temporarily neutralize Formosa was not a full commitment to permanently defend the Island and support Chiang Kai-shek, and it was left unclear just how close a relation the American government would have with the Nationalist regime. The Defense Department, encouraged by an increasing budget, must have argued for a permanent defense of the Island. Within the State Department, some persons must have argued for non-intervention in the Chinese Civil War in order to encourage Chinese Titoism, others must have argued for trading Formosa in exchange for good will and concessions, others must have argued for the setting up of an independent Formosa under United Nations auspices, and still others must have argued for the support of Chiang Kai-shek's government. It is not clear exactly what this "in-fighting" was like.

---

[17]"Military Situation in the Far East, Hearings before the Committee on Armed Services and the Committee on Foreign Relations," U. S. Senate, 82nd Cong., 1st Session (Washington: Gov. Print. Office, 1951), p. 3383.

According to President Truman,[18] on July 27 the Joint Chiefs recommended, at a meeting of the Security Council, that all-out aid be granted to the Chinese Nationalists so that they could defend Formosa. The President approved proposals to grant "extensive" military aid, to have the Commander's headquarters survey Chiang Kai-shek's requirements, and to carry out reconnaissance flights along the Chinese coast. If the President had really made up his mind, it is not clear why these decisions were not communicated to MacArthur until August 3.

Whitney[19] states that on July 29, the Joint Chiefs urged that the Nationalists be permitted to actively defend Formosa by attacking military concentrations on the mainland and by mining appropriate water areas. They asked the Commander to comment on these recommendations; he concurred with their judgment, arguing against the idea of a sanctuary for the enemy. (The problem, of course, was that the Chinese Communists were not really an "enemy," in that *they* had not attacked anyone except Chiang Kai-shek.) In the same concurring wire (evidently on July 30), the Commander added that he was *personally* going to Formosa on July 31. This appears to have taken the administration by surprise.[20] (He had not left Tokyo overnight in five years.) One can imagine the consternation of the State Department as they thought of the voluble Commander embracing Chiang Kai-shek. They could hardly tell the Far Eastern Commander not to visit a place which he was currently responsible for defending. He received a reply stating that Formosan policy was currently being discussed with the State Department and that he might "desire to send a senior officer to Formosa with the group on July 31 and go yourself later." This hopeful hint was somewhat offset by the end of the message, which stated, "Please feel free to go, since the responsibility is yours." It appears that this ambivalent message accurately reflected the state of conflict within the administration on its Formosan policy. The State Department evidently wanted to avoid a complete commitment to Chiang Kai-shek, while the Defense Department accepted such a commitment.

The worst fears of the State Department were realized when, directly after his visit, the Commander issued a statement in which he said that his mission was to prevent an invasion of Formosa, praised Chiang Kai-shek and stated that they both wished "that all people in the Pacific should be free — not slaves." In turn, the Chinese Nationalist leader

---

[18]Harry S. Truman, *Memoirs,* Vol. Two: *Years of Trial and Hope* (Garden City, N.Y.: Doubleday & Company, Inc., 1956), p. 349.
[19]Courtney Whitney, *MacArthur* (New York: Alfred A. Knopf, Inc., 1956), pp. 369, 370.
[20]Gunther, *op. cit.,* p. 195.

stated how much he admired the Commander and how he and the Commander had laid the foundation for "Sino-American military cooperation." While it is not clear how much this first faux pas affected the administration's decision making, it must have forced its hand to some extent — perhaps resulting in the decisions which the President communicated to the Commander on August 3. It also forced the administration to reassure persons in many nations that the United States had no permanent stake in Formosa. Finally, the Commander's statement struck the President as implying a rejection of his policy to simply neutralize Formosa.[21]

Seen in a mordant perspective, there is something terribly funny about this scene. Here is a group in the State Department desperately trying to maintain the knife edge balance of neutralizing Formosa without offending members of the United Nations or a communist regime whose independence from Moscow it would like to encourage. Furthermore, these men are in the midst of a United Nations debate in which they are trying to portray the imposition of the Seventh Fleet as a "neutralizing" measure that is not a permanent intervention in the Chinese Civil War or a commitment to Chiang Kai-shek. And here — thousands of miles away — is this independent seventy year old charismatic figure — a symbol of America — who, figuring that his country should support anyone who is fighting communism, honestly embraces Chiang Kaishek and throws everything into an uproar. Furthermore, there is absolutely nothing that can be done, because the Commander is the very soul of honor — with no political sense whatsoever — and stands amidst the ruin of this delicate policy structure without realizing that he has done anything wrong!

Amidst the ensuing inquiries from foreign capitals, the Secretary of State cabled the State Department Officer, who was attached to the Commander's staff, and asked him to send details of the talk in Formosa. Imagine his chagrin when that officer reported that he had not been taken along since the talk was "nonpolitical." Nor was this helped when he heard that the Commander felt that the defense of Formosa might be hindered by the unfriendly attitude of State Department officials towards Chiang Kai-shek!

As a result of this state of affairs, the President dispatched a trusted State Department official "so that the General might be given a firsthand account of the political planning in Washington." However, he was not as undiplomatic as to tell the Commander that he wanted to brief him on policy.[22] Rather, on the same day (August 3) on which he communicated his decisions to grant military aid to Formosa, he informed the Commander that he was sending his envoy to "discuss the Far Eastern political situation with him."[23] This is important to note, because the Commander was quite an egotist and has noted,[24] " A special envoy from President Truman, was sent to Tokyo to advise the President (sic) on political aspects of the Far Eastern situation." That is, in his world, the Commander was not being told Presidential policy — rather, *his* views were being sought!

Now, the envoy did spend a good deal of time obtaining information on conditions in Japan and Korea and the Commander's opinions on the Chinese, etc., but he also tried to explain the President's position on Formosa. In his report back to the President[25] he states that he relayed to the Commander the message that Chiang could not be permitted to start a war on the Chinese mainland. The Commander replied that he would naturally obey all orders and that he had refused to discuss political subjects with Chiang. However, the envoy goes on to say:

> For reasons which are rather difficult to explain, I did not feel that we came to a full agreement on the way we believed things should be handled on Formosa and with the Generalissimo. He accepted the President's position and will act accordingly, but without full conviction. He has a strange idea that we should back anybody who will fight communism, even though he could not give an argument why the Generalissimo's fighting communists would be a contribution towards the effective dealing with the communists in China. I pointed out to him the basic conflict of interest between the U. S. and the Generalissimo's position as to the future of Formosa, namely, the preventing of Formosa's falling into hostile hands. Perhaps the best way would be through the medium of the U. N. to establish an independent government. Chiang, on the other hand, had only the burning ambition to use Formosa as a stepping-stone for his re-entry to the mainland. MacArthur recognized that this ambition could not be fulfilled, and yet thought it might be a good idea to let him land and get rid of him that way. He did not seem to consider the liability that our support of Chiang on such a move would be to us in the East. I explained in great detail why Chiang was a liability, and the great danger of a split in the unity of the United Nations on the Chinese-Communist-Formosa policies; the attitude of the British, Nehru and such

---

[22]*Ibid.,* p. 353.
[23]*Ibid.,* p. 349.
[24]MacArthur, *op. cit.,* p. 341.
[25]Truman, Vol. Two, *op. cit.,* p. 349-353.

countries as Norway, who, although stalwart in their determination to resist Russian aggression, did not want to stir up trouble elsewhere.

In the remainder of his report the envoy mentions that the Commander was opposed to recognizing the Chinese communists, believed that State Department policies undermined Chiang's authority, and suggested that the President should threaten to attack airfields on the mainland if the Chinese communists continued to build up their positions. The envoy told the Commander that he would oppose any such recommendations because it would destroy the current unity within the United Nations. Finally, the envoy reports that the Commander advocated organized economic assistance for Asia, directed so that money got directly to the masses of people.

Fortunately, the Commander has left a brief record of *his* impression of the conversation with the envoy.[26] While we are not sure how much this impression was influenced by later events, it is well worth examining. He states:

> We discussed fully global conditions. I found him careful and cautious in what he said, but gained these very definite impressions: that there was no fixed and comprehensive United States policy for the Far East; that foreign influences, especially those of Great Britain, were very powerful in Washington; that there was no apparent interest in mounting an offensive against the Communists; that we were content to attempt to block their moves, but not to initiate any counter-moves; that we would defend Formosa if attacked, just as we had done in Korea; that President Truman had conceived a violent animosity toward Chiang Kai-shek; and that anyone who favored the Generalissimo might well arouse the President's disfavor. He left me with a feeling of concern and uneasiness that the situation in the Far East was little understood and mistakenly downgraded in high circles in Washington.

The above is a good example of the Commander's inability to enter the world of another. When the envoy stresses the importance of U.N. unity, the Commander does not accept this as a legitimate point of view; he thinks that "foreign influences . . . [are] very powerful." When the liability of Chiang Kai-shek is explained, he does not grant the possibility of this, he thinks that "President Truman [has] conceived a violent animosity toward Chiang Kai-shek." While he accepts the legitimacy of the President as his Commander and Chief, he does not really grant the legitimacy of the President's world.

---

[26]MacArthur, *op. cit.*, p. 341.

Now, again, there is something to be said in the Commander's defense. Certainly he was correct in perceiving that there was no comprehensive policy for the Far East. For if the Commander was being politically naive (rather than facetious) when he suggested putting Chiang on the mainland to get rid of him, the envoy was being rather obtuse in overlooking just how the American government was going to get rid of him. The administration had rather ignored Asia, ducked the problem of Asian communism, and failed to initiate an Asian Marshall Plan. It is also true that the envoy does seem to have given an awfully heavy weight to the importance of allied and U.N. opinion. This was precisely what the Counselor to the State Department had been afraid would happen if the United States responded through the U.N. — that policies might be rigidified because of the necessity of getting the approval of other nations. But the administration was no more interested in understanding the Commander's world than he was in really understanding the administration's.

Now, as we look at this communication failure, we are struck by the fact that the envoy failed to present a complete and honest picture of the President's world. We have already noted that one force that separates worlds is the fear that some of one's motives will be ill-received. The envoy emphasized the importance of Europe and the necessity of heeding the wishes of allies; he never mentioned China's need for social change, her dislike of Chiang, her possible use as a counterbalance to Russian power, and the reluctance of many Americans to risk a world war. If these were some of the reasons for not bombing the Chinese mainland, we may infer that they were not mentioned because the Commander might not have accepted these reasons — he might have become angry and considered the envoy a traitor and the administration the dupe of communism. But the consequence of not stressing these reasons was that the administration's position must have seemed logically indefensible to the Commander. It must have been infuriating to battle against apparent stupidity with the knowledge that his own case was stronger and with the suspicion that there were unspecified forces — perhaps communists in the administration — that were *really* influencing decision making. Might it not be better to encourage a social climate in which men can communicate that they value different things?

As a corollary to this, it appears that the envoy was not completely open to the Commander. It is difficult to be sure from a written memorandum, but I sense a kind of scorn for the Commander's (admittedly dramatized) world. For example: When the envoy states that the Commander believed Japanese pride had been aroused by his confidence in them, the envoy puts "his" in quotes. When the Commander tries to describe an oriental acceptance of death, the envoy's style of reporting becomes choppy as though to convey it is not of much importance, and he uses quotes as though to divorce himself from these silly views which he wants to convey only to show what a specimen the Commander is:

> He described the difference between the attitude towards death of Westerns and Orientals. We hate to die; only face danger out of a sense of duty and through moral issues; whereas with Orientals, life begins with death. They die quietly, "folding their arms as a dove folding his wings, relaxing, and dying."

The envoy even permits himself one judgment when he says, "He has a *strange* idea that we should back anybody who will fight communism" (my italics). I think it is a questionable idea but not a "strange" one. It would appear that the envoy was indicating disagreement rather than objectively reporting the Commander's feelings. One wonders if the envoy was somewhat insecure and maintained too much distance between himself and the Commander.

In summary, we have the impression that the envoy was not able to effectively bridge the gap between the President's and the Commander's world. He did succeed in conveying some of the administration's ideas to the Commander — certainly, he succeeded in robbing him of his illusion that there was a new aggressive Far Eastern policy — though he did not replace this with a new idea of what the policy was. Also, he noted the Commander's lack of complete understanding and fed this information back to the President. Rather than removing the Commander or making further attempts at communication, the administration decided to be careful in its orders and spell out limitations on the Commander's authority. The only problem with this solution was that it must have annoyed the Commander to sense this lack of trust in his judgment.

A number of news reports criticized the Commander's meeting with Chiang Kai-shek and some indicated that he had not informed Washington in advance of his trip. Annoyed, perhaps stung by the President's lack of confidence, and suspicious of enemies in the State Department, the Commander issued a public statement on August 10 to the effect that the trip was coordinated with the administration.[27] The statement concluded:

> This visit has been maliciously misrepresented to the public by those who invariably in the past have propagandized a policy of defeatism and

[27]Whitney, *op. cit.,* p. 275.

appeasement in the Pacific. I hope the American people will not be misled by sly insinuations, brash speculations and bold misstatements invariably attributed to anonymous sources, so insidiously fed them both nationally and internationally by persons 10,000 miles away from the actual events, if they are not indeed designed, to promote disunity and destroy faith and confidence in American purposes and institutions and American representatives at this time of great world peril.

The President, warned by his envoy and perhaps prompted by the above statement, had the Joint Chiefs tell the Commander on August 14 that the defense of Formosa was to be limited to support operations which could be conducted without committing any forces to the island itself. No forces were to be based on Formosa without the approval of the Joint Chiefs of Staff.[28] (It is not clear if this is the same message which Whitney states was sent on August 5 and directed the Commander to prevent any attacks on the mainland and cautioned him that only the President had the authority to order such attacks.)

The Commander wired:[29]

The June 27th decision of the President to protect the communist mainland is fully understood here and this headquarters is operating meticulously in accordance therewith . . . I understand thoroughly the limitations upon my authority as theater commander and you need have no anxiety that I will in any way exceed them. I hope that neither the President nor you have been misled by false or speculative reports, official or nonofficial, from whatever source.

While one suspects that the Commander must have felt annoyed and a little ironical about the administration's apprehensions, his phrase "protect the communist mainland," was rather outrageous and must have increased the President's apprehensions about how well the Commander did understand the limitations on his authority.

In the meantime, the President, who had been embarrassed by newspaper articles stating that the Commander disagreed with his policy of neutralizing Formosa, told the press that[30] "the General and I saw eye to eye on Formosa policy." This was a little unfair. The President knew very well that the Commander disagreed with his policy, and he was obviously using the Commander's prestige to present a unified bipartisan policy that did not really exist; he was playing politics. Perhaps the Commander saw this and resented it; but it seems more likely that he

---

[28]Truman, Vol. Two, *op. cit.,* p. 354.
[29]Whitney, *op cit.,* p. 376.
[30]Truman, Vol. Two, *op. cit.,* p. 354.

saw it and felt that their Formosan policy was really not that different. After all, the President and he agreed that the island had to be defended, and the President's envoy had mentioned having the U. N. establish an independent government so that it would not fall into "hostile hands." The only disagreements were on committing the country to Chiang Kai-shek and on letting him attack the mainland. What the Commander (having little political sense) failed to see, was that the President's private position — as stated by his envoy — was not his public position — as stated for the ears of the American people and the U. N. Publiciy, the President's position was that the "neutralization" of Formosa did not prejudice the final decision as to who should have political control over the Island.

In any case, on August 17, the Veterans of Foreign Wars invited the Commander to send a message to their annual encampment. The Commander responded with a statement about Formosa. It began,[31] "In view of misconceptions currently being voiced concerning the relationship of Formosa to our strategic potential in the Pacific . . ." and continued for six paragraphs that showed exactly why the Commander felt that it was strategically necessary to keep Formosa out of hostile hands. The last two paragraphs were controversial; the Commander stated:

> Nothing could be more fallacious than the threadbare argument by those who advocate appeasement and defeatism in the Pacific that if we defend Formosa we alienate continental Asia. Those who speak thus do not understand the Orient. They do not grasp that it is in the pattern of Oriental psychology to respect and follow aggressive, resolute and dynamic leadership — to quickly turn from leadership characterized by timidity or vacillation, and they underestimate the Oriental mentality. Nothing in the last five years has so inspired the Far East as the American determination to preserve the bulwarks of our Pacific Ocean's strategic position from further encroachment, for few of its people fail accurately to appraise the safeguard such determination brings to their free institutions. To pursue any other course would be to turn over the fruits of our Pacific victory to a potential enemy. It would shift any future battle area 5,000 miles eastward to the coasts of the American continent, our own home coasts. It would completely expose our friends in the Philippines, our friends in Australia and New Zealand, our friends in Indonesia, our friends in Japan and other areas to the lustful thrusts of those who stand for slavery as against liberty, for atheism as against God.

> The decision of President Truman on June 27th lighted into a flame a lamp of hope throughout Asia that was burning dimly toward extinction.

---

[31]Whitney, *op. cit.,* pp. 377-380.

It marked for the Far East the focal and turning point in this area's struggle for freedom. It swept aside in one great monumental stroke all of the hypocrisy and the sophistry which has confused and deluded so many people distant from the actual scene.

According to Whitney,[32] the Commander wrote the message because he saw:

> . . . an excellent opportunity to attempt to reply to whoever was whispering malicious charges against him in Truman's ear. Since there are 1,350,000 members of the V. F. W. and since a message from him to the national encampment would undoubtedly receive wide circulation, MacArthur decided that this was an excellent opportunity to place himself on record as being squarely behind the President.

One suspects that the Commander also may have thought that he was giving the President the moral encouragement to face down the nefarious State Department. In regard to the message, he states,[33]

> . . . I had sent messages to many other organizations in the past and regarded it as a matter of routine. The message expressed my personal opinion of the strategic importance of Formosa and its relation to our defensive position in the Pacific. There was nothing political in it. I sent it through the Department of the Army ten days before the encampment. The officials of that Department apparently found nothing objectionable in it. It was in complete support of the President's announced policy toward Formosa.

Now, the Commander may have perceived his message as a-political and as in complete support of the announced policy towards Formosa; but since American policy in "neutralizing" Formosa was currently on trial before the U. N. Security Council, and since the President had publicly stated that the neutralization did not prejudice any future political settlement, the Commander's intemperate words seriously embarrassed the administration. Again, the unthinking Commander had broken some of the administration's delicate China (policy). Since the Commander was a powerful personage in the Government — to say nothing of his being the U. N. Commander — the President was forced to do something to indicate that *he* set the nation's foreign policy and that the Commander was speaking out of turn and not for the govern-

---

[32]*Ibid.*, p. 377.
[33]MacArthur, *op. cit.*, p. 341.

ment. In like fashion, the President had just had to chastise the Secretary of the Navy for an inflammatory speech advocating preventive war.

Unfortunately, instead of taking the Commander's speech as evidence of his poor political judgment and correcting him, the President reacted to his message as though it were a personal attack. He saw the message as intentionally criticizing rather than supporting his policy. In summarizing the message, he states,[34]

> In other words, [the Commander] called for a military policy of aggression, based on Formosa's position. The whole tenor of the message was critical of the very policy which he had so recently told [my envoy] he would support. There was no doubt in my mind that the world would read it that way and that it must have been intended that way.

As we reread the Commander's message, it is not clear exactly why the President interpreted it as he did. The Commander simply intemperately amplified on the President's decision to defend Formosa. Why did the President interpret this as an attack?* There are three possible reasons, all of psychological interest, that probably contributed to the President's interpretation. One factor was the way in which the President first received the message. The Commander may have cleared his message with the Army, but its contents never reached the White House until the press room obtained a copy that had been publicly released by the Commander's public relations office and already printed (but not distributed) by two magazines. This may have led the President to perceive the message as something done behind his back.

A second factor was the inbred worlds in which the two men lived. From the record we have presented, one would think that the world was paying close attention to a conflict between two giants. This is not true. For example, if one scans *The New York Times* for June, July, and August, he does not find big stories about the conflict between the two men. To the contrary, the *Times* reports that the Commander saw Chiang Kai-shek in order to implement the President's policy. There are only hints in occasional back page articles that there may be a lack of coordination between the two. But each man's world was surcharged with an atmosphere that made little things big. When the Commander blasts out at his appeasing critics, he is responding to isolated left wing articles magnified out of all proportion by his zealous defenders. But the President thinks he is referring to him! He thinks that because the

---

*I am assuming that the President is correctly reporting his perception rather than evidencing a distortion of memory due to the succeeding events.

      Vol. Two, *op. cit.*, p. 354.

President's ingroup is scanning the news for criticism, sensitively alive to sparks that might ignite the political atmosphere. One cannot understand the President's reaction without reconstructing this atmosphere, without remembering that the war news was bad with American troops constantly retreating, that there was intense criticism of the lack of military preparedness — unjustly blamed on the President and his Secretary of State — and that the Democratic party was beginning to look poorly with a Congressional election just around the corner. In such an atmosphere, the Commander's statements felt hotter and more important than they actually were.

A third factor may have been the President's personality as it was brought out by the Commander. In the chapter on personality, we noted that President Wilson seems to have repressed part of his early relationship with his father. This relationship apparently was a submissive one, and forces from such a repression would account for Wilson's masking his own drive for power and his inability to accept pressure from another authority figure. Whenever such repressions exist, there is the possibility of "transference reactions," in which the person reacts to another person as if that other person were in the earlier relation. Such relations are characterized by inappropriate behavior.

Now, in the case at hand, the Commander was a very definite authority figure, and the President was not particularly close to his own father. Speaking of this relationship, Steinberg[35] notes,

> Although his mother adored him, his father often found him irritating. He never laid a hand on Harry, though he could scold him unmercifully. On one occasion, he bought Harry a Shetland pony and the two went for a ride with John Truman astride a lead horse. When Harry fell off the pony, his father would not permit him to climb back in the saddle but insisted that he walk the half mile home. John Truman was closer to [his younger son], whose facial features and mannerisms resembled his own.

When the President immediately interprets the Commander's message as purposely criticizing him before the world, we must recognize that the President may have been reacting to the Commander as if the Commander were his father — that is, it is possible that a transference reaction occurred. This interpretation receives some support from the President's statement of his reaction[36] in which he notes that he seriously considered relieving the Commander of military responsibilities in the

---

[35]Steinberg, *op. cit.* p. 24.
[36]Truman, Vol. Two, *op. cit.,* p. 355.

Far East, leaving him only with command of the Japanese occupation. However, the President decided against such a move because,

> It would have been difficult to avoid the appearance of a demotion and I had no desire to hurt General MacArthur personally. My only concern was to let the world know that his statement was not official policy.

Two aspects of this reaction seem suspicious: The strength of the reaction indicates that the President was a-typically insecure in his dealings with the Commander. The reason given for not relieving the Commander seems strangely personal. One would think that the President would say that he hesitated to remove the Commander because of the necessity to maintain bipartisan unity. When we consider that the President believed that the Commander was deliberately going against his authority, his solicitude seems strangely out of place. Furthermore, from our knowledge of the two men's personalities, we would guess that it is the President and not the Commander who would be hurt by an apparent demotion — another indication that some identification was taking place.

In any case, the President immediately instructed the Secretary of Defense to order the Commander to withdraw his message. According to Whitney,[37] the Commander was astonished. He wired back:

> My message was most carefully prepared to fully support the President's policy decision. . . . My remarks were calculated only to support his declaration and I am unable to see wherein they might be interpreted otherwise. . . . The message has undoubtedly been incorporated in the printed agenda for the Encampment and advance press releases thereof have already reached worldwide centers of circulation. Under these circumstances I am sure that it would be mechanically impossible to suppress the same at this late date, and I believe to attempt it under such conditions would be a grave mistake. Please, therefore, present my most earnest request to the President for reconsideration of the order given me in your message, as I believe that repercussions resulting from compliance therewith would be destructive and most harmful to the national interest.

In the same message, the Commander stated that if the decision remained unchanged, his withdrawal should be sent to the Commander-in-Chief of the V. F. W. Whitney notes,[38] "He soon received from Washington the cryptic note:

Your message to Clyde A. Lewis forwarded verbatim as requested."

---

[37]Whitney, *op. cit.*, pp. 380-381.
[38]*Ibid.*, p. 381.

While it is not clear whether or not the President saw the Commander's response to this withdrawal order, the President did write a rather apologetic letter which the Commander received on August 30. In his letter the President stated that he was sending a letter which he had written to the Ambassador to the United Nations on August 27 and that this letter would explain why it had been necessary to order a withdrawal of the message to the Veterans of Foreign Wars.

The enclosed letter[39] listed seven arguments to the U.N.'s Security Council in defense of the United States' position with respect to Formosa. It was the fourth of these points that seems to have finally jolted the Commander into realizing how differently the President saw the world. This point read:

The action of the United States was expressly stated to be without prejudice to the future political settlement of the status of the island. The actual status of the island is that it is territory taken from Japan by the victory of the Allied forces in the Pacific. Like other such territories, its legal status cannot be fixed until there is international action to determine its future. The Chinese Government was asked by the Allies to take the surrender of the Japanese forces on the island. That is the reason the Chinese are there now.

While the administration was simply trying to get flexibility in its position vis-a-vis Formosa, the Commander reacted to this statement as a repudiation of the Cairo agreement to restore Formosa to the Republic of China. Because this position sharply rubbed against his sense of honor, it emphasized the differences between the President's political world and his own idealistic world. The unfortunate result of the way in which the worlds met, is that it highlighted rather than reduced differences. Each world was different enough to begin with, and each began to increase its myth about the other. The President began to think of the Commander as scheming for power. The Commander began to think of the President as influenced by communists in the State Department. Neither had the perspective to see the misunderstandings that were actually taking place on top of their real differences in outlook.

The fact of real differences in interests and outlook, often masks the misunderstanding that accrues when men are in somewhat competitive positions. Thus, it is interesting to note that, two years later, a gesture of President Truman's was misunderstood. While waiting for the inauguration of his successor, Truman[40] notes:

[39]MacArthur, *op. cit.,* p. 342. See also Truman's *Memoirs,* Vol. Two, p. 356.
[40]Truman, *Mr. Citizen,* pp. 15, 20.

Suddenly General Eisenhower turned to me and said: "I wonder who is responsible for my son John being ordered to Washington from Korea? I wonder who is trying to embarrass me?"

I answered: "The President of the United States ordered your son to attend your Inauguration. The President thought it was right and proper for your son to witness the swearing-in of his father to the Presidency. If you think somebody was trying to embarrass you by this order then the President assumes full responsibility."

What was on my mind on that Inauguration Day, and since, has been regret that relentless grudges should so color the thinking and actions of men in trusted leadership.

While misunderstanding between the President and his Commander had sown the seeds for greater conflict and destructiveness, the growth was not apparent for several months because of the sudden upturn in the fortunes of the war. On September 15, the Commander successfully initiated the amphibious landing we described in Chapter 5. Since the maneuver was opposed by nearly everybody, its success was a tremendous personal success for the Commander. His judgment had prevailed over that of the Joint Chiefs of Staff, and he had been proved right.

On October 9, two planes attacked a Soviet air base. This indiscretion, together with the politics of the forthcoming Congressional election in November, probably account for the fact that the President announced, the next day, that he would meet his Commander at Wake Island. It is interesting to note that the President traveled twice as far as the Commander for the meeting. Each man obviously felt quite ambivalent about the other. Thus, the President later spoke of the Commander as "one of the great military men in our history" as well as a man whose statements all "had the earmarks of a man who performs for the galleries." And the Commander was to speak of the President as "a man of raw courage and guts . . . the little bastard honestly believes he is a patriot"; and, referring to Truman's response to the Korean Invasion, he said, "he reacted instinctively, like the gutter fighter he is — and you've got to admire him." But whereas the President looked upon the Commander as *big* and perhaps envied some of his qualities, the Commander evidently saw the President as *little,* and his admiration was mixed with contempt. It would be interesting to content analyze the statements of these men about each other. This can be done, as we saw in the second chapter with Holsti's analysis of the Secretary of State's view of Russia, or the statements could be rated by the emotion they expressed. In the latter case, we would expect to find the President feeling predominantly inhibited emotions such as envy, awe, and pity and the Commander feeling expressed emotions such as admiration, wonder, and contempt.

On October 15, however, the Commander had just won a great victory, and both men were inclined to the positive sides of their images of one other. The meeting was cordial. The Commander greeted the President with warmth, saying "Mr. President" and pumping his hand. The President smiled and said, "How are you, General, I'm glad you are here. I've been a long time meeting you, General." The Commander responded with, "I hope it won't be so long next time, Mr. President." The two men then talked alone for about half an hour. According to the President,[41] the Commander assured him that victory was won in Korea, that the Chinese would not enter the war, and that the Japanese were ready for a peace treaty. The Commander mentioned his statement to the Veterans of Foreign Wars and "said that he was sorry if he had caused any embarrassment." The President replied that he "considered the incident closed." The President noted that he told the Commander about the plans for further European development and stated, "The General seemed genuinely pleased at this opportunity to talk with me, and I found him a most stimulating and interesting person. Our conversation was very friendly — I might say much more so than I had expected." Note that while the President felt that he was including the Commander in his ingroup's plans, he did not ask for the Commander's opinions or speak of the future of Asia. In essence, then, the President graciously put the Commander in his place.

After breakfast, the two met with eight advisors for an hour and a half. One of the advisors had a secretary who was in the next room and took stenographic notes of the meeting. The Commander said that all resistance would end by Thanksgiving, that he had had complete support from Washington, and that there was little chance that the Chinese would intervene since at most they could get 60,000 troops into Korea and had no air support.* After a break and a second meeting with advisors present, the President proposed lunch but the Commander stated he would prefer to depart as soon as possible. The President notes[42], "the time differential between Wake Island and Tokyo would have thrown the General's return into the night hours if we had stayed and had lunch together, as I had planned."

One suspects that more than a night landing caused the Commander to leave the President as quickly as he could. The President's intimates described him as buoyant, whereas it was noted that the Commander kept looking at his watch and refused to stay for lunch, telling the President, "There are many pressing matters awaiting my return to

---

*The Commander was later to state that his judgment was based on the American ability to bomb Manchuria and cut any Chinese supply lines into Korea.

[41]Truman, H. S., *op. cit., Memoirs VII.* p. 365.

[42]*Ibid.,* p. 367.

Tokyo." He told correspondents that "all the comments will have to come from the publicity man of the President" and would not relent, even to give his impressions of the President. Mr. Leviero of *The New York Times* noted that the President "left Wake highly pleased with the results, like an insurance salesman who had at last signed up an important prospect while the latter appeared dubious over the extent of the coverage."

Later, the Commander interpreted the visit in terms compatible to his own position. He stated,

> The President's visit to the Pacific cannot fail to arouse great enthusiasm throughout the Far East, where it will be interpreted as symbolizing a firm determination that peace shall be secured in the Pacific, and that Asia shall be free, not slave.

It is hard to say exactly what the conference at Wake meant to each party. It appears that what bothered the Commander was not any new statements of policy or cautionary orders but the fact that he had personally met with the President and had to act in such a way that he acknowledged him as his superior. The Commander's attempt to play the role of an equal — note that he did not salute the President — was defeated by the President's security in his role as Commander and Chief. The President, on his part, was probably relieved to feel that the Commander acknowledged his authority. This probably prevented the President from having to believe that the Commander literally refused to accept his policy. He was so relieved that he did not inquire fully into whether the Commander really understood his policy, or how the Commander actually felt.

Methods of Communication and Reconciliation

While the President had temporarily conveyed his authority and strength to the Commander, he had still failed to communicate his policy. With our knowledge of their worlds, it is easy to see in retrospect how difficult this would have been. The President could imagine disagreements but could not imagine how an intelligent person could fail to understand what he said; so he assumed that the Commander understood. The Commander could imagine a person failing to understand what he said but could not imagine how an intelligent person could fail to agree with what he thought; so he assumed that the President had no valid policy. About all the two worlds had succeeded in conveying was that they were alien; they had clashed to provoke distrust and resentment rather than communication.

The difficulties inherent in communicating between two different worlds are usually underestimated. Most persons assume that their world is reality; consequently, they believe that the other's position must be based on the same "reality." They believe they understand the other's position, when in fact they have a pseudo-understanding achieved by distorting the other's motives. This illusion of understanding is preserved by the lack of contact that usually exists between alien worlds and the lack of motivation—since effective communication often requires changing one's own world. To overcome these impediments, special theories and techniques are currently being developed.

These ideas suggest that in order to communicate his policy to the Commander, the President (or an envoy) would have also had to try to understand the policy which the Commander desired. The Commander obviously resented the fact that the administration was not interested in his policy. And on his behalf, it must be said that he was not simply a theater commander but a powerful figure in his own right at a time when the administration needed bipartisan support. This does not, of course, mean that the administration would have had to follow the Commander's policy instead of its own. If the Commander had proved incapable of understanding and following the administration's policy, he could have been immediately but gracefully recalled.

Let us examine the different ways in which two conflicting worlds may interact. Lerner[43] has presented an excellent conceptualization of the various processes. He distinguishes among five basic outcomes.

1. One person may *dominate* the other, that is, force the other to give up his position. For example, the President ordered the Commander to cease public statements and ultimately dominated him by divesting him of his commands; likewise, the Commander might have dominated the President by a coup d'etat or by getting him impeached or (as actually happened) by using public opinion to force him into embracing Chiang Kai-shek.

2. One person may *capitulate* to the other, that is, abandon his own position. Thus, the President might have given in and allowed the Commander to formulate the administration's foreign policy, or the Commander might have passively accepted the administration's unwillingness to support Formosa.

3. The two persons may *compromise,* that is, both leave their positions in favor of a third position (which often does not meet the

---

[43]Melvin Lerner, personal communication.

values of either). Thus, the President and the Commander might have tried to defend both Asia and Europe — with disastrous results.

4. Both men may make an *"encompassing response,"* that is, both move to some new position that encompasses each previous position and integrates the values of both positions. For example, the men might have agreed on the present primacy of Europe but on the necessity of beginning a build-up of technical and military aid to Asia.

5. The two men may *agree to disagree,* that is, recognize each other's positions as different but legitimate and proceed to cooperate as best they can. In this case, the President and the Commander might have faced up to the fact that they strongly disagreed, and the President might have publicly acknowledged this in return for the Commander's public avowal of his intentions to submit to the President's authority in spite of his disagreement.

These distinctions are helpful in recognizing the different ways in which conflict may be resolved and in distinguishing between good and poor solutions. Also, it is possible to state some of the conditions under which the different outcomes will occur. For example, to generate an encompassing response, it is necessary to experience and understand the other's position and to accept it as legitimate. To do this, it is necessary to momentarily move from one's own position. This is facilitated if one's own position is stable and one feels secure; but if the person's own position is shaky, then he is afraid to move from it. It is interesting to note that an encompassing response is always a creative act; an excellent example is cited in Wertheimer's book[44] on the creative process.

To facilitate encompassing responses, Rapoport[45] has suggested a new method of debating. In the ordinary debate, which is designed to convince a third party of which position is correct, a person states his *own* position and rebutes his *opponent's* position by pointing out all the things *wrong* with it. In a "Rapoport debate," which is designed to facilitate the understanding of each other's position, each person states the *other* person's position until the other person agrees that his *partner* understands it. Then, the person states everything that is *right* with the other's position. He accepts everything that he can of the other's position. By trying to understand and accept the other's position, each person increases the possibility of making an encompassing response, and his

[44]M. Wertheimer, *Productive Thinking* (New York: Harper & Row, Publishers, 1959).
[45]A. Rapoport, *Fights, Games, and Debates* (Ann Arbor: University of Michigan Press, 1960).

support of the other's position helps the stability of the other's position and thus increases the likelihood of the other being able to make an encompassing response.

In order to study the effects of the two types of debating, a preliminary study by Eidlin and Oexle[46] asked students who belonged to the John Birch Society and students who belonged to the Young Democratic Club, to debate the propriety of President Kennedy's maneuvers to force manufacturers to retract steel price raises. Each student wrote out his opinions before and after debating with a student of opposite views. Analysis showed that students using the ordinary debate method changed their opinion so that there was even less agreement with their opponent than before the debate. Following a "Rapoport debate," students not only changed their opinions slightly in their opponent's direction but also showed a deepening of their own opinion so that their arguments were more consistent with their values. While no attempt was made to see whether these students would be more likely to produce encompassing responses, the students who engaged in a "Rapoport debate" showed much more respect for their opponents than the students who had used the ordinary debate method. In fact, the only drawback to the "Rapoport debate" was that it failed to provide an outlet for aggressive argumentation and, hence, was not as enjoyable to those students who essentially wanted to fight rather than understand their opposition. Would such a debate have helped the Commander and the President? We can, of course, hardly guess; but since it has been demonstrated that those subordinates who think highly of their supervisors are also more apt to understand them, it may not be too much of a generalization to suggest that if the Commander had undergone the equivalent of a Rapoport debate with the President, he might at least have learned more respect for him and perhaps have begun to understand his reasoning more than he evidently did.

It is, admittedly, idealistic to think of two people with quite divergent views really trying to understand each other. And it may be that unless we are socialized differently we cannot have more respect for values that appear alien to our own. But when government policy that may affect the lives of millions of people is being influenced by a conflict, we must encourage the most ideal solution to the conflict. Had the administration really considered the Commander's views and values, it might have paid more attention to Asia and might not have been forced into Congressional hearings that exposed its plans to the enemy.

---

[46]F. Eidlin and E. Oexle, "Ethical debate and the steel price rise crisis," unpublished paper, Dartmouth course, 1962.

Furthermore, if the Commander had been treated as a valued consultant, he would have been more a part of the group that made the decisions to fight in Korea and to avoid an all-out war with China. Experiments have repeatedly shown that if a person considers himself to be part of a group that makes a decision, he is more likely to implement that decision later on. Conversely, in Chapter 9 we shall see that by neglecting to consider a person's ideas, we reduce his "weight" and engender hostility. Clearly, the Commander was not made to feel part of the decision group — he later mentioned that while he agreed with the decision to resist the Korean Invasion, he regretted that his opinion had not been asked. While the Commander was repeatedly asked to come to visit Washington, the invitations mentioned receiving a hero's welcome and becoming better acquainted; they did not request his advice. If the Commander was powerful enough to be kept as a gesture to the bipartisan policy, he was also powerful enough to be consulted during the decision making. We have already noted the factors that determine the formation of the decision making group. It should also be noted that if a person is too alien to become part of the decision group, he is probably too alien to be trusted with the implementation of a decision from that group.

On the other side, if the Commander had respected his President, tried to understand the administration, and utilized his power to work through the administration rather than to muster opposing public opinion, he might have been able to exert a more positive pressure on American policy. Other subordinates have been able to change the policy of an initially hostile administration. For example, President Coolidge's Ambassador to Mexico managed, in 1927, to invent "moral guardianship," and have this genuine responsible interest in Mexico replace the President's and the Secretary of State's resistance to the Mexican nationalization of American property.

Now, it may be argued that since the Commander and the President represented different political parties, and since such conflicts are usually settled in favor of the party with the most power, the contenders could not afford to try to understand each other for fear that it might damage their power position. That is, the very fact of a power contest — whether it be about Congressional appropriations or an election — may prevent each side from exposing facts or values that are unpopular and, hence, necessitate secrecy. Furthermore, as we shall see in the next chapter, there is often a bargaining advantage in proving oneself intransigent and either unwilling or unable to move from one's position. Finally, some arguments are always based on superior force rather than on shared values; and these are bound to hinder agreement, even when the debate is performed in the best of faith. (For example, if one person or people suppresses another, there will inevitably be a fear of revolt that will distort arguments that are otherwise based on understandable values.)

While, undoubtedly, there are circumstances where a Rapoport type of debate (or any other attempt to arrive at an encompassing response) would endanger one's position, this should not detract from a description of the ideal or from attempts at its attainment. Certainly, at this time we seem to err in the direction of suspicion rather than trust. In the case histories examined here, I have not discovered one instance where there was a loss of power because of an attempt to honestly state one's values and to understand another's position, whereas there are several instances of a loss of power due to a failure to state one's own positions and to comprehend the positions of an opponent.

Dynamics of Authority

Just as incoming information is not only distorted by the perceiver but also biased by the sender's failure to transmit information which he knows the receiver will not appreciate, so outgoing orders are not only misinterpreted but also, sometimes, not given or not insisted upon because the sender knows the orders will not be appreciated by the receiver. Thus, in the everyday world of life, we often see a parent neglecting to give a command which the circumstances call for but which his child is sure to resist. Or the parent may give the command but not insist upon its execution. Often, this abdication of authority has serious consequences. For example, Gore[47] cites an instance where a fire chief saw his hose crew close in on an overheated gasoline storage tank and shouted for them to pull back. While he was sure they heard his order, they acted as if they had not, and he let them go ahead with what they thought was their duty. Unfortunately, the tank exploded and the men were killed. In spite of the common occurrence of this phenomenon, it is somehow startling to see an example in the highest levels of government. Let us see how the President (through his advisors) momentarily abdicated his authority as Commander in Chief.

On his return from Wake Island, the Commander decided to land the tenth corps on the northeast coast of Korea. Since this split both command and supply functions away from the ninth army on the west coast, it was opposed by most of the Commander's staff planners and the

---

[47]William J. Gore, *Administrative Decision-Making* (New York: John Wiley & Sons, Inc., 1964).

Commander of the eighth army, who had been having trouble coordinating the independent movements of the tenth corps. The Commander responded to these objections by saying that mountains would separate the two forces in any case and that *his* office could provide for their operational unity. It is probable that interpersonal considerations were a major factor behind the Commander's move. Observers have noted that while the Commander of the eighth army and the Commander of the tenth corps were devoted to the United Nations Commander, they disliked each other. Since the United Nations Commander was unsure of the capacity of the eighth army Commander and was very close to the Commander of the tenth corps, he probably hesitated to place the latter under the former's authority. It should also be noted that while the decision may have hindered coordination by the eighth army Commander, it effectively kept power in the hands of the United Nations Commander. The Joint Chiefs of Staff were to repeatedly urge that these forces be unified, but the Commander always refused to do so; and the Chiefs, keeping to the tradition of never interfering with a field commander, never insisted that their judgment be respected. The tenth corps itself became widely dispersed in order to capture as many of the fleeing North Koreans as possible. Thus, the net effect of the Commander's tactics was a tremendous scattering of troops — a dispersion that must be kept in mind as we review the succeeding events.

Earlier in October, as the victorious forces marched up into North Korea, the Joint Chiefs of Staff had instructed the Commander to use only Korean troops near the Manchurian border. The Commander went against this instruction and told his field commanders that all troops could go anywhere in North Korea. When the Joint Chiefs questioned this lack of obedience on October 25, the Commander replied that the use of American troops was a military necessity and that they would be replaced with Koreans as soon as it was feasible. He reminded the Joint Chiefs that he had been told to feel unhampered tactically.

In late October and early November, these advancing troops met stiffening resistance, and it became clear that some Chinese troops had entered Korea. By November 6, the Commander was afraid that the Chinese were intervening in strength. He requested and finally obtained permission to bomb the bridges crossing the Yalu River between Manchuria to Korea. At this point, the Chinese pulled back their forces, and it was not clear what their intentions were. It was clear to the participants of the National Security Council meeting on November 9, that the Chinese had the capability to defend the remainder of North Korea and that the United States would have to bargain with China if she hoped to unite Korea. Unfortunately, there were two difficulties with bargaining: the opposition party would protest any kind of recognition of China in the United Nations or relinquishing Formosa; and there was no direct contact with the communist regime in Peiping, because the communist government had not been recognized. Consequently, it was hoped that the Chinese were intervening merely in order to establish some kind of buffer zone to protect their border and their hydroelectric supply. The National Security Council reasoned that the Chinese could not push the United Nations off the peninsula without Soviet aid and that since the Soviet Union would not want to precipitate a world war, the Chinese would lack strength and show some restraint. As Neustadt[48] has remarked, "Why these Americans, who had proclaimed *their own* aversion to world war, should have thought Stalin would assume that *he* risked general war if Peking acted, I will not endeavor to explain." It is also difficult to explain why a hope should have replaced a realistic view of the situation, but we have considered such errors in the chapter on projecting the future. Here it suffices to note that it was assumed that the Chinese wanted some kind of buffer zone and that this idea was strengthened when the Chinese suddenly pulled back their forces. It was accordingly suggested that while the State Department was seeking ways to negotiate with the Chinese, the Commander should be free to make what advances he could (after all, he had done better than anyone had expected in his amphibious landing), as long as he did not provoke the Chinese by bombing Manchuria.

When the Secretary of Defense pointed out that the eastern front was widely dispersed and highly vulnerable to attack, the Secretary of State asked if there was a better line for defensive purposes. The Chairman of the Joint Chiefs of Staff replied that the farther back such a line was, the better it would be — but that a withdrawal might weaken the South Koreans' will to fight. The Council could not decide what to do. Letting the Commander advance might clarify Chinese intentions or help American bargaining power, but caution called for ordering the Commander to halt and regroup his forces. While the Council had just as much information as the Commander, it finally decided to let the Commander advance at his discretion. Such a decision — to relinquish control to a person with a different set of responsibilities — is structurally poor. By failing to make its own decision and thereby giving the choice of action to the Commander, the administration relinquished its control over the situation in one of its few non-courageous actions. It is noteworthy that the President was not present at this meeting of the National Security Council — though, of course, he was informed that the Com-

---

[48]R. E. Neustadt, *Presidential Power* (New York: John Wiley & Sons, Inc., 1960).

mander had been given the discretion to advance. The Council agreed that this decision should be kept under review pending clarification of Peiping's intentions — an excellent device for masking the abdication of authority that had actually taken place. This was an abdication rather than a delegation of authority, because the Council knew that the Commander's world differed greatly from the administration's and he could hardly be trusted to make decisions in an appropriate way. As Neustadt[49] emphasizes, from November 9 on, the Commander rather than the President became the judge of which risks the administration was willing to take.

Given this leeway, the Commander determined to launch a "home by Christmas" offensive to the very borders of China. He anticipated no resistance, believed that the Chinese had pulled back because they had been impressed by American firepower, and probably expected his boldness to convince the Chinese that nothing would dissuade the American government from unifying all of Korea. The creation of a buffer zone struck him as pure appeasement.

The Pentagon was aware that numerous Chinese troops might have already crossed the Yalu to hide in the Korean mountains. According to Neustadt,[50] "By mid-November some of these men [in the Pentagon] felt virtually certain of the real Chinese location and were becoming worried lest [the Commander] fail to concentrate his forces." Reportedly, the Secretaries of Defense and State and the Chairman of the Joint Chiefs of Staff were worried about a possible attack, and the British wanted to pull back and consolidate the scattered forces. Neustadt states that the Commander "was practically implored to show more caution. When he demurred, as under his instructions he had every right to do, the Chiefs of Staff lacked courage (lacking certainty) to seek their alteration from the President."

In spite of the fact that everyone wished the President would change the Commander's orders, no one went to the President. The Chairman of the Joint Chiefs of Staff (who the Commander believed was incompetent) felt that since this was a matter of "policy," the Secretary of State, as head of "policy," should go to the President. The Secretary of State (who was continually under fire from Congressional opposition and was aware of the President's idealism about generals) felt that since this was a "military" risk, it was a matter for the Defense Department. The Secretary of Defense did not wish to interfere either with the Commander (whom he had feuded with continuously in the army — it should be noted that each was the center of rival networks of mili-

---

[49]*Ibid.*
[50]*Ibid.*, p. 144.

tary leaders) or with the job of the Chairman of the Joint Chiefs of Staff. Thus, the buck was passed back to the Chairman, but if it really were a "military" rather than a "policy" matter, the Chairman was loath to argue with a man in the field who was closer to the situation (and who had just been right with his amphibious assault when the Chairman had said it was impossible).

These men knew that unless they had the President's backing, the Commander would do what he pleased no matter what they said. But none of the men were *certain* they were correct, and they could hardly go to a President who liked concrete arguments — it was easier, and safer, to do nothing. The President, unaware of the strength of the opposing arguments and not really thinking of the possible consequences, felt that "you pick your man and then you've got to back him up." In any case, he was publicly committed to the unification of Korea. As a consequence, the decision to review the Commander's decisions was never acted upon and the Commander kept the authority to do as he pleased. At first, his offensive worked well; then, on November 27, the Chinese attacked in full strength, swept down between the Commander's split forces, and forced a massive withdrawal with hundreds of American casualties.

Perhaps the most interesting psychological aspects of such abdications of authority is that once the superior has surrendered his will and tried to give his responsibility to the subordinate, he cannot seem to take his authority back. As in the above example, he is forced to be a bystander and to helplessly view the ensuing disaster. That is, even if more information comes in so that the superior would now definitely decide on a different course of action from the subordinate, he cannot seem to regain his decision making powers.

It is my belief that up until the Chinese entry into the war, the Commander did not really abrogate the authority of the President. While it can be argued that his behavior (such as his speech to the Veterans of Foreign Wars) constitutes a deliberate challenge or, at least, reflects indifference towards the attitudes of the administration, it seems more likely that a series of misunderstandings had occurred. When these misunderstandings were clarified the President and the Commander were aware that they disagreed on certain important matters; the Commander accepted these disagreements, and the two men had no trouble until the military situation changed. At this point, I believe, the Commander's behavior shifted qualitatively, and he began to ignore the President's authority.

Now we must digress for a moment to examine the nature of "disagreement." If two persons really disagree with one another but don't know it, then there is an obvious kind of misunderstanding. Therefore, we are likely to think that if they know they disagree there is no *misunderstanding*. While in a sense this is true, it is obvious that there still may be a complete *lack of understanding*. This was the case between the President and the Commander. As Hoare[51] has noted, the Commander never understood the evolving concept of limited war. He thought in a completely different frame of reference, and the President was unable to get the Commander to see the position of the United States in the world as he himself saw it. It was not just that the two worlds were different and that the men in them could not agree. It was also that neither party had any real understanding of the other's world and, hence, had no sympathy or tolerance for the other's world. It was as though the two men were from different cultures.*

The difficulties involved in empathizing with both of the two worlds is reflected in many accounts and perceptions of the Commander's later "disobedience" and "challenge of presidential authority." Many persons believe that the Commander deliberately disobeyed orders because he thought he could get away with it, or that the President's disposal of the Commander was an act of appeasement to communism. Actually, the situation appears to be much more complex than that and reflects the difference between the two worlds.

Once the Chinese had entered the war, the administration was now faced with a new situation. From its viewpoint, it preferred losing Korea (which was strategically insignificant and a poor place to fight) to getting involved in an all-out war with China and risking the eventual loss of Europe or Japan. Persons in the administration may also have felt some guilt about involving China in the war by blockading Formosa and crossing the 38th parallel. Furthermore, they sensed that the American people and its allies did not want to fight a war, and therefore they wanted to limit the war as much as possible.

The Commander, on the other hand, was in quite a different position. His world demanded an enlargement of the war in order to secure Korea and humble Communist China. Furthermore, *he* had been responsible for the disastrous offensive; he must have felt his defeat deeply and desperately wanted to redeem himself with an ultimate victory. (There is a striking parallel here with his defeat in the Philippines.) Finally, as a soldier responsible for the lives of his men, he felt that

---

[51]William W. Hoare, "Truman," in Ernest R. May (ed.), *The Ultimate Decision* (New York: George Braziller, Inc., 1960).

*In this regard, we should note some of the current research on understanding between cultures. See, for example, Bryant M. Wedge, *Planned Basic Research in International Contact* (Princeton, N. J.: Institute for the Study of National Behavior).

morally the nation should go all out to support the war effort until victory was achieved. He did not countenance the morality of a limited war of attrition. Therefore, the Commander laid plans for winning rather than limiting the war. He requested permission to bomb Manchuria, to use Chinese Nationalist troops, and to commit divisions of American troops that were currently slated to go to Europe. The administration, thoroughly sobered by the turn of events, turned down all of these requests. It instructed him, instead, to defend Korea with what forces he had and to retire to Japan if necessary.

These instructions did not sit well with the Commander, who pressed the administration to become more involved in the war. He argued that a defense line could not otherwise be developed across Korea and that unless there were "political decisions" he would be forced into purely defensive beachhead positions. Imagine his dismay when he received a reply that stated,[52] "We consider that the preservation of your forces is now the primary consideration. Consolidation of forces into beachheads is concurred in." Faced with this policy, the Commander publicly blamed the failure of his own misguided offensive on the administration and its orders to prevent a broadening of the offensive. Apparently, he simply could not tolerate the idea of a defeat — especially *his* defeat. Consequently, he kept talking and issuing statements that led allies to believe that the government might change its mind and broaden hostilities.

As a result of his remarks, on December 5, an order directed to all commanders (but aimed at one) stated that all press releases and speeches concerning foreign policy were to be cleared by the State Department and that publicity media in the United States were not to be communicated with.

The Army Chief of Staff was sent to Korea to check on the situation. He reported that the situation was not quite as bad as the Commander had portrayed. By December 11, the Chinese began to have supply problems, and it seemed possible that a line across Korea could be held.

The Commander argued that one should not be afraid of provoking China into a major war because all of China's resources were already committed to the Korean attack or were backing up the attack in Manchuria. This left China vulnerable in other areas. Therefore, the United States should blockade China, destroy its cities with naval gunfire and bombardment, and use Chinese Nationalist troops for a diversionary action against mainland China. He argued that an evacuation of Korea would have adverse effects upon all the people of Asia and would

---

[52]Truman, Vol. Two, *op. cit.*, p. 393.

release Chinese troops for action in places of greater importance than Korea (e.g., Formosa). He attempted to meet the administration's concern for Europe by arguing that the *preparations* for European defense would not be hurt by using more force in the *current* Asian emergency — indeed, it would ensure seasoned troops for later commitment in Europe.

His argument, however, ignored one of the administration's main concerns — that if American troops were all used in China, the Soviet Union could strike in Europe. Hence, on January 9, the Joint Chiefs of Staff informed the Commander that there was little possibility of any change in policy. He was, therefore, instructed to inflict maximum damage on the enemy — subject to the primary consideration of the safety of his own troops and the basic mission of protecting Japan. If evacuation was necessary for this main objective, it should be performed. (Note that the Joint Chiefs of Staff did not state that *they* felt policy should not be changed — although, in fact, they felt just that.)

On January 10, the Commander said that his forces were too weak to hold both Korea and Japan and that if heavy losses were to be avoided an evacuation should be instigated. Furthermore, he reported that troop morale was becoming low. The Commander tossed the question of evacuation back to Washington. This caused the Joint Chiefs of Staff to consider action against the Chinese mainland if the Americans were forced out of Korea. This responsiveness on the part of the Joint Chiefs of Staff encouraged the Commander in his misconception that they concurred with his general policy. The Army and Air Force Chiefs of Staff were ordered to visit Korea to check on the situation. And the President wrote the Commander a letter.

In this letter, the President did his best to present his world to the Commander and to reassure him of the worth of his limited war. He listed ten reasons that required a continued resistance in Korea. In essence, he concluded that if eventually an evacuation had to occur, it must "be clear to the world that the course is forced upon us by military necessity and that we shall not accept the result politically or militarily until the aggression has been rectified."[53] This letter was an elegant statement of the President's views and values; unfortunately, the Commander, stuck in his own world, was not able to understand and appreciate it.

By January 17, the Chiefs of Staff found that the Chinese advance had stopped. Their supply lines were now definitely too long, and it was clear that South Korea could be held. But at home, the opposition party

---

[53]MacArthur, *op. cit.,* p. 382. Also in Truman, *Memoirs,* Vol. Two, p. 436.

had won elections wherever it had challenged the administration's foreign policy. The opposition now put together an emotional coalition between isolationistic resentment at Euopean aid and demands for the support of Nationalist China. There were demands for either a withdrawal or an all-out fight. The administration was put on the defensive and was forced to embrace the Chinese Nationalists in order to insure support for continued European aid. On the other hand, the administration's holding of Formosa and refusal to seat China in the United Nations nearly disintegrated the North Atlantic Treaty Organization! The skillful insertion of terms which China could not accept and the intransigency of the Chinese themselves helped save the situation.

If the administration had been put on the spot by the Commander and the opposition party, the Commander was also tied by the administration. He could see the administration preparing to send four divisions to Europe instead of Korea, and it must have infuriated him. He gained an ally in the House Speaker, who favored the use of Chinese Nationalist troops. The Secretary of State strongly opposed this and many other measures which the Commander proposed — for example, the Commander was told that he could not bomb near the Korean border. In spite of these difficulties, the war progressed well; by the middle of March, the United States had recaptured Seoul, and the Joint Chiefs of Staff began wondering if a further advance might not be possible. While it now seems that advance would have been possible, and the Chinese were already pushed back beyond the 38th parallel, the administration and the allies had lost interest in unifying Korea. With their fingers burnt and their focus on Europe, they decided that the time was ripe for negotiations.

Accordingly, on March 20, 1951, the Joint Chiefs of Staff informed the Commander that a presidential announcement on negotiations was planned. Since any major advance across the 38th parallel would have to await the consequences of this negotiation attempt, they asked what authority he needed for the next few weeks. The following day, the Commander replied with the rather unhelpful request that "no further military restrictions be imposed upon the United Nations Command in Korea."

On March 24, the negotiation plans of the administration were completely broken up by one of the Commander's communiques. It declared that Communist China had been revealed as militarily weak. Not only had it failed to recapture Korea, the Commander proclaimed, but if the mainland were attacked it would collapse. Certainly, the unity of Korea should not be sacrificed to the desire for peace, and a truce could easily be obtained if it were not burdened by talk about Formosa or the admission of China to the United Nations. Within these limitations, the Commander stated that *he* was willing to confer with the enemy commander to find a solution.

This announcement virtually asked China to admit defeat; it preempted the administration's plans for negotiations. In essence, it completely disrupted peace plans and gave the administration a push into open war with China. While he did not perceive himself as disobeying orders, the Commander had ignored the intent of orders and in doing so had again affected American foreign policy. From the capitals of all the allies, inquiries poured in asking if the United States had shifted its policy. The State Department was forced to abandon its negotiations, and the President later noted that at this point he decided he could no longer tolerate the Commander's actions. He has said,[54]

> I can only say that on that day I was deeply shocked. I had never underestimated my difficulties with MacArthur, but after the Wake Island meeting I had hoped that he would respect the authority of the President. I tried to place myself in his position, however, and tried to figure out why he was challenging the traditional civilian supremacy in our government.

The President noted that the Commander's proposals had always received full consideraton and that he and the Joint Chiefs of Staff had "leaned over backwards" because of the Commander's military reputation. However, he observed that ever since the Chinese entered the war the Commander's statements "had the earmarks of a man who performs for the galleries." He concluded that the Commander's communique could only be explained by his desire to "prevent any appearance that the credit for ending the fighting should go elsewhere."

Note that the President tells us that the Commander was deliberately challenging the authority of the Presidential office — the office from which the President drew all of his confidence — in order to gain credit for ending the war. As we shall see, another interpretation seems more likely. We noted in the chapter on perception that a perception of another person's actions is always an interpretation. We must now note that the interpretation that is selected often jibes with aspects of one's own personality. This is particularly true when the perceiver has access to a limited amount of data. For example, a study done by Dornbusch, Hastorf *et al*[55] shows that when one person describes another, his description is more likely to tell us about how he perceives things than

---

[54]Truman, *Memoirs,* Vol. Two, *op. cit.,* p. 443.

[55]Sanford Dornbusch, Albert H. Hastorf, Steven A. Richardson, Robert E. Muzzy, and R. S. Vreeland, "The perceiver and the perceived; their relative influence on the categories of interpersonal perception," unpublished paper.

about what the other is really like. They show that when two persons, A and B, each describe two other persons, C and D, there is more agreement between A's descriptions of C and D (or B's descriptions of C and D) than between A and B's description of C or between A and B's description of D. Applying this reasoning, we note that the President was himself politically sensitive. *He* was the person who had called the conference at Wake Island, in part to associate his administration with the then victorious Commander and, hence, to share in his glory.

In saying this, I am not disputing the fact that the Commander's actions were undermining Presidential authority and that this had to be met by some Presidential action. I am suggesting that the attribution of *purposely challenging* and *to get credit* is more a reflection of the President's personality than the Commander's, and that the *way* in which the Commander's actions were met was biased by this faulty attribution.

How can we account for this flagrant lack of cooperation from a professional soldier who stressed duty and honor and viewed himself as loyal and obedient? First, it should be noted that the Commander never really disobeyed an order. After the "muzzling" order of December 6, the Commander sent his next communique to Washington and it was returned with the statement that it was not necessary to clear routine reports. The Commander's statement, published on March 24, was regarded by him as one of these routine communiques. He states it was written *before* the message from the Joint Chiefs of Staff, which he received on March 21. The Commander is thus to be charged with disregard for his President's policies rather than with deliberately disobeying him. The motives for this regard seem clear: First, from the Commander's view, the Administration's policy just did not make sense; in fact, since he had never understood the Administration's world, it looked to him as if the Administration had no policy at all and was simply being swayed by "politics" or puffs of wind from British imperialists or State Department Communists.

Second, his own confidence was of a charismatic nature and he lacked sensitivity, he did not comprehend the extent to which his actions were undermining Presidential authority. In his world, he thought of the President as separated from himself by a wall of advisors who deceived him as to the nature of his Commander and concealed timidity and defeat. According to the Commander, the meeting at Wake Island had lowered his opinion of the President. He states,[56]

> The defiant rallying figure that had been Franklin Roosevelt was gone. Instead there was a tendency toward temporizing rather than fighting it through. The original courageous decision of Harry Truman to boldly

---

[56]MacArthur, *op. cit.,* p. 363.

meet and defeat communism in Asia was apparently being chipped away by the constant pounding whispers of timidity and cynicism. . . . He seemed to be in the anomalous position of openly expressing fears of overcalculated risks that he had fearlessly taken only a few months before.

By viewing the situation in this way, the Commander managed to see himself as propping up Presidential authority rather than challenging it. Hence, he regarded it as his duty to speak out for the correct policy. To the extent to which the Commander was aware of asserting an independent policy which the President did not agree with, he rationalized his behavior by thinking that his loyalty was to the Constitution rather than to the President. This, of course, was the most dangerous trend in his thinking, since it did challenge the idea of civilian supremacy over military policy, and was an attempt to abrogate the authority of the President.

Third, he had been made responsible for deciding whether to retreat or advance in the face of Chinese opposition. When he chose to advance, he must have felt responsible for the ensuing disaster. He was not secure enough to admit to himself that he had made a mistake, so he viewed his defeat as a clever tactic that had exposed Chinese treachery. This view, however, was only possible to hold as long as he saw the war in the large view — as an all-out struggle with communism. If the war was conceived of as a limited war, he had made a serious tactical error. In fact, if he had conceived of the war in the way the administration did, he might not have begun that disastrous offensive. To follow the adminstration's policy exposed the Commander to guilt, and it was this personal involvement that summed with the objective facts of his world to cause the Commander to proclaim his policy to the public — a public that, he felt, had to see him as perfect if it were not to reject him: a mother-like public.

No matter what the Commander thought he was doing, the President had to quiet him in order to pursue his own policy. Therefore, on March 26, he instructed the Joint Chiefs of Staff to remind the Commander of the directive of December 6 that prohibited uncleared statements on foreign policy. They stated, "any further statements by you must be coordinated as prescribed in the order of 6 December."

Unfortunately, on March 8, the Speaker of the House had written to the Commander, "asking" if he agreed that Asia should be protected and Nationalist Chinese forces should be used to attack mainland China. On March 20 the Commander had replied that he agreed with the Speaker of the House and that "There is no substitute for victory." On April 5, the Speaker read the Commander's letter on the floor of the House. Again the question was raised as to who was conducting American Foreign

Policy. It is ironic that the time delays involved prevented the President from realizing that this last challenge was not as provoking as it looked.

On April 10, the President dispatched his last order to the Commander. It read:

> I deeply regret that it becomes my duty as President and Commander in Chief of the United States military forces to replace you as Supreme Commander, Allied Powers; Commander-in-Chief, United Nations Command; Commander-in-Chief, Far East; and Commanding General, U. S. Army, Far East. You will turn over your commands effective at once to Lt. Gen. Matthew B. Ridgway. You are authorized to have issued such orders as are necessary to complete desired travel to such place as you select. . . .

This way of dismissing the Commander was particularly unfortunate; it made him a martyr. While the abruptness of the dismissal was partly caused by a report that word had leaked to the press (the initial plan called for the Secretary of the Army to hand the Commander the orders), neither the manner nor the wording of the dismissal was gracious. While the Commander had not cooperated fully with the President since the reversal in the Korean War, he had led a lifetime of service to his country. He deserved better treatment.

In defense of the President, it must be pointed out that the action of dismissing the Commander and, hence, asserting the authority of the Presidency, must have taken a great deal of courage. The President was well aware of the storm it would cause, and he must have had to isolate himself somewhat at the expense of his feeling for the situation. It appears that the dismissal order took all of the President's emotional strength so that he had none left for diplomacy. We must point out, however, that *part* of the reason why it was so difficult to dismiss the Commander was the construction which the President had put on the Commander's actions. If he had regarded him as a stubborn old fool, he would have easily found a gracious way to dismiss him. Since he regarded him as a challenger and out for glory to boot, he found it harder to handle.*

---

*Another possibility is inherent in the hypothesis that some transference had occurred and the Commander had become a symbol for the President's father. Under this hypothesis, the President would unconsciously wish to hurt the Commander (father) whom he consciously admired. Because of the strong forces against this desire, he could not remove the Commander much earlier or in a straightforward way. Rather, the pressures of his insolence had to build up to such an extent that the President was obviously justified in relieving him. The resulting sudden dismissal was, of course, an excellent solution, since it must have hurt the Commander very much.

If the President had simply conceived of the Commander as politically dense, his communications with him might have been much more incisive. As it was, the Commander was able to retain his illusion that the President was not really running the show.

While we have tried to demonstrate how the personal emotions of both the Commander and the President somewhat biased their view of the situation and hindered their interaction, this contamination was small compared to the personal emotions involved in the ensuing public howl.

No doubt, the abruptness and apparent injustice of the Commander's dismissal contributed to the public outcry that followed the President's action. There are times when a nation is swept by a wave of sentiment, times when an event somehow triggers similar emotions in citizens of all walks of life — as when President Kennedy's death touched many Americans so personally that different ages and backgrounds were unified in their feelings, and flags spontaneously appeared from both hovels and mansions. When the Commander was recalled, such a wave (only it was a wave of indignation) swept the country. As Rovere and Schlesinger[57] have noted,

> . . . in the two or three weeks that followed the recall, the American citizen, as encountered in the street, in the railway coach, at the supermarket, the saloon, the gas station, and the barbershop, seemed a deeply aggrieved and affronted man. He took [the Commander's] recall as if it were an outrage to his own person.

Over 27,000 telegrams and letters poured into the White House; Congressional mail ran ten to one against the dismissal. State legislatures condemned the President, and he was publicly booed and burned in effigy. Opposition Senators talked of censure and even impeachment, and "McCarthyites" charged that the government was under the control of the Soviet Union. The Commander, on the other hand, was greeted by record breaking crowds and given the rare opportunity of addressing a joint session of Congress in a speech that demonstrated his strength to all. Worst of all, the opposition managed to force a Congressional investigation into "the situation in the Far East" — an investigation that kept public opinion aroused throughout the country, aided the rise of McCarthyism, and forced the administration to permanently embrace the Chinese Nationalists and publicly commit themselves to the defense of Formosa. In such ways — by the clash of political forces rather than by reason — is foreign policy molded.

---

[57]Richard H. Rovere and Arthur M. Schlesinger, Jr., *The General and the President* (Farrar, Straus & Giroux, Inc., 1951), p. 5.

Now, there is no doubt that when the President removed the General from all of his commands, he was simply asserting the rights of the Presidential office as determined by the constitution. The President has the right to have his in-group and not some other power make government policy. Had the Commander refused to relinquish his command and thus have begun a revolt, the majority of Congress would have united to support the administration and prevent a disruption of the government. However, it is quite clear that the President cannot lightly exercise this right. Once the Commander was removed and was no longer under the authority of the President, he could say whatever he pleased and was much more damaging to the administration than when he had been constrained by his duty to his Commander in Chief. Not only did the removal of the Commander from office free him from the restraints that had hitherto hindered him from saying whatever he pleased, but the mere fact of his recall gave him the entire nation for an audience. The manner of his recall provoked a reaction that did more damage to the administration's foreign policy than anything the Commander had been able to do while he was in the service.

The irrational reaction of the public reflected another gap between worlds, for the administration had failed to convey an important aspect of its world to the individual worlds of many American people. The rise of McCarthyism was a symptom of this educational failure. Just as the administration had failed to honestly state its views on Asia to the Commander, it had failed to state them to the American people — largely because it was afraid of a reaction from the opposition party that would doom its other programs. The boom in the Commander's neo-isolationism and the related rise of McCarthyism were the prices of this educational failure. It was the Commander, not the administration, who defined the enemy as communist ideology rather than Russian nationalism. The compromise between *his* definition and the administration's position continued to affect American policy in Southeast Asia and contributed to the heavy involvement in Viet Nam.

In this chapter, we have considered the problem of communication between the in-group and a dissident power it had to deal with. Policy formation is not usually quite so hectic, because most disagreements are contained by a common interest in obtaining less disturbing compromises. Ordinarily, competing perceptions of the truth are kept in control by large scale bargaining operations, and policy is formed by a quieter competition between different governmental coalitions. In the next chapter, we shall consider these inter-group factors and their interaction with the intimacy of the in-group.

CHAPTER 8

Interpersonal Relations: Consensus Formation Within the Organization

The way in which a nation is organized determines many characteristics of its foreign policy and makes some psychological processes more relevant than others. In the case of the United States, Schilling has woven the ideas of different political scientists into a compact description of these relationships; they may be summarized as follows.[1]

The United States is politically organized into an elite structure, which consists of a number of autonomous and competing groups, and a mass structure, which consists of a small informed stratum and a large base that is ordinarily ignorant and indifferent to foreign policy. Each elite group has a different opinion about how the nation should behave and different institutional responsibilities to mind. Finally, power is thinly and widely distributed among these different groups.

As a consequence of this organization, any person or group who advocates a policy must be able to interest a number of elite groups; he must form a consensus in order to develop his program. Consequently, the psychological process of consensus formation is of major relevance.

---

[1]Warner Schilling's integration of some ideas from Almond, Hilsman, Fox, Huntington, and Neustadt is contained in pp. 19-27 of Schilling, P. Y. Hammond, and G. H. Snyder, *Strategy, Politics, and Defense Budgets* (New York: Columbia University Press, 1962).

The process of forming a consensus is a struggle for survival; for if a policy advocate is unable to join numerous different groups to his cause, he will not be able to affect policy. The resulting battle to win power, gain allies, influence neutrals, and weaken opponents is comparable to the diplomatic struggle between nations. Discussions tend to be negotiatory rather than analytic. Their object is either to persuade the other that his own interests are best served by joining the policy advocate or, if the interests are incompatible, to find some way to compromise or bargain. The only difference between these negotiations and the diplomacy of nations is that the prospects for agreement are better and the conflict is marked by a much higher propensity to seek a solution. That is, since accommodation is necessary to obtain one's own goals and there is common desire to see the nation with some policy it can act upon, the conflict is checked by a strain towards agreement.

Presumably, nations with more autocratic governments are not as preoccupied with attaining consensus, and it has been noted that they tend to make more errors of commission and less of omission than democracies do. Unfortunately, there are no really good comparative studies on these points, and one does not know the degree to which they are true. However, it is clear that in the United States the fact that the political organization makes consensus formation of prime importance leads in turn to certain characteristics of the American foreign policy that is produced:

1. Since the very having of a policy depends on obtaining a consensus among diverse groups, there may be no policy at all, or an unstable policy, or a contradictory policy, or (if the consensus is not broad enough for effective implementation) a "paper policy."

2. The fact that time is necessary to build a consensus leads to a slow policy and creates large delays between the recognition of a problem and a solution.

3. Since it is difficult to build a consensus, elites are reluctant to disturb it. The time and energy of elites are limited, and solutions to policy problems are difficult to get and harder to get agreement on. The result is a "gyroscopic" effect on policy: once policies are begun, they tend to keep on going without regard for changes in the circumstances that first caused them. We saw a case of this in the decision to cross the 38th parallel. A policy may continue and contribute to the misperceptions we noted in Chapter 2, until the circumstances drastically change and dramatically challenge the policy. Outmoded policy and crisis oriented policy result.

4. The tendency for changes to occur only when there is a crisis is very pronounced when the required consensus needs the support of the mass structure. The masses, ordinarily ignorant of policy, can be convinced to give money, votes, or lives, only when confronted with grave problems. Since the public's response is more emotional than intellectual, its participation may create an over-reaction or a short-reaction; and since not all problems can be presented as crisis, there is often a noticeable under-reaction. As we shall see, this general ignorance of the public leads elites to produce overly simple or demagogic statements or to practice duplicity in manipulating public opinion. These practices, in turn, may make it hard to change the policy once the public is aroused.

5. The necessity of consensus diffuses responsibility and dampens initiative so that leadership may not be exercised and the various elites may assume a "radar approach" to policy formation with each power watching and waiting upon others.

6. As we observed in Chapter 3, consensus rather than rationality is the current selection test for policy. Hence, the process of mutual accommodation does not always lead to sound policy but may lead to a compromised policy that benefits nobody. Psychological dynamics are often crucial in determining whether or not the consensus is a sound one.

In this chapter, we shall examine four different aspects of consensus. First, we will consider some psychological research that is relevant to the development of a consensus between the leaders of groups and to the problem of whether or not the consensus is sound. Second, we will examine several factors that may impair communication between leaders, and consider what countermeasures may increase the occurrence of understanding. Third, we shall observe how consensus is affected by interpersonal dynamics within the State Department. Although policy is largely set from above, the bureaucratic organization provides the intelligence estimates, the policy analyses, and the planning on which the policy is based. While there are no good data on exactly how this affects policy, its effect could be considerable. Furthermore, the bureaucracy's lower level operational decisions may often be crucial in determining whether the policy succeeds in accomplishing what was hoped. We shall see how various structural and managerial factors have important psychological consequences that affect the efficiency of the bureaucracy. Fourth, we shall note the role of congressional and public opinion and examine some important psychological problems that are raised. While a consensus must be developed in a democracy, the

President has considerable leeway in defining the situation for Congress and the public to get the consensus he desires. To the extent that Congress and the public are apathetic, and to the extent that the President uses propaganda rather than education, the consensus process is bypassed, and the policy process may begin to resemble what occurs in autocratic countries. In recent years, the continual "crisis" of the "cold war" seems to have produced such a change in American foreign policy.

Psychology Aspects of Consensus Formation

The case histories of various decisions that affect foreign policy all demonstrate the importance of consensus formation and show some of the characteristics we have listed above. Schilling's[2] history of the formation of the 1950 defense budget is a virtual museum of examples. We shall examine one aspect of that case, on the one hand to provide a concrete example of what we have been describing, and on the other hand to suggest that the characteristics of the consensus process may not be as determined as they might appear to be at first sight.

As we noted in the introduction, the central conflict about the size of the 1950 defense budget was between the Director of the Bureau of the Budget and the Secretary of Defense. The Budget Director — as the head of an elite group with fiscal responsibilities — argued that a higher defense budget would be inflationary unless taxes were increased or wage and price controls were instigated. He pointed out that the public would not accept controls and that the Russians would win a major victory if the economy were hurt by an inflation. The Secretary of Defense — as the head of an elite group with defense responsibilties — argued that the present defense system was simply not adequate to contain Soviet expansion and that it was wiser to risk hurting the economy than to lose more territory to Russia. Both men, of course, represented agencies that felt the way they did, and both had many allies outside of their own groups and areas of responsibility; but the crucial person to win as an ally in order to establish a reasonable consensus was the Secretary of State — a man whom the President greatly admired and who held primary responsibility for containing the Soviet Union in a time of peace.

When the three men first met with the President, the Secretary of State took a position that supported the Director of the Budget more

---

[2]Schilling, *op cit.*

than the Secretary of Defense. He pointed out that the current foreign policy was based on the assumption that there would be no war. He himself felt that the Soviet Union would not attack if it was clear that the United States would resist. The best way to demonstrate the intention to defend Europe was to initiate universal military training, a measure less expensive than a budget increase and less likely to be seen as provocative. It is interesting to examine the reasons behind this position. Schilling notes that it reflected the Secretary's institutional responsibilities. That is, as Secretary of State he could not base his policy on the assumption of war — it was his responsibility to avoid it; likewise, it was his responsibility to consider the intentions of others and to try to influence these intentions. Universal military training would show the Soviet Union that the United States was serious — but without being provocative. In addition to these considerations generated by his role, two personal beliefs were important in determining the Secretary's stand. One belief was that the Secretary of Defense was not doing all he could to force a sound economy program on the armed services. The other belief (born from personal experience) was that the American public would continue to demand military economy in times of peace and splurging in time of war. The Secretary wanted to smooth out this "feast and famine" cycle so that the nation would be prepared for the "long haul" he foresaw. Here too, universal military training made more sense than a large defense budget in the coming year.

After this meeting, the Secretary of Defense refused to accept defeat and did his best to enlist the support of the Secretary of State. He arranged to have the Joint Chiefs of Staff brief the Secretary of State on defense plans and needs but was dismayed to find that he was not really interested. The Secretary of State asked very few questions and then launched into an hour long description of the military needs of the *European* nations for which he, as Secretary of State, was trying to obtain aid. When the Chairman of the Joint Chiefs asked if the United States should not be prepared to come to Europe's assistance, the Secretary of State replied, certainly — but *first,* French military strength should be bolstered.

Finally (after many wasted months) the Secretary of Defense tried to enlist the Secretary of State's support on the basis of *his* (the State Department's) needs. Noting that the State Department had once written a memo on "peace needs" — e.g., six thousand troops might be needed for U. N. action in Palestine — the Defense Secretary pointed out that the defense budget should be prepared not only to meet a war but also to assist the Secretary of State in negotiations to maintain peace. Since he believed that the Berlin Blockade and the Soviet development of the atomic bomb had led to a deteriorating situation, the Defense Secretary fished for support by asking the Secretary of State if the situation — on which the defense budget should be based — was better or worse or the same. Unfortunately, the Secretary of State did not respond to this belated reference to his needs and views. He replied that the situation was about the same, and he did not help the Defense Secretary get the budget increase he so desired.

Now, if the Secretary of State could have obtained the universal military training that had been *his* solution to defense problems, we could easily understand his failure to support the Secretary of Defense; but by this time Congress had definitely rejected his plan. Why, then, did he not now support a higher defense budget? Schilling notes three reasons: (1) the President's earlier budget decision had been in the form of an order, and the Secretary of State knew that his own reputation would be risked if he fought the Defense Secretary's battle. (2) He really did not know what his military needs were because it was hard to calculate just what would help him most. His one clear need was for European rearmament. Knowing the budget problem, he had to consider the possibility that if the Defense Department got additional funds he might not get the money for military aid, which he most wanted. (3) He balanced this view — which risked American unpreparedness — with a belief that the Soviet Union was now afraid that the United States would use atomic weapons. Also, he had seen the United States more poorly prepared in 1941 and yet recover quickly enough so that things had worked out satisfactorily.

The above interaction illustrates the consensus process and how, in this case, it created a delay between the problem of Russian expansion and a viable solution. The solution had to await a crisis — the Korean War — before the mass structure could see the problem and would agree to the tax sacrifice and controls that made it possible to increase the defense budget without ruining the economy. But it would be a mistake to consider that the obtained outcome was determined by the structure without being influenced by psychological aspects of the consensus process.

Two aspects of the interaction between the Secretaries of Defense and of State are worthy of further notice. First, the Defense Secretary failed to consider the needs of the Secretary of State until it was too late to build an alliance based on these needs. Second, the two Secretaries were essentially in a position where they could have cooperated to get a bigger budget with more money for each other; but this cooperation did not develop, because the Secretary of State chose to compete for what money there was in the current budget.

These same aspects were present within the Defense Department in the conflict between the services for whatever money there was to be in the defense budget. The Army chose to compete with the Navy rather than to ally itself with the Navy against the Air Force; and a crucial factor in this turn of affairs was the Navy's failure to consider the Army's needs in time and to persuade the Army of the vital contribution of tactical air support from carriers.

These aspects of consensus formation — the consideration of other's needs, the decision to cooperate or to compete, and the general problem of alliance formation—have recently become the object of psychological investigation. While the field is new, it is interesting to see what development has occurred and what is needed before principles can be generated that will be helpful in "real life" situations.

Consideration of others' needs.

It is relatively easy to create situations in which one person may or may not show a consideration for another's needs. We can then vary parameters of the situation in order to discover which factors influence whether or not consideration occurs. Consider the following experiment performed by Smith and Smith.[3] They worked with pairs of persons, giving each member of a pair a different job to perform with playing cards. One person had sixty-four cards and was told to form a complete deck of fifty-two cards and then as many additional four-of-a-kind booklets as he could in order to win bonus prize money. The other subject was given twenty cards and told to make twelve "tents" out of pairs of cards and as many additional tents as he could for bonus money. Since neither subject had the exact resources he needed, each subject had to bargain with the other. They were separated by a partition and initially had no knowledge of each other's task, although they were free to communicate with each other. They were under time pressure, and fourteen of the seventeen pairs that were run began to communicate only after they discovered their dependence on each other. Now, the point we wish to note is this: at the end of the play, in ten of the seventeen pairs, *neither* person had a clear idea of the other's task, nor had there been any effort made to discover what the other person needed. Consequently, most pairs failed to make optimal trades.

The experimenters varied the type of time pressure that was used. Eight pairs were told that once every minute the experimenter would turn over a card from a deck he held; when the ace of spaces was turned, their time was up. This created a constant moderately high

---

[3]J. C. Smith and Walton N. Smith, "Social relativity, motivation and problem solving," unpublished paper, Dartmouth course, 1962.

pressure on these subjects, as is shown in Figure 1(A). In fact, in order to insure comparability, the deck was "rigged" so that the ace of spades was always the twentieth card. The other nine pairs of persons were told that they had twenty minutes to work in. This created a low amount of pressure that gradually built up to an extreme amount of tension, as is shown in Figure 1(B).

Figure 1.   *Two Different Types of Pressure*

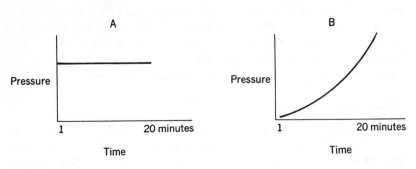

Now, although twenty minutes was ample time for completing the task, only nine of the thirty-four persons managed to do so because of the bargaining problems that arose through their failure to understand the nature of the other's task. That is, only about one-fourth of the persons took the time to really consider the other's needs. There is some indication that consideration is related to the type of time pressure. With the rising time pressure shown in Figure 1(B), nine of eighteen persons learned about the other's task. With the constant time pressure shown in Figure 1(A), only two of sixteen persons learned about the other's task.

The above experiment shows that persons in the laboratory who have a task and who are under constant pressure for time tend not to take time to understand the nature of the other's task, even when they are dependent on cooperating with the other. To return to the case of the 1950 defense budget, it is clear that persons in the field — such as the Secretary of Defense and the Naval Chief of Staff — faced with many tasks and little time — did not take the time to understand the needs of the State Department or the Army. This is not to say that they were unaware of specific needs, but they did not understand the why of these specific needs and, hence, they could not build their own plans around meeting the other's needs as well as their own. A person in the experiment would know that his partner needed the nine of spades, but he did not know that this was because his partner was trying to complete a deck of cards — after all, *he* was building card tents and didn't care about specific cards. It is noteworthy that not one person thought of building the tents with the faces of the cards turned out so that he could easily spot the cards his partners needed. Likewise, the Secretary of Defense knew that the Secretary of State might need some troops for Palestine, but he had no real conception of the Secretary of State's overall concern with limited wars. If part of the budget had been built around these needs instead of the needs of an all-out war, it might have received more support. Similarly, the Navy — arguing for super carriers to carry atomic weapons — did not build the Army's need for tactical air support into its stacking of the cards.

It would be interesting to know the conditions under which a person engaged in a task takes the time to understand the needs of his partners. While one factor seems to be the nature of the time pressure under which he operates, and while another interesting possibility would seem to be the emotional relationship between the persons, we shall have to await further investigation before these and other factors are clarified.

Cooperation and competition

The fact that government policy stems from a consensus process in which one party may choose to compete or cooperate with another party, suggests that game theory* may be as heuristically relevant to policy formation as to international relations. Indeed, one could argue that the bargaining within a government has more of the qualities of a game than the diplomacy between governments, since the rules of the game and the constraints to keep playing within the game may be more stringent.

In order to deal with the interaction between the Secretaries of State and Defense as though they were playing a game, we consider each of their possible choices as possible "moves" in a game. The outcome of a move depends on how the other person "moves," and all the possible

---

*Game theory initially developed from gambling theory. In the latter, one may rationally calculate the odds on a bet and determine how much a bet is worth and, hence, whether to accept it. In game theory, one adds a rational opponent and rationally calculates what move would be the best if one desires to maximize his gains and minimize his losses. The interested reader should consult Anatol Rapaport's *Fights, Games, and Debates* (Ann Arbor, Mich.: University of Michigan Press, 1961) for a thorough and understandable discussion. While game theory is normative and tells how a person *should* play, we shall see that some intriguing empirical studies have investigated how persons actually *do* play.

combinations of moves (and, hence, outcomes) may be portrayed in a "pay-off-matrix" that describes the game. In the simple game we are dealing with here, there are only two moves available to each player, and the game is decided by each player making only one move. Furthermore, if we view the conflict over the 1950 defense budget as a game, the Secretary of State appears to have been playing what is known as a "zero-sum" game.

In a zero-sum game, such as chess, what one person wins the other loses. Since the Secretary of State viewed the budget as a limited quantity, he feared that if the Defense Department got more money this money might come from the $3 billion allotted to his European military aid program. He therefore appears to have been playing a zero-sum game[4] (such as the one outlined in Figure 2 in which the pay-offs are determined by how he believes the President will respond to the advice of his two secretaries).

Figure 2.   *Pay-off matrix for the Secretary of State's game*

		Secretary of State Moves	
	Moves	A Support increase in U.S. & European strength	B Support increase in European strength only
Secretary of Defense	A Support increase in U.S. & European strength	$2 bil. for State $1 bil. for Defense	$3 bil. for State $0 bil. for Defense
	B Support increase in U.S. strength only	$0 bil. for State $3 bil. for Defense	$2 bil. for State $1 bil. for Defense

In Figure 2, we have arranged each of the pertinent choices available to the Secretaries as possible moves in a game and placed the consequences of a move in the body of the table. Note that the payoff of a move, in the body of the table, cannot be exactly foreseen unless one knows the other's move as well as one's own. This particular game is not very interesting, because clearly the Secretary of State should move B (supporting only an increase in European strength). In that way, regardless of what the Defense Secretary does, State will get most of the money.

---

[4]To be strictly accurate, we should call this a 3 billion dollar fixed-sum game, but the principle is the same.

Now, viewed in this light, it is clear that the Defense Secretary's only chance was to have convinced the Secretary of State to play a different game, a non-zero-sum game where both he and the Secretary of State could gain by cooperating with each other. Such a game might have had the pay-off pattern shown in Figure 3, where the pay-offs are determined by the Secretary of Defense's estimate of what each Secretary most needed.

Figure 3. *Possible pay-off matrix for the Secretary of Defense's game*

		Secretary of State Moves	
	Moves	A Support increase in U.S. & European strength	B Support increase in European strength only
Secretary of Defense	A Support increase in U.S. & European strength	4 for Defense, 2 for State	1 for Defense, 2 for State
	B Support increase in U.S. strength only	3 for Defense, 1 for State	0 for Defense, 0 for State

In Figure 3, the pay-offs are not in billions of dollars; they are in units of overall value for each man. Thus, the Defense Secretary might have believed that if he and the Secretary of State cooperated (both playing A), the Defense Department would benefit by an increased defense budget and from some European armament. Likewise, while the State Department would not receive as much support for European armament, it would benefit from a superior American defensive position that would adequately make up for this loss. Given the game shown in Figure 3, the Secretary of State would move A and cooperate, since that would maximize State's pay-off.

Now, in fact, one suspects that the Secretary of Defense *was* playing the game shown in Figure 3 and did not realize that the Secretary of State was playing the game shown in Figure 2. Certainly, he knew he needed the Secretary's support, and yet he does not seem to have any move to reassure him about a possible loss in money available for European armament. Thus, we apparently have another excellent example of the differences between the psychological worlds of two men, and this time the two men were reasonably close to each other within the administration. The Defense Secretary's failure to recognize that the Secretary of State was playing a zero-sum game, prevented him from serious attempts to persuade him that the game was really a non-zero-sum game and one in which he should cooperate since it would be the wisest move for him to make. It should be noted that the above analysis does not make use of the normative aspects of game theory (which is an attempt to prescribe the optimal way to play a game) but rather uses the terminology of game theory in order to describe a real situation from a different perspective. This reveals that the consensus process could have had a different outcome than that which actually happened.

Alliance formation

The fact that different groups within the administration try to ally with one another suggests that experiments on alliance formation will eventually be valuable in helping us understand which alliances form. To date, studies have focused on the role of relative power as a factor in alliance formation; as an illustration, we may consider the following experiment by Vinacke and Arkoff[5]. Three persons were given a modified Parchesi game to play. Each player had only one man to move; when the experimenter rolled a die each player advanced his man the number of spaces indicated by the dice *times* his "power weight," which might be 1, 2, 3, or 4. Since the same die throw was utilized by all the players, the important variable was securing a high power weight. One way to do this and, hence, win the game, was to form an alliance with one of the other two players. The alliance then had the power weight of the

Table 1   *The Percentage of Different Alliances Forming under Different Power Structures*

	Weights of persons A, B, C					
	A B C 1 1 1	A B C 3 2 2	A B C 1 2 2	A B C 3 1 1	A B C 4 3 2	A B C 4 2 1
Alliance Formed						
A with B	33%*	13%	24%	11%	09%	09%
A with C	17	12	40	10	20	13
B with C	30	64	15	07	59	08
None	10	01	11	62	02	60

---

*i.e. when A, B, and C had equal weights, 33% of the alliances were between A and B.

[5]W. E. Vinacke and A. Arkoff, "An experimental study of coalitions in the Triad," *Amer. Social Rev.*, 22 (1957), pp. 406-15.

two players combined, and the allies could divide the winnings. By offering to give a relatively large proportion of these winnings to a potential ally, a player could win another over to his side. The play thus represented an aspect of "real life"; and by varying the weights given to the players, the experimenters could study the relationship between the relative power structure and which alliances actually formed. The results of the experiment are shown in Table 1.

Table 1 demonstrates that, if there is a chance of winning, an alliance between the two weaker members or between a weak member and one of two strong members is two to three times more likely to form than an alliance between the strongest members. Now, while there is something intuitively satisfying about this result, it must be remembered that this bias occurs in spite of the fact that the strong member who fails to form an alliance is bound to lose. In other words, forces are at work that prevent the person with the most power from using this power to his advantage. In a situation where the relative power is 3-2-2 or 4-3-2, the most powerful person is actually at a considerable disadvantage. There seem to be two forces acting against the person with power. One of these is the implicit nature of the situation, which makes an alliance between the two weaker members the most "natural" solution. It is not that some mysterious force pushes the players to a "natural" solution. Rather, everyone present perceives an alliance between weaker members to be a common solution, and this common perception creates a force towards this common solution, since everyone knows that everyone else perceives this as common. The process has been described at length by Schelling, and we shall consider it in more detail later in this chapter. The second force present is the reluctance of the most powerful person to give away as much share of the profits as will a less powerful person. It seems to him that since he is contributing the most power, he has a right to the most profits. Under these circumstances, a fifty-fifty split seems the height of generosity. Very few people can bring themselves to realize that their power is worthless by itself and that in order to win an ally they may have to be willing to offer a greater share of the profits to a potential ally. Likewise, the weaker person is reluctant to ask for as great a share of the profits from the most powerful person as from an equal — hence, he does not — and he forms an alliance with the equal. It has been demonstrated that in the above circumstances the most powerful player is least likely, and the weakest player is most likely, to initiate the first offer of a coalition.

In evaluating the above experiment, it may be objected that since all three players moved their men in accordance with the same die throw there was no element of chance in the situation and that the presence of this element might yield different experimental results. Accordingly, Puklin and Goodman[6] ran the same experiment, with the exception that each player rolled a separate die and moved forward according to his weight times the number on his individual die. Faced with the vicissitudes of chance, the players did not behave substantially differently. When they were weighted equally (1-1-1), most players delayed the formation of an alliance until the end of the game. Here their different positions on the board — some having done better than others — made the situation into essentially a 4-3-2 situation with 3 and 2 forming an alliance. When the players began with a 4-3-2 weight, the players with 3 and 2 almost always formed the alliance. This occurred even more frequently than in the earlier experiments, because the player with a weighting of 4 knew he had *some* chance of winning, even if he were not in an alliance. Similarly, when weighted 3-1-1, the two players weighted 1 would immediately form an alliance, since they had some chance of beating the player with the 3 weight.

It would be interesting to see what proportion of alliances within the government could be predicted on the basis of this one variable of relative power. A classic instance that comes to mind is the Presidential election of 1824, where no candidate had a majority of the electoral votes. The names of the three candidates with the largest number of votes went to the House of Representatives for a decision. Jackson had the greatest number, Adams somewhat less, and Crawford and Clay had smaller numbers.* In this situation, with Crawford incapacitated with a paralytic stroke, Clay threw his support to Adams and was later appointed Secretary of State in Adam's Cabinet. While one can think of other reasons for this event, the instance fits the experimental results nicely, and one wonders what a systematic search would reveal.

The two experiments we have just considered had persons play only one game. We might wonder what new factors would be introduced into the bargaining process if the players had to interact with each other repeatedly in successive games. For example, would there be any tendency for a stable alliance to form that would repeatedly be used against the third party? Lieberman[7] has performed an experiment that differs slightly from the ones we have described but suggests some answers to these questions. Rather than varying relative power, he varied

---

*The electoral votes were: Jackson 99, Adams 84, Crawford 41, Clay 37.

[6]James Puklin and James Bennett Goodman, "A Second Experimental Study of Coalitions in the Triad," unpublished paper, Dartmouth course, 1962.

[7]B. Lieberman, "Experimental studies of conflict in some two-person and three-person games," in Joan H. Criswell *et al., Symposium on Mathematical Methods in Small Group Processes* (Stanford, Calif.: Stanford University Press, 1962).

the value of the alliance. His players were told that if A formed a coalition with B, C would have to pay their alliance ten cents; if A allied with C, B would have to pay them eight cents; and if B formed a coalition with C, A would have to pay them six cents. After all of the players had communicated with each other, made various offers to divide the pay-off in tempting ways, and finally established a coalition between two of them, the game was ended, the loser paid his money, and a new game immediately began. A total of forty successive games was played by each of eight groups of three men.

The groups behaved quite differently, with three of the eight groups showing remarkable stability and changing coalitions only twice over the forty games. On the other hand, three of the groups changed coalitions over twenty-two times during the course of the games. While Lieberman does not give us information that would fully account for these differences, he does point out that a new factor — reputation — began to play an important role in the alliance formation. Thus, one player might call on another to trust him to not break their alliance even if the other player approached him with a better offer. If he kept his word, he built up an enviable reputation that was valuable to him, since he became a very desirable partner regardless of his relative power or of how much of the pay-off he offered.*

While the experiments on alliance formation are most encouraging in advancing the objective study of this field, there is still a wide gap between the present experiments and the complexity of real alliances. By this, I do not mean that experiments should be models of reality — if they were, they could hardly serve to point up the fundamental relations between variables that the grime of reality often masks. Rather, I mean that there are still variables and relations that are essential in understanding alliance formation and that have not yet been uncovered by the experiments.

---

*There is one very intriguing point that strikes the peruser of Lieberman's data. While power was not directly varied, it would appear that player A was the most powerful, since the average alliance he formed would be worth nine cents, whereas B's average alliance would yield eight cents and C's only seven cents. Because of this, we might either expect A to make the most profits or, following the lead of the earlier experiments, expect A to fail to form coalitions and hence make the least profits. However, the data show that the average A player earned thirteen cents over the forty games, whereas the average B subject earned fifty-three cents over the forty games and the average C subject lost sixty-five cents! Examination shows that these results are due to the low probability of a coalition between A and C (it formed only half as frequently as either of the other coalitions). Although one can think up a few ad hoc explanations, none of them seems very satisfactory. It is difficult to think of any logically impelling reason why the A-C coalition should not form, unless for some reason B was in a better position to build up a good reputation. Here the matter will have to await further research.

For example, none of the experiments which we have considered prepares us for the failure of the Army and Navy to ally themselves against the Air Force or for the United States to be the instigator of the North Atlantic Treaty Organization. This is because the current experiments have varied distribution of power and touched on reputation but have assumed common interests and have not considered the role of perceptive reasoning in convincing another party of the existence of common interests. Schilling's account of the congressional debate over the 1950 arms budget provides some examples of this variable.

A member of the House's Subcommittee on Armed Services Appropriations wanted to amend the defense budget to allow $300 million more for the Navy. He had the support of the majority of the subcommittee and the Chairman and ranking minority member of the Armed Services Committee itself. The purpose of the additional money was to maintain the Navy's supply of operating aircraft and to prevent a decline of naval air power. When the amendment came to the floor of the House its supporters tried to get allies on these grounds but failed to make a case for why naval air power should not decline (by showing how naval air power fit into current strategy). Schilling notes that in the absence of this information most House members imagined their own strategic context — the delivery of atomic bombs on Russia — and asked if carrier based or land based bombers could do the job better. Once the debate was put into this context, the amendment was lost, because land based bombers had more capacity and were less vulnerable to attack. The final vote was 125 to 65 against the amendment. Had the supporters of the amendment made a case for the strategic value of naval air power, argued the importance of maintaining a foothold in Western Europe, shown that what was needed was tactical air support in Western Europe, and pointed out that this could be better secured by carriers, then they might have been able to win the allies they needed. In this case, potential allies were lost because of a failure to develop good reasons that would shape the bargaining along lines that would convince others that they had interests in common with the supporters of the amendment.

A second case occurred shortly afterwards. The House did pass a 800 million dollar increment for the Air Force. When this came to the Senate after a downturn in the economy, a member of the Senate's Subcommittee on Appropriations fought to keep this increase. But while it was clear that the money could purchase ten more air groups, it was not clear why these were needed. The supporters for the increase were asking others to overrule a committee report and to forget an immediate consequence on the economy for a potential increase in security, yet they failed to develop clear arguments that could win allies. Good arguments for the strategic purpose of the increase were available — in general, these would have been along the lines of increasing the Air Force's capacity for ground support — but to have developed these arguments, the Subcommittee on Appropriations would have had to become much more familiar with strategic arguments that were masked by the executive's budget format.

In general, when one person is attempting to convince others to join him — whether it be in a formal alliance or a cooperative strategy or a vote — a crucial factor (in addition to factors such as the distribution of power, one's reputation, and personal friendships) is the ability of the person to present his cause in a way that will convince the other that his own values will be served if he joins. While this factor may seem obvious, it is often masked by the great importance of power considerations and, consequently, often overlooked — even to the extent that a well reasoned argument is relatively rarely heard, in spite of its power to influence. In psychology too, the force of the rational is neglected in favor of the apparently more interesting irrational forces that often govern behavior. This may be a mistake, for there may be some very interesting properties to the great force which a rational argument sometimes creates.

In summary, we may note that the study of alliance formation, like the study of consideration of the others' needs and of the choice between competition and cooperation, shows that the consensus process does not *necessarily* produce those poor characteristics that are so often its hallmarks.

Factors Affecting Understanding

Intergroup conflict and bargaining

The fact that there are many semi-independent groups in the government, and that policy is formed from a consensus growing out of the conflict and alliances between these groups (with public opinion a sought-after weapon) suggests that any development in the field of intergroup conflict might be useful in our understanding of policy formation. Industrial psychology has been interested in intergroup conflict for the same reason. As Cyert and March[8] have noted, the decisions of firms are the outcomes of conflict within the firm — with each subgroup working towards its own operational goals. However, the con-

---

[8]R.M. Cyert, and J.G. March, *A Behavioral Theory of the Firm* (Englewood Cliffs, N.J.: Prentice-Hall, Inc., 1963).

flicts within a firm are not as pervasive as those within a government, since there is an agreed-upon standard — profits — that is much less ambiguous than "national interest." Consequently, there have been relatively few attempts to conceptualize the intergroup conflict within an industrial organization.

One such attempt is the work of March and Simon,[9] who have catalogued a number of factors that affect conflict. They point out that the probability of conflict between individuals is increased as the situation grows more complex, as the individuals have less experience with the situation, and as the munificence of the environment decreases. (For example, the conflict within the Defense Department was aggravated by the scarcity of money for the budget.) Likewise, the conflict between groups is decreased by the lessening of individual conflicts across the groups, by a felt need for joint decision making (because of a mutual dependence on limited resources or an interdependence of timing activities), and by similar goals and perceptions of reality. March and Simon note that conflict may be reacted to in one of four ways: A group may attempt to solve the problem that is creating the conflict, or they can take the easier route of trying to persuade the other group, or bargain with it, or gain a power advantage over it.

Unfortunately, there is no available conceptualization that helps one understand *when* groups will expend effort to come together to solve their problems in a creative way rather than simply persuading or bargaining or seeking more power.

It is clear that there are great difficulties involved in two groups trying to really understand each other's needs so that they can reach an integrative solution. We saw some of these difficulties in the last chapter. There, however, the two groups involved had completely different sets of beliefs. When groups believe they are similar, Manheim[10] has shown that they have less conflict. What hinders communication when the groups are reasonably compatible? One important factor seems to be the mere presence of competition between the groups.

Blake and Mouton have performed a number of studies on the biases that result from membership in competing groups. In one such experiment,[11] they had competing groups form solutions to a problem and then listen to each other's ideas. Enough time was allowed for discussion

[9]J.G. March and H.A. Simon, *Organizations* (New York: John Wiley & Sons, Inc., 1958).

[10]H. L. Manheim, "Intergroup interaction as related to status and leadership differences between groups," *Sociometry*, 23 (1960), pp. 514-27.

[11]R. R. Blake and J. S. Mouton, "Comprehension of own and of outgroup positions under intergroup competition," *J. Conflict Resolution*, 5 (1961), pp. 304-309.

so that each of the adversaries believed that he understood the other's solution as well as his own. At this point, the participants were given a true-false questionnaire based on the objective properties of each other's solution. It was found that *in fact* members understood their own group's solution better than the solution of the competing group. Thus, the average person fails to gain a complete understanding of the position held by a competitive group, even if he is given the opportunity to learn that position until he believes that he understands it. Furthermore, he may even overlook or deny points of communality between the solutions if he thinks that his group's solution is best and he does not want to recognize the other group's worth.

In a related study,[12] Mouton and Blake examined the effect which group membership had on the evaluation of a solution produced by a group. They had pairs of judges perform the evaluation. Pairs that were completely neutral were contrasted with pairs of judges who had one member of the pair belonging to one of the groups whose solution was being evaluated. They found that when a judge had a vested interest, he affected the joint judgment so that a solution produced by his own group was evaluated higher and a solution produced by a competing group was evaluated lower. This effect was most striking when the biased judge's group actually had the poorer solution. The experimenters also showed that a person in competition may overlook or deny points of communality between his group's solution and the solution proposed by a rival group.[13]

While competition between groups may directly hinder an attempt to understand the other's position, may prevent the realization that one does not understand, and may lead to a failure to comprehend points of communality, there is an even more potent factor that is sometimes associated with competition — the desire for greater power. In order to understand why a concern with power may drastically interfere with intergroup communication, we must examine Schelling's[14] analysis of bargaining.

Suppose two persons, A and B, are told that each must choose either heads or tails. If they both choose heads or both choose tails, they will win money. If their choices conflict, they win nothing. If they may not communicate each person will search the situation or past traditions or

---

[12]J. S. Mouton and R. R. Blake, "Influence of partially vested interests on judgment," *J. abnorm. soc. Psychol.,* 66 (1963), pp. 276-78.

[13]R. R. Blake and J. S. Mouton, "Comprehension of points of communality in competing solutions," *Sociometry,* 25 (1962), pp. 56-63.

[14]Thomas Schelling, *The Strategy of Conflict* (New York: Oxford University Press, 1963).

his knowledge of common habits for clues as to how to choose. In this case, the cultural choice is "heads." Each person knows that somehow heads is predominant over tails and that he must choose heads because the other person will choose heads and will expect him to choose heads.

Now, suppose both A and B are told that if heads are chosen, A will win ten dollars and B will win one dollar; whereas if tails are chosen, A will win one dollar and B ten dollars. In spite of the fact that B would now like to choose tails, he still must choose heads if he wants any money. There is an impelling structure to the situation that forces this choice; for B knows that A will choose heads, and B knows that A will expect him (B) to choose heads — it is the only "obvious" choice. Now, if the situation were different — if a coin were to be flipped in order to determine who received ten dollars and who received one dollar — it would not matter to a person whether he was assigned heads or tails. But in the above situation, it matters a great deal whether one has heads or tails; and, hence, this apparently trivial matter may be the occasion of conflict. Schelling points out that there is often an "obvious" place to compromise and that before the bargaining begins both parties will jockey to set the stage for this obvious compromise to benefit them. Much conflict about the agenda of a meeting is of this nature.

Schelling develops this point of tacit communication — based on things which everybody knows everybody else knows — to account for many other phenomena of interest in the bargaining process.

Thus, suppose the persons playing the above coin matching game know that if heads are agreed on A will get ten dollars and B one dollar, and if tails are agreed on, both A and B will get five dollars. Now the structure of the situation has changed so that "heads" is not the obvious answer. In fact, most people will probably recognize "tails" as the preferred choice — because it is the "fair" compromise and, hence, an obvious choice. A knows that B will probably insist on tails and will choose tails, and he knows that B knows that A knows this; therefore, A will have to choose tails. If, however, A can communicate with B and say, "I am going to choose heads because heads comes before tails," then B is placed in a difficult position. If A manages to communicate that he is really going to choose heads, then B has to choose heads too or he won't even win one dollar. There are several devices which A can use to his advantage in this game. He may break off communications immediately after he has announced his intention. This puts B in the awkward position of not being able to argue that he doesn't believe it, that tails is the only fair solution, and that he is going to stick with tails no matter what — better nothing than injustice. Of course, the break-off of communications can be literal (A might be physically impossible to reach), or it can be psychological (with A refusing to understand B's protests). Another device available to A is to commit himself to his position so that B cannot doubt that he is going to carry out his choice. Thus, if A not only says that he is going to choose heads but also bets twenty dollars with a friend that he will choose heads, or writes "heads" and throws away the only pen, etc. — then he cannot go back on his choice, and B is forced to acknowledge it and act accordingly. A commitment sacrifices choice in order to gain power over the other.

Knowing all this, B has a few counter-weapons of his own. He may break off communications before A can say anything. He will be successful in this even if he gets the communication from A, as long as B does not let A know that he has understood the communication. That is, B may read a message which A hands him, and A may even see him read it; but unless B responds to this — by indignation or shocked surprise or some indication that he understands — then A is thwarted. The avoidance of looking at a person in the eyes is one type of this resistance to a communication, a communication which, if it were acknowledged, would force the recipient to act in a way he does not wish to act. The other counter-weapon available to B, is to resist A's choice with an even stronger commitment of his own to his choice. If he bets thirty dollars that he will choose tails and severs communication, then A is undone. But to be able to do this even when there is a probability that A may not perceive one's action is yet another matter. We have here the battle of wills in the purest sense, and a battle that is inherent in the strategy of deterrence.

Unfortunately, no analysis or experiment has yet been performed that disentangles the factors involved in this battle of wills. However, it should be clear that if two groups are involved in a power struggle, communication (or the absence of it) becomes a weapon, rather than a tool to increase understanding.

Schelling's analysis stresses the fact that for their common good, both parties must recognize some limits to their conflict so that they avoid destroying each other or can come to some agreement that allows them to act. Since each knows that the other recognizes these limits, the bargaining seeks to take advantage of this fact. Unfortunately, this sometimes causes such a preoccupation with gaining subtle bargaining advantages that conflict is prolonged and settlements that would be of mutual advantage are missed. Many observers have noted the bad effects which political officers — who are sensitive to subtle power advantages — can have on conferences of scientists, health officials, and engineers who would otherwise cooperate easily.

In summary: if two groups are involved in bargaining and begin jockeying for a bargaining advantage, then — no matter how compatible their positions might be — they may never get together to find an integrative solution, because the communication between them will have the characteristics of a weapon and their attention will be focused on subtle details of the maneuvering rather than on creating a mutually profitable consensus.

Governmental efficiency and intellectual intimacy

When two persons are not able to integrate their different views, they are apt to produce quite a poor joint response. This has been neatly demonstrated by Bauman and Roman.[15] Working with husbands and wives, they first gave each spouse a separate intelligence test and then asked them to take the test together as a joint project. Some couples managed to successfully integrate their answers so that their joint intelligence score was superior to their individual scores, but a substantial number wound up with a lower joint score. In these cases, the couples were unable to constructively cope with disagreements and had to resort to poor compromises. Within an organization, these problems are heightened by the existence of real differences in responsibilities and interests that make effective consensus difficult to attain.

The difficulties inherent in policy that depends on consensus have led to numerous investigations on governmental efficiency. One of these that focuses on foreign policy is a penetrating inquiry by the Senate's Committee on Governmental Operations. Its report, "Organizing for National Security,"[16] was prepared by the subcommittee on National Policy Machinery chaired by Senator Jackson. The first interim report[17] by the Committee made several important points, which are listed below:

1. Interdepartmental committees have a built-in bias towards compromise and can not substitute for planning by the State Department.
2. Various proposals for reorganization should be considered. These include: a national security planning staff of Presidential advisors, more responsibility for the Secretary of State (perhaps by creating a Secretary of Foreign Affairs, combining several different agencies that are now independent), a joint State-Defense planning staff, a shorter budget cycle, a budget stated in functional terms, a mes-

---

[15]G. Bauman and M. Roman, "Interaction testing in the study of marital dominance," *Family Process*, 5 (1966), pp. 230-42.

[16]Senate Committee on Governmental Operations, "Organizing for National Security" (3 vols.) (Washington: U. S. Government Printing Office: 1961).

[17]Published in 1960.

sage from the President to Congress on foreign policy requirements and resources, a joint Congressional committee to study this
report, the assignment of scientists to the NSC's policy planning
staff, and the creation of civilian research groups for White House
and State Department aid.

3. Government personnel might be improved by training methods
   that would develop non-parochialism (perhaps by joint careers in
   different departments), by the attraction of better people through
   pay raises and the easing of conflict of interest laws, and by a
   decrease in the high rate of turn-over (there is, on the average,
   a new Secretary of Defense every two years).

4. In a democracy, the public sets the limits of the possible in policy
   making. Thus, public understanding must be increased — particularly in view of the unprecedented length of the "cold war"
   with its lack of the unifying stimulus of a "hot war."

After an exhaustive literature research and numerous hearings (there
are 1,300 pages of testimony,) the final report of Jackson's committee
reaffirms the importance of the Secretary of State and makes specific
suggestions on improving the State Department and recruiting government personnel. However, the committee fails to mention ways to increase public understanding and rejects *all* of the various proposals for
reorganization of the Department. It is not clear how the neglect of
public education occurred. The rejection of proposals for reorganization
seems to me to be both an advance and a failure. An advance, because
the panacea of reorganization is rejected and is replaced by the recognition of the need for good persons and good relations among them. A
failure, because the committee failed to sufficiently develop this point
and to ask which organizational structures — or educational programs —
could help achieve good persons and relationships.

To be specific, let us examine the committee's treatment of the
National Security Council. While the Council itself has since been
disbanded, it serves as an example of any sort of interdepartmental
apparatus. The committee concludes:[18]

> *First:* The real worth of the Council to a President lies in being an
> accustomed forum where he and a small number of his top advisers can
> gain that intellectual intimacy and mutual understanding on which true
> coordination depends. Viewed, thus, the Council is a place where the
> President can receive from his department and agency heads a full
> exposition of policy alternatives available to him, and, in turn, give them
> clear-cut guidance for action.

---

[18]*Ibid.* p. 38.

Second: The effectiveness of the Council in this primary role has been diminished by the working of the NSC system. The root causes of difficulty are found in overly crowded agenda, overly elaborate and stylized procedures, excessive reliance on subordinate interdepartmental mechanisms, and the rise of the NSC system for comprehensive coordination and follow-through responsibilities it is ill suited to discharge.

To help the Council serve the primary role of mutual understanding, the committee suggested that meetings should not be regularly scheduled, should strive to present alternative positions in sharp relief, should be much smaller, should use the Planning Board to criticize the policy initiatives developed by the Departments rather than to negotiate departmental compromises, should insure that policies were related to their budgetary requirements, and should rely on the Secretary of State to propose major new departures in national policy.

Each of the above points are suggested meeting procedures designed to sharpen mutual understanding. They open up a very interesting psychological question:[19]

Under what conditions can intellectual intimacy and mutual understanding be achieved?

If the Jackson committee is correct in its judgment that coordination and policy development can only flow from intellectual intimacy, then the above question is most important. Since one cannot force persons to be intellectually intimate — that is, to really understand how one another thinks — achieving this goal requires indirect methods which we might divide into two groups. The first of these methods is educational in nature. If governmental leaders can be trained to recognize intellectual intimacy, then they will be more inclined to select subordinates with whom they can achieve this, and they will strive harder to achieve it. The second method is by induction. If the correct conditions can be created, then intellectual intimacy will tend to flourish naturally.

The educational method

One of the first points that must be stressed in training persons to appreciate intellectual intimacy is that it does not mean thinking the same way or having the same values. Rather, it means understanding how the other thinks and what he values. It implies having a knowledge of the partner's need, and knowing what game he is playing, and being

---

[19]I am indebted to Robert Boyles for phrasing the question this way.

a responsible member of the alliance; but it does not imply having the same needs or even playing the same game. Consequently, it should not only occur between the President and those members of his staff who have no interests or responsibilities that may conflict with the President. It should be able to occur between the President and cabinet members who have many conflicting interests. Intellectual intimacy does not require a person to give up his interest for a "nation-wide" point of view — on the contrary, he should defend his own point of view; what it requires is a genuine understanding of the perspective of others. A pseudo-Quaker meeting where everyone has veto power and complete consensus is demanded, results in the poor compromises; it is an unsuccessful attempt to gain true intellectual intimacy. In true intimacy, the thoughts and values of others are really considered, but a decision is made by a person who is responsible and is in an authority position that is legitimatized by the consent of the others. An excellent example of such intimacy is the relation between President Truman and Secretary of State Acheson.

Speaking of this relationship, Acheson[20] says,

> . . . these talks [with the President] enabled us not only to keep one another informed but to see events and choices each from the other's point of view. This, I venture to suggest, can play a more effective part in developing a coherent national policy than the multiplication of staff and what is called, 'coordination.'

Unfortunately, there is no way to institutionalize this type of relationship, and no series of case histories has made the point so convincingly that future Presidents will bear it in mind.

An interesting example of the development of at least a small amount of intellectual intimacy is provided by the December, 1950, conference between the President of the United States and the Prime Minister of Great Britain.[21] The Prime Minister came to the conference worried about the United States becoming involved in an all-out war with China and hoping for a cease fire in Korea and the development of Chinese "Titoism." The President was concerned about the possibility of losing the British as valuable allies but was determined to grant no concessions to the Chinese. At the end of the conference, the President and Prime

---

[20]Dean Acheson, "The President and the Secretary of State," in *The Secretary of State*, American Assembly, Columbia University (Englewood Cliffs, N.J.: Prentice-Hall, Inc., 1960).

[21]The following is based on an account in Chapter 25 of Harry S. Truman's *Years of Trial and Hope: 1946-1952* (Garden City: Doubleday & Company, Inc., 1956).

Minister agreed that an all-out war would be avoided but that there would be no concessions to the Chinese and that troops would remain in Korea unless they were forcibly driven out. They agreed to disagree on the issue of seating China in the United Nations and to not let this difference of opinion interfere with their "united effort for our common objectives." Aside from the by-play of arguments — which are interesting in their own right — there are three items worthy of notice. The first is the role of emotions in showing depth of conviction. Remarks such as the following are illustrative:[22]

British Prime Minister:

"I think if China were in the United Nations, there would be a possibility of discussion. That I know is distasteful to you. But I think if there is to be a settlement, it is better to have it come through the United Nations . . ."

American President:

"I think in the long run the Chinese will realize that their real friends are not in Moscow and Siberia; they are in London and Washington."

British Prime Minister: (without smiling)

"You won't bring them to that realization if you keep fighting them."

American President:

"No, but I won't back out of Korea . . ."

British Prime Minister:

"I am with you there."

American Secretary of State:

"My own guess is that it wouldn't work. All we might get would be time, but never enough time to do any good. Just enough time to divide our people bitterly. Just enough time to lose our moral strength."

Such deeply felt statements must communicate the limits of how far a person can shift his position. Emotions, like actions, are better at communicating values than are mere words.

The second is the role played by the British Ambassador to the United States. In meeting after meeting, at certain crucial points he would summarize the discussion, pull threads together, emphasize agreements, and bring the conferences back to specific points. The President noted that "his keen mind and friendly approach helped us keep on track."

---

[22]*Ibid.*, pp. 406-409.

The third is the role played by informed conversation. The most important of these occurred at a small dinner party at which the President told the Prime Minister about the opposition he was encountering in the Senate and the Prime Minister explained to the President about the nature of his opposition in the British Parliament. The President notes that "after this conversation we understood better what many of our real problems were."

Emotional exchange, a sympathetic coordinator, and a chance for the informal discussion of private problems are all aspects of a meeting that can greatly aid the achievement of intellectual intimacy. Likewise, as we mentioned in the last chapter, working with the Rapaport debate method and understanding Lerner's ideas on position taking might be very helpful training procedures; and, in the next section, we shall see that certain group laboratories may help trust to develop. It is conceivable that an educational program could be developed and taught in foreign service schools and to interested executives and congressmen. Once introduced, it would rapidly spread as one would have to grasp the ideas in order to retain status. An awareness of the importance of these issues would be forced if Senate committees such as the Committee on Government Operations and the Committee on Foreign Relations would ask the President to defend his appointments on the grounds of potential intellectual intimacy. A follow-up of the history of these appointments would also serve a most worthwhile critical function which the committees could undertake.

The induction method

The second way to encourage intellectual intimacy is to create conditions under which it can flourish. We have no systematic knowledge about what optimal conditions would be. Routine meetings between different pairs of two men might be better than committee meetings. A paper summarizing a Rapaport debate might be better than either alternative texts or a consensus text. Likewise, we are not familiar with the issue of what sorts of people can achieve intellectual intimacy with each other.

One of the few available pieces of research is Katz's[23] experimentation with one aspect of intellectual intimacy between husbands and wives. He asked different marital teams to maneuver a ball up a curved inclined plane. The position of the plane was controlled by the movements of both the husband and the wife. Hence, success required each to

---

[23]Irwin Katz, J. Goldstone, M. Cohen, and S. Stracker, "Need satisfaction, perception, and cooperative interaction in married couples," *Marriage and Family Living*, (1963), pp. 209-213.

know what the other was about to do and to coordinate their actions accordingly. Katz showed that if the husbands and wives had complementary need structures (so that, for example, one partner's need to nurture fit with the other's need for succorance), they cooperated better than if their need structures were in conflict. Such an experiment suggests that there may be certain guidelines which an official could follow even if he were not personally acquainted with a potential appointee.

In suggesting that appointments should be made with an eye on whether intellectual intimacy will be possible, we are not forgetting the importance of power considerations. Certainly, every appointment affects the distribution of political power. Each appointee is himself a small center of power that will ultimately affect whether or not the appointer can accomplish his goals. Because of this, the appointer must name men who will maximize the probability that the distribution of power will favor his programs. However, we would insist that wherever any choice exists, the appointer will be more successful if he attempts to maximize the amount of intellectual intimacy that will be possible.

In a similar way, any suggested change in an organization is bound to affect the distribution of power. As Schilling[24] notes,

> The design of organization thus turns on the question of which problems one wants to be highlighted by conflict and the question of by whom one wants the critical choice to be made. . . . The choice of organization is a political choice. The "best" organization is that which distributes power and responsibility in such a fashion as to facilitate the policies you favor . . ."

Nevertheless, some organizational *atmospheres* will be much more conducive to intellectual intimacy than others, and one might be able to hold power relatively constant and yet greatly affect intimacy. Let us consider what sort of an atmosphere is needed.

Since intellectual intimacy requires full communication, it demands trust and loyalty. If trust may be betrayed and the knowledge which a person furnishes can be used to weaken his power, then a person cannot afford to give his knowledge. Thus, the organization must have norms that enable open interpersonal relations to exist in the midst of competitive politics. The dynamics of power politics must be held within bounds that permit the open communication necessary for the benefit of all.

As we discussed earlier, communications and commitments can be used as a lever in the bargaining process and therefore create a problem

---

[24]Schilling, *op. cit.*, pp. 229-30.

for the development of intellectual intimacy. To develop an understanding of another's position one must be open to communications from the other and must recognize the other's commitments — but these are precisely the two things which one must *not* do if one is trying to avoid entanglements with a person who is trying to secure a bargaining advantage. Likewise, if one has to maintain a power advantage in order to control other persons, then understanding the position of the other may lead to a loss of control. It is much harder to turn down a request which the other knows that you understand, than to be a step removed and turn down a request which you have never had the opportunity to grasp. If, then, one wishes intellectual intimacy to develop between two persons, one must not place them in a situation where they have to bargain with each other or where one has to control the behavior of the other. Or, if these conditions cannot be met, one must establish norms that prohibit the pre-bargaining maneuvers and illegitimate uses of understanding that we have described.

Interpersonal Dynamics within the State Department

With a dozen different groups, each pressing for the kind of foreign policy of benefit to itself, the way in which the government is organized may be an important factor in determining whether any consensus occurs and whether the resulting policy has good or poor characteristics. Whenever there is an important question of policy, different groups will take sides on the issue involved. As an example, we may consider Haas and Whiting's[25] list of the groups taking a stand on the recognition of the Soviet Union in 1918. Favoring recognition were: military and Red Cross personnel, who wanted to keep Russia in the war to oppose Germany; some leading presidential advisors, who wanted to use Russian claims to oppose Japanese expansion; some economic and financial interests, who wanted to increase markets or develop industries in Russia; some Senators, who wanted a stable, peaceful world and, hence, wished to recognize every non-aggressive government; many citizens, who desired to transform the Soviet Union into a more democratic and less anti-capitalistic country by the inducement of recognition and aid; and most communists and socialists, who wanted a Soviet victory to be recognized. Against recognition were: lumber and manganese companies, who wanted to exclude Russian competition; segments of labor, who were opposed to Soviet slave labor; some railroad interests, who

[25]E. B. Haas and A. S. Whiting, *Dynamics of International Relations* (New York; McGraw-Hill Book Company, 1956).

wished to obtain the Chinese Eastern Railway; some businessmen, who wished to undermine the Soviet government in order to get American business enterprises operating in the country; the American Federation of Labor, which was concerned about creating a good name for unionism; some Senators and State Department Officials, who were opposed to communist ideology and wished to change the government by external pressures; and various financiers, whose bonds had been canceled by the new government.

Such an assortment of groups often cuts across governmental divisions so that some State Department officials are allied with some Congressmen while others are allied with members of the Defense Department who have the ear of a different set of Congressmen. This pluralism serves to prevent any governmental group from becoming too extreme. Thus, in the past debate over "massive retaliation" policy, Janowitz[26] has noted,

> . . . the internal political balance in the military establishment has had a discernible consequence in stabilizing trends in foreign policy. Implementation of the massive retaliation doctrine was crucially resisted and modified by the persistence and effectiveness of opposition groups within the military establishment.

However, the same pluralism also creates problems in achieving the integration necessary for a group to take an effective stand. In order to see how group organization affects consensus formation, we shall examine one small part of the bureaucracy that is involved in foreign policy. Then we shall consider certain management problems within the bureaucracy that affect its ability to achieve productive consensus, and some personnel and training problems that may affect the type of consensus that is achieved.

Pruitt[27] has provided us with a detailed picture of one office in a geographical Bureau with the Department of State. This particular office was composed of seventeen officers (and their support personnel) and handled United States affairs with three friendly countries. A representative portion of its organizational chart is shown in Figure 4.

In addition to communicating American interests to the pertinent American embassy abroad, it is the job of the XYZ office to comprehend and represent the needs of the friendly countries under their super-

---

[26]M. Janowitz, *The Professional Soldier* (Glencoe, Ill.: The Free Press, 1960), p. 313.

[27]D. G. Pruitt, *Problem Solving in the Department of State*, Social Science Foundation Monograph Number 2 (Denver: University of Denver, 1964).

Figure 4.   *Organization of the "XYZ" Office in the Department of State*

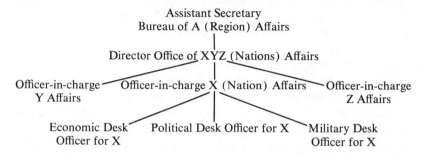

Assistant Secretary
Bureau of A (Region) Affairs

Director Office of XYZ (Nations) Affairs

Officer-in-charge   Officer-in-charge X (Nation) Affairs   Officer-in-charge
Y Affairs   Z Affairs

Economic Desk   Political Desk Officer for X   Military Desk
Officer for X   Officer for X

vision. In doing this, the office presses for policies that respect these needs as opposed to policies that may be more considerate of the needs of other countries or of other Departments within the government.

The XYZ office does not really engage in the creative design of new proposals but rather reports, evaluates, and "pushes" proposals that are devised somewhere else. The problems and the proposals ordinarily come from the United States Embassies in the foreign countries, and it is interesting to note that the Embassies' problems, requests, and proposals usually take a much longer range view than is ordinarily found in the Washington bureaucracy.

There is a rule that any agency affected by a policy must be consulted. Consequently, the Desk officer for X must clear all dispatches to his country. The more important the policy, the more desks will have to clear the decision and the more chance there will be for a conflict of interests to arise. If a conflict is anticipated, the "policy pusher" may attempt to get allies called in on the proposal by requesting them as consultants or getting them to make the proposal in the first place. He will also attempt to avoid probable enemies. For example, if the officer in charge of one country anticipates that the officer for another country may object to his proposal, he may first route the proposal to his Office Director so that it will have momentum before the other officer is called in on the proposal. It is expected that an officer will only communicate with other officers who are on his own level or who are his immediate superior or inferiors. If the reader begins to feel "bogged down" in this morass of details about consensus formation, he will realize exactly the same feeling which many State Department officials experience as they cope with the task of trying to create a consensus.

The strength with which an officer "pushes" or blocks a proposal, is an important factor in determining whether or not a consensus will be achieved. It is generally true that if an officer is willing to push hard for his proposal or position, he has a greater chance of seeing it adopted. A deadlock develops only if he meets an opponent who feels as strongly as he does. When an officer exhibits strong feelings about an issue, he essentially communicates a threat to those who oppose him. He is willing to expend more action, to push the decision higher, and to bargain with an opponent who may refuse to clear his policy.

The "strength of push" is a function of several different factors. Since the major responsibility of a desk officer is to indicate how a proposed action will affect the country he is responsible for and American relations with it, and since (at least for those dealing with friendly countries) he values keeping these relations good, the strength with which he pushes for (or against) a policy will depend on how much effect the policy will have on the country which he is responsible for.

A second factor is probably the degree of certainty with which an individual feels his policy is correct. While this feeling of certainty may be unwarranted and may simply depend on the individual's confidence, there is some evidence to suggest that, other things equal, certainty is associated with correctness of insight. Bavelas[28] had two persons separately guess the number of beans in a jar. Then the persons were put together without the jar and told that they had to agree to choose one of their guesses to submit for a prize that would be given to the team with the best guess. In this experiment, no compromising was permitted. Bavelas found that the person on the team who pushed the hardest for his guess — and, hence, had his guess become the team's guess — was, in fact, more likely to be closest to the correct answer.

A third factor is inherent in the personality of the officer involved. In maneuvering for allies and in avoiding enemies, each officer is faced with the power of other officers who may object to his calling in a superior to settle an argument in his favor, or not routing a message to them first, etc. Pushing a proposal always takes effort, costs good will, and incurs obligations. Pruitt reports that there are wide personality differences in the willingness to offend others by not consulting them, or to push one's ideas in the face of another man's personal opposition, or to assume the risk of being blamed for a decision rather than spreading the responsibility for the decision by bringing others in on a proposal. Since the average proposal involves opposition from others (this was true in fourteen of the twenty-five proposals studied), one imagines that energetically advancing a proposal would be a source of personal conflict for some officers. Differences also exist in how powerful an

---

[28]Alex Bavelas, personal communication.

individual makes his office. If an officer wants to be consulted, he can establish precedents, build up his knowledge, create cooperative relations with others, and insist on being consulted. Because of this, Pruitt hypothesizes that if officers are rotated too quickly in an agency, they will lose influence through a lack of time to build up the necessary reputation and contacts.

Still another factor is the extent to which an officer believes he has a chance of his push being successful. This factor is of great importance in setting the bounds for possible policy. Each officer develops an opinion about what other officers will accept and reject and sets his aspirations accordingly. He also develops expectancies about what people outside of his office will accept, and (needless to say) he may misjudge what is possible. While there is no objective evidence to indicate how much of a restraint this poses, Jones[29] notes,

> To a degree far greater than is healthy, each subordinate officer in the State Department operates and makes recommendations on the basis of a personal estimate of what Congress or the American people will accept, and usually there are enough low estimates along the line to keep policy and action flying low, if not grounded.

When consensus is prevented by a strong push meeting a strong objection, there is an intra- or inter-agency deadlock that can either result in a dropping of the proposal until a periodic policy review brings it up again or a referral up to higher level. In the latter case, the conflict may go to an officer who is over both of the disputants, or it may go to higher officers who are still separated in responsibilities and who will either settle the conflict between them or pass it up to a still higher level, where eventually it will either be resolved by an inter-agency committee (where compromise will occur) or by the President. With or without conflict, a proposal must go up the chain of command until an officer feels he has enough authority to make a decision. The greater the possible risk to the United States' interest, the higher the decision goes. It may never come back down. In these cases, the issue is never really resolved and is settled by the press of circumstance.

Pruitt believes that as a decision goes up the hierarchy, it is less likely to be handled by officers with dissimilar perspectives. That is, the closer two officers are — the fewer vertical lines of authority that stand between them — the more similar is their outlook. Because of this, the

---

[29]J. M. Jones, *The Fifteen Weeks* (New York: The Viking Press, Inc., 1955), p. 149.

heads of two departments may often have a more common perspective than two subordinates in the same department. While higher officers take a broader view, a consensus between them may be hindered by a reluctance not to "back up" their subordinates. It is also possible that when a consensus is achieved at higher levels, it may be relatively conservative. Higher officials are likely to be more concerned about the danger of setting precedents and more likely to be influenced by Congressional opinion and other political factors.

Although conflicting subordinates who are unable to attain consensus are reluctant to send problems up in the hierarchy (there is a sense of failure, a fear of being considered inept, and a desire to avoid overburdening superiors), there is a constantly increasing overload towards the top of the hierarchy. Thus, Elder[30] reports that in 1954 there were approximately five hundred staff studies a month that reached the Secretary and Undersecretary of State, and in 1958 the load averaged 850 papers a month! This overload appears to stem from several factors: (1) The "Wristonization" program, which was designed to give officers a more varied experience by shifting them from position to position, created a high rate of turn-over in the lower level positions; in two years, twelve of the seventeen offices studied by Pruitt had new occupants. Unfortunately, these positions require a fair amount of specialization, and the program may have had the undesirable consequence of causing officers to pass decisions up the hierarchy because of their inexperience. (2) The involvement of more agencies in decisions creates more chance of conflict and, hence, more chance that a decision will be pushed up to a higher level. (3) The increasing involvement of the United States in foreign affairs creates more problems.

The need to coordinate an increasingly broad spectrum of diverse interests, the failure to obtain consensus at low levels, and the consequent overload at higher levels have not been dealt with adaptively. Rather than increase the delegation of authority within their organization, higher officers have tended to form more committees with a consequent loss of time, an increased number of poor compromises, a high degree of inaction, and less flexibility to change a course of action. On the other hand, because of the increasing difficulty of initiating new programs within a department, independent agencies are arising and acting on their own initiative when their action really should be coordinated by Department officers. In short, higher departmental officers are so busy they are failing to maintain real control over policy.

---

[30]R.E. Elder, *The Policy Machine* (Syracuse, N.Y.: Syracuse University Press, 1960).

Management

Pruitt's description of the bureaucracy within the State Department lends itself to Golembiewski's[31] analysis of the Civil Service. The latter's general thesis is that in the process of developing a competent civil service which functions independently of the spoils system, an unintended consequence has been the reduction of *both* the supervisor's and the subordinate's power and effectiveness. Golembiewski argues that the doctrine of simplifying job content decreases the worker's control over his environment. It has been shown that in units which have high productivity, subordinates feel that they as well as their supervisors have a lot of power. Golembiewski notes that this is paradoxical only if one assumes that there is only so much power to be had. However, this is not so; ". . . a high-power supervisor can afford to (and usually does) allow his subordinates to exercise greater power also. A low power supervisor is in such an insecure position that he can seldom bring himself to be so generous."[32] Operators who produce defective goods when there are outside inspectors may produce decent goods when they are allowed to do their own inspecting. Civil service jobs are often so limiting that the person does not have power which he could effectively use.

To amplify on this point, Golembiewski contrasts the typical job organization in Figure 5 (A) with that which he favors in Figure 5 (B).

Figure 5.   *Two Ways of Organizing Jobs*

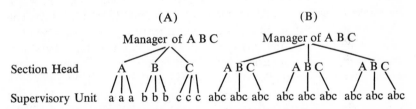

Whereas the hierarchy shown in (A) reduces supervisory power, that in (B) provides job enlargement at all lower levels. In (A), decisions will be pushed upward since only the manager oversees all the components that must be integrated. Therefore, little delegation will be given to lower level supervisors. Since poor performance in any one of the sections will greatly hinder overall production, there is pressure

---

[31]R.T. Golembiewski, "Civil service and managing work: Some unintended consequences," *Amer. Pol. Sci. Rev.*, 56 (1962), pp. 961-73.
[32]*Ibid*, p. 964.

on the manager to insure the integration of all the sections — and this pressure is exerted downwards. This, in turn, discourages upward communication. The manager's effort to get honest information and achieve integration undercuts efforts by the lower level superiors to get the power they need. In contrast, the (B) type hierarchy of responsibility frees the manager of pressure so that he can attend to the most important decisions and devote himself to the motivation, training, and counselling functions with which good managers raise production.[33]

If Golembiewski is correct, the way jobs are arranged forces different styles of supervision to emerge. An (A) hierarchy encourages detailed instructions and persistent attempt to direct and observe performance — this lowers performance — while a (B) hierarchy encourages freedom of control at lower levels with the supervisor monitoring his subordinates' production. He can easily do this, since each subordinate is doing approximately the same job and is in more or less direct competition.

Let us ask whether the above analysis can be applied to the upper echelons of the State Department. We must, of course, make a translation, for Golembiewski's analysis is based on the output of goods rather than the management of ideas; and, perhaps more important, the direction of influence comes entirely from the top down. Now, this holds for most businesses and for the lower levels of civil service work, including clerks and typists; but at the level of desk officers in the State Department, Pruitt's data indicate that something else is happening. The desk officer is not deriving his recommendations only from broad policy directives coming from above; he is also proposing recommendations which he thinks he can persuade his superiors to accept. There is an inversion here, because the desk officer is a political force representing a point of view — in this case, that his superiors should consider the goodwill of the country he is responsible for. Yet it is true that the job hierarchy of the State Department's "office" (shown in Figure 4) is like Figure 5 (A); and it is true that decisions are being pushed up until higher level officers are so overloaded that they cannot supervise enough work properly and must surrender authority to autonomous agencies rather than delegate it to their own subordinates. If we accept the analysis as relevant, then one possible solution might be to broaden the perspectives of officers by enlarging their jobs instead of increasing their rotation from job to job. Of course, the limit to a Figure 5 (B) job hierarchy occurs when specializiation is needed. In the absence of information about how

[33]R. L. Kahn and D. Katz, "Leadership practices in relation to productivity and morale," in *Group Dynamics*, ed. D. C. Cartwright and A. Zander (Evanston, Ill.: Row, Peterson, 1960).

much knowledge officers now gain on their job and how much they could gain if they were rotated less but given a broader job, we can make no decision. However, it might be worthwhile to experiment with organizing an office in the way Golembiewski suggests. There has been an increasing number of interdepartmental exchanges. It might be possible to organize some jobs across departments. This might prove a solution to the constant problem of how to achieve coordination between departments.

It is somewhat surprising that the burgeoning development in industrial psychology has not yet effectively penetrated the State Department. Elder[34] comments, "Unfortunately, the Department has never had funds to analyze its own documents used in past negotiations as a means of learning what or what not to do in the future . . ." One wonders if the Department has ever really tried to evaluate its efficiency. What rating systems do exist are apparently based on having a unit rate itself rather than having an objective outsider make the evaluation. Now, it must be noted that there are some essential differences between the State Department and a business enterprise of equal size (the Department employs about 35,000 persons). Perhaps the most essential is that the shared value in a business — to increase profits — is much less ambiguous than the shared value in the State Department — to advance the interests of the United States. While it is hard enough to measure the profits resulting from a policy in business, it is very difficult to measure the advantage resulting from a governmental decision that will advance the values which some hold and will retard the values of others. Neverthless, it would appear that the Cuban Invasion was a relative failure and the Peace Corps a relative success. It should not be impossible to measure efficiency if one really tried. Because of the lack of evaluation, one finds numerous instances of inefficiency. To take just one example, the Brookings report[35] shows that many embassies have no organized system for getting to know either key officials or important non-governmental leaders.

Management is becoming increasingly important, both within the State Department proper and within embassies. Within the State Department, the techniques of management and leadership vary considerably from one Secretary to another. According to Jones,[36] President Truman's third and fourth Secretaries of State were both excellent man-

[34]Elder, *op. cit.*, p. 165.

[35]H. Field Haviland, Jr., *The Formulation and Administration of United States Foreign Policy* (Washington: The Brookings Institution, 1960).

[36]Jones, *op. cit.*

agers, although they ran the Department somewhat differently. The third Secretary insisted that his subordinates propose alternative solutions to a problem. After hearing each of the solutions argued out, *he* would then choose the one he preferred. Morale was kept high because of the effectiveness of the Department and because of the competition between teams arguing the various alternatives. The fourth Secretary preferred to have problems tackled by group discussions in which he would freely participate. His personality was such that he was successful in drawing forth different views and in making everyone feel that his view had been a contribution. While both of the Secretaries were sensitive to the factors stressed by Likert[37] and Argyris[38] — that is, they interacted with a subordinate in a way that built his sense of personal worth — other Secretaries have not been so skillful interpersonally and have, of course, paid for this by a loss of organizational efficiency.

It is encouraging to note that the State Department has begun using "group laboratory training" in a series of management conferences for senior Foreign Service officers.[39] In such training, as conducted by members of the National Training Laboratories,* about ten persons meet in a group for a week or two with a professional leader who encourages them to organize themselves and to examine their own behavior. There is an emphasis on expressing feelings openly and in analyzing the experiences that occur as the group struggles to organize itself. In this process, each of the group members discovers how his behavior affects the other persons present and how his own behavior reflects the impact which others have on him. If the training is successful, the individual emerges with a greater sensitivity to the needs of others, a more flexible control over his own behavior, and an increased understanding of the dynamics that create an efficient group.

One of the first products of this training within the State Department is an article by Chris Argyris[40] that describes some of the problems discovered by members of the State Department when they examined their own behavior and the forces acting upon them in group laboratory ses-

---

*The training of the Tavistock Institute is similar, but the group functions within a somewhat more structured routine. Also, members are not encouraged to disclose their perceptions of each other.

[37] R. Likert, *New Patterns of Management* (New York: McGraw-Hill Book Company, 1961).

[38] C. Argyris, *Interpersonal Competence and Organizational Effectiveness* (Homewood, Ill.: Dorsey Press, 1962).

[39] Alfred J. Marrow, "Managerial revolution in the State Department," *Personnel*, 43 (Nov.-Dec., 1966), pp. 1-12.

[40] Chris Argyris, "Some causes of organizational effectiveness within the Department of State," (Washington: Government Printing Office).

sions. As with many groups, but perhaps with particular strength, men from the State Department subscribed to a norm of withdrawing from open discussion of interpersonal difficulties and conflict. During the group laboratory, they became aware that while this withdrawal was safe and might lead to promotions, it had unintended psychological effects. These included the creation of an underlying sense of personal inadequacy and failure in the self, and loneliness and manipulation in others. As one participant said:[41]

> "During this week many of us have complained about _____ (back in Washington). All of us have admitted that we have never leveled with him. We have withdrawn.
>
> Up to now, I felt this was right. Now I realize that I may be running away from my responsibility. As I thought of this, I suddenly wondered what would happen if people reacted to me by withdrawing. So I began to wonder if Mr._____feels lonely; if he senses the withdrawal. Does he feel that many of us feel that like death and taxes Mr. _____ will always be with us. If he feels this withdrawal and hostility, no wonder he manipulates us. What else can he do?"*

When a system is dominated by a high level of withdrawal, members play safe and group meetings are less effective. Leaders focus on protecting their department and make a reputation as skillful in-fighters who do not lose bureaucratic struggles. They concentrate on this rather than on making effective decisions on the merits of the case, for the system does not reward the taking of real initiative and responsibility. Furthermore, communication problems develop, and groups cited examples of how these led to misleading cables and poor advice. Finally, a lack of openness may affect the conduct of diplomacy itself. Argyris notes,[42]

> It frequently occurred in our small group meetings that one ambassador felt certain that he was hiding his anger. However, the rest of the group experienced him as angry but did not tell him so. . . . Another example was given by many middle and younger officers who felt that they had

---

*Note how this type of self-knowledge complements the more personal kind of knowledge associated with group or individual therapy. That this latter type of knowledge may also be increased in group laboratory training is indicated by the following quotation from Argyris' report: "I learned that it is one thing the mistrust people when one is capable of trusting and quite another to mistrust when one is not capable of trusting. I was in the latter group."

[41]*Ibid*, p. 30.
[42]*Ibid*, p. 51.

learned to write official documents whose tenor fitted with the defenses of their boss. They reported that the resulting language was not as clear as they felt it could be.

Personnel research and training

There is a recognized need in the Department for personnel research, and perhaps the important job of improving the recruitment, selection, and training of personnel will open the door for other studies. While the knowledge accumulated in these important fields of psychology is outside the scope of this book, we may note two interesting related problems that have not received the research attention that has been devoted to selection and training.

The first of these problems is how to evaluate and control the effects of selection biases. Several of these operate. For example, a young man going into a foreign service career is probably an upper-middle class white who majored in history, political science, or a language. Tradition, recruitment procedures, and the foreign service examination all contribute to this selective bias. Certainly, one wants a person who has attended a good college and studied material that may be useful to him. However, there may be unintended consequences. An upper-middle class white is likely to hold fairly conservative social values, and a history major is likely to be unfamiliar with the quantitative techniques useful in evaluation and in systems analysis. It would be useful to trace out some of the impacts which these factors have on policy.

As Sapin[43] notes, a modern diplomat needs to know more than the language and history of an area in order to produce a good analysis of its contemporary situation. He should also be familiar with the concepts and methods of the behavioral sciences. Furthermore, he has an enlarged number of tools for influencing the actions of a foreign government. He needs to know how to use economic aid, military assistance, information programs, cultural exchanges, etc., to produce the results he wants; and with the increasing number of overseas programs, he needs to develop managerial skills. Finally, if one agrees with Rossow[44] that the "new diplomacy" must be able to communicate across the cultural boundaries that separate the West from the rest of humanity, a diplomat should know something of cultural anthropology and comparative social

---

[43]B. M. Sapin, *The Making of United States Foreign Policy* (New York: Frederick A. Praeger, Inc., 1966).

[44]Robert Rossow, "The professionalization of the new diplomacy," *World Politics*, 14 (1962), pp. 561-75.

and philosophical analysis. These needs must be met by changing either selection or training procedures.

It is quite possible that definite policy biases are introduced by the type of persons attracted to and selected by the State Department. For example, in an investigation of altruism, Sawyer[45] had college students make a series of choices similar to those involved in the "non-zero-sum" game we considered earlier. Each person could choose his moves so as to maximize his own pay-off (an individualistic orientation), the joint pay-off (a cooperative orientation), or the difference between his and the other's pay-off (a competitive orientation). Sawyer showed that such choices are always affected by whether one is dealing with a stranger or an antagonist. However, students who are training for social service positions (such as YMCA work) are generally more cooperatively oriented; business students are the most individualistic; and students in the social sciences differentiate the most between friends and antagonists. Since most persons entering the State Department are from the social sciences, if the above findings can be generalized we might expect the average officer to make more of a distinction between friendly and antagonistic nations than the average person would.

In a similar vein, Halpern[46] noted that the Central Intelligence Agency is attractive to men who are power oriented, energetic, and conservative in doctrine. While such men are clearly needed, they are not likely to be systematic thinkers or to have a keen moral sense. With the current lack of control over the CIA, this appears to have led to some unfortunate actions.

Similarly, men in policy making positions are often lawyers. Halpern believes that the average lawyer thinks of foreign policy in terms of discrete cases rather than in terms of a continuous flow where one policy is seen as influencing the future. This may partly account for the low weight that is given to long range planning.

On a more general level, Elder[47] notes that most men who reach high governmental positions have a need for power, and attempt to create empires of responsibility for themselves — often at the expense of others who seek power. After the leader departs, the responsibilities of his empire decline; but the physical jobs remain. As a result, there are more subordinates to do less and less of a job. These empires also result in decentralization and compartmentalization and, hence, loss of control

---

[45]Jack Sawyer, "The altruism scale: A measure of co-operative, individualistic and competitive interpersonal orientation," *Amer. J. Sociology*, 71 (1966), pp. 407-416.
[46]Manfred Halpern, *The Morality and Politics of Intervention* (New York: Council on Religion and International Affairs, 1963).
[47]Elder, *op. cit.*

over policy; they lead to the interagency committee which is so deadly to constructive policy formation. Elder charges that Congress encourages this splitting of authority because it enhances its own power relative to the Executive. Little is known about how to control this splitting of authority and to what extent selection biases contribute to it. Nor do we know the effects which a need for power must have on decision making.

The second (and related) problem concerns the effect which a job has upon the men who hold it. The most obvious effect is that the nature of the job may cause them to leave. Within the government, Sapin suggests that the need to coordinate different perspectives often waters down differences and blunts analysis to an extent that it is possible that some of the most imaginative officers may leave the foreign service.

Several observers have noted that a man's job influences his style of thinking. In his evaluation of the "military mind," Janowitz[48] observes, "Clearly, action and responsibility for one's actions are more valued than reflection in any organization where combat is the basic goal." And, after discussing the conflict within the military over massive retaliation, Janowitz[49] notes, "All evidence indicates that both [those for and against massive retaliation] — in varying degrees — overemphasize the potentials of force." Likewise, whether as cause or effect, businessmen seem more competitive than others and politicians more sensitive to power.

It is difficult to evaluate the negative effects of job training because any training director concentrates on teaching what the job itself requires and does not look for side effects. Acheson[50] has stated that foreign service training "makes men cautious rather than imaginative," and several observers have charged that being part of a bureaucracy tends to generate hostility and cynicism. If these observations are correct, then some corrective action or, at least, open recognition may control the dilatory effects that must follow. As yet, we have no general principles about the formation of such emotional sets, but a recent study by Winter and his associates[51] successfully traces the development of cynicism in a boy's prep school and gives some hope that we can eventually control these unwanted byproducts.

It should be noted that a number of interesting psychological problems are associated with the foreign service and should be considered in any training program:

---

[48]Janowitz, *op. cit.*

[49]*Ibid.*, p. 429.

[50]Acheson, *op. cit.*

[51]D.G. Winter, R. Alpert, and D.C. McClelland, "The classic personal style," *J. Abnorm. Soc. Psychol.*, 67 (1963), pp. 254-65.

1. When an officer serves in another country, he may begin identifying with that nation. This is particularly true if he has more than a superficial knowledge of the country and understands that what is good for his own country is not necessarily good for the country he is in. Yet he must remain loyal to his own country and retain perspective. An officer who begins to identify may start basing his reports on the views and hopes of the local government rather than on an objective analysis of the situation. Furthermore, Nicolson[52] notes how such an identification places the diplomat in subtle conflicts: He observes:

It not infrequently occurs that a diplomatist, when instructed by his government to make a communication which he knows will cause irritation and pain, so waters down his instructions that an inaccurate and flaccid impression of their purport is conveyed. Even if he be sufficiently loyal and conscientious to carry out the strict letter of his instructions, he is sometimes tempted, in order to avoid giving offence, to accompany the delivery of these instructions with such intonation of voice, such conciliation of gesture, as to imply that he himself does not really agree with the intimation which he has been instructed to make.

It is not clear how to conceptualize the delicate balance that must be struck between empathy and loyalty, or when empathy becomes identification, or exactly when a diplomat should be rotated in order to preserve his perspective.

2. Here are three other temptations which a good diplomat must overcome: (a) hedging predictions so that one's judgment will never be in error; (b) reporting what one's superiors would like to hear instead of what they ought to hear; (c) lying in order to avoid detection. Nicolson[53] quotes Lord Malmesbury,

If, as frequently happens, an indiscreet question, which seems to require a distinct answer, is put to you abruptly by an artful minister, parry it either by treating it as an indiscreet question, or get rid of it by a grave and serious look; but on no account contradict the assertion flatly if it be true, or admit it as true, if false and of a dangerous tendency.

3. Within an Embassy there is a compartmentalization of function so that each officer has distinct responsibilities which he guards as

---

[52]Harold Nicolson, *Diplomacy* (3rd ed.) (London: Oxford University Press, 1963), pp. 115-16.
[53]*Ibid.*, p. 112.

his personal bailiwick. There is a reluctance to interfere with another officer's job or to question his professional judgment. When officers return to the State Department, they carry back this pattern of behavior so that they are reluctant to intervene in disputes within the Department. It may be these professional norms that inhibit higher officers from adjudicating disputes between lower officers with specific area responsibilities, thus producing what appears to be indecisive behavior.

4. Because of the wide diversity of jobs within the foreign service, an officer is required to fill many different roles (which his personal disposition may or may not fit) and to make difficult transitions between these jobs. At one time, he may be in the obscure role of quietly and privately analyzing reports; in the next assignment, he may be in the midst of the action of an operational job and called upon to manage a team of specialists. He may have to move from a job as Ambassador, where he has immense individual responsibility and is accorded great respect, to a job as office director, where he must bargain with others and is one among many equals.

5. While he may enjoy cooperative counseling and view himself as an advisor, the foreign service officer may be placed in the rather disagreeable position of having to *advocate* measures before a Senator who is acting as a judge or who wants to get information to make some political point.

6. The foreign service officer is faced with a barrage of specialists in the economics of aid, in engineering, communications, etc., who are certain that they can do things to improve certain aspects of the situation. He is often placed in the position of having to restrain and point out limitations which are imposed by the situation when it is viewed as a whole. This, combined with his knowledge of the difficulties involved in really affecting a foreign government, to say nothing of a foreign culture, may make him feel that he is acting negatively — which is un-American! — and may even lead him to feel that foreign policy is about as efficacious as an icepick on an iceberg. There is a danger that he will fail to look for what *can* be done with the tools of diplomacy and will retreat into hardshell opposition or play along with activists to "keep them out of mischief."

All of the above problems would be more manageable if they were frankly and personally discussed in the course of foreign service training. In this way, each officer could have an adequate conceptualization of the problems which he could relate to his own experience. Such awareness would facilitate each officer's control over his behavior and would encourage members of the service to help each other in meeting these common problems.

The Role of Congressional and Public Opinion

Robinson[54] has made a detailed study of the role of Congress in the formation of foreign policy. In general, he found that Congress did not recommend foreign policy but (through its control over money, treaties, and appointments) acts as a modifier and legitimizer rather than an initiator. Even this role was lessened when the policy involved potential violence and the requirements of speed and secrecy preempted public discussion. A wealth of behavioral data on these matters has now been collected by political scientists. For example, Robinson's study includes information about the 614 bills pertaining to foreign aid that were introduced in the Senate over a ten-year period. The analysis of this data clearly shows the impact of the committee structure and the influence of the committee's chairman. Thus, the thirteen (to fifteen) men of the Committee on Foreign Relations introduced 304 of the 614 bills, and fifty-five percent of the bills that were introduced by committee members were reported out by the committee, as contrasted with eleven per cent of the bills introduced by non-committee members. Of the 219 bills reported out of the committee, 201 were passed on the floor. The power of the committee's chairman is shown by the fact that ninety-two of these bills were sponsored by him; while many of these were handled by him for the administration, this role requires the administration to consult him.

Aside from the role played by members of the Committee on Foreign Relations, the average Senator or Congressman does not usually participate intellectually in the consensus process. Data on the communication between Congress and the State Department and case studies on Congressional-Executive interaction in twenty-two important foreign policies show that Congressional support for foreign policy is generated more by the implicit trading of favors (a postmastership for a vote for foreign aid) than by arguments from the State Department (whose orientation towards the needs of other nations does not mesh with Congressional concern for the needs of their constituents).

---

[54]James Robinson, *Congress and Foreign Policy Making: A Study in Legislative Influence and Initiative* (Homewood, Ill.: Dorsey Press, 1962).

According to Robinson's analysis, the power of the executive lies in his chance to choose the problem and the alternatives for debate. He states,[55]

> The definition of alternatives is the supreme instrument of power; the antagonists can rarely agree on what the issues are because power is involved in the definition . . . the definition of the alternatives is the choice of conflicts, and the choice of conflicts allocates power.

Thus, an initiator of policy can propose the policy as an answer to a problem which he defines so as to admit no other answer. This interesting aspect of power, implicit also in Neustadt's analysis of Presidential power, is quite different from the usual conceptions that emphasize the ability to reward or punish, to provide charismatic leadership, or to legitimately decide another's fate in some way. It recognizes that since a person often chooses how to act or whom to support, control over the definition of this choice is power over how the person behaves. This type of power is also of crucial importance in the administration's dealings with the public. While policy is shaped by the elite groups, these groups derive their power from the public and must fashion a consensus which the mass structure will support with votes, taxes, and lives. In fact, in today's world, Hartshorne[56] notes that a people's tolerance for austerity and willingness to meet the demands of their government are more important than climate, resources, or geography in limiting the policy and ambitions of a government. Since the public is somewhat ignorant of the real situation which its leaders are facing, it puts a constraint on adaptive policy — a constraint which the leadership often tries to cope with by exaggeration or other forms of deception.

There is a considerable body of evidence that indicates that public opinion does not *directly* affect foreign policy.[57] Because of its power to take the initiative in defining the situation and the alternative courses of action, the administration can focus opinion to support a wide variety of policies. However, there are three indirect ways in which public opinion influences foreign policy: by the distortions it requires from the administration, by its response to the case made by the opposition, and by the general limits it sets on what is viable. We shall consider each of these in turn.

---

[55]*Ibid.*

[56]Richard Hartshorne, "Political geography in the modern world," *J. Conflict Resolution*, 4 (1960), pp. 52-66.

[57]James N. Rosenau, *Public Opinion and Foreign Policy* (New York: Random House, Inc., 1961).

Distortions by the administration

Lippman[58] has argued that any democratic government has a difficult time managing foreign affairs because it must cope with public opinion that is years behind the time. In its effort to cope with this, the government may be forced to define the situation in a somewhat distorted way so that it can mobilize the necessary public support. Unfortunately, this distortion may pose a problem for policy formation in succeeding years, because then it must cope with the public opinion generated by the earlier policy. The distortion also seems to have an effect on the policy makers themselves as they respond to and come to believe their own definition of the situation. We may see this effect quite clearly in Jones' description of the development of the Truman Doctrine to support nations against communist expansion and the Marshall Plan to aid Europe.*

When economic pressure forced Great Britain to abandon its commitments to Greece and Turkey in 1947, the administration faced the situation squarely and decided that it would attempt to fill Britain's shoes and give aid to those countries. The President called a group of Congressional leaders to the White House to seek their support for his plan. The Secretary of State conveyed to the group the plight of the countries involved and how this would be increased by the British withdrawal. He indicated that aid should be extended out of American loyalty to these people who had resisted Hitler, and out of our common humanity.

Now, the average Congressman is not a slave to public opinion. Bauer, Pool and Dexter[59] have shown that the Congressman is not under direct pressure on most issues and actually invites most of the pressure he receives. He signals which pressures he wants and ignores those he does not want. Furthermore, his freedom is greater than it appears, because he selects much of the pressure by the way he builds the bloc of voters who elect him and the issues in which he involves himself. However, almost every Congressman is sensitive to taxation. The Congressional leaders who were listening to the Administration's plan believed that their constituents were more concerned about a tax reduction than the plight of Greece, and they were not impressed with the Secretary's concern with loyalty and humanity. Their questions

*cf Jones, *op. cit.*

[58]Walter Lippman, *Essays in the Public Philosophy* (Boston, Little Brown and Company, 1955).

[59]R.A. Bauer, Ithiel de Sola Pool, and Anthony Lewis Dexter, *American Business and Public Policy* (New York: Atherton Press, 1963).

346   *The Psychological Dimension of Foreign Policy*

ranged from "How much will it cost?" to "Why should we pull British chestnuts out of the fire?"

Things were going badly when the Undersecretary of State asked the Secretary if he could speak. For ten minutes he fervently advocated the aid plan. He pointed out that in the past eighteen months the democracies of the world had lost strength, while communism had gained power. He described Soviet pressures on Turkey, Iran and Greece. He pointed out that if the Soviet Union managed to get control over any one of these countries, she could get control over the Eastern Mediterranean and the Middle East — how from there she could begin to influence South Asia and Africa. Europe was being lost, and Great Britain was being forced to retire. Only two great powers remained, and an unbridgeable ideological chasm separated them — not since the days of Rome and Carthage had there been such polarization. The United States had to protect freedom from Soviet aggression. It was not a question of whether to be loyal, or humanitarian; it was a question of whether to safeguard freedom. The United States had to act — or lose.

When he had finished, there was a long silence broken at last by the leader of the opposition party, who said that he had been impressed and shaken by what he had heard. It was clear, he said, that aid to Greece and Turkey was only part of a grave situation, and he believed that this message should be given to Congress and to the people.

The administration responded to this opinion. It was clear to the administration that in order to maintain American power it would eventually have to help people all over Europe, and that such an aid program would eventually cost billions of dollars. It accepted the judgment that the majority of Americans were still isolationistic and did not care to have the United States playing the role of a leader who would give aid to all governments that were trying to meet the needs of their people. While the Soviet Union was aggressively pushing to attain a nationalistic aim of old standing — control over its entrance to the Mediterranean — it was obviously necessary to overcome American isolationism by selling the aid program in terms of supporting the "free" world against communist aggression. The only way a consensus could be formed was by creating an ideological confrontation. Consequently, the administration went to Congress and to the people with speeches written in this vein.

Now, it would be hard to overestimate the importance of speech making in the formation of public policy. Great care is taken in speech making because a speech made by the President or his Secretary of State publicly commits the administration to a course of action. Jones[60]

---

[60]Jones, *op. cit.*

describes the process by which an important speech is made with its conferences between key officials, the give and take about whether certain points should be included, and the final top level clearance of the speech. Thus, the making of a speech can be an occasion for that close communication so essential to good policy. But in order to fully appreciate the importance of speech making, we must remember Bauer's[61] thesis that the audience has an effect on the communicator by causing him to select and emphasize those facets of his knowledge that he feels will be effective.

Since the administration saw it could sell its program by emphasizing the conflict with communism, its public information program and all its speeches portrayed the world conflict between free and totalitarian governments. These speeches, in turn, became basic documents that were used in drafting the bill to aid Greece and Turkey and, later, in laying the basis for the development of the Marshall Plan. In this way, the "mass structure" exerted an influence on foreign policy. The price for overcoming its isolationism and securing a consensus was the emphasizing of the cold war — a slight deception that was to bear evil fruit.

While the needed aid program was obtained, we must note two unfortunate consequences that resulted from the means by which it had to be obtained. First, this somewhat distorted view of reality that was presented to the public necessarily limited the government's future freedom of action. While statements such as "the free world must be supported against communist aggression" and "cold war" reflected some truth, they also encouraged the kind of inaccuracy that leads to war. It is a good example of the type of ideological phrase that, as Morgenthau[62] has noted, always masks a struggle for power. For large segments of the "free" world were dictatorships rather than democracies, what was "aggression" when performed by the communists was viewed as "the assertion of responsibility" when performed by the allies, both the United States and the Soviet Union supported social reforms such as increased literacy and population control, and it was not communism as much as the the Soviet Union that had to be stopped. To be accurate, then, the statement should have been, "All independent status-quo countries must be supported against Soviet expansionism." This version of reality would have permitted more mobility in later foreign policy. It would, for example, have facilitated aid to Poland or Yugoslavia. Two years after the Marshall Plan, the Secretary of State was to try futilely to get rid of the term "cold war." He told newsmen, "It is not a

---

[61]R. A. Bauer and C. L. Zimmerman, "The effect of an audience upon what is remembered," *Publ. Opin. Quart.*, 20 (1956), pp. 238-48.
[62]Hans Morgenthau, *Politics Among Nations. The Struggle for Power and Peace* (New York: Alfred A. Knopf, Inc., 1960).

good term and might as well be dropped. We are not engaged in war, but in peace."[63] The alarm over sweeping communism was the ground in which McCarthyism was rooted; and the exaggeration of the communist threat, which was necessary to get aid for Europe, was later to prevent decent relations with China. Even today, the preoccupation with communism and American national power has encouraged public attitudes that are antithetical to cooperation between nations and to the development of world law. One can neither cooperate with revolutionary governments that are portrayed as evil nor work towards world law when the nation believes it has to expand national power rather than establish and abide by international law.

Second, a chance may have been missed. The United States could have defined itself as a nation genuinely interested in the welfare of other nations — it could have been the moral leader of the world. Because public opinion was not ready for this role, the United States had to settle for defining itself as the leader of the status quo countries; and while its aid programs attempted to encourage social change, this goal became clearly secondary to that of stopping communism. Jones[64] states that after the aid bill was introduced, a study of public opinion showed that ". . . . most public support was based on the conviction that the security and well-being of the United States required resistance to Soviet or communist expansion."

It must be noted, however, that it is not clear exactly what the public's initial opinion was; it might have been far more conducive to liberality than congressional opinion reflected. It is interesting that the main opposition to the aid bill was that the aid was not funneled through the United Nations. This kind of opposition took the administration completely by surprise. While Jones considers that support for the United Nations was a sort of half-way stop on the road to taking real responsibility, it may also have reflected a genuine positive feeling towards world law and the desire for constraints on power politics. Had the men in power within the Administration and in Congress been less power oriented and more oriented towards developing the United Nations,* they might have found a public willing to follow. While the administration recognized that the public could be led out of apathy in order to stem the advance of communism, it *might* have been possible to lead the public out of apathy in order to advance democracy, build world law, and prevent starvation.

---

*Such an effort would not have been impracticable if it had been focused through the Secretariat.

[63]*The New York Times,* June 6, 1950, p. 3.

[64]Jones, *op. cit.,* p. 176.

The foregoing may seem to detract from the very real accomplishments of the elites who put together the Truman Doctrine and the Marshall Plan. It should not. The administration recognized the problem at hand, courageously tackled it in spite of a bleak political situation, and came up with a successful plan that prevented the Soviet Union from gaining control over the Mediterranean and Europe. While it may not have fully capitalized on latent potentials in the public, it did enter into a fairly meaningful dialogue with the public so that it utilized some of the strengths inherent in the mass structure. Jones[65] indicates this correct relation of leaders to the public when he writes,

> Democratic statesmanship, as contrasted with the mere conduct of public affairs, consists in gauging an objective situation accurately, in selecting the proper psychological moment to expose it to the public, in pointing towards solutions in policy terms and concepts capable of evoking wide public interest and discussion, and finally in drawing from that discussion — to which the best brains in the country have contributed — ideas as to how to carry policy into execution and support for specific measures . . . a working alliance between leadership on the one hand and bureaucracy and the people on the other.

In Chapter 3, we saw how such open communication was essential for the occurrence of creative planning.

It is unfortunate that there is so little of this sort of consensus construction. Administrations are often distrustful of the public and feel that distortion is necessary or, at least, much easier than education. Huntington[66] has noted that a President ordinarily fears public debate because the decision has already been made within the Executive and a great deal of trouble may have been involved in working out a rather fragile consensus. He is therefore interested in implementing the decision and in not having uncontrollable pressures change it or the opposition exploit it. Therefore, he tries to limit public interest by reassurance, minimizing information, and discouraging disquieting testimony.

Obviously, then, if discussion is going to be broadened, it must be done *before* key decisions are made. Huntington[67] observes,

> At present, one way in which issues are brought to the top and forced upon the President for decision is through the lobbying activities of Congressional committees. Broader and earlier public discussion of strategic

[65]Ibid., p. 225.
[66]Samuel P. Huntington, "Strategic planning and the policy process," *Foreign Affairs,* 38 (1960), pp. 285-99.
[67]*Ibid.*

programs would in all probability have a similar effect, and instead of interested guesses we would be provided with concrete evidence of what "the public will support."

Such discussions would have to be considerably more sophisticated than they are today. McClelland's[68] analysis of the public debate during the crisis with China over Quemoy shows that much of the discussion failed to take into account the limited opportunities that were actually available. While arguing for a wider debate of policy, he notes that the difficulties with a valid discussion include the maneuvers of domestic partisan politics, the secret aspect of diplomacy, and the habits of the press, as well as the leadership's deceptive, mollifying statements and the concealment of policy history which we have mentioned.

Officials often feel that public opinion is a dangerous and restrictive influence. While this may be true, it may also be that public attitudes are much more sophisticated than the public opinion which the best of our current surveys can measure, and Rosenberg has suggested that it would be desirable to have measuring devices that can tap the potential of the public as well as its current state. Such a device would tie in closely with educational programs, for it would probably operate by measuring the capacity of the public to learn new concepts. At the present time, a President (or any leader) must estimate how malleable public opinion is by watching the reactions of those about him and noting how his decisions appear to those writing in newspapers and magazines.

It is often argued that the public has so little interest in and knowledge about foreign policy that there must always be a large gap between its opinions and the situation the administration actually confronts. Scott[69] has even suggested that the average person's attitudes towards foreign affairs may be quite non-rational. My own conversations with the "man on the street" have been more encouraging. While there are many facts which he does not know, he seems to be quite aware of the administration's position and has his own rational view of the position. If he were only given a less distorted picture of the situation, I believe, he would do justice to it. As Rosenberg[70] notes,

---

[68]Charles A. McClelland, "Decisional opportunity and political controversy: the Quemoy case," *J. Conflict Resolution,* 6 (1962), pp. 201-213.

[69]W. A. Scott, "Rationality and non-rationality of international attitudes," *J. Conflict Resolution,* 2 (1958), pp. 8-16.

[70]Milton Rosenberg, "Images in relation to the policy process," In Herbert C. Kelman (ed.) *International Behavior.* (New York: Holt, Rinehart and Winston, Inc., 1965), pp. 330-31.

. . . the potential threat that public opinion poses for the pursuit of rational policy is in part due to the fact that governmental and communication elites have been so ready to hide the facts, and to misrepresent or oversimplify the actual justifications for policy choices. In consequence, public opinion has remained far more uninformed and rigid than it need have been.

While we have only considered the "gap" between the actual situation in 1947 and the picture presented by the administration in order to galvanize the Congressional leadership, it should be evident that various kinds of gaps are a common occurrence. In the course of decisions about Korea, there was often a gap between what the administration knew and what the public knew. Thus in Chapter 4, we noted that the administration's decision to destroy the power of North Korea was made several weeks before the public thought the administration was considering whether or not to cross the 38th parallel. Let us consider some other instances.

Before the war, there were several times when concerned Congressmen asked the administration if South Korean strength was as great as North Korean. In spite of the fact that the CIA had information available that indicated a serious discrepancy in strengths, the inquiring Congressmen and the public were told there was no difference.

When the invasion began, it was apparent by Monday night that at least a partial mobilization would be necessary. But key Congressmen were not informed of this, and on Friday the Secretary of Defense told the press no mobilization was planned. On Friday, when the administration knew that mobilization would be necessary and that at least two divisions of troops would be sent immediately to fight Korea, the public was told, "General MacArthur has been authorized to use certain supporting ground troops." The press was told that these troops would not be used in combat. It is clear that the administration was afraid of Congressional and public opinion and hesitated to use infantry as early as it should have — therefore, only air and naval forces, which seemed "more natural," were called for Monday night. A presidential advisor later said, "We were scared of the Hill in this thing. If we had tried to put ground troops in at the start there would have been a great deal of trouble."

This same fear was involved in the President's decision to avoid asking Congress for a joint resolution in favor of American intervention. There was fear of a debate on alternate measures — awkward questions as to how involved the United States might become, and so forth. The Secretary of Defense said that discussion about U.S. ground strength would help the enemy. Perhaps these were legitimate fears but in the light of future developments it seems clear that Congress should have been consulted before troops were committed to Korea. The administration claimed there was not time, but this is simply not true — four days elapsed between the first serious thought of troops and their commitment. At the Congressional conference only one Senator complained of the failure to consult Congress, and a leading Senator called for unity in the Senate so that the U.S.S.R. would not be encouraged. Not until months later did several Congressmen start complaining.

The administration knew that the United Nations would not support the decision to blockade Formosa, so there was agreement that the United States should "assume sole responsibility" for this questionable act. The fact that it was preventing a successful communist invasion was disguised by referring to the fact that Chinese Republican forces would not be permitted to attack the mainland and that the intervention's main purpose was "to insure Formosa's military neutralization." As Hoyt points out, this action casts doubt on the asserted feeling of legal obligation in consulting the United Nations on the Korean action. As we have noted, one unfortunate result of this "covering-up" operation was that the American public (and even much of the administration) could not understand why India did not fight in Korea. The reason, of course, was that the Indians felt the Formosan action was going to anger the Chinese and that the moral issues were not clear.

When fourteen leading Congressmen were informed Tuesday of Monday night's decision to intervene in Korea and Formosa, there was no criticism. Several wished to be assured that American actions were in accord with the principles of the United Nations. The President said that they were. He then, however, pointed out that the Formosan action was taken on "our own responsibility." This point seemed to not be salient to the Congressmen; it was overlooked and never conveyed to the public. Thus, Smith's[71] authoritative article reports:

> Wiley wanted to be sure that the orders to MacArthur were in accord with U.N. resolutions. The President said they were, and added later that we were pressing that afternoon for an additional U.N. resolution recommending "such assistance to the Republic of Korea as may be necessary to repel the armed attack and to restore international peace and security to the area." We had been assured of the necessary support for the resolution.

[71]Beverly Smith, "The White House story: Why we went to war in Korea," *The Saturday Evening Post*, (Nov. 10, 1951), pp. 22, 76-88.

A similar gap between government and people occurred several years later and explains why the American people never realized that the idea of massive retaliation was not needed to stem Russian nuclear aggression but rather to meet a limited budget that could not pay for limited wars. The ethics of this policy were not publicly debated.

A democracy cannot endure with a large separation between government and people. A large separation leads to a government that has to manipulate the public with false images, support programs under false fronts, and conduct all social welfare from health to road building in the name of defense and without constructive debate. When the government is a democracy, it becomes the victim of its own propaganda as its freedom to act is limited by the image it has built up. So, to act effectively, it must demand more powers. Under the continual stress of the "cold war," more power continually goes to the Executive. War is no longer debated in Congress. There is inadequate Congressional control over the CIA. The Executive can launch invasions and commit assassinations without public debate and consent. What will it be able to do in the future? This "atrophy of democratic control"[72] is occurring because it seems necessary for keeping American power and avoiding a third world war. It is necessary only if the public is uneducated. To the extent that the public is aware of the facts and issues in international relations, a democracy can be preserved.

Response to the opposition

If the administration's policy fails to accomplish its implied goals, the opposition party will make the best case it can for the administration's incompetence. In doing this, it will usually have to accept the administration's definition of the situation, because information campaigns and the nation's actions will have solidified this definition. However, it can take advantage of any problems that arise, and it will not hestitate to seize on weaknesses in the definition and create its own distortions in order to reap some political advantage. In the case of the Truman Doctrine, the immediate policy was completely successful in halting Soviet expansion. But when the Chinese Communists won all of mainland China, the Republican opposition had a field day. In spite of the fact that there was really nothing the administration could have done, and in spite of the fact that the Secretary of State was obviously committed to the security of the United States, the opposition

---

[72]Hans J. Morgenthau, "Decision-making in the nuclear age," *Bul. Atomic Sci.,* 18 (Dec., 1962), pp. 7-8.

charged that the administration in general and the Secretary of State in particular were "weak on communism." Witch hunts began for traitors in the State Department, and, as we have seen, the administration was forced to commit itself to Chiang Kai Shek.

Notice how the opposition exploited the distortion in the administration's definition of the situation. Since the administration had presented Soviet expansion by portraying an ideological struggle against communism in general, it left itself open to a false attack when a largely independent communist movement was successful in China.

Since the administration and Congress are well aware of the destructive uses of public opinion, they are much more cautious than the current public attitudes would seem to warrant. In a democracy, the mass structure is always influencing policy much more than one would suspect if one restricts his attention to the power politics of the elites. It is the hidden part of the iceberg, constantly influencing what the elites can do. On the one hand, it constrains or frees the current administration's policy. Its power is reflected in Jones'[73] remark:

> To those interested in how foreign policy is made, it may be pointed out here that no atmosphere is more conducive to official action than that created when public figures on the Right and on the Left happen to agree, even though for different reasons, that a daring, even 'visionary' course of action should be taken: it raises their sights; it opens the psychological and political doors to action . . .

On the other hand, it determines the elites of the future and what their attitudes will be. It does this by rewarding and punishing various actions. This may occur when the public applauds the action of a recognized leader. Thus, in Chapter 2, we noted how the public's response encouraged a leading Senator to swing to internationalism. It may also occur when a man who wants to become a leader seizes on some potential attitudes in the public and creates his own constituency. This, of course, is true whenever something becomes a political issue. A politician seizes on corruption or on a poor foreign policy or on some public need that becomes an issue when the public appears to be responding to that line of attack. McCarthy's attitude would not have been developed into a political force if segments of the public had not rewarded him and if the press had not responded to his charges as newsworthy. At one point, polls showed that more people knew about McCarthy's charges of communist infiltration in the State Department than any other domestic issue. Only fourteen per cent of those ques-

---

[73]Jones, *op. cit.*, p. 234.

tioned were uninformed, and thirty-nine per cent felt that McCarthy was doing the country a service. Once a political issue has been built up, it serves to give certain officials power and to constrain others, because officials cannot make policy that would expose them to a political attack. Thus, the administration could not encourage the Chinese Communists to turn towards the United States, because it would be exposed to the political issue being developed of "communists in the government."

The tragedy of distortion on the part of either the administration or the opposition is that the real issues are masked and the public debate that should occur is never achieved. With a focus on whether Russia would launch a global attack or whether or not there were traitors in the State Department, there was no public debate on whether or not Formosa should be "neutralized" or whether the United States should become committed in South East Asia or whether massive retaliation should be used to contain communism. Until the public is trusted and educated, productive debate will not occur and unscrupulous politicians will be able to manipulate public opinion for their own ends.

Public limits on policy

While the government of a country has wide leeway on how to define a situation, it is constrained by certain emotional factors that influence the mass structure in such a way that certain policies are impossible or almost inescapable. A few of these emotional factors are listed below. The first four are selected from Kennan's[74] *Russia and the West.*

1. At the end of any period of turmoil, a people desires to stop sacrificing for causes and becomes occupied with its private life (page 181). Thus, after both World Wars, all participants found it difficult to prepare new armies.
2. During a conflict, a people's allies become idealized and their enemies degraded (page 348). Thus, during the Second World War, the potential danger of Russia and the potential good of Germany were overlooked by Americans.
3. A people tends to concentrate all of its problems on one source of evil so that a black-white dichotomy occurs. They forget that "No other people, as a whole, is entirely our enemy. No people at all — not even ourselves — is entirely our friend" (page 369). Thus, during the expansion of communism, the American people had a tendency to blame all their losses on Russian aggression and communist infiltration in the government.

---

[74]George F. Kennan, *Russia and the West under Lenin and Stalin* (Boston: Little, Brown and Company, 1960).

4. In a period of frustration and hopelessness, a people becomes ready for emotional enthusiasms and impatient with moderate measures (page 289). Thus, in 1932, the German public could no longer remain patient and, hence, responded to Hitler's demagoguery.

5. In a period of external stress, a people stops tolerating internal deviancy. Thus, Crespi[75] has shown that tolerance for conscientious objectors was lowest at the beginning of World War II, then rose as the war was being won; and Janicki and de Rivera[76] have shown that during the Cuban missile crisis, American students began objecting to anti-war ads, White House pickets, and refusal to serve in the armed forces — objections that slackened as the crisis passed over.

6. When a people has been frustrated by the constraints imposed by an alien government, a lessening of the constraints leads to an explosive discharge rather than an appreciative relief.[77,78] It is not clear under which conditions this energy can be harnessed.

7. Regardless of whether a people has experienced turmoil, is being frustrated, or has real economic needs, if it perceives opportunities for expansion it usually seems to expand. Thus, the British and French colonial empires, the western expansion of the United States, and the recent expansion of Russian influence have occurred in spite of the absence of frustrating need to expand.

The above statements are not as accurate as we wish. For one thing, there has been no systematic attempt to find negative instances that would force a modification of the statements. For another thing, the way the statements are worded sometimes masks important variables. Thus, the word "people" masks the important variable of common identification. If there were no common identification, the nation would split up under external pressure rather than resist deviancy. Likewise, the word "frustrated" masks the importance of the formation of expectancies and rights, which are the things that become frustrated. Still, the statements serve to demonstrate how one might begin to predict policy on the basis of mass rather than elite factors. Two further statements are:

---

[75]L. P. Crespi, "Public opinion toward conscientious objectors: V National tolerance, wartime trends and the scapegoat hypothesis," *Jl. Psychol.*, 20 (1945), pp. 321-46.
[76]P. Janicki and J. de Rivera, "Political attitude during the Cuban missile crisis," unpublished paper, 1960.
[77]Robert Le Vince, "Anti-European violence in Africa: A comparative analysis," *J. Conflict Resolution*, 3 (1959), pp. 420-29.
[78]Judson Brown, "Principles of intrapersonal conflict," *J. Conflict Resolution*, 1 (1957), pp. 135-54.

8. When tensions increase and the level of anxiety is raised, the public becomes more nationalistic rather than more internationalistic. Kaplan and Katzenbach[79] have pointed out that the lives of most persons are bound up in the nation where their hopes and values are lodged. They are identified with it and give it their loyalty. Hence, the defeat or humiliation of one's nation is an extremely threatening event. Thus, when a nation is challenged, its people tend to *react* and thus may lose perspective. Note, for example, that the immediate response to news of China's hydrogen bomb was "build anti-ballistic missiles" and not "perhaps we should admit China to the U.N."*

9. General ethnocentrism exerts a force towards belligerent rather than cooperative policies. Thus, Campbell and LeVine[80] suggest that Presidential candidates who advocate belligerent policies tend to enjoy more popularity and feel less need to be apologetic about their position because their loyalty is never in question. In his investigations of altruism, Sorokin[81] has demonstrated how charity decreases with distance. He asked his classes to donate money for three different worthy causes: a computing machine for the class, students at the University who were financially hurt by a recent catastrophe and would have to leave school if they were not helped, and students in a foreign country who were dying in a current famine. The number of students who donated and the

---

*Dana Bramel (personal communication) has conducted an interesting experiment that illustrates this effect. He administered two different questionnaires to different groups of college students. One questionnaire contained anxiety arousing items such as:

If, after an atomic war, you were becoming weak and knew that you were slowly dying from the effects of radiation, how likely is it that you would:
  a. desperately seek physical pleasure?
  b. be paralyzed by fear?
  c. turn your attention to God and prayer?
The other questionnaire had neutral items such as:
  How often do you go to the movies?
Both groups then were given questions such as:
  Do you favor an increase or decrease in U.S. government expenditures next year for the development and production of missiles and nuclear bombs?
Protestant male students show a clear tendency to favor more armaments and more nuclear weapons testing when they have first been exposed to the anxiety producing questions.

[79]Morton A. Kaplan and Nicholas de B. Katzenbach, "The patterns of international politics and of international law," *Amer. Pol. Sci. Rev.*, 53 (1959), pp. 693-712.

[80]Donald T. Campbell and Robert A. LeVine, "Propositions about ethnocentrism from social science theories," unpublished paper, March, 1956.

[81]Pitrim Sorokin, *The Ways and Power of Love* (Boston: Beacon Press, 1954).

amount that was donated decreased as the cause shifted from own class, to other students, to foreigners.

Another type of emotional factor that often affects policy is the "national character" of the people. While we cannot explore the various approaches to this interesting topic in this book, we will consider one example of its possible application to policy formation.

One approach to national character has been emphasized by Almond's[82] categorization of the major attitudes of the American public that have consciously influenced foreign policy. Snyder has applied some of these to an analysis of the climate of opinion surrounding defense budgeting during the Eisenhower administration. Snyder[83] sees the administration's policies as ". . . a modern version of isolationism, or at least as a thought pattern which grew from the same emotional soil which fostered the isolationism of the past."

The latter seems more appropriate, since (as Snyder notes) the administration accepted the need to defend overseas interests and the need to have alliances. Since this makes the policy appear internationally inclined, why does Snyder say that is grows from the same emotional soil that produced isolationism? What he is observing is that the way in which the administration was defending overseas interests and forming alliances could best be described by characterizations that also fitted isolationism.

For example, the Eisenhower administration came up with the doctrine of "massive retaliation" as a way to contain the enemy. That is, the enemy was threatened with a nuclear war if he expanded. This doctrine can best be understood as the product of a desire to become as uninvolved as possible. It helped, in the President's words, "to keep our boys at our side instead of on a foreign shore." The acceptance of the idea of using strategic atomic weapons and pulling American troops back to a "central strategic reserve" in America, indicates the same emotional needs that generated isolationism. Likewise, the doctrine drew support from the idea that the attack could be by means and at places of American choice, and thus tied in with the desire for freedom to determine policy without regard to the policy of others. Furthermore, it tied in with American moralism. Thus, Snyder notes,[84]

[82]Gabriel Almond, *The American People and Foreign Policy* (New York: Frederick A. Praeger, Inc., 1960).

[83]Glenn H. Snyder, "The 'new look' of 1953," In W. R. Schilling, P. Y. Hammond, and G. H. Snyder, *Strategy, Politics and Defense Budgets* (New York: Columbia University Press, 1962), p. 495.

[84]*Ibid.*, p. 502.

. . . Americans, when forced to war, have generally not prosecuted the war with the aim of bringing about the most desirable set of external power relations, but rather with the aim of punishing the enemy thoroughly for his transgression of civilized norms.

When policy is influenced more by national character than the structure of the situation, it is not apt to be successful. In the case of "massive retaliation," it was not too long before it was realized that the other side could issue counter-threats and make small aggressive moves that could only be appropriately countered by localized defenses rather than a massive retaliation.

Ironically, the isolationist tradition (with its impatience with foreign affairs) and the reformist tradition (with its interest in world integration) often find themselves combined against international power politics. Whereas the Johnson administration, for example, operates within international power politics and is opposed to both "drop the bomb" and "get out" believers, the Eisenhower administration showed the reverse pattern. Snyder[85] states,

> There is no contradiction in saying that Eisenhower's policies can be related both to the tradition of isolationism and to the tradition of "reformist-pacifism," since both of these traditions are themselves closely related. The one wishes to withdraw from power politics, the other, to do away with power politics by reforming the international system in the image of a national community. Both reject the concept of applying power in limited, calculated ways so as to promote a configuration of power in the external world most favorable to United States security interests.

While we cannot delve into the fascinating field of comparative politics with its psychological dimension of how the individual relates to the nation, we must briefly mention a related emotional factor that may affect foreign policy and yet is often overlooked — the quality of the interpersonal relations that exist within a society. Interpersonal relations are important, not only because they may affect an underlying level of hostility that works towards belligerent foreign policy, but also because they provide the models which the average person must use in order to think about international relations. If a person is only familiar with dominance-submission relations and has never experienced a free relationship governed by mutual love and respect, he will only be capable of thinking of international relations in terms of dominance and sub-

---

[85]*Ibid.*, p. 501. Snyder credits this idea to William T.R. Fox.

mission; an idea such as the freely accepted authority of law, will not be available for him to think of as a possible relation between nations.

Summary

While the often poor characteristics of American foreign policy are not a direct result of American national character, they are the result of a consensus process that is necessitated by a diverse governmental organization which, in turn, is directly related to American character and history. Any attempt to reform American foreign policy by increasing control and direction of policy, runs afoul of this fact. As long as the United States has a democratic form of government, it is going to have consensus made policy with all of its possible weaknesses. But policy by consensus is not necessarily bad policy. It can be good policy, but *only* if the leaders enjoy intellectual intimacy, if the bureaucracy is open and innovative, and if the gap between the leaders and the public is not too large.

We have now sampled three different views of the interpersonal relations that lie behind foreign policy. In the chapter on the small group, we viewed policy as initiated by a small Presidential "in-group" and modified by that group's confrontation with other powers within the Executive and Congress. Hence, we focused our attention on the dynamics of the "in-group." In the chapter on commands and communications, we viewed policy as the resultant of a clash between the basic forces within the nation. There, we focused on the communication between the leaders of these forces. In this chapter on consensus formation, we viewed policy as the product of a consensus that is formed between numerous competing groups within the government. Therefore, we focused on the process of consensus formation. Each of these perspectives has merit in helping one to grasp how policy comes to be formed.

From our own psychological standpoint, all of these views show one similarity. The policy is well formed if it is based on good interpersonal relations, it is poor to the point of being non-existent if it rides on poor ones.

Whether we are dealing with the relations between members of the in-group, between rival forces with nothing in common, or between groups competing to form a consensus, lack of communication is a tragedy that produces misunderstandings and poor policy.

Poor communication is much more frequent than we realize. In the chapter on perception, we noted that the very fact that men have different personalities, backgrounds, and responsibilities, makes them see the same stimulus in different ways and become opponents, each arguing for his own perception. When the situation the other person is responding to is perceived differently by an outside observer, he attributes incorrect motives and characteristics to the other. The other, not realizing why the observer is acting as he is, begins his own misperceptions, and the cycle builds on itself.

A democracy is dependent on good internal communications. It cannot afford to take them for granted when they are often demonstrably poor. We need to instigate much more research on the improvement of communication between leaders, we need to label and become much more aware of communication failures, and we need to create a class of specialists who can cope with these failures when they occur.

CHAPTER 9

Interactions Between the Representatives of Nations

Foreign policy is responsive to the actions of other nations and involves efforts to influence who the leaders of these nations will be, what decisions they will make, and how they will define the relationship between their nation and others. These attempts at influence may involve the manipulation of objective economic, military, political, and public opinion factors. However, these are usually accompanied by diplomatic agreements and communications that attempt to insure that the officials of the other nation will give these acts an appropriate *meaning*. These symbolic devices often attempt to preserve or obtain some relationship which the leaders of one nation desire to have with the leaders of the other nation.

Such communications may occur directly between key decision makers or via the prolonged contact of professional diplomats. In preceding chapters, we have observed such interactions in conferences (eg., the conference between the President of the United States and the British Prime Minister on Korean War policy) and via cables (eg., the cable from the German Ambassador conveying the British Foreign Secretary's warning to the Kaiser). In this chapter, we shall examine the interactions between representatives of the United States and the Soviet Union towards the end of World War II as they attempted to deal with conflicting interests over Poland. This interaction resulted in a decline of friendly relations between the nations, and we shall apply various psychological conceptualizations in an attempt to increase our understanding of why this occurred. Then we shall examine a number of factors that affect all negotiations, and observe some difficulties in post-war negotiations between Americans and Russians. A consideration of these psychological factors has led social scientists to think about conflict in a particular way and to propose certain strategies for American foreign policy. In the latter part of this chapter, we shall briefly examine some of these ideas.

Analysis of American-Soviet Interaction in 1945

Details of the interaction

From 1942 through 1944, Great Britain, the Soviet Union, and the United States successfully collaborated to defeat the Axis and begin the United Nations. Stalin's resentment over the delay in opening a second front in Europe had apparently been replaced by good will and trust; and while there were a number of obvious problems, they were held in check by the desire to keep united against Germany. As the war in Europe was being concluded, these problems began surfacing and a number of conflicting interests became apparent. Still, the three nations seemed determined to cooperate with each other. No one dealt with the Germans behind the back of others. Stalin took what he could get but recognized British prerogatives and carefully refrained when Churchill quelled a communist uprising in Greece. The British, in turn, kept quiet when Russia essentially took over Bulgaria and Rumania. Then, however, the cooperation began to slacken. As we shall see, the problem was not one of misunderstanding, but (as in the case between Truman and MacArthur) the difficulty involved a lack of real understanding. The various parties did not sympathize with each other's interests and did not really agree on what "cooperation" meant.

The difficulty in resolving conflicts of interest became most apparent in the disagreement over the nature of the Polish government. By the time of the Yalta Conference, the outlines of the problem were clear.[1] As its troops advanced, the Soviet Union had unilaterally established a provisional government in Poland that, it was sure, would cooperate with Russian policy. It refused to have any dealings with the more nationalistic Polish government in exile, in spite of the fact that that government had hundreds of thousands of Polish troops fighting with the

---

[1]Herbert Feis, *Churchill, Roosevelt, Stalin* (Princeton, N. J.: Princeton University Press, 1957).

British army and a large underground movement in Poland. Churchill and Roosevelt had argued strongly but submitted in order to keep the allied coalition. They recognized that the government in exile opposed border changes which the Russians demanded and, in their opinion, deserved; but at Yalta they hoped to persuade Stalin to make the provisional government more representative. Stalin was firm, and the best Churchill and Roosevelt could do was to pressure him into an agreement with rather ambiguous wording and without any real teeth. The final statement read:[2]

> The Provisional Government which is now functioning in Poland should therefore be reorganized on a broader democratic basis with the inclusion of democratic leaders from Poland itself and from Poles abroad .... (it) shall be pledged to the holding of free and unfettered elections as soon as possible on the basis of universal suffrage and secret ballot. In these elections all democratic and anti-Nazi parties shall have the right to take part and to put forward candidates.

This left Stalin able to argue that the Soviet sponsored government should be the nucleus of any reorganization and it failed to provide for any supervision of the elections. The Americans and British were simply not able to do any better; still, their own intentions were on the record, and it had been agreed that their Ambassador should meet with the Russian Foreign Minister to bring about the reorganization of the Polish government. In the subsequent months, it became clear that no agreement could be reached, because the Russians insisted that any additions to the provisional government had to be acceptable to current members of that government. Since all of the more nationalistic leaders were hostile towards Russia and the current provisional government, there was nothing that could be done.

Roosevelt, under persistent pressure from Churchill, finally wrote Stalin on April 1, 1945, to protest the "veto power" of the Soviet sponsored provisional government. On the 7th, Stalin replied that the current provisional government had to be the kernel of the new government. With Roosevelt's death on April 12, the new President was immediately confronted with the problem.

After reviewing all the documents and speaking with the Americans who had been involved, President Truman joined Churchill in protesting that the Soviet government was reverting to its original position at Yalta and ignoring the compromise that had been reached. Confronted

---

[2]*Ibid.*, p. 528.

with a note that the Russians were about to recognize the provisional government, Truman has noted,[3]

> I was disturbed. This was another Russian maneuver aimed at getting their own way in Poland, and I made up my mind that I would lay it on the line with [the Foreign Minister].

On April 20, the American Ambassador returned from Russia and met with the President. The President asked him to indicate the major problems he was having with the Russians. According to the President, the Ambassador replied[4] that the Soviet Union thought it could pursue a policy of cooperating with the United States and Great Britain at the same time it independently extended Soviet control over its neighbors. Some of Stalin's advisors interpreted American generosity and cooperativeness as indicating a softness that would allow the Soviet government to do what it pleased without risk of a challenge from the United States. The Ambassador listed a number of difficulties he was encountering in dealing with the Russians. He felt that in order to reconstruct their country the Russians needed American help and, hence, the United States could be firm without risking a break in relations.

When the President observed that he would be firm but fair and that "the Russians needed us more than we needed them," the Ambassador agreed but pointed out that a number of Russian officials believed that American business had to increase exports to Russia if it were to survive. The President replied that such a notion was "ridiculous" and that he intended to be firm and not try to win their favor by making "concessions from American principles or traditions." He stated[5] that sound relations could only be established on a "give-and-take basis."

The Ambassador pointed out that the Soviet Union would attempt to extend its influence in Eastern Europe and that this would mean not only Soviet influence over each nation's policy but also a secret police force and no freedom of speech. He observed that the United States would have to decide what its attitude would be toward this.

On the 22nd, the President met with the Russian Foreign Minister and told him that the solution of the Polish problem "was of great importance because of the effect on American public opinion." The Foreign Minister replied that he understood that but that the matter was

---

[3]Harry S Truman, *Memoirs,* Vol. One (Garden City, N. Y.: Doubleday & Company, Inc., 1955), p. 15.

[4]*Ibid.,* p. 70.

[5]*Ibid.,* p. 71.

even more important for the Soviet Union. He pointed out that Poland was far from the United States but bordered on the Soviet Union.

On the 23rd, the President met with his top advisors[6] and told them that American agreement with Russia had "so far been a one-way street and that this could not continue." He then asked for their opinions.

The Secretary of War stated that the Russians had kept their word on all major military matters. He said that "without fully understanding how seriously the Russians took this Polish question we might be heading into very dangerous waters. . ." He felt that the Russians were being realistic in regard to their security, and he wanted to avoid any break with Russia that would prevent its cooperation in fighting Japan. Later, the Army Chief of Staff expressed the same point of view.

The Secretary of the Navy said that he felt that the Russians thought we would not object if they took over Eastern Europe and that we had "better have a showdown with them now rather than later."

The Ambassador to Russia stated that the real issue was whether "we were to be a party to a program of Soviet domination of Poland."

In answer to a question, the President said, "The issue was the execution of agreements entered into between this government and the Soviet Union."

In the late afternoon, the President again met with the Soviet Foreign Minister and said he regretted that he and the Secretary of State had made no progress on the Polish question. He pointed out that economic aid measures could not pass Congress without public support and asked him to keep that in mind (a hint). He then gave the Foreign Minister a message to transmit to Stalin. This message pointed out that there was an agreement at Yalta to reorganize the provisional government by means of consultation between the current government and other democratic leaders. The message stated:[7]

> The United States Government cannot be party to any method of consultation with Polish leaders which would not result in the establishment of a new Provisional Government of National Unity genuinely representative of the democratic elements of the Polish people. The United States and British Governments have gone as far as they can . . . .

The Foreign Minister stated that the Soviet Union wished to cooperate as it had been doing. However, he said that it was the view of the Soviet Government that[8] in the past the three governments had equal

---

[6]*Ibid.,* p. 77-79.
[7]*Ibid.,* p. 81.
[8]*Ibid.,* p. 81.

status and that in no case had one or two of the three attempted to impose their will on another. This was the only acceptable basis for cooperation.

The President replied that all he wanted was for the Soviet government to carry out the Yalta agreements. The Foreign Minister said his government stood by these agreements and was convinced that all difficulties would be overcome. The President "replied sharply," and an exchange followed that concluded with the Foreign Minister saying, "I have never been talked to like that in my life." The President notes, "I told him, 'carry out your agreements and you won't get talked to like that.' "

The following night, the President received a reply from Stalin.[9] The Marshall noted that the President continued to view the Provisional Polish government as one of many equally legitimate Polish groups. He stated that at Yalta he, Churchill, and Roosevelt had considered the Provisional government as the kernel of any future Polish government. Mentioning that Poland bordered on the Soviet Union rather than on Great Britain or the United States as observed:

> Poland has the same meaning for the security of the Soviet Union as the question on Belgium and Greece for the security of Great Britain. You, apparently, do not agree that the Soviet Union has a right to make efforts that there should exist in Poland a government friendly toward the Soviet Union, and that the Soviet government cannot agree to the existence in Poland of a government hostile toward it. Besides everything else, this is demanded by the blood of the Soviet people abundantly shed on the fields of Poland in the name of liberation of Poland. I do not know whether there has been established in Greece a really representative government, and whether the government in Belgium is really democratic. The Soviet Union was not consulted when these governments were being established there. The Soviet Government did not lay claim to interference in these affairs as it understands the whole importance of Belgium and Greece for the security of Great Britain.
>
> It is not clear why, while the question of Poland is discussed it is not wanted to take into consideration the interests of the Soviet Union from the point of view of its security . . . . you demand too much of me . . . .

It should be noted that the disagreement over Poland was taking place against the background of the defeat of the Axis armies and the possibility of separate "deals" with Germany. In March and early April, Stalin had been very upset by a report of separate peace talks between

---

[9]*Ibid.*, pp. 85-86.

the Axis and the British and Americans. He was worried that the Germans might take advantage of cease fire agreements to move troops to the Eastern front, and his suspicions of underlying British hostility were enhanced by the fact that the Germans were obviously more reluctant to surrender to Russian forces than to American or British forces. In actuality, the Americans and British were playing fair. This probably became clear to Stalin by early May, when the Americans and British clearly rejected German offers of a separate surrender on the Western front. On the other hand, in the middle of May, an American executive error had resulted in a sudden stopping of lend-lease aid. Amidst protests from numerous nations, the error was corrected, but the Russians interpreted the action as especially aimed at them.

In late May, the President sent a personal envoy, who had worked closely with Roosevelt and Stalin, to try to come to some agreement with Stalin over Poland and some other issues. Stalin brought up the sudden stopping of aid as an example of how America was growing colder towards Russia as Germany was being defeated. He felt that if the stopping of aid was intended as pressure on the Russians to make them comply, this was a fundamental mistake. The envoy explained that the stopping of aid was an error and was not intended as a manipulation. Working with the Ambassador, the envoy presented the American case in the best way he could and tried to increase Russian understanding of the American position. He reported back that he had conveyed the gravity of the Polish situation and that Stalin had listened attentively to the state of American public opinion. The Ambassador cabled that the envoy had done a "first-rate job" in presenting the President's views and explaining the situation. He noted, however:[10]

> I am afraid that Stalin does not and never will fully understand our interest in a free Poland as a matter of principle. The Russian Premier is a realist in all of his actions, and it is hard for him to appreciate our faith in abstract principles. It is difficult for him to understand why we should want to interfere with Soviet policy in a country like Poland which he considers so important to Russia's security unless we have some ulterior motive. He does, however, appreciate that he must deal with the position we have taken.

Finally, on June 6, the envoy achieved an agreement with Stalin on the names of a number of Poles who would be invited to Moscow to meet with the Polish commission and set about broadening the pro-

---

[10]*Ibid.,* p. 263.

visional government. The commission met on June 15, and a satisfactory agreement was reached. The provisional government was broadened by the addition of several Polish leaders who had indicated that they would cooperate with the Soviet Union. The American and British Ambassadors received a pledge that the government would hold free elections, with freedom of assembly and discussion. On June 28, the new provisional government was formed and, on July 5, recognized by the American and British governments.

In spite of this sign of accommodation, it was not long before the new members of the provisional government found they were not getting their share of government positions. For an election, the pro-Soviet members of the government suggested a single list of candidates supported by all parties with a predetermined number of seats allotted to each party in advance. When the leader of the opposition objected, the police began interfering with the activities of his party. A multi-party election was eventually held in January of 1947, but lists of candidates were invalidated, and pro-Soviet delegates received 392 of 444 seats. By a series of forced mergers, the communists eventually obtained a single "unified" party.[11]

The problems over Poland were duplicated in a score of different interactions between the United States and the Soviet Union. Suspicions grew, Russia became withdrawn, the unexpected success of communism in China made the West defensive, and, with the advent of the Korean War, cooperation completely ended and the Russians became enemies instead of allies. Initially, both the Americans and the Russians wanted to "cooperate" with each other, to minimize and work through any conflicts of interest. How can we analyze the interaction to account for the destruction of these good intentions?

While it is possible that the Soviet government simply decided to take whatever it could get and began to deliberately mislead the Americans in order to take advantage of their gullible generosity, it appears that the situation was more complex. From a detached perspective, we may note at least three interesting features of the interaction that may account for an unintended decline of the relationship.

First, neither party seems to have understood the other's meaning of "cooperation" or sympathized with the other's interests. In the chapter on perception, we noted that persons form different views of reality; and in the chapter on commands and communication, we saw how difficult it was for the President and his Commander to really

---

[11]Cf. Samuel L. Sharp, *Poland* (Cambridge, Mass.: Harvard University Press, 1953).

understand each other's worlds. Imagine, then, the differences in perspective that may exist when the persons are from completely different cultures.

Second, neither party fully trusted the other, and both began attributing bad motives to each other. In the last chapter, we observe some difficulties in achieving good bargaining outcomes within the government. We shall see that a fuller exposition of these difficulties involves us in these problems of trust.

Third, both parties felt the other *should* behave differently. The different conceptions of what was fair led each party to feel injured by the other. We shall see that different estimates of each other's power and desires contributed to this feeling and led to the decline of friendly relations.

Differences in perspective

A central cause of the lack of understanding between the Russians and the Americans appears to have been their completely different meanings of "cooperation." These different meanings stemmed from the different ways in which each party was accustomed to handling conflicts. The Russians settled conflicts within any given unit (such as a nation) by the dictates of a central authority; the power of different parties within the unit was used simply in determining who the central authority would be. Hence, there was no such thing as a compromise between parties within the unit, and cooperation between units simply meant the recognition of different spheres of influence and the arranging of mutually profitable "deals." The Russians felt that dividing Europe into non-conflicting spheres of influence was cooperation. The Americans settled conflicts within a unit by setting up a structure — such as the principles of an election, or the rules of law, or a market — and then let the different parties arrive at a solution within this framework. The power of the different parties would govern where this solution would lie, and all parties would cooperate in forming the principles that would govern the conflict. Cooperation between units involved setting up principles within which the units could bargain. It meant "compromise" rather than "deals". The Americans felt that setting up a multi-party system in Poland with the assurance of a strong communist party was cooperation.

One advantage of the American method is that different parties can be insured varying amounts of power by rigging the framework within which the conflict will occur. Thus, certain undesirable outcomes can be prevented. (A related disadvantage is that circumstances may unjustly penalize some parties.) The Americans were sincere when they advocated both free elections and a government that was friendly towards the Soviet Union. They thought this could be obtained by having all the leaders cooperatively agree on an unwritten rule — respect for the desires of the Soviet Union—and by carrying out all election campaigns within this framework. The Russians could not grasp this idea. In their world, the only way to insure cooperation was to set up one leader who would be subordinate to Moscow. They understood direct control and did not know how to use the sort of indirect control — the setting of checks and balances — which the Americans used.

Parentheticaly, it should be noted that because of the past conflicts between Russia and Poland, the Soviet Union may well have been more realistic in feeling that it would have to insure cooperation by dominating the Polish government. This is not to say that no system of checks and balances could have worked, but it would have had to have been more stringent than the one the Americans were preposing. Had the Russians understood how to control the situation in the American way, they might have been able to propose some system; as it was, they could only view the American proposal as completely inadequate for their own security. It should also be observed that domination may be necessary under some objective conditions. When the other country is between oneself and a powerful neighbor — as Poland was between Russia and Germany—a "puppet" kind of government may be required. In different conditions, the Soviet Union has managed to work with a relatively independent nation, namely Finland.

The same misunderstanding poisoned many different attempts at cooperation. The United States, with the best of intentions and good will, wanted to move to a truly international position. It wanted to cooperate to achieve this framework and was willing to compromise within this framework. The President wanted to give less powerful nations a genuine voice in decision making and was displeased with Stalin's view that America, Britain, and Russia should settle all the world's affairs. Truman wished to *internationalize* certain important waterways. Stalin wanted *control* over the waterways important to Russia.

From a distance, both parties appear quite ethnocentric, each feeling their system to be *the* system for anyone with intelligence. To an American, a "deal" seemed cynical and immoral; it seemed realistic to a Russian, whereas a "compromise" appeared as a putrid selling-out. The Russian does not understand that by subscribing to principles, an individual can compromise without risking his identity. He is suspicious of being trapped in the American's web of principles and taken over by his brand of cooperation. The American does not understand how immoral and selfish his individuality appears to a Russian. Of course, both systems have real weaknesses; the Soviet system hinders individual expression, whereas the American system may fail to encourage deprived peoples to seize the initiative, gain control over their fate, and come into a genuine partnership with the rest of the nation. In Chapter 7, we reviewed the difficulties that interfere with two worlds understanding each other and mentioned that the "Rapoport debate" technique is one way of bridging the chasm. (In Rapoport's[12] book, there is an interesting sample debate between an individualist and a collectivist, and the reader who fails to understand the merits of either side will find it to be profitable reading.)

The situation was further complicated by the fact that each nation's system offered power advantages to that nation. It was generous for the United States to offer to internationalize waterways and atomic energy; but with a strong navy and a pluralistic society it would be in a much better position of strength than the Soviet Union, where the necessary compromises would weaken her internal security. Stalin wanted control over the straits between the Black Sea and the Mediterranean (a traditional Russian desire). Truman offered to internationalize these straits with a three-power guarantee of free access. But it was obvious to Stalin that Churchill was not about to give up British control over the Suez and internationalize it.

On the other hand, it was all very well for the Soviet Union to control some waterways and accept a limited sphere of influence; but such a deal would have required the British to surrender some control over the Mediterranean, and the dominance of Poland would have strained the very principles on which the strength of the democracies were based. It was unfortunate that the American leaders always argued in terms of "public opinion." Not only did Stalin not comprehend why they could not manipulate such opinion the way he could, but also it really was a much deeper security issue, since the fabric of principle that holds together a democracy would have been weakened. Since this issue was not consciously conceptionalized, Stalin could not see that a security problem *was* involved, even though Poland was miles away from Western borders. He must also have felt confused by the lack of American concern over Spain's undemocratic government. While there was a greater identification with Poland because of the number of

---

[12]Anatol Rapoport, *Fights, Games, and Debates* (Ann Arbor: University of Michigan Press, 1961). For some additional arguments, see Rapoport, *Strategy and Conscience* (New York: Harper & Row, Publishers, 1964).

second generation Poles in the United States and the large Polish army that was fighting with the allies, Stalin could hardly escape noting that the Americans and British objected to communist governments more than to right wing dictatorships.

To Americans, the Russians were unprincipled opportunists, and within the American frame of reference, this was an accurate perception. But this description carried a negative evaluation that imposed American standards on a government that operated in a completely different fashion. It was correct to see the Soviet government as different and appropriate to try to teach it what Americans felt to be a more desirable way of doing things; it was inappropriate to treat the Soviet government as similar and then react with contempt and fear when it behaved differently from the way the British government behaved.

To Russian eyes, on the other hand, the American behavior seemed to be unwarranted interference. Since they had no understanding of principles, they could not grasp why Americans kept pushing the Polish issue unless they were being opportunistic. Rather than realize that the Americans were different from themselves, the Russians believed the Americans were being high handed, mistrusting the Soviet Union, and wanting to surround it with hostile countries that would minimize its influence.

Trust and the attribution of motives

In the last chapter, when we examined the way in which consensus was formed within the government, we noted that the bargaining and negotiation process was quite similar to what occurred between nations. Everything that was said in that section about intra-governmental relations, can also be applied to inter-governmental relations. For example, the research that demonstrated that groups fail to really understand each other's proposals, probably applies to the Russian perception of the *intent* behind the American proposals for a Polish government. According to the American Ambassador, in May, 1945, Stalin actively complained ". . . about our misdeeds and aggressively indicated that if we did not wish to deal on a friendly basis with the Soviet Union, she was strong enough to look after herself."[13]

However, in making the translation from the last chapter, one important factor must be kept in mind: bargaining within the government is constrained by the fact that all the participants have a common fate and identity and know they must reach agreement in order for the gov-

---

[13]Truman, *op. cit.,* p. 262.

ernment to survive. The research of both Hilsman[14] and Bauer and his associates[15] has touched on the importance of this factor in limiting the extent of the conflict between groups within the government. There is a "damper" over negotiations *within* a group that does not exist in the relations *between* groups, and this makes the conflict within a marriage or an administration or a management-union unit somewhat different from the conflict between unions, industries, or nations.

In the last chapter, we noted that during the bargaining over the 1950 defense budget, the Secretary of State seemed to be playing a different "game" than the Secretary of Defense. The former's game was a "zero-sum" game in which one person wins what the other loses, whereas the latter's was a "non-zero-sum" game in which some moves lead to gains or losses for both parties. This latter type of game has recently been the center of many experiments because it can be a very simple game (with each player having only two possible alternatives) yet capturing important points about trust and cooperation.

The game can be set up in many different ways, but the following is typical: Two persons, separated by a partition, are each given a red button and a black button. Pushing either of these buttons is a move in the game. Typically, each person makes his move without knowledge of the other person's move. As soon as both persons have moved, the game is over. What happens — whether both win or lose or one wins and the other loses — is determined by the pattern of the moves. There are only four possibilities: Both players could have pushed the red button, both the black button, player one could push red and player two black, or player two could push the red button and player one the black button.

The experimenter makes up a "pay-off matrix" that determines how much each player wins or loses in each of the four conditions. Typically, this pay-off matrix is arranged to put each player in an interesting dilemma. For example, consider the matrix used by Scodel and his associates,[16] shown in Figure 1.

In this matrix, the first number in a cell is Player I's pay-off, and the second number is Player II's pay-off. For example, if Player I pushes his red button and Player II pushes his black button, Player

[14]R. Hilsman, "The foreign-policy consensus; an interim research report," *J. Conflict Resolution,* 3 (1959), pp. 361-82.

[15]Raymond A. Bauer, Ithiel de Sola Pool, and Lewis A. Dexter, *American Business and Public Policy* (New York: Atherton Press, 1963).

[16]Alvin Scodel, Sayer J. Minas, Philburn Ratoosh, and Milton Lipetz, "Some descriptive aspects of two-person non-zero-sum games," *J. Conflict Resolution,* 3 (1959), pp. 114-19 and 4 (1960), pp. 193-97.

Figure 1. *Pay-off matrix with a dilemma*

		Player II	
		black	red
Player I	black	3,3	0,5
	red	5,0	1,1

I wins five points and Player II wins zero points. Each player is given a copy of the pay-off matrix so that he can decide which move is better for him to make. A moment's study of the above matrix will reveal the dilemma that confronts each player. If one decides to push his red button, he will win the most points and will be ahead of the other player *if* the other player pushes his black button. But if the other player also pushes his red button, both will win only one point. If one decides to press his black button — make a cooperative move — both players will benefit *if* the other player also pushes his black button; but if the other pushes red, then the first player will win nothing. The dilemma is amplified because each player knows that the other player must be thinking the same thoughts which he is thinking! Often a player will have thoughts such as "If I want to push red, he will want to push red also, so we will wind up winning far less than if we both pushed black. But if I push black and he doesn't, I'll be a sucker. He doesn't want to be a sucker any more than I do, so he'll probably push red. In that case I'd better push red too and at least make one point, etc." Suppose the pay-off was quite large and each point represented a thousand dollars — what would the reader choose to do?

Scodel and his associates gave twenty-two pairs of persons the above matrix and had each of the pairs play the game fifty consecutive times. The points stood for pennies and each person was told, "Here is a chance for you to make some money." The investigators found that in seventeen of the twenty-two cases, the players wound up in the red-red cell of the matrix! Thus, in spite of the fact that players would be better off if they cooperated with each other, something about the situation forced them not to. The investigators compared the last twenty-five games with the first twenty-five to see if the persons were gradually learning to extricate themselves from the poor situation they were in, but found that the last twenty-five trials were even worse.

We might expect that if the players had a chance to talk with each other, they would be able to resolve their difficulties. Accordingly, the investigators had another eleven pairs of persons play the game, allowing them to talk with each other for two minutes between the twenty-fifth and twenty-sixth games. While the amount of cooperation increased slightly, most of the persons used the conversation to try to discover the other player's plans rather than to arrange a joint cooperative strategy.

The investigators next tried more extreme matrices, such as the one shown in Figure 2.

Figure 2. *An extreme matrix*

		Player II	
		black	red
Player I	black	4,4	1,3
	red	3,1	0,0

Here the cooperative strategy is clearly superior — if it can be achieved. While the amount of cooperation rose, the average subject still pushed the red button forty-seven percent of the time.

The reader should note that there are a number of political situations in which the heads of nations may be in an essentially similar dilemma. In such a situation, some persons argue for cooperating when the other cooperates and competing when he competes, while others advocate complete and undiscriminating cooperation. Accordingly, two other manipulations were tried. In one of these, the second player was secretly instructed and always pushed the same button as the first player. In the other, the second player was instructed to always push the black button regardless of what the other player did. Neither of these conditions produced a cooperative strategy on the part of the first player. In the first condition, thirty-six per cent of his choices were black, and in the second condition, thirty-nine per cent. We must conclude that something about the situation — either lack of trust or lack of coordination, or too much competitive drive — leads persons to press the red button in spite of the fact that they could make more money by cooperating.

Persons might approach the game with a number of different intentions. Morton Deutsch* has varied this systematically by giving persons different types of instructions about how to play the game. He used the rather extreme matrix shown in Figure 3.

One-third of the persons playing the game were instructed to compete — to try to do better than the other person; a third were asked to

---

*Morton Deutsch, 'Trust and suspicion," *J. Conflict Resolution,* 2 (1958), pp. 265-79.

Figure 3. *Matrix used by Deutsch*

Player II

		black	red
	black	9,9	−10,10
Player I	red	10,−10	−9,−9

cooperate with the other person and think of his gains as well as their own; and a third were told to think only of their own absolute gains — to be individualists — neither caring about the other person's welfare nor trying to do better than him. As might be expected, the competitively oriented persons chose black only twelve per cent of the time, while the cooperatively oriented chose black eighty-nine per cent of the time. The persons who were instructed to maximize their own gain could easily do so by playing black and getting the other player to play black; but, as in Scodel's experiments, only thirty-six per cent of their choices were black. Once again, even though we know that the persons were trying to maximize their own gain, the situation forced them to act in a way that was not in their own interests.

When Deutsch permitted the players to communicate before each game, he found that the individualistically oriented players were able to increase their black responses to seventy-one per cent. In examining *how* these players tried to communicate their desire to cooperate, Deutsch noted that some managed to communicate much more effectively than others. The better communicators not only proposed cooperation but also discussed how to react to violations of trust and even proposed a method of absolving the guilty party. To study this, Deutsch made up five types of communications. He then had a different group of players communicate before the game but substituted his own notes for those written by the players. In this way, he carefully controlled what was communicated. The notes and the percentage of cooperation they elicited are shown in Table 1.

These results clearly demonstrate that there are ways in which one player can induce cooperation in spite of the situational pressures towards harmful moves. It should be noted that a person cannot induce cooperation by always pushing the black button. The other is too likely to believe that he does not know what he is doing and deserves to be taken advantage of.

It is obvious that if one does not trust the other and believes that the other may take advantage of one's cooperative moves, one may become

Table 1. *Different communications and the cooperation which they elicit*

Communication	Elicited Cooperation
None	11%
I expect you to push black	31%
I intend to push black	39%
I intend to push black and I expect you to	47%
I intend to push black, I expect you to, if you do not I will push red next time	61%
I intend to push black, I expect you to, if you do not I will push red next time but will give you another chance the time after that	80%

so suspicious that opportunities for cooperation may be lost. For example, consider this report from *The New York Times:**

The United States and West Germany are considering a proposal by Poland and Czechoslovakia to extend international atomic energy controls in both Eastern and Western Europe.

The two Communist countries have offered to place their atomic power reactors under the inspection safeguards of the International Atomic Energy Agency if West German does the same.

When the proposal was advanced *last month* at the annual general conference of the United Nations agency in Vienna, the initial West German and American reaction was negative, largely because of suspicions about political motives.

. . . . Some Administration officials, particularly in the disarmament and atomic energy fields, believe the proposal could be of far-reaching significance in extending the principle of international atomic energy safeguards to Communist countries.

In turn, they argue, such a step could help establish the precedent of international safeguards for enforcing a treaty barring the spread of nuclear weapons and prevent atomic power plants from being used for military purposes.

. . . . Several nonnuclear Western states accepted agency controls but until the Polish-Czech initiative, the Communist states supported international controls in principle but generally resisted such safeguards for their own programs.

*John W. Finney "U. S. is considering Polish-Czech plan on atom controls," *The New York Times,* Oct. 24, 1966, p. 1.

The change in the Communist attitude, presumably made with Soviet approval, has caused suspicion, more in Bonn than in Washington, that there were some political "booby traps" in the Polish-Czech proposal, aimed at West Germany and the European Atomic Energy Community.

. . . . One interpretation is that the Communists sought to cause further diplomatic complications for West Germany and the North Atlantic Treaty Organization by seeming to impose an additional constraint on West German desires for a "voice" in its own nuclear defense.

But West Germany has formally renounced the production of atomic weapons and already has placed its atomic program under the inspection of the European Atomic Energy Community, known as Euratom.

Thus [sic] another suspicion arose: that the Communist move was designed to interfere with the European movement by promoting a role for the United Nations agency that might undermine the authority of Euratom, particularly over West Germany.

But American officials point out that in the past both West Germany and Euratom have accepted the principle of two systems of inspection — one by Euratom and the other by the United States. Therefore, it is argued, there should be no jurisdictional objection to having parallel inspection systems.   (italics mine)

Such suspiciousness is far less prevalent when the parties to the conflict feel that they have something in common.

Thus, Deutsch shows that the probability of cooperation increases if the players shared the common experience of being exposed to an obnoxious third party before the game began. Likewise, Tottle and Kolman[17] have shown that cooperation is increased if the players have had the experience of successfully working together. In their experiment, before any game was played, some of the pairs of players were told that they would be given a simple task designed to measure their ability to work together as a team. While one player read a paragraph aloud, the other wrote his words down as quickly as he could. Then the players switched jobs and copied a second paragraph. When they had finished, the paragraphs were read to the experimenter, who checked for errors and compared their time against college norms. The players were always told that their time was better than average. After this successful teamwork, the players were introduced to a non-zero-sum game with the matrix shown in Figure 4.

---

[17]John W. Tottle, III, and Mike Kolman, "The effects of previous frustration and previous cooperation on the playing of the two person game," unpublished paper, Dartmouth course, 1962.

Figure 4.   *Matrix used by Tottle and Kolman*

Player II

		black	red
	black	25,25	10,35
Player I			
	red	35,10	0,0

Those players who had worked together made significantly more black (cooperative) choices than did the players who had had no common experience before the game. It is interesting to note that when the players were questioned about why they had chosen black more frequently, they did not answer in terms of "wishing to cooperate" but were apt to reply, "obviously *we* would both earn the most money if *we* pressed black." The results of this one experiment could be explained by postulating that a success simply left each player feeling more secure and less in need of competition to prove his superiority over the other player. But, together with Deutsch's experiment, the results suggest that if persons share a common emotional experience, they begin to form a unit and, hence, share an identification with each other that makes it more desirable or safe to cooperate.

The difference which this would make is shown in an experiment by Wilson, Chun, and Kayatani.[18] Using the matrix shown in Figure 5 they had two-men groups first play against other two-men groups and then play against their fellow group members.

Figure 5.   *Matrix used by Wilson, Chun, and Kayatani*

Group or Player II

		black	red
	black	2,2	0,4
Group or Player I			
	red	4,0	0,0

The game was played twenty consecutive times. Each time, the teammates (separated by a screen from the other team) would first get together to make their out-group choice and then make an in-group choice to determine how their winnings (if any) would be divided. A public record of all past choices was available. When playing against the

[18]Warner Wilson, Natalie Chun, and Myra Kayatani, "Projection, attraction, and strategy choices in intergroup competition," *J. Personality and Social Psychol.*, 2 (1965), pp. 432-35.

other group, an average of nine of the twenty choices were black, as opposed to an average of only 15 black choices within their own group.

The experimenters also had the players rate each other, both before and after the game, on personality traits such as "gullibility," sociometric traits such as "attractiveness," ability traits such as "intelligence," and motive traits such as "hostility." Neither personality, sociometric, nor ability traits were affected by playing the game. There was, however, a large impact on the differential perception of motives. In spite of the fact that the lack of inter-group cooperation was as much one group's fault as another's, members in the other group were perceived as more hostile, competitive, greedy, mean, and stubborn — and less generous, cooperative, fair, and kind. In short, the other group — rather than one's own group or the nature of the situation — is blamed to explain the poor results.

The explanation for this bias may lie in how the individual rationalizes his own choices. We may assume that he is in some conflict about whether or not to "cooperate." If he tries cooperation and is not rewarded, he is likely to oversimplify his opponent's motivation as being uncooperative. This, in turn, justifies his own non-cooperative choices in the future. This process may differ from individual to individual, and it may often rely on the person looking at his own *intentions* and the other's *acts*. In any case, the experimenters point out that it poses a basic problem for intergroup harmony.

We have seen that the failure of American-Soviet cooperation was due to a fundamental difference in outlook — that the Russians desired to cooperate in a different sense than the Americans did. Yet when American attempts at cooperation failed, many officials attributed this to Soviet hostility. For example, at the Potsdam Conference (in July), Truman made an unsuccessful attempt to get Stalin to cooperate (in the American sense of the term). In his memoirs, he notes,[19]

> The persistent way in which Stalin blocked one of the war-preventative measures I had proposed showed how his mind worked and what he was after. I had proposed the internationalization of all the principal waterways. Stalin did not want this. What Stalin wanted was control of the Black Sea straits and the Danube. The Russians were planning world conquest.

"Should forces" and "weight reduction"

While the type of game we have just considered is useful in investigating a number of basic points about cooperation, there are a number

---

[19]Truman, *op. cit.,* p. 412.

of additions that would have to be made in order to deal with some of the factors that appear to have been important in the exchange over Poland. While the games have a clearcut cooperative move, what was a cooperative move to the United States (arranging a multi-party system in Poland) was an unconscionable demand to the Russians, and what was a cooperative move to the Soviet Union (recognition of Soviet dominance in Poland) appeared to the Americans to be a nefarious deal. In short, the *meaning* of each move differed so that the interaction produced a new relationship. In the game, each party attempts to maximize his interests, and a cooperative strategy is usually the best way to do it. If the parties cannot get together, they may attribute hostility or stupidity or ulterior motives to each other, but they do not necessarily get angry — it is all in the game. In the case of Poland, however, there seems to have been a feeling of what one *should* do. President Truman felt the Soviet Union *should* honor their agreements, the Ambassador wondered if the United States *should* make a deal with barbarians, Stalin may have felt that the Americans *should* not press him on a country affecting Russian security, all the parties involved seem to have felt the others *should* pay more attention to their needs. It is these feelings of "shouldness" that are not captured within a game (though one *should* not cheat — go outside the rules of the game.)

In the chapter on decision making, we observed that emotional forces guide one's choices; that every rational act takes account of the emotions that would arise if a certain choice were made. In interpersonal behavior, one may also be concerned about the emotions he will provoke in others, and he will be affected by the emotion produced in himself. When a person makes a decision that violates the dictates of a "should-force," he experiences anxiety or guilt. When another person violates a "should-force," he may produce anger, hostility, or contempt in the wronged person.

Now, of course, we must separate the feelings which Stalin and Truman had for each other as persons, from their feelings as the chief decision makers of the Soviet Union and the United States. When Truman first met Stalin at Potsdam, on July 16, he writes,[20]

> I was impressed by him and talked to him straight from the shoulder. He looked us in the eye when he spoke, and I felt hopeful that we could reach an agreement that would be satisfactory to the world and to ourselves.

During the conference, the President appears to have maintained a friendly, detached attitude towards the Marshall and appreciated

---

[20]*Ibid.*, p. 341.

several examples of his wry humor. He did not, however, sympathize with the positions which Stalin took as the leader of the Soviet Union. Likewise, Stalin seems to have appreciated Truman as a person but found the American position not understandable. We cannot, therefore, say that the men were *personally* offended. On the other hand, they did not react with the detachment of two businessmen who impersonally conclude that some arrangement would not be mutually profitable. Both Stalin and Truman seem to have felt that the other *government* should behave differently. The best way to precisely conceptualize this sort of relationship is not clear. However, if we set this dilemma aside for future clarification, there are a number of interesting ideas that may be applicable.

A government may or may not care about the welfare of other nations. Karl Deutsch[21] has termed this factor "responsiveness." When one party is responsive to the other, it perceives the other's needs and responds to them by giving them adequate weight in its decision making. In the last chapter, we observed that there were men in the State Department whose jobs required them to represent the needs of the nation they were assigned to. Pruitt[22] has noted that these men are an important link in American responsiveness to other nations. Ultimately, the amount of American responsiveness to another nation depends on how that nation's needs fare in the internal bargaining process that determines American policy. The United States is likely to be more responsive to the needs of an ally that has strong connections with the American government.

Working in the area of interpersonal relations, Horwitz[23] has noted that a person feels that his desires *should* be accorded a certain amount of weight. If another person makes a decision without giving the first person's desires an adequate weight, then the first person will become hostile. In part, this is due to the fact that one's weight is an important long term consideration that will affect how one is treated in many future decisions. Hence, if one's weight is reduced — if the other ceases to be as responsive as one feels he should — one acts immediately to have weight restored. Since, when a person makes a decision, he gives weight to his own and the other's *desires,* in order to estimate the amount of weight one has received, one must make a judgment about the relative strength of these desires. If a person underestimates the strength

---

[21]Karl W. Deutsch, *et. al., Political Community and the North Atlantic Area* (Princeton, N.J.: Princeton University Press, 1957).
[22]Dean G. Pruitt, "An analysis of responsiveness between nations," *J. Conflict Resolution,* 6 (1962), pp. 5-18.
[23]M. Horwitz, D. J. Glass, S. Giniger, A. Cohn "Hostility and the obligation of openness as a function of interpersonal weight," Mimeographed paper.

of the decision maker's desires, he may believe that a decision adverse to his own desires indicates that the other has underweighted him.

How much weight does one expect to be given? Clearly, one important factor is how much power one possesses, while a second factor is the extent to which one is in a "unit" with the other. A member of the "in-group" — whether it be a family, a nation, or an alliance, feels that his desires deserve a greater consideration than the desires of parties who are not in the unit. Similarly, one's responsiveness is ordinarily increased if the other has the power to reward or punish one's choices and if the other shares membership in a unit.

There is a clear advantage in having the other be responsive, for in order to influence his decisions, one may simply need to communicate one's needs rather than make promises or threats. On the other hand, one will avoid being in a position where the other has all the power; in such a situation, only oneself will be responsive, and one may thus be in danger of being used. Because of the long range importance of responsiveness, if both parties are responsive, negotiations are much simpler. Either party can yield a point here or there, secure in the knowledge that this will be appreciated and ultimately returned.

We have been talking of responsiveness as a general set to attend to the other's needs. The motivation behind this set is important. If the person or nation is responsive simply because the other can influence what happens to him — simply for selfish reasons — then the other cannot rely on his concern continuing if the situation changes so that he is no longer dependent. Contrariwise, if the person or nation is responsive because of a genuine concern for the other's welfare — out of love—then the other can count on a stable concern that will not fluctuate with circumstances. We have seen how Stalin was concerned that once the war was over and the United States had no further use for Russia, its relations would cool off. Long range cooperation and the development of a unit depends on a sentiment of genuine concern for the other. Cooperative acts are most useful when they contribute to the development of the sentiment. Because of these considerations, Morton Deutsch[24] concludes his analysis of cooperation and trust by stating:

> We must each develop a genuine stake in the other's security and welfare, in the other's doing well rather than poorly, and we must promote cooperative endeavors which will foster the development of an interest in the other's successes rather than failures.

---

[24]Morton Deutsch, "Cooperation and trust: some theoretical notes," in Marshal R. Jones (ed.), *The 1962 Nebraska Symposium on Motivation* (Lincoln, Neb.: University of Nebraska Press, 1962), p. 316.

Now, returning to the interaction over Poland, we can note how some of the above factors may have been relevant. First, it is evident that each nation felt that it was powerful, that the other needed its help, and that it should accordingly be given a good deal of weight. Beginning with the latter part of 1943, the American government had begun negotiations with Russia on post-war aid to help Soviet reconstruction. The Americans appear to have been motivated by a generosity towards their allies, a belief that a good standard of living would increase their tolerance, and by a desire to insure Russian cooperation with internationalism. But Feis[25] notes:

> It was thought that Russia would find it very hard to manage after the war without the raw materials, chemicals, electrical and railway equipment that the United States could provide; and that the wish to secure these would induce it to want to keep American good will.

While, on the other hand,[26]

> Stalin and his associates, in accord with Marxist-Leninist doctrine, believed that when the war ended capitalist societies were going to run into a crisis of adjustment and great unemployment. Hence they thought that merely to save itself the United States would be eager to send the Soviet Union its products on almost any loan terms.

Since both governments were mistaken in their belief that the other nation needed them more, they both inflated the weight they felt they should receive.

Second, both nations seem to have underestimated the strength of the other's desires as to the nature of the Polish government. The United States, having never been invaded, and with different methods of securing friendship, could not really comprehend Russia's insistence on a puppet government in Poland. In spite of the fact that Russia had been invaded by Germany through Poland twice in thirty years and that the Polish government had been continually hostile towards the Soviet Union (albeit often with good reason), the Americans could only perceive the Russians as motivated by greed rather than a strong desire for security. The Soviet government, lacking the moral principles so essential in a democracy, could not understand how strongly the American and British people felt about a democratic Poland and could only perceive an unwarranted expansion of American power in the Russian sphere of influence.

---

[25]Feis, *op. cit.,* p. 645.
[26]*Ibid.,* p. 641.

As a result of the overinflation of the weight each government thought it should have and of the underestimation of the other government's desires, when the Americans decided to insist on representative government the Russians felt underweighted and when the Russians decided to unilaterally recognize the provisional government the American government felt underweighted. Both reacted by decreasing their responsiveness to each other's needs. This threatened the unit relation between the governments, and the decrease in trust hindered proposals for cooperative moves. In the course of a few years, the overall relation became one of hostility. The Soviet Union changed its policy of cooperation between separate spheres of influence to a competitive policy of expanding its influence wherever possible. The United States changed its policy of cooperating within a world unit to a policy of containing communism at almost any cost.

In choosing to emphasize that Stalin was not living up to the Yalta agreement rather than focusing on the type of deal Stalin desired, Truman maintained a continuity of American policy and protected Roosevelt's image, but he may well have somewhat maligned Stalin and hurt relations between the Soviet Union and the United States. It is possible that Stalin reneged on the Polish agreement because he saw that elections would go against him; but it seems more likely that he was never really committed to the American interpretation of the agreement in the first place. The Soviet position was clear at the beginning of the Yalta Conference, and Stalin seems to have reluctantly accepted the wording but not the meaning of the compromise agreement in order to pacify American and British public opinion and smooth relationships among the three governments. If Roosevelt believed he was getting a free commitment, he was probably incorrect. Actually, he probably realized that if he had insisted on a real commitment to a democratic Poland, the Russians would have pulled out of the alliance. Confronted with two unacceptable alternatives, he chose an unrealistic course of action in accepting a paper agreement without insisting on adequate compensation. The Soviet Union was quite capable of keeping agreements that were in accord with their notion of cooperation.

Now, of course, even if the interpretation of events presented in this chapter is correct, the United States might have decided against making the sort of deal the Soviet Union desired. Even though the United States could do nothing to prevent the Soviet domination of Poland, it could have protested that move as vigorously as was possible. Nevertheless, a correct perception of Russian motives and a real understanding of their desires would have made "coexistence" possible back in 1945.

In the long run, truth is always advantageous. If the American people had realized the terms of Soviet cooperation, they probably would have supported the Truman Doctrine and the Marshall Plan without having to view the Russians as diabolic enemies or generate the hysteria that produced McCarthyism. And when the economic recovery of the Soviet Union and its independent development of atomic weapons demonstrated that it did have power commensurate with the weight it demanded, the American government would have been free to develop the sort of limited cooperation which it is only beginning today. In the chapter on perception, we saw how the American Secretary of State's perception of the Soviet Union as diabolic prevented the development of controls on atomic arms in 1955. Relaxed coexistence with limited cooperation was possible years before it was obtained, and that time might have been well used. By failing to realize the Russian meaning of cooperation, by attributing bad intentions and feeling that the Russians *should* act differently, American leaders appear to have seen only two possible alternatives — a hostile enemy or a world partner — and American policy neglected other possible steps toward world order.

In the foregoing pages we have examined one example of an interaction between governments and noted a number of psychological features that were important. We must now consider negotiations in a more general way. While it will be necessary to introduce some new variables the reader will be able to note the presence of all the features we have examined up to now.

Negotiations

We have been concentrating on how the interactions between two national decision makers affected the relationship between their governments. However, it should also be clear that whatever relationship exists greatly affects the interaction between government representatives. If the relationship is a friendly one, officials within the executive will be attuned to the other nation's needs, the Congress will be responsive to aid requests, and a general atmosphere of trust will cause decision makers to cooperate with the other nation. If the relationship is unfriendly, officials will ignore the other nation's needs, the Congress may be hostile and the public threatened, and decision makers will look for ways to exploit the other nation's weaknesses. These effects become quite clear when we examine the impact which relationships have on negotiations.

The influence of different relationships

The dynamics of negotiations vary according to whether the other is perceived as an enemy, a competitor, or a friend.

To the extent that the other is an enemy, he will use the negotiations for subsidiary ends. That is, he may use them to stall for time, to gather information about what he can or cannot get away with, to deceive his opponent into believing that he is friendly, to create a propagandistic effect on the world at large, or to intimidate his opponent. At this level, the "negotiations" are not really negotiations but rather a form of warfare.

To the extent that the other is a competitor, he will use the negotiations to strike the best bargain he can. That is, he will try to get the other to agree to an outcome that is highly favorable for him. While he has no real concern for how much the other likes the outcome, and will take what he can get, the mere fact that he depends on the other's *agreement* forces him to be somewhat concerned with what the other likes. The other must at least find the outcome more satisfactory than no agreement at all.

Sawyer and Guetzkow[27] have summarized a number of maneuvers with which a negotiator can attempt to obtain a favorable agreement. One can attempt to persuade the other to agree by pointing out advantages he had overlooked, by threatening, or by mobilizing public support in favor of the agreement. One can jockey for a favorable bargaining position by arranging the agenda or a *fait accompli* so that a favorable alternative seems like the "natural" or "reasonable" solution to the bargaining. One can trick the other into thinking that one will not agree to anything less than a relatively favorable alternative.

Since the other party is engaged in the same sort of enterprise, the result depends on a kind of competition. Both sides will try to negotiate from strength — that is, from a position where only a relatively favorable agreement is better than no agreement. Such a position must be credible, causing each side to commit itself in such a way that unfavorable alternatives are clearly ruled out.

Since one's credibility will affect other negotiations at other times, it may be worthwhile to take a loss — to pay the price of lack of agreement in order to sustain one's reputation. Thus, a person or side that is willing to take some punishment has an advantage over a competitor who is unwilling to undergo sacrifices.

Experiments on bargaining by Siegel and Fouraker[28] show that opening the bargaining with high requests, making small concessions,

[27]Jack Sawyer and Harold Guetzkow, "Bargaining and negotiation in international relations," in Herbert C. Kelman (ed.), *International Behavior* (New York: Holt, Rinehart & Winston, Inc., 1965).
[28]Saul Siegel and L. E. Fouraker, Bargaining and Group Decision Making (New York: McGraw-Hill Book Company, 1960).

and having an intense desire and expectancy to win a good alternative tend to produce relatively favorable bargains.

Unfortunately, these competitive maneuvers detract from the negotiations as an attempt to find a common ground for agreement. As Sawyer and Guetzkow indicate, this aspect of negotiations involves the creative innovation of alternatives that may be more favorable to both parties than any of the obvious ones are. If the negotiators are busy maneuvering and building up strength and credibility, they may be too wary and exhausted to openly explore creative alternatives. In the last chapter, when we examined bargaining within the government, we observed that creative solutions cannot occur without an adequate understanding of the other's position — of what his values and needs really are. Thus, Siegel and Fouraker[29] demonstrate that when both bargainers have information about the pay-off matrix, they achieve a maximum joint pay-off more often. Similarly, Pilisuk and Rapoport[30] show that the number of cooperative responses in a non-zero-sum game are substantially greater when the players know the exact values within the pay-off matrix. Unfortunately, understanding how another person values certain alternatives requires open communication; and, as we have noted, this is not likely to occur when one is afraid that the other will use this information to gain a competitive advantage.

To the extent that the other is a friend (or partner), one can trust him and have the open communication that facilitates the search for creative alternatives. One is secure in the knowledge that the other has one's own interests as well as his own at heart. While this collaboration is not necessary in order for cooperation to occur, and while one may cooperate simply for one's own advantage, we have noted that a firm collaborative relationship provides the best reassurance that cooperation will continue if conditions change.

Clearly, whether one is in a hostile, a competitive, or a friendly relationship* makes a great deal of difference in how one will negotiate. If one would like to be a friend but thinks that the other may be an

---

*The distinction we have drawn between bargaining with the other as an enemy, a competitor, or a friend, seems parallel to Rapoport's distinction between a fight, a game, and a debate. *(Fights, Games and Debates,* op. cit.) He suggests that when a conflict is a fight, it is unreasoned and goes out of control in a Richardson process. A conflict that is a "game" — like the game of diplomacy, with war as one possible move — is kept under control by implicit agreements. Certain common interests or rules are recognized, within which the competition occurs. When a conflict is a debate, each side recognizes that it is worthwhile to try and understand each other's position so that a more valid position may eventually emerge.

[29]*Ibid.*

[30]M. Pilisuk and A. Rapoport, "A non-zero-sum game model of some disarmament problems," *Peace Research Society (International) Papers,* 1 (1964), pp. 57-78.

enemy or a competitor, one hardly knows how to act. While Fedder[31] has pointed out that one need not trust the other if the negotiations can produce an alternative that is advantageous to both parties; if one perceives the other as an enemy or an unscrupulous competitor, one's suspiciousness may prevent the finding of such an alternative.

There are certain basic factors that must exist in order for negotiations to ever occur. After an examination of the history of bargaining between unions and management, Diesing[32] listed four such factors:

1. The weaker side must be strong enough to be able to inflict damage on the other side. Otherwise, the other side will simply take what it wants.

2. Although each side will try to weaken the other's power, it must be understood that neither side will try to destroy the basic power resources of the other. That is, each side must demonstrate a respect for what is vital to the other side and accept the existence of the other side. This crucial factor is often missing when hostility exists and the other side is perceived as an enemy. We shall return to this difficulty in the next section.

3. It must be possible to find *some* goals and principles that can be shared. Diesing notes that each side usually tries to do this by urging its ideology on the other. Each supposes that its own principles are adequate for all purposes and, hence, that the only obstacle to cooperation is the failure of the other side to recognize the nature of reality. We have seen how this occurred in the bargaining between the Soviet Union and the United States. The former insisted that the recognition of three independent spheres of influence was the only realistic way to run the world, while the latter presumed that democratic internationalism furnished the only principle on which a stable world could be based. Diesing observes that in union-management relations the resulting contest in persuasion usually leads to disappointment and, finally, suspicion. The basic problem is that each side's principles and beliefs are actually inextricably bound with their own personal interests and are not really suitable for sharing. Likewise, in our examination of the relations between the Soviet Union and the United States, it was clear that national interests were interwoven with the ideology that was being advocated.

---

[31]Edwin H. Fedder, "Communication and American-Soviet negotiating behavior," *Background,* 8 (1964), pp. 105-120.
[32]Paul Diesing, "Bargaining strategy and union-management," *J. Conflict Resolution* 5 (1961), pp. 369-78.

Fortunately, it is usually possible to arrive at some shared values (such as procedural rules that give each side equal participation); standards that have an objective reference that limit exploitation (such as wages equal to the industrial average); and goals which both believe in (though often for different reasons).

4. There must be a certain amount of honesty. We have noted that open communications facilitate creative bargaining but can only occur when a friendly relationship exists. The amount of honesty that is useful depends on the type of bargaining relationship that exists, and this, in turn, depends on certain situational factors. These may be delineated as follows:

(a) If there is a sort of truce — a relation of power bargaining — then bluffing is useful. This sort of relationship is most likely when one side is in danger of losing cohesiveness and needs a fight to unify its members, or when a strong internal opposition forces the attainment of immediate results and downgrades the priority of long range cooperation.

(b) If a relationship of working harmony exists — each side wants a "fair" solution — enough honesty is required to establish what each side's true positions are.

(c) If there is enough opportunity for joint problem solving, this relation may develop into a relationship of genuine cooperation — where each side really cares about helping the other side. In that case, complete honesty is useful so that each side may help the other.

Problems created by cultural differences

While we have been speaking of the *general* dynamics governing negotiation, Nicolson[33] notes that variations in national character, tradition, and political objectives, produce quite different types of diplomacy. Some attempt to inspire fear, others confidence; some take "tricking" for granted, while others assume honesty. He observes:

All diplomatists (the professionals scarcely less than the amateurs) are inclined to assume that their own conception of the art of negotiation is shared more or less by those foreigners with whom they are negotiating. This fallacy leads to misunderstanding. It might be admitted, incidentally, that British statesmen are peculiarly prone to this illusion. They are so accustomed, in domestic controversies, to invoke the principle of fair dealing and to rely upon settlement by compromise, that they do not

---

[33]Harold Nicolson, *Diplomacy* (London: Oxford University Press, 1963) p. 128.

understand that such conceptions are not always present in the minds of foreign negotiators.

Nicolson suggests that serious problems may arise from assumptions of similarity. On finding that a foreign statesman does not behave "fairly," a British statesman (or American) may feel that a gross deception has been practiced on him. At the same time, unless his counterpart discovers the Englishman's principles, he interprets the Englishman's actions as deceitful. Certainly, our observations on some of the difficulties between Stalin and Truman lend generality to these points.

There have been a number of studies of negotiations between the United States and the Soviet Union. In the period immediately after the Second World War, most American negotiators were eager to establish good working relations with their Soviet counterparts. They perceived them as friends and were quite willing to compromise and work together in a partnership to build a new world order. They were stunned to discover that the Soviet Union did not have the same broad goals as the United States but wanted to work completely independently for a different sort of world.

As the cooperative relations between the nations declined, the Soviet representatives tended to become enemies and to use negotiations as a weapon — for propaganda, to gain time, to confuse issues, etc. — rather than as a device to reach areas of agreement. Furthermore, as Mosely[34] has described, the Russian negotiators were not familiar with Western politics, were not really free to negotiate very independently from their overworked central authority, and were unable to appreciate compromise as a working method. Incorrectly accused by the public of "not trying hard enough," the hurt and dismayed Americans regrouped, changed their attitudes towards the Soviet Union, and, of course, over-reacted to the opposite extreme of believing the Russians unwilling to sincerely negotiate anything. The scars of this sobering encounter are still with us today, in part because the realization of Soviet differences worked towards the selection of "tough minded" negotiators; and in part because of negotiators who "converted" to a belief in the intransigency of the Soviet Union — with all the rigidity that sometimes accompanies conversion.

Now that the dust has settled, a new and more reasoned consensus is beginning to form. It is clear that the Soviet Union is not the partner

---

[34]Mosely, Philip E. "Some Soviet techniques of negotiation," in R. Dennett and J.E. Johnson (eds.), *Negotiating with the Russians* Boston: World Peace Foundation, 1951).

that had been hoped for, but neither is it an intractable enemy. The Soviet Union does not want to be a junior partner; it wants to be a full grown competitor. While not as satisfactory as partners, competitors do have some common interests, and there are many fields where limited cooperation would be feasible. The problem is not unlike that presented by the non-zero-sum game. Both sides would like to win as much as they can; neither side wants to be taken advantage of; the facts of the situation dictate certain cooperative moves; and the pressures of the situation have thus far prevented adequate cooperation.

It should be clear that the Soviet Union is a competitor that has different interests than the United States. It is nonsensical for Americans to think the Soviet Union is going to cooperate with the United States to get what the United States wants (a strong United Nations, for instance, or world law). If the Soviet Union can use negotiations to win points for itself or to gain needed delays, etc., one should not be shocked when it does exactly that. On the other hand, it is just as un-thoughtful to fail to see that the Soviet Union and the United States have certain common interests, such as preventing nuclear war. In these areas of interest, the two nations should cooperate with each other. (Parenthetically, it should be observed that such cooperation might create other areas of common interest.)

There are pressures working against this cooperation in the same way that pressures work against useful cooperation in the non-zero-sum game. Nations should work against these self-defeating pressures, and we even have *some* knowledge about how to begin, since we know that certain ways of communicating are more effective than others. Unfortunately, in dealing with Soviet representatives, another set of problems arise because of differences in basic assumptions and in styles of thinking. That is, not only do Americans have to deal with a competitor rather than a partner, but both sides have to deal with competitors who are basically different in certain ways from themselves. Some of these differences have been described in a report by Wedge[35] in the course of his investigation into the problems of student exchanges in 1958.

Both governments believed (for completely different reasons) that student exchanges would be beneficial to them. After much negotiation, an agreement was reached to exchange twenty graduate students in 1958. In the Soviet Union, the citizen is subordinate to the State. Therefore, the Soviet government expected to choose the students it would

---

[35]Bryant Wedge, "A note on Soviet-American negotiation," *Proceedings of the Emergency Conference on Hostility, Aggression and War, 1961* (Washington, D. C.: American Association for Social Psychiatry, 1961).

send to represent its country, and to be able to reject students sent to it who had undesirable political views, etc. In the United States, the government represents its citizens. Therefore, the American government expected to send whatever students were best qualified and had the most need to go, and to request academic information so that it could place incoming students in the appropriate universities. The Soviet program was run through its Ministry of Higher Education, whereas the American program worked through an independent civil agency, the Inter-University Committee on Travel Grants. It was not long before serious problems began to arise.

The Soviet government rejected some of the American candidates because their study proposals were ideological unacceptable. While this may have struck some Americans as an amusing example of Soviet defensiveness, the Russians were not amused when, in the following year, eight Soviet candidates were rejected because they "were found either to lack educational qualifications or the minimum information needed to place them in American universities." The rejections were regarded as a slap at the Soviet government. (Note that it would not have been so regarded if the rejections had been for ideological reasons.) When the Americans kept sending students who had unacceptable study proposals (such as a plan to write the political biography of Mikhail Kathow, "a reactionary and odious figure in the history of our people"), tempers began to rise on both sides. This was not helped by a *New York Times* article charging that "Soviet authorities have dashed American hopes for an expanded exchange of graduate students." Once again, American hopes for fellowship were crushed.

In retrospect, it seems clear that the Soviet Ministry approached the exchange as a business between governments that could speak for their citizens, whereas the American Committee was trying to deal with individual problems and the requirements of private universities. Neither side could understand why the other could not operate in the way it did, unless it was for "political reasons." Thus, Wedge notes,[36]

> . . . when I spoke with responsible officials on each side in May, 1959, . . . each side felt the other was sabotaging the agreement and each was quite vigorously trying to impose its standards on the other. If the Soviets spoke of "forces in America . . . interested . . . in breaking (contacts in the field of education) and misinforming the American public," the Americans were insisting on a standard for "all universities everywhere." There could be no doubt, in speaking to these officials, of the perfect

---

[36]*Ibid.*, p. 3.

genuineness of their feelings, of their hurt disappointment and their anger. There could be no doubt of the sincere efforts of each side to make the program work, to be maximally accommodating to each other, and there could be no doubt that, sophisticated as they were and try as they might, each side believed that the other was being deliberately obstructionistic.

Wedge's examination[37] of the verbatim records of the first 160 sessions of the Conference of the Eighteen-Nation Committee on Disarmament (March, 1962-April, 1963) reveals further problems. The records were examined with the view of discovering Soviet assumptions, attitudes, and approaches. They revealed the following factors:

1. The sovereignty of the state is of the utmost concern. Wedge notes, "Hardly a session goes by in which Soviet sovereignty is not perceived as threatened or in which it needn't be asserted." The Soviet representatives also project this point of view on others and seem to believe that other States wish to assert their sovereignty at the expense of the Soviet Union. They are, therefore, extremely suspicious of American motives. Suggestions of subordinating any national authority to a world body such as the United Nations, meet with vehement objection.

2. This concern with self-determination seems to also be reflected in an unwillingness to accept any suggestion by the other side, even when there is no discernible difference in position: "If the United States representative suggests completing a task on Tuesday, the Soviet spokesman may insist on Monday." Occasionally, a representative will make an identical suggestion but will ignore the earlier mention of it. Likewise, once a position is taken, the Soviet representative cannot yield it. Yielding appears to represent a giving-in to the other's will. Similarly, there is an insistence on equality in all State issues — right down to equal speaking time, regardless of how much time might be needed.

3. The concern with sovereignty and protection of willpower seems to be related to the high value attached to secrecy. The Soviet government is almost obsessed with the idea that the United States wants to discover its secrets. It is as though a penetration of its secrecy would render the government vulnerable to American control. Wedge notes,[38]

---

[37]Bryant Wedge and Cyril Muromcew, *A View from the East: A Study of Psychological Factors in Soviet Disarmament Positions* (Princeton, N. J.: Institute for the Study of National Behavior, 1963).
[38]*Ibid.*, p. 24.

As we have scrutinized this record, we have been struck by the unreasoned quality of the expression of this concern, the regular reversion to the vocabulary of Communist vituperation when it is expounded, the failure to discuss means to obviate espionage risks in inspection procedures. It seems to us that these characteristic responses speak for an emotional basis for this anxiety . . . especially by comparison with other issues which may involve strategic or political considerations but which are subject to rational discussion even though there may be no concession of position.

As we read this material, we have the distinct impression that if we were dealing with a person with these characteristics, we would be dealing with a person who was desperately trying to assert himself; a person who was afraid of being overwhelmed by reasoning from the outside; afraid of having to give in to an argument which he believed to be basically false; afraid, in short, of losing his identity. Whether this reflects some facet of the Russian national character and/or is a result of their means of government, we cannot as yet say.

It may be objected that the Soviet representatives are not *really* concerned about the sovereignty of the State and worried about being tricked, not *emotionally* unwilling to accept suggestions, not *genuinely* concerned about giving in to the other's will; they are putting on a calculated act to confuse and harass the American representatives and obscure the fact that they do not really want disarmament or whatever else is talked about. This is certainly possible and, if it is true, then there is nothing we can do about it; it indicates that there are no common areas of interest on which cooperation could be based. But it does appear that there are areas of common interest, that the Soviet government is aware of them. What if they are revealing genuine emotional concerns, while the American negotiators — aware that these concerns are unwarranted — are responding as though they were being tricked by unscrupulous men? Might not the Russians think in turn that the American representatives were not negotiating in good faith?

Perhaps Soviet negotiators really are concerned about their national sovereignty — as well they might be, considering the extent of their control over other nations. If they really are afraid of being swallowed up by an alien capitalistic culture, how must they feel when Americans keep insisting on international supervision and moralistically asserting that the only way to have peace is through an effective world organization? If Wedge is correct, when America keeps trying to make the Soviet Union a *partner,* that government must feel as though a noose is being put about its neck. When it angrily throws off what it sees as a noose, Americans are hurt at their rejection of an embrace. If Soviet negotiators are really concerned about national sovereignty, how must they react when American negotiators talk about "freedom in the world" instead of American interests. They *must* react with suspicion to such talk; they cannot imagine that it could be sincere. Americans really believe that they have the only right and reasonable view of what the world should be like. Imagine how infuriating it must be to have to deal with such people, *particularly* if there might be something to what they say.

American negotiators have been telling their government that the Russians do not really want to negotiate. They view Russian intransigency as a calculated maneuver. Wedge's careful, objective analysis of Soviet negotiating behavior has suggested that the Russians have genuine fears that must be taken into account. This does not mean that American negotiators should give in to Soviet demands; it does mean that they should not react to them as false issues but should give them due consideration. Then, accommodation may become possible. To continue with our list of important differences between Soviet and American attitudes and assumptions:

4. Soviet negotiators have a style of thinking that is unlike their American counterparts. They approach problems from the most general and universal position. First, general principles must be agreed upon, *then* one proceeds to the particulars. This absolute, deductive way of thinking clashes with the pragmatic, legalistic approach of the Americans, which starts with a specific issue and ultimately expands into a general principle.

   For example, consider the Soviet reaction to empirical data that shows the existence of social classes in the Soviet Union: "Inasmuch as social classes are based on ownership of the means of production it is impossible to speak of social classes in the Soviet Union." In concurrence with this approach, the Soviet delegations usually have no instructions about details and, hence, cannot discuss them. The Soviet negotiators use this absolute approach to gain a bargaining advantage. They try to bribe and threaten their opponents to agree on principles so that negotiations can proceed.

5. The Soviet negotiators would rather *barter* than compromise. Compromising is a concept that is foreign to Russian culture. It cannot be a practical means of adjusting issues by partial concession, because, in their style of thinking, one starts with inviolable principles. There is only one right way to proceed. Deviation from

this is not "compromising"; it is yielding. Any concession is regarded as a sign of weakness, a falling under the opponent's influence. Furthermore, the Soviet negotiator works under instructions from Moscow. This, like his way of thinking, is not conducive to "making do." On the other hand, bartering — old Yankee horse trading — seems to be compatible. Bartering involves a direct exchange of tangible advantages that may be in widely different areas; hence, no compromise need be involved. The negotiation starts with lengthy generalities and finally, very cautiously, approaches some issues that may be tradable. Both seller and buyer are careful not to show interest in the item.

Wedge states that the Russian language lends itself to "this kind of vague and oblique exchange of ideas without making any unequivocal statements." This protects the negotiator from the humiliation of a direct rejection of a proposal. Once a price has been set, the technique is to repeat it endlessly in the hope of wearing the opponent down. Bluffing, threatening, and lying are considered legitimate facets of conducting a trade.

Wedge suggests that American negotiators should try to learn the Soviet style of thinking while they simultaneously continue to ask for the specifics which the pragmatic style requires. He also feels that it should be possible for Americans to barter as well as compromise. It would be interesting to set up a bargaining game or simulation in which these ideas could be tried out.

Regardless of whether Wedge is correct in the details of his interpretation, his central idea should be evaluated most seriously:[39]

> ... the limitations imposed by the Soviet pattern of thought and political perception are a very real obstacle and should not be considered as mere unwillingness to negotiate or an attempt to wreck attempts to reach an agreement. There are certain Western concepts which are truly beyond the Soviet conceptual scheme of reality. What they don't understand they are very suspicious of and condemn on principle. Also, being absolutistic in their reasoning, they refuse to acknowledge many basic Western social and political concepts and principles.

Thus, Wedge is urging both sides to stop attributing bad motives to one another and, instead, to view difficult behavior as a problem that is not under the other's deliberate control. He suggests that in order to keep conflicting positions from getting out of bounds, negotiators should

[39]*Ibid.*, p. 49.

review a negotiation at the close of every day, using a disinterested observer who could point out extraneous motivational issues.

The misinterpretation of motives

In many situations, the average bargainer or negotiator is apt to misinterpret the motives of the other. For example, Horwitz and Loomis[40] found that when industrial supervisors played a non-zero-sum game (with a matrix similar to that shown in Figure 3), each man seemed to believe that he cared about the other player, but the other was concerned only with his own selfish gains. Consequently, each played uncooperatively and obtained joint losses.

When pairs of subjects were asked to discuss their feelings with each other, they discovered that both had underestimated each other's concerns and failed to show their own concern in their moves. Subsequently, they behaved much more cooperatively; whereas pairs who had simply been instructed in cooperation and exhorted to do so, continued to defeat each other.

Horwitz postulates that, unless there is contrary information, a person tends to assume that a person who frustrates him is motivated by his own desires and does not care about him. Given an opportunity to exchange information about the reasons that actually motivated the actions and about the feelings which they generated, the parties will discover and increase concern for each other.

Horwitz points out that these tendencies are particularly true when the persons are representatives of competing groups. In the first place, a representative cannot be as flexible as an individual, because he is often representing a compromise within his own group that cannot be disturbed without reopening internal conflict. As a result, the representatives will frustrate each other for no apparently good reason and, hence, will appear rigid and selfish. In the second place, neither representative will divulge the reasons for his position, in part because information about conflicts within his own group is private and dangerous to give, in part because he finds it difficult to articulate the complicated bargains, likes and dislikes, etc., that produced the compromise position. In the last chapter, we saw how the American President and the British Prime Minister derived great benefit when they managed to exchange this sort of information at an informal meeting. This is not easily done when the other party is one's main competitor.

---

[40]Reported in Murray Horwitz, "Power, identification, nationalism, and international organizations," working paper for the Pittsburgh Seminar in the Social Science of Organizations, 1963.

When negotiators begin to perceive each other as lacking in consideration, they act to restore the consideration that is due them. They usually do this by becoming inflexible and maneuvering for power. Since they do not reveal their true concerns, they are perceived as even less considerate than before and, finally, negotiations cease because the other side is not "sincere."

The attribution of motives to another person or nation is an important determinant of how we will interact with him. A number of recent studies have shown that our judgments about another's motives depend not simply on his behavior but also on the context of the situation. In the chapter on perception, we noted how Strickland[41] demonstrated that a person who has to rely on a subordinate will develop more trust in the subordinate if he cannot keep him under surveillance. In order to develop trust in another person, there has to be some opportunity for him to let you down. If the situation happens to be one where a person is under constant surveillance, then, through no fault of his own, trust will not be developed.

We are often unaware of the ways in which a situation influences our judgment. Consider the following experiment by McGrath and Julian.[42] They worked with a number of experimentally created "negotiation" groups. Each group consisted of four men: a Catholic, a Southern Baptist, a Unitarian, and a "neutral" chairman. In order to be eligible for prize money the groups had to achieve unanimity on various Church-State issues such as whether or not the King James Bible should be used as a text in public schools. The issues were arranged so that at different times each of the religions members would find himself in a group where he had the minority position. (Thus, on the above issue a Southern Baptist would be a minority arguing for the use of the Bible.) The experimenters demonstrate that the person who happens to be in the minority position argues about twice as much as the other religious members of the group. A person in the minority position may, therefore, appear quite rigid and dogmatic.

Now, when the issue is very important and the negotiator represents a group dependent on his endeavors, he may be forced into a dogmatic position and the character of his ideology may appear rigid and unamenable to change. At the close of the second world war the Russians were often in a minority position that was opposed by the Americans and the British, and communism was a minority viewpoint.

---

[41]Lloyd H. Strickland, "Surveillance and trust," *J. Personality,* 26 (1958), pp. 200-215.

[42]Joseph E. McGrath and James W. Julian "Interactions process and task outcome in experimentally created negotiation groups," *J. Psychol. Studies,* 14 (1963), pp. 117-138.

It is quite possible that this situation accounted for part of the rigidity shown by the Soviet delegates. While rigidity may be self-defeating, it is hard for the party in a minority position to become aware of the forces playing upon him, and it would seem that those in the majority should do their best to make the minority as secure as possible. In the future, this point (and all the others) may have to be applied to China.

Strategies for Conflict

In the preceding pages, we have noted a number of psychological factors that influence conflict. Among these are: the differences between individual worlds and the lack of understanding of these differences; the fact that a person's behavior may be perceived to be a characteristic of him when actually it is influenced by the situation in which the person finds himself; and the fact that certain kinds of relationships permit the openness that leads to creative solutions to conflicts of interest. Knowing these factors, respecting the differences between individuals and peoples, and valuing the creative solution of conflicts, psychologists and other social scientists have advocated that certain strategies or approaches should be built into American foreign policy and that certain ideas should be kept in mind at all times. We may consider these approaches by focusing on three central ideas: changing the other, affecting one's own society, and managing conflict.

Changing the other

While another government may commit unfriendly acts because of conflicting interests, it sometimes occurs that a government is actively *hostile*. In these cases, the attacks are directed at what the other *is* rather than what it *does* or what it possesses. Kennan observes that this was true in the early days of the Soviet Communist regime. If the Americans performed some generous act, it was either viewed with suspicion or it was believed that the Americans *had* to do it out of some kind of economic necessity. As a result of this hostility, other governments reacted by excluding the Russians from conferences, refusing recognition, and encouraging actions which were offensive to the Soviet government. These acts of rejection contributed to the rise of Nazi Germany and to various pacts between the Soviet Union and Germany. Today, the Soviet Union is no longer hostile, but America is confronted with the growing power of a hostile Chinese government. How can one deal with such hostility? We may make several suggestions.

First, rather than viewing the hostility as a basic character trait in a government that must be destroyed, rejected, or excluded, view the hostility as a behavior that can be changed. Meet the hostility with firmness rather than counter-hostility. An attack on the other's ideology is essentially an act of counter-hostility that is performed because the government or people have seen the other's hostility as a character trait — caused by his ideology — rather than as a behavior which it can change. A nation's ideology is its most sensitive point. Wheeler[43] points out that ideologies are important in holding a nation together and that a people can tolerate having to give up national goals and behaviors more readily than abandoning the central national ideology. When Americans attack "communism" and try to change a nation's commitment to that ideology, they threaten the government more than if they attempt to change some specific institution or behavior.

The potential for change is increased by establishing as relaxed an atmosphere as is possible. The other nation can become open and have more respect for the individual, only if it is not threatened. Korten[44] has drawn a distinction between nations with low and high "goal structure". When there is low goal structure a people expect progress but have no specific terminal goals that should be met in a specified period of time. On the other hand, the stress of war, famine, or rapidly rising expectations creates demands for specific goals in short periods of time and sets a high goal structure. Korten postulates that when a low goal structure exists, governments will naturally move towards democracy with an emphasis on the goals of the individual citizen. When high goal structure exists, governments will move towards authoritarianism with the individual being important only insofar as he contributes to the all-consuming group goal. These shifts, from democracy to autocracy and vice-versa, are not smooth ones in perfect time with the situation. There is always a resistance to change, because of traditions and vested interests; and an autocratic leader may attempt to force a high goal structure in order to resist democratic tendencies. Nevertheless, in the long run the shifts will occur in the indicated manner.

Second, since threatening, negative behavior may increase the opponent's cohesiveness, justify his hostility, and decrease his perspective, it is necessary to focus on the rewarding of positive behavior. Milburn[45] has suggested that deterrence is effective only when one presents the opponent with acceptable alternative behaviors that can permit him

---

[43]Harvey Wheeler, "The role of myth systems in American-Soviet relations," *J. Conflict Resolution,* 4 (1960), pp. 179-84.

[44]David C. Korten, "Situational Determinants of leadership structure," *J. Conflict Resolution,* 6 (1961), pp. 222-35.

[45]Thomas W. Milburn, "What constitutes effective deterrence?" *J. Conflict Resolution,* 3 (1959), pp. 138-45.

to achieve functionally similar goals. His choice of these positive paths will then meet some of his own needs and can be rewarded by trade concessions, treaties, public applause, etc.

It should be observed that by firmly resisting negative behavior (but refusing to attack) and rewarding positive behavior (even when it increases the opponent's power), one has an effect not only on immediate decisions but also on long term policy and on who is in office. Within any nation, there are always different groups pressing for different policies, some more belligerent, some more cooperative. Which of these groups triumph depends largely on the reality of the situation confronting the nation. If the advocated policy can meet the objective situation, it survives; otherwise, it dies out and a new policy emerges with a different set of leaders.

Third, since attempts to directly control the opponent's policy may be resented even if they are positive and based on rewards, the most reliable way of changing another's behavior is by one's own behavior. If a nation does well internally, it may become a model which others will begin to follow. Since this may not occur if the other nation's problems are substantially different, it may be necessary to work with some third nation whose problems are similar but that can be encouraged to develop into a model which others can follow.

Effects on one's own society

Conflict with another nation can have beneficial effects internally. Sumner[46] has observed that long periods without conflicts create a stagnant society with vested interests and privileged classes that cannot be attacked; reform may only come about when it is forced by the efficiency required by a conflict. Thus, within the United States, programs for civil rights and mental and physical health have been helped immensely by the need for America to be competitive. It is also true that if a nation is open to change, it may learn something from the culture that is imposing on it.

However, unless conflict is handled properly, it may have a dangerous internal side effect; in their attempt to assert themselves, a nation and its people may lose their identity. This may occur whenever the means used to win a conflict creates internal change. Given democratic values, success is helping another people to become themselves without dominating them; failure is to lose one's own identity — and this may occur, without being physically dominated.

---

[46]William Graham Sumner, *War, and Other Essays* (New Haven: Yale University Press, 1911).

Identity is a complex concept that is bound up with the concepts of freedom and responsibility. Here we need merely note that it refers to what a person, a nation, or a people *is*. Most American citizens identify with their nation, which is a democracy. Part of their identity as a people is a belief in the worth of the individual. Americans feel proud when they perceive their nation to be acting correctly and ashamed when it fails to do so. If they do not have these feelings, then they are alienated from the nation or its government.

We may illustrate the dynamics of the internal changes accompanying conflict, by noting how the United States is currently in danger of losing some of its identity as a democracy, while its citizens are becoming alienated and losing some of their identity as a people.

The prolonged character of the "cold war" has led the authority of the central government to increase at the expense of the authority of the individual. The individual is subject to what is becoming a perpetual draft at the same time that the Congress is giving up its power to declare war. As we noted in the last chapter, the average citizen is committed to policies without his knowledge. When he can no longer influence the actions of his government, he is no longer responsible for these actions and the government is no longer a democracy. In fact the nation is becoming less of a democracy.

Since the average citizen still believes in democracy, he resents being separated from policy formation. The increased importance of foreign policy and the gap between the executive and the people, which we noted in the last chapter, has prevented the average citizen from influencing an important segment of governmental actions. This causes an increasing number of persons to feel ineffectual, and they are being alienated from the government.

As long as a government is in a position that necessitates threatening other nations with nuclear retaliation, it must maintain a certain gap between itself and the people in order to make its threat credible. No government is going to believe that a people will willingly expose itself to a nuclear attack. Only if the government can operate independently can it hint that it would be willing to have a nuclear war and, hence, secure a good bargaining position. Likewise, as long as a government must portray itself as inflexibly committed to certain policies, it exerts a force to stifle opposition to these policies on the grounds that such opposition encourages the opponent. This prevents a responsible opposition from forming. Because of these factors, it is in the best interests of a democracy to create a situation where it does not have to take these positions.

The identity of the German people was severely damaged by the policy of genocide. The identity of the American people is being changed by the nature of policies such as "massive retaliation" and "pacification of the countryside." Rapoport[47] has observed,

> The basic question in the strategist's mind is this: 'In a conflict how can I gain an advantage over him?" The critic cannot disregard the question, "If I gain an advantage over him, what sort of person will I become?" *

We have noted that part of the American identity is a belief in the worth of the individual. When one threatens to kill masses of civilians in a nuclear strike, this belief is weakened — even if the deaths are euphemistically called "population response".** When one begins an *offensive* against guerrilla forces in the countryside, one has to kill more civilians than guerillas. When one destroys crops, one creates a famine that kills the young and the old rather than the fighting man. When one reports the number of enemy killed rather than territory secured, one highlights these deaths as the objective. These actions downgrade the worth of the individual and begin to change the American identity.

A consideration of the above points will show that there is more than one way to lose a conflict with a hostile opponent. In order for the United States to defend against the possibility of a deleterious change, it is necessary to attempt to change the opponent rather than defeat him, to involve the citizenry in policy formation, and to work towards limiting the intensity of the conflict so that harmful policies are not invoked.

Unfortunately, we have often had the occasion to note factors that work against new policy. These same factors will work against any of the suggestions made in this book. Any such suggestions will probably be implemented only if they are adopted by some incoming administration. For this reason I believe we must develop the concern for improving foreign policy into a *political* concern. We must work to get organizational reforms and a more positive foreign policy built into political platforms. But now let us turn to examine problems in limiting the intensity of conflict.

---

[47]Anatol Rapoport, *Strategy and Conscience* (New York: Harper & Row, Publishers, 1964), p. 189.

*During the Cuban missile crisis, a number of decision makers argued for a surprise air strike against the missile sites. This movement was checked when a key member of the group said (in effect) "We are not that kind of country . . . sneak attack would betray our heritage and ideals." (Cf. A. M. Schlesinger, Jr., *A Thousand Days* (Boston: Houghton-Mifflin Company, 1965.)

**This delightful term was used to label the abscissa of a system's analysis graph. The ordinate was "megatonnage."

The Management of Conflict

We have noted that conflict between nations produces internal effects that may be beneficial or destructive. It also affects other nations. The current competition between the more developed nations has helped the progress of many underdeveloped areas by freeing them from colonialism and stimulating foreign aid. On the other hand, it has hurt areas that have become battlegrounds for the larger conflict and areas where internal instability has been encouraged by the flow of arms and the general lack of stability in the world. Conflict itself is not a bad thing; it is a fact of life that lies behind a good deal of progress. However, when it becomes too intense or widespread, it becomes very destructive. Therefore, the challenge is not to eradicate conflict but to discover how to manage it and keep it productive.

One sign that a conflict has gotten out of control is when it erupts into violence. In order to get a picture of the magnitude of the problem, we can simply count the number of acts of violence that occur in a given period of time. Richardson[48] has compiled such a list for the period between 1820 and 1945.

He decided that a good measure of the size of a conflict would be the number of persons killed in the fighting. This could range all the way from one — a murder — to about thirty million — the number killed in the Second World War. As the number of dead increases, we get inaccuracies in the count. For this reason, a better measure is the logarithm of the number of dead — an index of the magnitude of the conflict, similar to the magnitude of star brightness. His figures are given in Table 2.

Table 2. *Number of conflicts of varying magnitude between 1820 and 1945*

Magnitude Index	Range of Deaths	Number of Conflicts
7	3, 162, 278-31, 622, 777	2
6	316, 228-3, 162, 277	5
5	31, 623-316, 277	24
4	3, 163-31, 622	63
3	317-3, 162	188
2	33-316	?
1	4-32	?
0	1-3	6,000,000 (estimated)

[48]Lewis F. Richardson, *The Statistics of Deadly Quarrels* (Pittsburgh: Botwood Press, 1960).

The figures for magnitudes 7 through 4 (Table 2) are exact. A few conflicts of magnitude 3 were probably not discovered. Murder statistics are fairly good in most countries, and the estimate is probably reasonably accurate. (Murders per million population ranges from 0.3 in Denmark in 1911 to 610 in Chile in 1932). The gap in the table is in the range from 4 to 316 deaths. Richardson wryly notes that these riots and isolated disturbances are often too small to come to the attention of the historian, and since it is nobody's professional duty to take note of them, they are quickly forgotten. Ghandi once observed that most evil was not caused by cruelty but by indifference. The reader may examine his own "indifference" by attempting to name the five wars of magnitude 6 in Table 2. He should also try to name the two nations that fought the most wars in the period from 1820 to1945.*

If we ask about the distribution of wars in time, we discover that during some years no wars occur, while in others as many as four may begin. Defining a "war" as a conflict of magnitude 4 or greater, Richardson shows that his data follow a Poisson distribution.

A Poisson distribution is generated when there is a small probability of some chance event but a large number of chances. Thus, if one dumped a few raisins into some cookie dough and made a large number of cookies, the number of raisins in each cookie would follow a Poisson distribution. Richardson's finding leads us to infer that there is a small probability of war occurring at almost any given time. Richardson also shows that there are periods when this probability is larger or smaller than would be expected by chance, but that these variations do not follow any clear cut cyclical pattern. The probability of war shows no consistent increase or decrease over the last 432 years. While the magnitude of wars is increasing in modern times, it should be noted that this may be due to the increasing population.

In its desire to control conflict, a nation tends to fixate on its principal challenger and believe that if *it* could only be controlled, peace would be insured. Thus, during the Second World War, the United States focused its attention on how to control Germany and Japan. These plans were soon upset by the emergence of Russia as a rival. While focusing its attention on Russia, China began to emerge as a

---

*The wars are:
  Taiping Rebellion, 1851-64
  U.S. Civil War, 1861-65
  War in La Plata (Paraguay, Uruguay, Brazil, and Argentina), 1865-70
  First Chinese Communist War, 1927-36
  Spanish Civil War, 1936-39
The nations that have engaged in by far the most wars are Great Britain and France. Most of these wars were "colonial wars."

potential rival; and we may be assured that after the rivalry among China, Russia, and the United States, some new power will emerge as a challenger. Richardson has demonstrated this continuous upsurge. He divided the period from 1820 to 1945 into six consecutive blocks of twenty-one years and then noted which nations or groups were involved in the period's wars. For each block of twenty-one years, he counted the number of new belligerents who had not appeared in any previous block of time. It is difficult to believe, but the data clearly demonstrates that the number of these new belligerents does not decrease from block to block (about thirty per cent of the belligerents are always new-comers). Richardson[49] noted,

> ... the problem of keeping the peace is not merely to prevent future aggression by Germany and Japan, nor only to prevent aggression by any of the states at present established, nor even aggression by other dissatis-fied groups with names at present well known, because there is likely to arise a steady supply of new dissatisfactions, and of new groups organiz-ing those unrests; . . . aggression is so widespread that any scheme to prevent war by restraining any one named nation is not in accordance with the history of the interval AD 1820 to 1945.

In an attempt to discover factors that ameliorate conflict, Richardson examined a number of different variables. His statistics show that nations sharing a language or a religion have just as many wars as those with differences. On the other hand, having a common government does decrease the number of wars. Although fully forty-five per cent of the wars between 1820 and 1945 were civil wars, Richardson demonstrates that when one takes into account the physical opportunities for persons to fight,* there are significantly fewer civil wars than one would expect from the number of foreign wars. Furthermore, half of the civil wars occurred after less than twenty-four years of common government. Richardson shows that for each decade of common government, there is a decrease in the probability of an outbreak of civil war. In fact, the data fit a geometric progression with $r = .75$. That is, after each decade of common government, there is only seventy-five per cent as much chance of civil war as in the preceding decade. This finding seems to fit with our observation that persons who are placed in a game situation when there is a conflict of interest, find it easier to achieve a cooperative solution when they are in a common "unit."

The search for ways to manage conflict has given rise to a number of interesting suggestions. Some of these center about the promotion of

---

*The technique is an ingenious mapping procedure utilizing Euler's theorem and counting cells of equal population density within nations and across frontiers.
[49]*Ibid.*, pp. 171, 174.

cooperation between groups, others accept enmity and concentrate on innovations which may control its ill effects, still others focus on the necessity of maintaining communications between the groups in conflict. In the succeeding sections we shall examine each of these types of suggestion in turn.

Cooperation for shared goals

Levi[50] has noted that war occurs because it is an accepted institution, and it is accepted easily because there is no common loyalty to one community and no agreed-upon procedure for settling conflicts. On this shrinking globe, the need for larger political units seems quite apparent. Harvey,[51] in her description of one such larger community — the British Commonwealth — points out that the Commonwealth is not really a formal international organization but is largely knit together by tradition, responsiveness to each other's needs, and the principle of equality. She states that a community depends on a set of common beliefs. In the case of the Commonwealth, these common beliefs occurred because of similar histories and center about the common law as symbolized by the British Crown.

On the other hand, Angell[52], pointing to the diversity of institutions in the Western bloc of nations, argues that common beliefs are not essential for international unity. He states that if nations with different values begin to cooperate on tasks of mutual concern, they will gradually learn to trust one another so that more important joint undertakings can occur and a greater trust can be established.

There is one interesting field experiment that bears on this matter and demonstrates that when two separate "ingroups" cooperate to achieve a common "superordinate goal," they begin to lose their hostility towards each other and even begin to join together in a larger group. The "robbers' cave" experiment was performed by Sherif and his associates.[53] They took twenty-two boys, created conditions that led them to form two in-groups, brought these groups together in a way that created hostility, and then tried several methods of reducing this hostility and breaking down the in-group/out-group distinction. Let us consider this in detail.

---

[50]Werner Levi, "On the causes of war and the conditions of peace," *J. Conflict Resolution,* 4 (1960), pp. 411-20.

[51]Joan Heather Harvey, "The British Commonwealth: a pattern of cooperation," *International Conciliation,* 487 (1953), pp. 1-48.

[52]Robert C. Angell, "Defense of What?" *J. Conflict Resolution,* 6 (1962), pp. 116-24.

[53]Muzafer Sherif, O. J. Harvey, B. Jack White, William R. Hood, and Carolyn W. Sherif, *Intergroup Conflict and Cooperation: The Robbers' Cave Experiment* (Norman, Okla.: Institute of Group Relations, University of Oklahoma, 1961).

The subjects of the experiment were eleven-year-old boys, all from middle class established Protestant families, and all with satisfactory academic and social records. None of the boys were acquainted with each other before they were selected to go to a summer camp, which was well isolated from the outside world. The boys were divided into two equal groups and used different facilities so that they were isolated from each other for the first seven days of the experiment.

During these days, each group of boys did numerous things together that appealed to them and required cooperation — such as building campfires, playing ball, and swimming together. Under these conditions, they gradually formed themselves into two structured groups. That is, leaders emerged (who controlled their groups; suggestions were made to them, and their choices were accepted by the others), other roles developed (a deviant, a baseball captain, etc.), a status hierarchy and other stable attitudes formed (some boys were perceived as strong, others were not expected to do well, some boys' suggestions were listened to while others' were not). Each of these groups took on certain *different* standards and norms that determined "acceptable" behavior (to be tough, not to swear, to swim in the nude, etc.). Each developed different "group realities" (they agreed to call certain places by given names, they invented different games, they decided to install screens on their windows, they determined that certain places were better for swimming than other equally good places). It is interesting to note that the leaders developed by following and implementing this group reality as much as by suggesting it. Members who refused to comply were simply ignored. Finally, partly as the result of becoming aware of outsiders, each group was possessive ("our" field, "our" song), obtained names (the "Rattlers" and the "Eagles"), wanted to compete with the other group as soon as they learned of its presence, and increased its solidarity (helping everyone in the group learn to swim, electing a ball captain, and stabilizing the leadership hierarchy — on one occasion, in an *intra*-group ball game, a group member *held* the ball so that the leader could get home safely).

Certainly, these boys had established in-groups; and until a new boy had learned and accepted the group reality, he would have been "different" and not fully accepted. It is not clear to what extent these groups also felt superior to out-groupers. When the groups learned of each other's existence, a few of the lower and middle status boys made derogatory or possessive comments; but the major reaction was one of wanting to compete and to be the better group. As the investigators note, the boys all came from the same class and culture and had the security afforded by having adults around. These facts undoubtedly influenced their competitiveness, some of their norms — (such as taking turns), and perhaps even the fact that they became a structured in-group.

In order to insure a condition of inter-group hostility (rather than either cooperation or dominance), the experimenters created conditions under which each group would see the other as a competitor and a source of frustration. They note that in an earlier experiment, hostility did not develop if the source of the friction was attributed to the camp administration.

As we have noted, when the boys became aware of each other they were already inclined to challenge each other in baseball. The following day, the experimenters amplified this idea by suggesting a tournament with a whole series of competitions (baseball, tug of war, tent pitching, cabin inspections, etc.) and medals, pocket knives, and a trophy as a prize to the best group. Both groups were most interested in this proposal, and the "Rattlers" were especially enthusiastic. They improved the ball field and put their flag on top of the backstop. On the next day, the first contests were held. The baseball game was opened by an exchange of derogatory names and questionable sportsmanship and was narrowly won by the Rattlers. In the afternoon, a tug of war was also won by the Rattlers, who enthusiastically grouped around and then gave three cheers for the Eagles, their leader saying, "that shows that *we* are good sports." They then razzed the Eagles and went away.

The Eagles were thoroughly dejected and "stood around discussing how big the Rattlers were." Noticing their rivals' flag on the backstop, they took it down and burned it. This had a considerable effect on their morale, and hopes for ultimate victory returned.

On the next day, the Rattlers were furious, confronted the Eagles, and grabbed their flag. While they were doing this, the Eagles destroyed a second Rattler flag. Several fights broke out, and the staff stepped in to stop the physical encounters and to get the second baseball game going. This was won by the Eagles, who now became the jubilant good sports to the dejected Rattlers. The Eagles considered this victory due to a before-game prayer and the fact that they didn't cuss the way the Rattlers did. Their leader concluded that since "the Rattlers were such poor sports and such 'bad cursers,' the Eagles should not even talk to them any more." The Rattlers began blaming each other for the loss, and several of those criticized wrote letters to go home. The Rattler leader made a joke out of the affair and pulled the group together.

In the afternoon, the Eagles won the tug of war by adopting a strategy that wore out the over-confident Rattlers. After the event, the leader of the Eagles started to shake hands with the Rattlers but was told to "shut up" and called various names. The Rattler leader bought a suggestion for a night raid on the Eagle cabin and led a most successful attack on the sleeping Eagles. This recouped the Rattlers' spirits but, of course, provoked retaliation from the Eagles, who were now called "communists." The struggle continued with growing intensity, checked only by ministrations of the adult staff, during the three days of contests (which were manipulated so that they were finally won by the Eagles). After a day's cooling-off period, during which the groups were kept separated, the experimenters obtained several measures to demonstrate the extent of the in-group/out-group differentiation.

When the boys were asked to choose — from the entire camp — who they would like to have for friends, the Rattlers made ninety-four per cent of their choices from within their own group, while the Eagles made ninety-three per cent of their choices from within their group. When the boys were asked to characterize the two groups as to whether none, a few, some, most, or all of the group were: brave, tough, friendly, sneaky, smart alecs, stinkers — they characterized their own group favorably (one hundred per cent by the Rattlers and ninety-four per cent by the Eagles) and the other group unfavorably (fifty-three per cent by the Rattlers and seventy-seven per cent by the Eagles). When the boys were asked to estimate how well different boys did in a contest between the groups, they over-estimated the performance of in-group members in comparison with members of the out-group. Finally, and perhaps most decisively (though quantitative data was not obtained), the groups did not want to be near each other in any way for any reason.

A number of dynamics may be stressed:

First, the inter-group competition had an effect on the internal structure of each group. In the Eagles, the leader before the contest was replaced by a boy with better athletic ability who was more enthusiastic about the competition and pulled the group together to meet it. A friend of his rose from middle status to become his lieutenant, and the old leader fell to middle status because of his lack of support in the competition. In the Rattlers, the leadership was maintained because the leader — with only mediocre athletic ability — threw himself completely into the competition and maintained control of decisions. A middle status boy who was viewed as a slacker was scapegoated and fell to low status.

Second, it is clear that when a group felt discouraged, its morale and solidarity were maintained by action taken against the other group.

Third, this action was supported by the development of stereotypes. Members of the in-group were portrayed as heroic, while actions by the out-group were seen negatively. Both groups viewed themselves as good sports, and the others as poor sports; themselves as "resourceful," the others as "unfair."

While Sherif and his associates demonstrate that the two groups of boys developed negative stereotypes of each other, it is not clear that the groups really began to think of each other as "different," rather than simply "poorer" members of the same class. That is, there is no evidence that the boys ever ceased to apply the same standards to the other group; the Eagles believed that they were better than the Rattlers because they did not curse so much, but they seemed to have felt that the Rattlers *ought not* to — that they had the capacity to do better. Similarly, there is no evidence that either group began to deny the other's basic rights as persons. The experimenters produced hostility and stereotyping rather than inhumanity.

Having achieved a degree of inter-group hostility, the investigators proceeded to try to reduce the conflict and unite the groups. They rejected utilizing a common enemy (successful in earlier studies) or trying to emphasize individualism within the groups, because both of these approaches have quite limited utility. Instead, they decided to attempt utilizing goals that had appeal to both groups and would necessitate their working together.

First, the experimenters established that simply bringing the groups together so that they had an opportunity for contact, did not reduce the hostility. On seven separate occasions, the groups were brought together to eat, see movies, shoot fireworks, etc. They stayed in their separate units (sitting together, etc.) and simply used the occasions to interchange hostile remarks or throw food at each other. However, it should not be concluded that "contact between equals" is always ineffective. It is shown to be ineffectual in reducing hostility between groups that are equals. It may be effective in reducing inhumanity in some group that considers itself superior to some "inferior" group.

After the failure of simply providing opportunities for contact, the experimenters introduced a number of "superordinate" goals. The first of these was created by sabotaging the camp's water supply. The two groups of boys were thus placed in a position of having to work together to find out what was wrong. In trying to fix a plugged valve, the boys cooperated well together. But after another aspect of the work was completed, there were contradictory claims as to who had discovered the trouble. That night, the groups began to throw things at each other in a good-natured way, but this began to develop into a fight and had to be stopped.

On succeeding days, the experimenters introduced other goals that required cooperation — the purchase of a movie, pulling one of the camp's trucks that had "broken down," separating intermixed camping equipment, and so on. After each of these successful cooperative endeavors, the inter-group tensions gradually abated. This was soon evidenced by the lessening of derogatory name calling and, finally, by the crossing of group lines to eat with each other. During this period, inter-group relations were in a state of flux, with some individual members still expressing hostility and with group lines reappearing sharply in some situations.

Good relations were finally cemented when the Rattlers generously allowed the Eagles to use their truck and, later, used some prize money to buy drinks for everyone. After six days of common goals, the boys were again asked to choose friends and to rate each other on bravery, sneakiness, etc. The percentage of out-group friend choices rose from six to thirty-six in the Rattlers and from seven to twenty-three in the Eagles. Stereotyping also slackened. Though favorable characteristics were still attributed to the in-group (there was a slight contraction of five percentage points for the Rattlers and seven for the Eagles), the out-group was now unfavorably described in only four per cent of the Rattler ratings and twenty-three of the Eagle ratings—as contrasted with fifty-three and seventy-seven, respectively, in the previous questioning.

It must be noted that the dynamics of this tension reduction were clearly influenced by the behavior of the groups' leaders. The Rattler leader often played an important role in starting cooperative activity — sometimes simply *beginning* the activity when discussions had bogged down. On the other hand, the leader of the Eagles, who had first come to power as a result of his leadership during the competition, noticeably dragged his feet.

In planning the experiment, the investigators rejected the idea of working only with the groups' leaders. They reasoned that since a leader is often the prisoner of his group's desires, they could make their point more effectively by manipulating super-ordinate goals for the entire group. Unfortunately, however, this limits the application of their finding to situations where one is in the position of being able to manipulate group goals. As McNeil[54] has pointed out, the boys were not allowed the freedom to purposively strive to reduce hostility. On the other hand, since there was an adult staff present, it is quite possible that the boys sensed what the adults wanted them to do and were guided by these implicit hopes and expectations.

It is not clear to what extent the results of the "Robbers' Cave Experiment" can be generalized to international relations. While each group of boys developed somewhat of a "culture" of its own, there were

---

[54] Elton B. McNeil, "Waging experimental war! a review," *J. Conflict Resolution,* 6 (1962), pp. 77-81.

few important differences between these cultures because of the boys' similar backgrounds. Nations are likely to have quite different cultures, and we have seen how such cultural differences interfered with the American-Soviet unit that was built up by the cooperation during the Second World War. Still, it would seem that the basic demonstration — that barriers between groups can best be broken down by means of common work towards shared goals — may well be applicable to nations.

It has been observed[55] that attempts at European integration failed as long as they were structured in terms of global ideals and politics. It was simply impossible to get enough consensus and enough willingness to give up national power. The Schuman plan for a coal and steel community had the advantage of being a concrete plan to accomplish a definite task. On this simple base, the greater integration involved in the European Common Market could be built, and this in turn may eventually provide a basis for greater political integration. Whereas it took six years to ratify the treaty setting up the coal and steel community, its successful operation led to a ratification of the Common Market treaty in only three years. Integration is thus quietly being achieved, not by appealing to ideals or making sweeping declarations but by gradually resolving competitive interests in the process of successfully meeting practical economic needs.

In the interest of meeting concrete needs, the administrative organ of the coal and steel community was given various concrete supra-national powers: to abolish tariffs, quotas, and supports; to discontinue monopolies and cartels; to provide housing and retraining programs for workers; to supervise migration and production methods; to promote better transportation; and to impose a tax. The governments involved had a tacit agreement to let the community's administration work without hindrance. A court was established to judge complaints made against the community's authority, and this freed the authority to extend its regulatory power firmly. The court tested whether or not the administration was within the limits granted to it by the treaty. Actually, the loss of national sovereignty turned out to be less than was anticipated, and the benefits that have resulted may make the coal and steel community a model for further attempts at international integration.

While the United Nations has not approached the effective integration of the European Common Market, it has achieved many significant cross-national projects through the operation of its Secretariat and may

---

[55]Jan J. Schokking and Nels Anderson, "Observations on the European integrating process," *J. Conflict Resolution*, 4 (1960), pp. 385-410.

be laying the groundwork for cooperation in the future. Alger[56,57] has pointed out that while public attention is focused on formal assembly votes, the greatest impact of the United Nations may be on the attitudes of its participants. For example, the 1,400 national officials who are in the General Assembly spend most òf their time in committee work where there is continuous interaction between the various delegates. This interaction is more "parliamentary" than "diplomatic"; that is, the delegates have more contact with each other, communicate much more frequently, pay less attention to rank and protocol, and talk informally about possible bargains and compromises. Perhaps most important, they are much more likely to have contacts with diplomats from unfriendly countries. In the press of working together on a committee, of having to chair a meeting fairly and meet professional standards, the delegates learn to understand and appreciate the positions of unfriendly governments. They must deal with information that dispels stereotypes and oversimplified and exaggerated beliefs. Friendships are developed, and lines of communication are opened. Countries that are on the same side in one committee will be on opposite sides in another committee. Because of these events, tension reducing communication occurs, extremist tendencies and commitments are prevented, and the possibility of cooperation is enhanced. Alger suggests that if we paid more attention to these consequences of the United Nations, we might be able to promote small procedural changes that would have even more beneficial effects.

Some of the most promising avenues for development have been sketched by Jackson.[58] He suggests, for example, that the United Nations begin to develop its own source of independent funds by instigating international canal taxes and that the United States consider making its chief delegate a cabinet member rather than an ambassador.

There are also several opportunities for international collaboration. In his discussion of the Antarctic Treaty, Taubenfeld[59] shows how the International Geophysical Year provided an impetus for internationalizing the Antarctic — a development that was resisted by Argentina and Chile but agreed to by the United States and the Soviet Union. He points out that it is far easier to bar weapons from a new area than to remove them from existing defense systems, that an international administration

[56]Chadwick R. Alger, "Non-resolution consequences of the United Nations and their effect on international conflict," *J. Conflict Resolution,* 5 (1964), pp. 128-45.

[57]Chadwick F. Alger, "Face-to-face relations in international organization," paper delivered at the American Orothopsychiatric Association Meeting, March 6-9, 1963).

[58]Elmore Jackson, "The future development of the United Nations: some suggestions for research," *J. Conflict Resolution,* 5 (1961), pp. 119-27.

[59]Howard J. Taubenfeld, "A Treaty for Antarctica," *International Counciliation,* 531 (1961), pp. 245-322.

should be developed, and that the entire venture sets an interesting model for the control of outer space. Yet another cooperative endeavor could be focused around the collection of international social data such as the data on wars we considered in this chapter or the kind necessary for the cross-cultural research suggested by Campbell and LeVine.[60]

Cooperation towards common goals helps the control of conflict by containing it within a single unit. A related approach is to control conflicts by a set of agreed-upon rules. This approach is illustrated by the endeavor to promote international law. While law may be used to settle certain conflicts, it may also be used to set limits within which a conflict can be contained. Strikes, business competition, elections, and most contests of power within a society, take place within the frameworks of law. If a nation, such as the United States, would agree to adhere to international law, it would help prevent miscalculation as to what actions might be taken and thus would help keep wars limited.

Persons often criticize the idea of international law because there is no body to enforce that law. Actually, enforcement is not as crucial as confidence. Parties can *agree* to be bound by the decision of a court in order to have an orderly way to contain conflict. If the parties keep their agreement, their trust in each other and their confidence in the law is sustained. Confidence in the law (and, hence, its power) grows when it is used. There is a substantial number of nations that would like to enter upon an agreement with the United States whereby cases would be submitted to an international court. Unfortunately, the Connally Amendment prevents the American government from agreeing to submit all cases. It essentially reserves the right for the government to decide whether or not each given case will be submitted. Needless to say, this prevents the growth of international law.

Unfortunately, there has been little psychological research in this important area. Investigations are needed on such factors as impartiality, confidence, and compliance. In this regard, it should be noted that Pruitt[61] has published a list of hypotheses as to when nations are more likely to comply with international law.

Strategic innovations and simulations

Conflict can get out of control in many different ways. The First World War developed out of a spiral of threats and counter-threats.

---

[60]Donald T. Campbell and Robert A. LeVine, "A proposal for cross-cultural research on ethnocentrism," *J. Conflict Resolution,* 5 (1961), pp. 82-108.

[61]Dean G. Pruitt, "Foreign policy decisions, threats and compliance to international law, *"Proc. Amer. Soc. Internat. Law* (1964), pp. 54-60.

Everyone was "firm" and expected someone else to back down. When nobody did, a war resulted which no nation really wanted. On the other hand, the Second World War developed when a failure to be "firm" permitted an aggressive leader to manipulate the desire for reconciliation.

The desire to avoid being caught in either a threat spiral or a manipulation, has led to a number of strategic innovations that attempt to meet the obvious objections to either appeasement or rigidity. We shall consider two of these: increasing the capacity to delay a retaliatory response, and initiating a "graduated reciprocal tension-reduction"

Since both of these innovations have been tried in inter-nation simulations, we shall pause for a moment to describe what this simulation process is like.

In simulations, an attempt is made to build a situation that will mimic the real world in all its crucial aspects. Of course, what aspects are crucial vary with the problem one is interested in, and there is always a danger that the model will fail to incorporate an important aspect of reality; but one can only learn by trying. In the inter-nation-simulation technique developed by Guetzkow and his associates,[62] there are usually from five to seven "nations." Each nation is represented by a team of decision makers. Typically, there may be a central decision maker who corresponds to a President or Prime Minister, a decision maker for internal affaris who reflects the pressures of the nation's own internal interests as would Secretaries of the Interior, Labor, etc., and an aspiring decision maker who would like to replace the central decision maker in his role of leadership. There may also be an external decision maker for force who corresponds to a Secretary of Defense or War Minister.

This miniature world of nations is carefully structured to conform to some interesting international situation. In the simulations run to date, the world has been structured as a bi-polar rather than a balance of power world.[63] That is, there have been two major nations, each with a cluster of smaller allies. The participants are given a brief history of the world (usually a history of conflict) and know that they are about to add a page to this history, which may then become the starting point for some future teams of decision makers.

---

[62]Harold Guetzkow, Chadwick F. Alger, Richard A. Brody, Robert C. Noel, and Richard C. Snyder, *Simulation in International Relations* (Englewood Cliffs, N.J.: Prentice-Hall, Inc., 1963).

[63]Cf. Norman Kaplan, "Balance of power, bipolarity and other models of international systems, "*Amer. Pol. Sci. Rev.,* 51 (1957), pp. 684-95.

Each nation begins the simulation with a designated amount of natural resources, industries, workers, and so forth. These amounts are represented as numbers (from seven thousand to forty thousand) of "Basic Capability Units." Each nation also has growth rates that determine the development of future capability units, and varying amounts of armed forces (both conventional and nuclear, in the case of the two major powers). The central decision maker may decide to invest his basic capability units in research and development, in the direct production of more basic capability units, in building up his armed forces, or in units of consumer satisfaction. He must be careful in his decisions, because if he distributes the nation's basic capability unwisely, he will be replaced by the aspiring central decision maker. Whether this replacement occurs is determined for each nation by an elaborate system of "validator satisfaction" indexes that are kept up to date by a research staff. If consumer satisfaction drops or if the nation begins to lose too much military power relative to the other nations, then the validator indices drop and there is a higher probability of the office holder being displaced by an orderly turnover in government or by a revolution. While the *probability* of turnover is set by the validator indices, whether a turnover actually occurs is determined by die throws. Some attempt is made to reflect different types of governments by allowing some central decision makers more latitude in their decision making.

The "nations" can behave towards each other in any way which real nations can. They may fight, trade, call conferences, form new alliances, give aid, release propaganda, and just about everything else. A world newspaper is regularly put out by the simulation's staff and provides a vehicle for general communication, news leaks, and so forth. In most of the simulations to date, some of the "nations" have also belonged to an international organization — an equivalent of the U.N. — and have faced the problem of new admissions and the possible changes in voting strength that might result. Usually, the participants spend two days becoming thoroughly acquainted with all of the variables of the "world" and trying a few trial runs. Then the simulation proper begins and lasts for two or three days.

Returning now to our strategic innovations, we shall first consider increasing the capacity to delay a retaliatory response.

If one's competitor makes a threatening move and one is afraid of being manipulated but unwilling to react quickly (because of the possibility that one is mistaken and will simply cause a threat spiral), there is a clear advantage in being able to delay one's retaliatory response until one is sure of the situation. More specifically, it has been argued that if a large segment of a nation's nuclear forces could be made invulnerable, the nation would be less likely to become involved in an accidental war. For instance, it would not have to quickly respond to an alarm of an impending nuclear attack but could afford to delay its response until it was sure it had been attacked and by whom. Furthermore, since an opponent would know that a preemptive attack could not possibly succeed in destroying that nation's retaliatory capacity, it would not be likely to try a preemptive attack. While no system is completely invulnerable to attack, hardened missile bases and polaris submarines are relatively invulnerable and, hence, help the nation have a "capacity to delay response." Though the above arguments sound completely valid, it was felt that an empirical test would be desirable.

Consequently, Raser and Crow[64] used the inter-nation simulation technique to see what would happen. They used twelve five-nation worlds. In six of these worlds, the two nuclear powers began without invulnerability. One-quarter of the way through the simulation, one of these nations gained invulnerability for its nuclear forces (the experimenters introduced this by having the nation's research program pay off in this way) and kept this invulnerability until the last half of the simulation (when a research program of the other nation turned up a way to break through the supposedly invulnerable defense). In the other six worlds, one of the nuclear powers began with invulnerability, lost it for a while, and then regained it. It should be noted that in all cases, the invulnerability referred only to the nation's nuclear forces and not to the rest of the nation.

Six of the twelve worlds enjoyed peace throughout the two-day simulation, three worlds had one small scale war each, and three worlds were marked by almost continuous fighting. The capacity to delay response, as indicated by an analysis of the data, did seem to help prevent some potential accidental wars. On the other hand, it seems to have increased the number of intentional wars! This unexpected result occurred because some of the decision makers viewed the invulnerability of their nuclear force as giving them the power to attempt to dominate other nations by threats, and, of course, this tended to lead to wars.

In retrospect, it seems unfortunate that the experimenters decided to alternate periods of nuclear invulnerability and vulnerability rather than simply having half the worlds characterized by nuclear vulnerability and half by invulnerability. Unfortunate, because it seems as though the participants were affected by their previous states of vulnerability and

[64]John R. Raser and Wayman J. Crown. *An Inter-Nation Simulation Study of Deterrence Postures Embodying Capacity to Delay Response* (La Jolla, Calif.: Western Behavioral Science Institute, 1964).

invulnerability, and it is difficult to be sure just what caused what. In the future, it would be desirable to run some "worlds" in which both nuclear nations have invulnerable nuclear capabilities. Until these worlds are run, it is only possible to say that the capacity to delay response does not automatically lessen the probability of war, because of the danger that the power it confers may be used in an attempt to dominate others.

Let us now turn to a second possible technique. If one believes that his nation is caught in a threat spiral but one is unwilling to be conciliatory because of the danger of possibly appeasing a manipulator, there is a clear advantage in being able to gradually reduce tensions without taking inordinate risks. Charles Osgood[65] has evolved a method for doing precisely this. He points out that when a system is under tension — once threats have begun to spiral — it is very difficult to decrease the tensions by negotiation or verbal reassurance, because neither side trusts the other. Hence, there is need for one side to take the initiative in creating an atmosphere of trust in which threats can be removed. This can most easily be done by unilaterally initiating a series of actions that will be to the advantage of the other side.

The *way* in which these actions are initiated is extremely important. If a nation simply acts in a nice way, it is likely to be misinterpreted. Thus, in the chapter on perception, we observed that when, in 1955, the new Soviet leadership reduced the size of their army, moved out of Austria, promoted better relations with Finland, and engaged in a number of other tension reducing acts, they were perceived as *weak* rather than *nice*. Osgood states a number of guidelines to prevent this and other misperceptions:

1. Each unilaterally initiated act should be announced publicly before its execution.
2. Each act should be a part of a series of actions that are identified as part of a deliberate policy to reduce tension.
3. After each act, there should be an explicit invitation for the other side to reciprocate with some act of its own.
4. The entire series of acts must be executed whether or not the other reciprocates; but the magnitude of the acts should increase if there is reciprocation, decrease if there is not.
5. The series should be continued even if the other attempts an aggressive move in some other area. However, any such attempt must be met with firm resistance.

---

[65]Charles Osgood, *An Alternative to War or Surrender* (Urbana, Ill.: University of Illinois Press, 1962).

6. Each act should be non-ambiguous and verifiable.
7. The acts should be planned so as to take advantage of mutual interests and opportunities for cooperative enterprises.

If the other nation is manipulating, the series of actions will fail; but this information on the state of the relationship will be purchased at a low cost, because the actions can be spread apart, incurring little risk to security. To the extent that the other nation was participating in a threat cycle, the series of actions will reduce tensions by creating an increment of trust and promoting the credibility of friendship rather than hostility. Note that there is no danger of appeasement; aggression is met with firmness, and the unilateral acts are not concessions to get the other side to stop negative actions. Nor is the series of actions a manipulation that tries to directly control the other's actions by rewards after each of his positive actions. Rather, the series of acts is taken independently of the other side in order to create trust, and the other side is *asked* to reciprocate, enabling one to progress to actions of a larger magnitude. One sometimes hears the Osgood proposal dismissed as "being nice in the hope that the other will be nice back." This misses two points: First, such a hope is quite reasonable if one is caught in a threat spiral where both sides have begun to distort each other's intentions. Second, the *how* of being nice is quite specific — it is a *graduated* plan calling for *reciprocation in tension reduction* (GRIT) — and is quite precise about the conditions in which it will be effective and the way in which it must be initiated.

Crow and Solomon[66] have given the GRIT proposal a preliminary test in an inter-nation simulation. They set up a bi-polarized "world" of five nations. The "world" had two major powers — "Omne" and "Utro" — and their respective alliance systems — Omne with "Erga" and Utro with "Algo" and "Ingo." The world had a "history" of previous war between Omne and Utro and continued hostility with Omne and Erga resisting Utro's attempt to get Ingo into a world organization. During the first day of the simulation, tension gradually mounted because of Omne's defense of the status quo, discriminatory aid and trade patterns, and a gradual world wide arms build-up. When a research program suddenly paid off for Omne and she granted Erga a substantial amount of military aid, tension reached a peak; Utro and her allies were quite challenged, perceived Omne as the world's villain, and determined to "restore the balance of power."

At this point in the simulation, the experimenters instructed Omne's leader to begin the GRIT strategy. His announcement of a "march

---

[66]Wayman J. Crow and Solomon N. Lawrence, *A Simulation Study of Strategic Doctrines* (La Jolla, Calif.: Western Behavioral Sciences Institute, 1962).

towards peace" and the initial unilateral actions were received with extreme suspicion by Utro and her allies.

When a Utro research program paid off, she launched a massive nuclear build-up to "catch up" and took advantage of a diplomatic error by Erga to seat Ingo in the world organization. In accordance with GRIT strategy, Omne resisted this move by boycotting the world organization while at the same time continuing small friendly acts. One of these acts — a contribution to the world organization's development fund (which helped *all* of the smaller nations without discrimination) —began to create trust, and Utro's allies began to place pressure on her to follow Omne's lead. When Omne announced a curtailment in arms production, Erga objected, and there was some internal unrest; but these problems were satisfactorily met by using the money saved from arms to build up consumer satisfaction. Utro's leader was finally convinced of Omne's good will by the statistics on their arms curtailment. Under some pressure from world opinion, in the closing period of the simulation, Utro responded by announcing that she would "try out" a cessation in her arms build-up.

One successful simulation does not establish the worth of a strategic method. But it would certainly appear that the GRIT strategy is worthy of being tested in the field. Of course, there may be problems with biased perceptions of what are equitable reciprocations. The major practical problem may be to determine those situations in which GRIT is applicable — that is, those situations in which the nations are caught in a threat spiral. It may well be that neither threat spirals nor manipulations exist very frequently. The average conflict between nations may be a competitive power struggle in which winning is more important than reducing tensions. This is the case, for example, in the current Viet Nam conflict. In these situations, however, the very fact that the GRIT strategy is available but is not being used, serves to remind us that the struggle is a competition in which both nations are equally implicated. If there is a desire to reduce tension and there is any doubt how much of the tension is created by mutual fear, then the GRIT strategy should be applied.

Let us examine yet another suggestion for controlling conflict. When nations are in a competitive relationship, they tend to gird themselves for the ensuing fight by perceiving only those aspects of the conflict that will help their own cause. Diesing[67] notes that these distorted perceptions begin to create secondary conflicts that are not really necessary and hinder effective bargaining. When relations are strained, there is a tendency for every small conflict to be viewed in the context of the

---

[67]Diesing, *op. cit.*

larger basic conflict between the two sides. This almost inevitably prevents the solution of small conflicts, and this leads to the exacerbation of the main conflict. In this way, the conflict gets out of bounds and has unfortunate consequences.

In order to maintain control over conflict, Fischer[68] has proposed that subsidiary conflicts that arise should be "fractionated," that is, split off from the central core of contention and treated as separate matters, each in its own right. He points out several ways in which a conflict can be fractionated or enlarged. For example, the parties to a dispute can be defined in a small or large way. If a Polish fishing vessel damages a transatlantic cable, the party in the ensuing dispute can be the ship's captain, or the department of fisheries, or the Polish government, or the Soviet government, or the communists in general. If a Soviet editor criticizes the New York stock exchange, it can be reported as such or as "Soviet Union attacks West." Likewise, the size of the dispute can be scaled up or down. The stopping of a truck going to Berlin can be treated as such or can expand into the issue of the reunification of Germany. Similarly, the precedent that is set by an action can be limited by specifying the situations under which the action is permissible. Fischer points out that concessions do not lead to more concessions unless they produce accommodation. A poor concession such as Munich did not lead to further concession; rather, it strengthened the will of the British people so that they declared war when Hitler invaded Poland. The United States may define recognizing a government as an act that signifies approval of that government, or as an act that simply signifies that the government has, for the moment, control of the country.

When conflicts are fractionated so that they are not enlarged to become nation-to-nation or ideological conflicts, it is much easier to recognize what common interests exist. Fischer argues that the expansion of conflict or the escalation of an issue is basically a defensive tactic that is useless offensively. Thus, arguing for a "free and democratic Cuba" is not as effective as quietly working towards an agreement that stops armed subversion from Cuba. He concludes,[69]

> Instead of identifying every issue as a part of the cold war to be dealt with as part of a single major conflict, it would seem wiser to insist that each issue, whether or not it reflects basic and fundamental differences, be dealt with independently on its merits. By separating out its Antarctic problem, and by dealing with it outside the context of the cold war, the

---

[68]Roger Fischer, "Fractionating conflict," unpublished paper.
[69]*Ibid.*, p. 16.

United States accomplished in the Antarctic Treaty a significant victory for the objectives of the United States.

Maintaining communication

The tendency to enlarge conflict and attribute bad motives to one's opponent, is but one aspect of a more general problem: the tendency to oversimplify the other's motivation, over-rationalize his decisions, and neglect his completely different frame of reference. It is this fundamental process that leads to the error of overemphasizing the "good" motives in an ally and ignoring the evil in a manipulator, as well as completely mistrusting a competitor.

The tendency to over-rationalize one's opponent and to simplify his motivation, may be seen in the average American official's reaction to the invasion of South Korea. If the Soviet Union instigated the invasion it was responding to many factors: a shift in its internal power heirarchy, indications that the United States was going to maintain a permanent military establishment in Japan, prospects of an easy victory in an area to which the United States was not deeply committed, and the emergence of China as a power and a potential rival. Yet the President and the majority of his advisors interpreted the invasion as part of a Soviet strategic master plan.

In the preceding pages, we have often noted how difficult it is to have accurate communications between different worlds. When the relations between two nations are bad to begin with, hostility may lead to rejection and the severance of what little communication exists. A recent statement on psychological aspects of foreign policy* noted, "It is psychologically dangerous to limit communication or break off contact with adversaries as ways of putting pressure on them. Hostility tends to rupture communication, which, in turn enhances hostility by increasing mutual fear and mistrust." We may see the consequences of disrupted communication by examining the Chinese decision to fight the United States in Korea.

In Chapter 4 we saw how the Chinese warned the United States that they would enter the war if American troops crossed the 38th parallel, and we observed how this warning was ignored and how the Chinese attacked. At present, it is impossible for us to know all the forces that led the Chinese to enter the Korean War. The secrecy of an autocratic government and the current hostility between the United States and China, prevent the interviews and examination of documents

---

*By the Council of The Society for the Psychological Study of Social Issues.

that would be necessary to reconstruct exactly what occurred within the Chinese government. However, some facts seem clear and allow us to guess the broad outline of what transpired. Whiting[70] has made a serious attempt to do this, and his outline is backed by Tsou's[71] account of Chinese-American relations over a longer time span.

In the first place, it is clear that there were many different reasons for entering the war and many arguments against it, and that the top Chinese decision makers reflected these different pros and cons and were by no means unanimous in their final decision. Thus, when the Vice-Secretary General of the democratic league fled Peking in 1956, he reported that for several days after the Foreign Minister's warning on September 30, there was high level discussion of whether or not to enter the war and that several top generals were opposed to entry.

The men who were opposed to entry must have argued that manpower was needed elsewhere for reconstruction, that the war would tax China's resources, delay admission to the United Nations, postpone the invasion of Formosa, and perhaps lead to defeat at the hands of the powerful American forces. The possibility that atomic weapons might be used was also considered. Tsou states,[72]

> What made the Chinese Communists willing to take these grave risks ... appears to have been their estimate of the threat of their security posed by an American victory in North Korea. In making this estimate, they were influenced not only by the geopolitical importance of Korea to China but also by their image of the United States as the foremost imperialist power.

Tsou points out that Japanese expansion had come through Korea in the 1930's, and he states,

> Their ideological perspectives did not permit them to distinguish between the Japan of yesterday as an expansionistic nation and the United States of today as a status quo power.[73]

While Americans may have had good intentions, the actions of the government must have confirmed the views of any Chinese whose communistic training emphasized Western imperialism over China. The in-

---

[70]Allen A. Whiting, *China Crosses the Yalu* (New York: The Macmillan Company, 1960).
[71]Tany Tsou, *America's Failure in China: 1941-50* (Chicago: University of Chicago Press, 1963).
[72]*Ibid.*, p. 576.
[73]*Ibid.*, p. 577.

tervention in Formosa, the aid to French forces in Indochina, the hostility towards seating China in the United Nations, the equipping of Nationalist forces on Formosa who could invade the mainland, the progressing friendliness with Japan that was obviously leading to a peace treaty that would permit Japanese rearmament, the violations of the Yalu border line, and finally the invasion of North Korea, which entailed the marching of Amercian troops up to the very borders of Manchuria, hardly looked like the actions of a friendly power.

To add to these actions, there were enough hostile words. The Commander of the United Nations Forces, with his statements for Chiang Kai Shek, his "Asians respond to aggressive leadership," and his frequent references to restoring "freedom" to Asia, must have sounded ominous indeed. The Commander's ultimate intentions did not look benevolent. When the Commander charged that China had aided the North Korean Invasion, it might well have been taken as the development of an excuse to invade China itself. Had Chinese officials been aware of the workings of a democratic government, they might not have been so alarmed, although the forthcoming elections seemed to auger more support for the Commander. However, as Whiting notes,

> Peking ignored the pluralistic political process in the West and failed to differentiate between the true locus of power in Washington and the confusion of voices on both sides of the Pacific Ocean.[74]

Consequently, the voice of the Commander of the United Nations forces may have been given greater weight than that of the President and Secretary of State, whose words might have appeared designed to lull Chinese suspicions.

In addition to this fear of growing American-Japanese resistance and possible expansion, the Chinese must have also weighed their own prestige and pride. Certainly, the Chinese had been excluded from the debate on Korean unification in spite of the fact that they had a clear interest in a bordering country. Whiting notes,[75] "It is difficult to think of any single course of action that could have so enhanced the stature of the new regime as did intervention in Korea." The pride and confidence of the new Chinese government must have played some role in their final decision to fight. Perhaps there was also a desire to unify the nation and to solidify the new regime in a war with an outside power. It is simply not clear how much the force for intervention came from

---

[74]Whiting, *op. cit.,* p. 169.
[75]*Ibid.,* p. 166.

fear of American expansion and how much from the felt power to expand Chinese influence at the expense of the Americans (and of the Russians, who had controlled North Korea previously).

Finally, we must note that the new Chinese government was somewhat dependent on the Soviet Union, and the latter may have played a considerable role in urging Chinese intervention. As a result of the intervention, the Soviet Union provided China with an excellent air force; and one imagines that many other concessions were gained as well.

With all these forces behind a commitment to intervention, it is not surprising that the arguments against commitment soon became undervalued. The possible American use of atomic weapons was dismissed by considering the atomic bomb of little strategic use in China. China was said to live on the farms rather than in the cities, and the potential devastation of the bombs was underestimated. The possibility of defeat was recognized but was considered to be the sort of defeat suffered at the hands of the Japanese. Having experienced this, the Chinese felt that at the very worst, they would simply retreat as before, using the vast land to prevent any real ultimate defeat.

Nevertheless, Chinese decision makers had a rather sober view of the war. They were unwilling to encourage hopes for a quick victory, and they did make some preparations for possible atomic attack. A clinching factor in the decision must have been the fact that China did not have to become committed all at once. The reader may recall that some Chinese forces engaged United Nations forces along a wide front from October 27 to November 7, tested the enemy's strength, and then withdrew. This provided Chinese authorities with an opportunity to assess the situation and the American reaction. The skirmishes showed them that their troops were capable of fighting American troops. Had the United States regrouped its forces into a defensive position, stated that it would not advance farther but that if it were attacked it would bomb mainland China, then the Chinese would have been faced with a difficult decision. If they did not attack, they would still obtain a useful buffer zone; while if they did attack, the United States would feel free to blockade China and subject at least Manchuria to bombing. As it was, the American decision to advance provided the Chinese with a perfect opportunity to trap their forces and to win large amounts of territory — a much easier decision to make.

Clearly, neither the Chinese nor the Americans understood each other very well. Whiting states,[76]

---

[76]*Ibid.*, p. 168.

Inadequate communications, or the failure to convey accurately to an opponent one's intentions and one's probable responses, played a pivotal role between August and October 1950 in precipitating war between C.P.V. and U.N. forces.

At least three factors contributed to the poor communication. First, Whiting states,[77]

> One obstacle to successful communication, particularly between Communist and non-Communist regimes, is the difficulty each side has in projecting itself into the frame of reference within which the other operates.

While the image of America as an expanding imperialistic power permitted the Chinese to act, and the image of China as a basically weak friendly country permitted the Americans to act, the fact that these images were both incorrect produced a needless loss of life and bitterness.

Second, communications were hindered by the lack of direct diplomatic contact between Washington and Peking. Chinese threats and American reassurances had to come indirectly through persons who were not trusted by both parties. This situation was compounded when the constraints of publicity caused diplomats to talk to the public rather than to each other. Whiting asserts that when the American ambassador to the United Nations spoke, he was often interpreted as replying to the Soviet Ambassador when in fact he was speaking to the American public or its allies.

The third important factor hindering communication was composed of two types of time lag. In the chapter on decision making, we noted how the preliminary decision to cross the 38th parallel was made as far back as September 11, before the triumphant amphibious assault. Had the Chinese threatened to enter the war at that time, the American decision makers would probably have modified their decision. But the Chinese did not know of the decision until much later — at the end of September — when American forces were on the 38th parallel. Then their threats were formulated in a manner designed to influence a decision that was currently being made; that is, they failed to realize that the decision had already been made. The time offset between private and public decision — with one nation attempting to influence a decision which another nation has already made — may have also been true in

---

[77]*Ibid.*, p. 169.

the United States' attempt to dissuade Chinese entry by offering some sort of buffer zone in North Korea. Had this offer come earlier, it might have had more promising results.

A second type of time lag often occurs between one nation's offer and the other's response. If a long delay intervenes, not only may the situation change and support for the offer crumble, but men will also speculate as to the cause of the delay, perhaps attributing it to treachery on the part of the other nation. In fact, it may be hard to decide whether a delay is due to a lack of consensus or to an attempt to gain power at the other's expense. When there is adequate diplomatic contact, the the offering nation can be reassured; but when there is not, or when feelings have polarized, the time lag may be misinterpreted.

Years later, we who were not involved in the decision process can observe that the Chinese attack was due to many factors; at the time, the American decision makers over-rationalized the attack. They perceived the Chinese as single minded, rational, and aggressive. It is only in perspective that we can see the Chinese misperceiving American intentions, distorting probabilities, being influenced by poor communications, and being motivated by *both* fear and expansionism.

Conclusion

I will now attempt to provide a very brief overview of the material we have examined. Then I shall point out how the psychological dimension adds to an analysis of foreign policy and what a study of foreign policy contributes to psychology. Finally, I will review the improvements which our study suggests the government should undertake.

In the first part of this book, we saw that each of us constructs his own reality. While we are confronted with objective situations, there are always a number of different meanings which we can give to these situations. First, we noted that the meaning that was selected to be reality was the meaning that least disturbed our beliefs; and later we discovered that, in a conflict situation, it was also the meaning that permitted us to act by satisfying most of our interests. More generally, the entire way in which we construct our reality reflects our individual personality and the way we can maximize whatever strengths we possess. We also observed that we are quite likely to limit our grasp of reality by attending to what is compatible, and that we are capable of distorting reality away from the objective situation — and are quite likely to do when all the realistic alternatives have negative consequences.

In each of these chapters, we noted that a person is always a member of a group and that there is a group or organizational reality that stabilizes the reality of each of its members and acts to prevent radical shifts of beliefs. Part of this reality is the "climate of opinion," and we saw how that and other factors restrict the creative anticipation of possibilities that would disrupt the group's plans.

In the second part of the book, we looked at how these different realities or "worlds" interacted with each other to affect foreign policy. Accepting the fact of real conflicts of interest, we asked what governed whether the conflict resulted in the domination of one party by the other, a disruptive war, a weak compromise, an agreement to coexist, or an integrative solution that benefited both parties. We concentrated on one key factor: the quality of the communication between the worlds and whether or not it resulted in a sympathetic understanding of the other's position.

We noted the many difficulties involved in grasping the other's reality: the pseudo-understanding that prevents a realization of real differences, the fact that an action may have completely different meanings in different worlds, the false attribution of motives that occurs, our lack of consideration for the needs of others, the fact that each side attempts to use *its* principles or ideology as the basis for an understanding, and the fact that open communication may be a disadvantage in competitive bargaining.

Most of the above factors are affected by the type of relationship existing between the two worlds. Hostility may lead to a complete breakdown of communications, and competition tends to promote suspicion, a lack of consideration for the other, and many incorrect motive attributions. On the other hand, when the worlds are responsive to each other or in a common unit, much more openness is possible. Some evidence suggests that such relations are enhanced by joint cooperative endeavors.

Finally, we observed that a consideration of the above points has led many social scientists to advocate the fostering of cooperative endeavors, the building of world law, and the active maintenance of communications with other worlds (no matter how hostile they may be). There is a feeling that a hostile opponent should be met with firmness but that pressure should not be attempted and attacks on ideology should be discouraged. Change is most likely to occur by the creation of acceptable alternatives that meet the opponents' needs, and by the establishment of systems which he may use as a model.

The analysis of foreign policy gains an interesting sort of depth when we add the psychological dimension. The political scientist is apt to consider the political leader as an independent variable affecting policy — policy that he forms by considering economic, political, and strategic factors and making decisions that may show either good or poor judgment. Viewed in this way, the leader is rather God-like (or Devil-like) in his endeavor to create an international environment that is the national interest.

By considering the individual as a dependent variable, the psychologist adds questions about *how* the economic, political, and strategic factors were considered, and *why* the decision was good or poor. The political leader is revealed as another person subject to the same forces that play upon ourselves.

Let us consider two examples: The interposition of the Seventh Fleet between Formosa and Communist China can be analyzed simply in political-strategic terms. We might say that the decision was made because, having decided to resist communist aggression in Korea, the administration naturally resisted communist expansion in a nearby area. It is not until we examine the behavior of the decision makers that we think to inquire why they reacted to communism as a unit rather than distinguishing between North Korea or the Soviet Union and China.

Likewise, the decision to unify Korea and trust the judgment of the Commander of the United Nation's Forces, can simply be considered a bad decision. But when we add psychology, we ask why the decision was made that way and note the powerful motivational forces preventing the correct decision.

When we add the psychological dimension, we become aware of the importance of the individual and his behavior, and we realize that events did not *have* to come out the way they did. When the right hand is palm down, one's little finger is doomed to be to the right of one's thumb as long as movement is restricted to the two-dimensional surface of the table. A third dimension adds a degree of freedom and allows us to see that the finger can be to the left of the thumb. Likewise, the addition of the psychological dimension permits us to realize that our foreign policy does not have to remain in its present state but could be much more positive and effective.

In attempting to add the psychological dimension to foreign policy, the subject of psychology is also enhanced. The psychologist becomes aware of the other dimensions of human behavior — dimensions which he is apt to overlook. Furthermore, the attempt to account for the behavior of persons in natural life, challenges his models and demands sophistication from his explanations. In the course of this work, we have shown the limitations of several different psychological models, proposed a number of new hypotheses, and presented data from several studies inspired by the problems we have encountered. I shall not review these here but would like to note a few interesting problems raised by our analysis.

First, we should like to know more about the conditions that seem to force persons to give a situation a distorted or inaccurate meaning.

Second, we would like to understand exactly when political considerations disturb "intellectual intimacy" and impede cooperative endeavors.

Third, we should like to explore the resolution of ideological conflicts. Using the Rapoport debate method, we would like to study the tensions involved in entering another's world.

Fourth, we wonder how the very analysis we have presented may be culturally biased, and whether agreement can be reached with investigators from different cultures.

The material we have examined seems to suggest certain procedures that might improve the quality of American foreign policy. These may be summarized as follows:

1. As we noted in Chapter 2, there should be an institutionalized procedure for gathering and presenting data that goes against current policy.
2. As observed in Chapter 3, there should be a group of "impractical" planners who are a step removed from the current policy planners in the State Department.
3. As was demonstrated in Chapter 5, the government should provide its officials with secret access to mental health facilities.
4. In Chapter 6, we observed that no officials are currently charged with the responsibility of advocating a concern for the welfare of other peoples (as opposed to governments) or the consideration of international law. This should be remedied.
5. In Chapter 9, we noted the desirability of stimulating cooperative projects with "unfriendly" nations. A group should be charged with this responsibility. Such a group could also insure the development of as much communication as is possible.
6. In Chapter 6, 7, and 8, we often saw extremely poor communications *within* the government. It is clear that a number of professionals should be selected and trained in the art of improving communications within the government. They should be available upon the request of designated officials.
7. In Chapter 8, we noted that Congressional committees passing on appointments should make it a practice to inquire whether intellectual intimacy is possible between the appointee and the men he must deal with.
8. The government should encourage the participation of public debate on general issues *before* forming a consensus within the administration on specific policies.

INDEX

MacArthur, Douglas
  occupation of Japan, 199
  personal history, 187, 248
  relations with Truman, 3, 247-297
  strategy in Korea, 175-180
  views, 188, 252
MacIver, Robert, 93
Maier, N. R. F., 73
Management, 333-338
Maneuvers of the advisor, 238-239
Manheim, H. L., 316
Manson, Frank A., 258
March, J. G., 315, 316
Marlowe, David, 170
Marquis, D. G., 140
Marrow, Alfred J., 336
Marshall, George, 13, 226
Marshall Plan, 9, 13, 76, 103, 212, 345
Marshall, S. L. A., 147
Massive retaliation policy, 328, 353, 358
May, M. A., 182
McCarthy era, 6
McCarthyism, 93, 354
McClelland, Charles A., 350
McClelland, David C., 169, 340
McGrath, Joseph E., 400
McGuire, William J., 255
McKinley, William, 186
McNeil, Elton B., 414
Meaning, 120
Means, 113
Meeker, Robert J., 7
Megatonnage, 405
Michelangelo, 44
Milburn, Thomas, 166, 402
"Military Situation in the Far East," 262
Miller, Whitney, 161
Minas, J. Sayer, 173, 374
Minnesota Multiphasic Personality
  Inventory, 169
Momentum, 89
Moore, William H., Jr., 7
Morgenthau, Hans, 347, 353
Mosely, Philip E., 392
Motives, 399-400
Mouton, J. S., 316, 317
Muromcew, Cyril, 395
Muzzy, Robert E., 292

National character, 358
National Security Council, 15, 101-102,
  284-286, 321-322
National Security Council—68 Paper,
  10, 14, 70, 79, 161, 191, 212, 260
National Training Laboratories, 336
"Need for Support" factor, 208
Negotiations, 387-401
Nelson, Admiral, 45
Neustadt, R. E., 81, 145, 158, 167, 223,
  225, 285, 299
Newsweek, 167
New York Times, 272, 348, 378, 394

Nicolson, Harold, 341, 391
Nixon, Richard, 182
Noel, Robert C., 418
Nomethetic approach to personality
  measurement, 168-181
Norms of a committee, 240-242
North Atlantic Treaty Organization, 13
North Korean invasion, 141-145
North, Robert C., 78, 44, 153

Objective probability, 108
Oexle, E., 281
Ogburn, Charlton, Jr., 59, 99
Operational Approach to personality
  measurement ,169
Opinion, 70-73
Orders, 229, 257-261
Organizational atmospheres, 326
Organizational constraints, 59
Organizational momentum, 89
Osgood, Charles, 421
Overrationalization, 28

Paige, Glenn D., 10, 31, 51, 184
Parsons, T., 221
Patterns of communication, 83
Peace Corps, 103
Pearl Harbor, 21
Perception, 40
  creative, 44
  determinants, 19-39
  distorted, 43
  organizational, 46-52
  transactional, 20
Permanent group dynamics, 239
Personality development, 185
Personality variables, 166-167
Personnel research and training, **338-343**
Pervasiveness of group, 212
Peterson, Basil, 174
Phenomenal approach to personality
  measurement, 183-193
Pilisuk, M., 389
Pinckney, Charles, 3
Planning, 98-104
Pluralism, 328
Poisson distribution, 407
Poland, 363-373
Policies, 95-96
Policy criteria, 91
Policy Planning Council, 99
Policy Planning Staff, 99
Pool, Ithiel de Sola, 39, 137, 345, 374
Population response, 405
Potsdam Conference, 381
Power, 242
Preferences in decision making, 166
Presidential abilities, 184
Presidential decisions, 129
Pressure, 306
Pretending, 78-82
Price, Don K., 234